European Society
1500–1700

European Society 1500–1700

Henry Kamen

Hutchinson

London Melbourne Sydney Auckland Johannesburg

Hutchinson & Co. (Publishers) Ltd

Brookmount House, 62-65 Chandos Place,
Covent Garden, London WC2N 4NW

Hutchinson Publishing Group (Australia) Pty Ltd
16-22 Church Street, Hawthorn, Melbourne, Victoria 3122

Hutchinson Group (NZ) Ltd
32-34 View Road, PO Box 40-086, Glenfield, Auckland 10

Hutchinson Group (SA) (Pty) Ltd
PO Box 337, Bergvlei 2012, South Africa

Original version published as *The Iron Century*
© Henry Kamen 1971
European Society 1500–1700 first published 1984
Reprinted 1986

© Henry Kamen 1984

Set in Times

Printed and bound in Great Britain by
Anchor Brendon Ltd, Tiptree, Essex

British Library Cataloguing in Publication Data
Kamen, Henry
  European society 1500–1700.
   1. Europe — Social conditions
   I. Title
   940.2′2   HN 373

ISBN 0 09 156990 7 cased
     0 09 156991 5 paper

for my mother, in gratitude

Contents

Preface

Although it closely follows the format of my *Iron Century* (1971), this is a substantially new book. The text has been shortened, revised and almost completely re-written; the period covered has been extended by one century; new sections, particularly on the family and on popular culture, have been added; and the bibliography has been brought up to date. Unlike the previous work, this includes no graphs and diagrams: so many of these are available at the moment that to choose a handful seemed quite arbitrary. In using this book readers must remain aware of the dangers of accepting any generalization that claims to apply to the whole of Europe, which contained within itself so many different societies that it must appear rash to try to talk of 'European society'. Despite the inherent difficulties, it is essential that we should look beyond narrowly national history to a broader perspective of the life of early modern Europeans.

This book would never have appeared but for the generosity of Eulàlia, who provided the peace and shelter that allowed me to write it. I am scarcely less grateful to Anthony Turner, who generously put both his house and his desk at my disposal. Both are responsible for the appearance of the book; I alone am responsible for its defects.

H.K.

1 Population structures

> . . . and the life of man, solitary, poor, nasty, brutish and short.
> Hobbes, *Leviathan* (1651)

By the early sixteenth century the traders, adventurers and explorers of the Atlantic seaboard had immeasurably extended the horizons of Europeans. The brief and fragmentary medieval contacts between Europe and Asia were replaced in the Renaissance epoch by direct and profitable exchanges between the traders of Europe and the Asian monarchies. 'What on earth have you come seeking so far away in India?', Vasco da Gama was asked in Malabar. 'Christians and spices', was his prompt reply. Spices, particularly pepper and ginger, became the chief source of wealth of the Portuguese crown, which in the first half of the sixteenth century pioneered the European discovery of the East Indian territories and China and Japan. It was the Portuguese Magellan, who had spent seven years in the Indies, who eventually passed over into the service of Spain and helped to give the latter a definitive role in the struggle for overseas possessions. Between them these two small nations, some nine million in population, opened up the globe.

The riches harvested by Portugal – between 1500 and 1520 some 10,500 tonnes of spices from the east, some 410 kilograms of gold a year from West Africa – stimulated rivalry. The Portuguese exercised strict control over information about their trade, but the Spaniards were never so secretive and allowed free exchange of ideas, for otherwise, as the historian Antonio de Herrera argued, 'the reputation of Spain would fall rapidly, for foreign and enemy nations would say that small credence could be placed in the words of her rulers since their subjects were not allowed to speak freely'. After mid century the great collections of travel literature, notably the Venetian Ramusio's *Delle navigazioni* (1550) and Hakluyt's

Principall Navigations (1589), began to dispel old myths about the overseas territories and presented the literate public with realities far removed from the tales of bisexual monsters and dog-headed men with which their fathers had been regaled.

Trade and exploration were the first stage, largely limited to the early century, of Europe's discovery of the outside world. In that early period the sense of wonder was still paramount: many realized with a shock that Asia and America frequently outdid any marvels that Europe might offer. Antonio Pigafetta, who sailed with Magellan in 1519 on the first European circumnavigation of the globe, claimed to have heard that the emperor of China was 'the greatest in all the world'. Cortés, writing to his own emperor after entering Tenochtitlán in 1521, claimed of Moctezuma's palaces that 'there is not their like in all Spain'. The great temple, he said, was one 'whose size and magnificence no human tongue could describe', and the city itself he called 'the most beautiful thing in the world'. Recalling in his old age the splendours of Mexico, Bernal Díaz said that even the market-place was such that 'some of our soldiers who had been in many parts of the world, in Constantinople, in Rome, and all over Italy, said that they had never seen a market so well laid out, so large, so orderly, and so full of people'.

In the course of the century this awareness of Europe's modest part in world civilization was superseded by a more aggressive attitude. Confident in his own superiority, the European moved forward into the colonial epoch. The aggressiveness was in part fed by the conviction that Christianity must be taken to the heathen. The most remarkable achievements in this respect were of men like St Francis Xavier (d. 1552), whose global vision took him to Goa, Malabar, Malacca, Japan and the Chinese coast; and of Fray Toribio de Motolinía, who in 1524 landed in Mexico with eleven other Franciscans to begin the first large-scale conversion ever undertaken by Christians outside Europe. In part, however, the attitude sprang from an assumption of inherent racial superiority. 'How can we doubt', wrote the Spanish humanist Sepúlveda in 1547, 'that these people – so uncivilised, so barbaric, contaminated with so many impieties and obscenities – have been justly conquered by a nation so humane and excelling in every virtue?' This may be compared with the words of Jan Pieterz Coen, seventeenth-century creator of the Dutch East Indies. 'May not a man in Europe', he asked a critic of his policies, 'do what he likes with his cattle? Even so does the master here do with his men, for these with all that belongs to them are as much the property of the master as are brute beasts in the Netherlands.' European perception of the outside world was thus rooted in a supreme confidence. 'All has now been traversed and all is known', proclaimed the historian López de Gomara in 1552. And in tune with this confidence came the growing urge to dominate, as stated firmly in 1590 by the Jesuit José de Acosta when, applauding the possession by Spain of America, he affirmed that this was entirely 'in accord with the desire of Providence that certain kingdoms rule others'.

Space and time

Not the least amazing feature of the expansion of Europe was the conquest of distance. A look at the distances covered by the ships trading to Asia round the Cape, the voyages made by the English settlers to north America, the territory traversed by Francis Xavier or Pizarro, might lead to the suspicion that technological progress had made it possible. Yet, for all the improvements in nautical science, time was barely attacked, and the endurance of man alone was a decisive factor in the conquest of distance.

Water, horse or coach were the three means of transport, and their efficiency varied. Over long distances the sea was beyond all doubt the quickest method of communication, but over smaller overland areas the horse was faster and more reliable, making it the obvious basis for the nascent postal services of Europe. Governments took a special interest in improving the quality of the postal service, which, however, remained very expensive and therefore used less by private individuals than by the state and by merchants. In any case, there was no significant increase in speed during the early modern period. Uncertainty of conditions meant that in the sixteenth century the post from Antwerp to Amsterdam normally took from three to nine days, and to Gdansk from twenty-four to thirty-five days. An English regulation of 1637 specified that mail was to travel in summer at 7 miles an hour and in winter at 6. A generation later, in 1666, the average speed of letters was not more than 4 miles an hour. Compare this with the New World, where the Inca postal system attained speeds unequalled until the invention of the internal combustion engine. The distance from Lima to Cuzco by mail-runner took three days, whereas a post-horse in the seventeenth century doing the same distance took twelve. So efficient was the delivery that the Inca used to have fresh fish run up from the coast, a distance of some 350 miles, in two days.

Outside Europe the vastness of distance required measurement in terms of endurance rather than time. The heroes were those like Columbus, who informed Queen Isabella in 1503 that 'the world is small: I mean that it is not as large as people say it is'. Few would have agreed. The expedition of Magellan and Sebastián del Cano, which set out from Seville with five ships in 1519 and returned in 1522 with only one vessel containing eighteen men, after having sailed round the world, was proof of the high cost of any attempt to make the globe smaller. When Francis Drake made the same voyage fifty-five years later the difficulties were still prohibitive: he had five ships when he set sail from Plymouth in 1577 and only one when he returned in 1580. The long absence is deceptive, for in most voyages far longer periods were spent in harbour than at sea. The ships of the American passage, the *carrera de Indias*, took on the average seventy-five days to cross from Seville to Vera Cruz, and 130 days to cross back; the entire journey, however, including long waits in Vera Cruz and Havana, might mean that a ship leaving Seville in July one year did not normally return before October in the subsequent year. The fortitude of the explorers was acclaimed by the historian Cieza de León, who asked what other race but the Spaniards could have penetrated 'through such rugged lands, such dense forests, such great mountains and deserts, and over such broad rivers'? We can reply that the Russians in Siberia, the Puritans in New England, the Dutch and Portuguese in Africa and Asia, the French in Canada, were each in their own way, and often with methods that few would approve, bringing the outside world closer to Europe and thereby conquering the great gulf imposed by time and space.

The government of a world empire was made peculiarly difficult for Philip II by the inability to communicate speedily with his administrators. 'I have not heard anything from the king about the affairs of the Netherlands since 20 November last', complained the governor of that region, Requeséns, from Antwerp on 24 February 1575. Businessmen no less than politicians had an investment in overcoming distance and time. Any delay in the payment of bills of exchange, the arrival of the galleons, the shipment of perishable cargo, might spell ruin. Yet when all the evidence for the urgent demands of these men of the world is considered, there can be little doubt that they were only a minority group. Time was not yet a universal pacemaker, and the age appears to move at a casual pace, regulated only by the movements of the sun, the cycle of the seasons, and an occasional clock.

Clocks were a relative novelty in the early sixteenth century. The population still took its division of the hours and minutes from the Church: the day was measured by liturgical hours, church bells tolled their passing and called the faithful to prayer. Protestantism helped to liberate time from its clerical dress, and clocks completed the process of secularization. By the end of the sixteenth century the clock industry was booming, particularly when the clockmakers from Catholic countries fled as refugees to Protestant states. In 1515 there were no clockmakers in Geneva, after 1550 they came as refugees from France, and by 1600 the city had twenty-five to thirty master clockmakers and an unknown number of apprentices. In the mathematical universe of early seventeenth-century intellectuals, clocks played an essential part. In contrast to the genial pace of earlier decades, in contrast to Gargantua's protest, 'I never rule myself by time!', the seventeenth century began the subjection of humanity to the clock. It was the astronomer Kepler who looked upon the universe and pronounced it 'similar to a clock', Boyle who considered it 'a great piece of clockwork'.

Clocks and watches remained the preserve of a minority. Industrial time was measured by daylight hours, a winter working day being shorter than a summer one by about two hours, with wages consequently lower. In sixteenth-century Antwerp, building workers had a seven-hour day in winter but a twelve-hour day in summer; winter wages were one-fifth lower. Concepts like 'from sunrise to sunset' were written into work regulations, but were inevitably imprecise. Only a few trades had their hours of work laid down by the clock rather than by daylight: in 1571 the printers of Lyon complained because their working day was timed to begin at 2 a.m. and ended only at 8 p.m. For most workers, especially on the land, imprecision of time took strict discipline out of work. Rest from labours was both recognized and encouraged. In the diocese of Paris at the beginning of the seventeenth century there were fifty-nine obligatory religious holidays, which together with the Sundays made up well over 100 days a year. It was normal in much of Catholic Europe not to work for nearly a third of the year. La Fontaine commented at the time that 'on nous ruine en fêtes', but the system was not necessarily as harmful as it might appear: in a largely agricultural economy, there was not enough work to employ people continuously, so that holidays provided a festive alternative to what might otherwise have been days of unemployment. All classes, not merely the leisured part of the population, accepted this casual attitude to time. There were, however, objections when attempts were made to change the calendar. In France, the king in 1563 decreed that the year should start in January instead of at Easter; the Parlement of Paris refused to register the edict until January 1567, a refusal which made the year 1566 only eight months long. A definitive international reform of the calendar did not come until 1582, when pope Gregory XIII abolished ten days from the year; most Protestant countries refused to accept the change, which led to the operation of a dual calendar in Europe.

Communities

Early modern Europe was a rural society. In western and central Europe in about 1600 less than 5 per cent of the people lived in some hundred 'cities' of over 20,000 inhabitants each. A further fifth of the population lived in small country towns; all the rest lived in rural communities. The great developments of early modern society – the elements of economic, social and domestic change – thus occurred less in the great metropoli and seats of government than away in the often forgotten corners of the European countryside. It was in the local communities that the social life and solidarities of a European were concentrated: 'state' and 'nation' were abstracts with which he almost never came into contact.

The units of organization in provincial society varied according to region. In most of Christian Europe the village community coincided with the parish unit, so that the Church played a leading role in defining the character of the community. In more feudalistic areas, the authority of a seigneur might be more decisive, particularly if he controlled most of the land. The community proper, however, was definable not in terms of outside influences such as Church and lord, but solely by the bonds between its members. Some villages, as in England where the peasantry were free and land distribution equitable, gave the appearance of being happy, self-sufficient units, with a full spectrum of social classes. By contrast, over much of eastern and Mediterranean Europe the villages could be depressed one-class communities, unable to survive out of their own resources. Contented or not, few villages existed as a viable community within themselves: all had to have close links with other nearby villages for such basic needs as marriage partners and commercial exchange. In a very real sense, then, the village was not always a proper community, which could be identified more exactly in the broader cultural area embracing the village: within this area people grew the same crops, experienced the same environment of soil and weather, did the same types of labour, dressed similarly and spoke the same language. Thus, in England one might think of a village and its district for ten miles around as a community, but in the Pyrenees or in Norway one could apply the term to several villages encompassed within the broad sweep of a mountain valley.

Though the basic unit within each village was the household or family, the importance of kinship as a social bond was not always paramount. In smaller communities, and in areas from which people tended not to move, endogamy might be high and the links of parentage strong. But in those many villages of northern Europe from which there was constant movement, family bonds were weaker and people were held together more by relationships of neighbourliness. Whatever the nature of the bond, the sense of 'belonging', the feeling of 'solidarity', was always intense and profound. Community feeling, of a sort seldom experienced today in our more individualistic world, was indeed perhaps the most powerful social force in early modern Europe. All human activity was judged by norms created by the community: disapproved marriages were mocked by the 'charivari', 'witches' were driven out by hostile neighbours, unfair taxes were resisted with revolt.

The focus of loyalties in the community in turn created intense conflicts. Very small quarrels might lead to the growth of factions, some based on kinship, some on status. It was possible for such low-level conflict to last from generation to generation, particularly in the Mediterranean where the notion of 'honour' (or one's 'reputation' in the community) was always deeply cherished. Others might spill out beyond the local level, as in the Sussex village of Cuckfield in the 1570s, when a quarrel between the vicar and the squire split first the community, then the county and was carried to national level, ending when Sir Francis Walsingham intervened in 1582 to secure the vicar's deprivation. Communities were naturally jealous of each other: in France and Spain the youths of one village would show their resentment at any of their girls being married to a man from another village, by creating a riot, extorting money or even resorting to violence. In times of distress, however, the village could unite remarkably well; and popular revolt, particularly against the local seigneur, often reinforced local loyalties.

Over much of Europe, even where clerical and lay lords dominated, the forms of ancient communal government were still preserved in the sixteenth and seventeenth centuries. A village would be governed by its 'assembly of inhabitants' (France) or its 'general council' (Spain), consisting in theory of all adult inhabitants but in practice of the propertied heads of households; even these did not all attend, and decisions fell more and more into the hands of an élite. Assemblies could coexist with seigneurial authority: in eastern Europe the lord sanctioned assembly meetings, and in England a jury of villagers might help to dispense seigneurial justice. Meetings were called only for exceptional business, sometimes as infrequently as once a year: in Spain bells were rung and the council met after mass on a Sunday, in a traditional or symbolic location (the Basque national assembly met under the famous tree at Gernika). In Swedish and Savoyard villages the vote at meetings had to be unanimous.

The community and the village assembly played a crucial role in all aspects of economic and social life. The assembly set times for ploughing, decided what crops should be planted and what cattle should be kept. Exploitation of the soil would sometimes be on a communalist basis: ploughland and pasture was periodically redistributed among households, since it belonged in some areas to the community as a whole and not to each family. A village with communal holdings – such as arable, pasture, woods, a mill – might be economically strong; though a dominant feature of early modern Europe was the steady alienation of these assets to pay taxes and debts. In France the process of alienation became so great a threat to economic viability that Colbert forbade sales, and ordered intendants to try and recover property alienated since 1620. Law and order was communally enforced: in Valencia the Tribunal of the Waters, composed of village elders, still meets weekly outside the cathedral to deal verbally with disputes between peasants of the region. Often the community would intrude into family life: in Russia village elders had a say in the arrangement of marriages.

By the end of the seventeenth century the autonomous village community was decaying throughout Europe. The single most important cause was the polarization of wealth within the village, creating on one hand a propertied and often tax-exempt élite, on the other a growing number of landless families. Control of the assembly fell into the hands of the minority. At the same time capitalization of the soil by outside interests (the lord, the city) and the growing demands of the state (for taxes and military service) helped to undermine the fragile economic supports of the community.

The intense localism of community feeling penetrated upwards into all levels of the state. The loyalty of a man to his hearth was basic: solidarities were with family, kin, lord and village, and throughout the early modern period there was little sign that they had been shaken. Local loyalties preceded those to the state, as in 1513 when villages on the French and Spanish sides of the Pyrenean border agreed to keep the peace between themselves and not participate in the wars between their respective countries. From one political level to the next, regional loyalties threatened the emergent centralized state. Throughout the early sixteenth century the self-governing city states of northern Italy remained the political ideal of Europeans, being proposed during the Comunidades in Spain in 1520 as the model for government. Even within themselves, the cities broke down into constituent communities, as with the 'communes' in Paris in 1588 and 1648, in Bordeaux in 1650. Persistent particularism everywhere – in Spain, in the Netherlands – delayed the formation of national identities. For most people, the village community of one's birth was one's 'country' (*pays, pais*), not the nation state of which it formed a tiny part. So fluid were loyalties that Marseille in 1591 and again in 1660 proclaimed itself independent of the nation: when Henry IV recaptured the city in 1596 he exclaimed, 'Only now am I king of France!' The parochialism of local communities must not, however, be exaggerated: most were integrated at some point into the wider world. The link was often provided by the nobility and gentry, who were equally at home in their local countryside and in the capital city, and indeed frequently acted as agents for central government in the provinces, helping to collect taxes and recruit troops.

The family

In its most traditional sense a family was a kinship group based on lineage. This concept was particularly important among the upper classes, who traced their descent, and assured the survival of their property, from father to son; it was less common among classes which had little property to transmit. A family was also a household, a group of people living together on the basis of marriage. Until recently it was held that the traditional west European household was a multiple or stem family, comprising more than one generation and including servants as well. An influential book by Ariès argued that this multiple household gradually gave way by about the sixteenth century to the emergent nuclear family, consisting only of parents and children. The evolution from multiple to nuclear family was accompanied, it was argued, by a major change in emotional attitudes. Unlike the large household, in which relationships were very impersonal and children received little affection, the nuclear family brought with it what has been called 'sentiment', 'affective individualism', or more simply 'love': the parents esteemed and respected each other and also their children. This conclusion has been contested by English demographic historians, whose research shows that in pre-industrial England the normal structure of households was the conjugal family: husband, wife and children; with extended or multiple familes numerically quite insignificant. Their conclusion can be applied to northern France: in Brueil-en-Vexin in 1625, for example, 85 per cent of households were nuclear and only 7 per cent extended. It can be argued that in north-west Europe there was no transition from one type of family to another, that even in medieval times the conjugal family may have been predominant, and that the changes in sentiment within the family have been exaggerated by some writers.

Our detailed knowledge of household structure is based on the technique of 'family reconstitution', which involves the arduous collation from parish records of all data on baptisms, marriages and burials, to give a full profile of life and death in the community. The demographic data, however, need to be set beside other historical evidence. It can then be seen that household size is dependent closely on economic and social conditions. In northern France and in England, where the size of landholdings was small, it was logical that small family units would be required. But in southern France, over a large arc stretching from Béarn and Gascony to Provence, and in other parts of the Mediterranean, farms were larger and family life tended to concentrate around the large house: here multiple units were far more common. In Montplaisant in Perigord in 1644 simple families were 50.8 per cent, multiple or extended families 36.5 per cent, of the population. In Altopascio in rural Tuscany in 1684, 58 per cent were simple, 36 per cent were multiple. In Provence, in Franche Comté, multiple families were between one- and two-fifths of the population. Thus, the larger estates of southern Europe helped the survival of communal forms of exploitation, and this encouraged branches of the same family to live together. But as property division proceeded and as laws of inheritance changed, the multiple tended to be replaced by the nuclear family. In Europe east of the Elbe, for which our knowledge in this period is extremely fragmentary, the large multiple family (known as the *zadruga* in Slav areas) was more common.

Marriage was a major step, particularly among the upper classes where it tied up property. Gentry who married beneath their station, contracting *mésalliances* and so putting the family fortune in danger as well as causing inter-family conflicts, prompted the state to take an early interest in the question. In France the king by edict in 1556 banned marriages that did not have the consent of parents, and in 1639 Louis XIII formulated the view that marriage was the cement of the state. These attempts to protect the social order, however, were counterbalanced in two respects: the Church (even after Trent, when the rules were tightened up considerably) recognized all marriages validly agreed between the two contracting parties; and social custom for most people outside the aristocracy allowed a surprising degree of freedom in courtship. In traditional society, courtship and sexual practice was far freer than has been thought. The allegedly cold English were not so in 1499 when Erasmus commented delightedly that 'wherever you move, there is nothing but kisses'; while a native said in 1620 that 'for us to salute strangers with a kiss is counted but civility, but with foreign nations immodesty'. At a popular level courting might involve 'bundling', or petting. Evidence from France and Germany shows a considerable range of tolerated sexual practices, usually stopping short of intercourse.

A powerful argument against the theory that love, and the corresponding freedom to choose one's mate, was a late phenomenon identifiable with the evolution of the nuclear family, is that most young people in western Europe did have some freedom of choice. In Spain the consent of parents for those marrying under the age of 25 was not made obligatory until 1776. In the seventeenth century in Spain a young man with legitimate claims on a girl could ask the vicar-general of the diocese to send an official to remove a girl from parental custody in order to wed her. In any case, in Spain, England, France and elsewhere the fact that young men of the lower classes were usually independently employed, had probably left the family home and had possibly lost at least one parent through early mortality, freed them in practice from dependence on parents in the choice of a partner. Many, moreover, had to go out of their own villages in search of a husband or wife, thanks to the high level of consanguinity in some country parishes. These elements of freedom must, of course, be balanced against strong traditional controls exercised by the head of the family, by the local community, and even by the feudal seigneur.

Once a choice of partner was made, the betrothal could assume great importance, particularly in Catholic countries where the engagement was deemed to be more solemn and binding than the nuptial ceremony, and could no more be broken than a marriage could. In many parts of France, Switzerland and Spain it was accepted that a betrothed couple could, with parental consent, sleep together under the family roof until they were financially ready to marry and set up their own home: the custom helps to explain high prenuptial pregnancy in some villages. The Counter-Reformation Church denounced the practice strenuously, but failed to alter it. In England the custom was almost unknown: a young married couple there would immediately set out to create their own conjugal unit. The informal approach to marriage and sex in many European peasant households arose largely from economic causes: the lack of enough space to afford privacy. Communal beds, in which both family and servants slept, were traditional. A French noble, Noël du Fail, commented in the late sixteenth century: 'Do you not remember those big beds in which everyone slept together without difficulty? All the people, married or unmarried, slept together in a big bed made for the purpose, three fathoms long and nine feet wide, without fear or danger or any unseemly thought, or serious consequence; for in those days men did not become aroused at the sight of naked women. However, since the world has become badly behaved, each has his own separate bed, and with good reason.'

Though the innovative role of the nuclear family has been justifiably called in question, there can be little doubt that important changes in family relationships occurred during the early modern period. Both tradition and common practice tended to give wife and children a very subordinate role: in 1587 a jurist of Tours commended 'domestic discipline where the father is as a dictator', and in 1622 an English writer described the husband as 'a king in his owne house'. There were extreme cases where customary law allowed men to beat their wives or kill them for infidelity. But by the early seventeenth century attitudes, at least in western Europe, were changing. The three great controls over family behaviour were the state, the Church and the community; all three modified their attitude between the fifteenth and the eighteenth centuries. Perhaps the two most significant influences favouring change during this period were, on the continent, the Counter Reformation; and, in the Atlantic world, the Puritan tradition.

The intervention of the state aimed invariably to strengthen the patriarchal authority of the father, with particular concern for the protection of family property. A revival of Roman Law among jurists stressed both the rights of property and the father's authority over his family: in some parts of France disobedience to parents came to be regarded as a crime, and in Spain the Madrid city police arrested disrespectful sons. On the other hand, the state ceased to tolerate the power over life and limb that husbands had once exercised over wives and children; and 'divorces' or legal separations were granted by state and Church courts both in France and Spain when the wife could prove systematic beating (in Protestant Basel, where divorce was granted to 16.7 per cent out of 1356 marital cases in 1550–92, the parties were exceptionally allowed to re-marry after a year). The Church, by its unique control over the sacrament of matrimony, was a powerful agent of change. Protestants, including Anglicans, reacted against Catholic teaching on the virtues of chastity by stressing the high calling of marriage, 'a state' (according to the Puritan William Perkins) 'in itself far more excellent than the condition of a single life'. At the same time Protestants emphasized (as the Catholic state in France also did after 1556) that the consent of parents was essential for marriage. The Catholic Church after the Council of Trent (1563), however, reaffirmed the complete liberty of young people to marry if need be without consent, though at the same time emphasizing the authority of parents and the obligations of children. In practice, the rules laid down by Church and state varied widely in their application.

Historians have frequently presented the traditional family as one in which wives suffered, children were beaten, and husbands ruled. Though all this undoubtedly happened, it is important to remember that a profound control was exercised over marital conduct by community norms. No village remained ignorant of the virtues or misdeeds within families, which were always vulnerable to the interference of kin and neighbours. In 1617 when the villagers of

Yardley in Worcestershire petitioned against a householder, they included the accusation that he 'did beat his wife most cruellie'. Throughout western Europe the custom of the charivari (or 'rough music' as it was also called) allowed members of the community to deride cuckolds, henpecked husbands, second marriages and unfaithful spouses. It was a custom disapproved of by both Church and state, mainly because of the conflicts to which it gave rise, and was disappearing by the end of the sixteenth century. Community control of other types survived: in Granada, for example, the people annually elected a *juez del barrio* (suburb warden) whose task it was to oversee the behaviour of families, and battered wives in the same region could obtain the arrest of their offending husbands. At the very time that the process of social and political change began to diminish the influence of the community over the lives of families, other moral norms were being brought into play. The Puritans in England and America may not have innovated radically in their approach to marriage, but they certainly shifted opinion towards a more respectful relationship within families. The Council of Trent also had a decisive influence: manuals for confessors published before its sessions contain no references to the duties of parents, whereas all manuals published thereafter devote considerable space to the subject. Cardinal Richelieu reflected the new trend when writing that the commandments impose 'obligations not only on children towards their fathers, but also on fathers and mothers towards their children, inasmuch as love should be reciprocal'. One of the most influential Catholic works exalting marriage was St François de Sales's *Introduction to the Devout Life* (1609): for him marriage was 'a great sacrament, to be honoured by all and in all ways'.

Although affection and love had probably always been important in match-making, there seems every reason to believe that their presence in family relationships was relatively new. This had less to do with evolution of the nuclear family than with the evolution of religious teaching. Church manuals before the mid sixteenth century do not use the word 'love' in a conjugal context; by the late seventeenth century most do so. In the early sixteenth century it was almost impossible to break an engagement to marry; by 1665 in France it was possible for Jeanne Pluot to be officially released from her engagement on the grounds that she 'has never loved and still does not love the said Lasnier, and would choose death rather than marry him'.

The encouragement of intra-family respect and affection by the Reformation and Counter Reformation, was one of the ways in which broad external influences helped to modify the character and development of the family. The evolution of work patterns was another powerful influence. Before early modern times there was no significant distinction between place of work and place of leisure: the family worked where it lived, as peasant families would continue to do for centuries to come. As work became dissociated from the home (through urbanization and later through industrialization), the family evolved into a centre where the wage-earner retreated for leisure. This helped to privatize the family, and servants, who had hitherto always been considered members of the family-household, were gradually excluded from the domestic circle.

Population structures

Early modern European society was dominated by death. Life expectancy at birth was alarmingly low: in the seventeenth-century nobility the average male expectation of life at birth was 28 years, the female expectation 34 years. In the English peerage in 1575–1674 the average male expectation at birth was 32 years, the female 34.8 (in the early twentieth century, by contrast, a male peer could expect to live to 60, a female to 70). The lot of the poorer people, for whom records are more difficult to come by, was inevitably worse. A study covering 3700 children of all classes born in Paris at the end of the seventeenth century arrives at an overall life expectancy of 23 years.

These figures are statistical abstracts, but are borne out by the all too real data for infant mortality. In the demographic system of early modern Europe it was almost a rule that one out of every four or five children born failed to survive the first year of life: in England the average was a fifth of all children, in France a quarter. Survival beyond infancy continued to be extremely hazardous. In the Castilian villages of Simancas, Cabezón and Cigales in the sixteenth century, up to 50 per cent of children died before their seventh year; in the nearby city of Palencia the figure was 68 per cent. In England less than two-thirds of all children born survived to the age of 10, in northern France barely a half. Almost one child in two in early modern Europe failed to live to the age of 10, and two live births were required to produce one human adult. The example of the Capdebosc family in the Condomois (France) is instructive. Jean Dudrot de Capdebosc married Margaride de Mouille in 1560. They had ten children, of whom five died before their tenth year. Odet, the eldest son, married Marie de la Crompe in 1595: of their eight children five did not reach their tenth year. Jean, the eldest, married twice. Jeanne, his first wife, had two children, one of whom died at 9 years, the other at five weeks. Marie, the second wife, had thirteen children in the twenty-one years 1623–45. Of them, six died in infancy, one was killed in war, two became nuns. Of the thirty-three children born to this prolific family during the century, only six founded a family. The principal reason: infant mortality.

Because life was short, the Europe of around 1600 was predominantly youthful. Children and young people must have been everywhere more in evidence than the aged. Sebastian Franck claimed (1538) that 'the whole of Germany is teeming with children'. In four parishes of Cologne in 1574, 35 per cent of the population were aged under 15; in six districts of Jena in 1640 the proportion was about 38 per cent. Leiden in 1622 had around 47 per cent in the same age group. Gregory King in 1695 estimated that over 45 per cent of the people of England and Wales were children, and that the average age of the population was 27 years. In Geneva in 1561–1600 the average population age was as low as 23, rising to 27.5 in 1601–1700. In the table below, seventeenth-century data are set beside those of twentieth-century England.

The predominance of youth in the population had important cultural effects. Young men, whose numbers often exceeded those of women, played a leading role in communal activities: at harvest

Age group	Venice 1610–20 (%)	England and Wales 1695 (King) (%)	Elbogen circle (Bohemia) late seventeenth century (%)	England and Wales 1958 (%)
0–9	18.5	27.6	26	14.8
10–19	18.2	20.2	20	14.2
20–29	15.4	15.5	18	13.8
30–39	15.7	11.7	14	14.1
40–49	11.0	8.4	9	13.9
50–59	8.3	5.8 }	13	13.2
60+	12.9	10.7 }		16.9

time, in festivities, at weddings. Organized youth groups – called 'abbeys' in southern France, 'cencerradas' in southern Spain – were to be found both in villages and big cities (Lyon in the sixteenth century had some twenty 'abbeys'), and gave scope to the disorderly propensities of the young. Despite the large numbers of young people they did not, as was once thought, marry young. Limited evidence for Spain tends to suggest that in the sixteenth and early seventeenth centuries girls married at the age of 20, men at about 25. In Altopascio (Tuscany) in the seventeenth century girls married when just over 21. These ages are exceptional. Over most of western Europe women's first marriage occurred between the ages of 24.5 and 26.5; the men were usually two to three years older. Among the élite, the age at marriage tended to be lower, since an early and profitable wedding helped to secure property: in the sixteenth century daughters of the Genevan bourgeoisie wed at about 22 years, English noblewomen at just over 20. The lower orders, on the other hand, probably delayed marriage until they could afford to set up their own family unit; though some couples, as we have seen, were allowed to live together after betrothal.

The relatively long wait for marriage raises interesting questions about how a young person who remained unmarried until the age of 29 spent his sexual energy. Sexual dalliance short of intercourse appears to have been tolerated quite freely among the common people of western Europe. None the less, illegitimacy rates were fairly low: in England in twenty-four parishes studied, the rate was 2.6 per cent of live births; in Spain the level at Talavera de la Reina was 3 per cent, though in Galicia it rose to some 5.6 per cent. Communal prejudice against mothers of illegitimate children were strong enough to restrict levels. On the other hand, the rate of pre-marital conception was everywhere quite high, and more in the cities than in the countryside. In the seventeenth century the rate in Amiens was nearly 6 per cent of first births, in Lyon up to 10 per cent; in one village in Galicia (Spain) 7.5 per cent of children were born within seven months of marriage. German towns appear to have had a high level, up to 21 per cent for Oldenburg in 1606–1700. England provides the most startling evidence: one-fifth of all first births in the sixteenth and seventeenth centuries were conceived before marriage, and in some villages as many as one-third.

Of course, not everyone married. It has been suggested that different marriage patterns existed in east and west Europe: in the 'west European pattern' a high proportion of women, possibly up to one-fifth, abstained completely from marriage; in the east, virtually all women married. At any given moment in the west, and thanks to religious ideals (convents, for example), economic disability, widowhood or simply the unavailability of men, up to half of all women up to 50 years old might not be married. Although in general the population was fairly balanced between male and female, the men too would suffer difficulties in finding mates: Rome in 1592 had only fifty-eight women for every 100 men, and in Nördlingen during the Thirty Years War the authorities allowed unlimited immigration to women (even before the war, in 1581–1610, immigrant girls were 22 per cent of brides) but restricted entry of males.

Marriage, moreover, was seldom for life. Thanks to the high mortality rate, the average couple could look forward to a relatively short married life: at Basel in the 1660s the mean length of a marriage was just over twenty years. A nuclear family would thus be thrown adrift by the untimely death not only of half the children but also of one parent. It became the rule rather than the exception to re-marry, though poorer and older women had less hope of doing so, which explains the high proportion of widows in the rural Mediterranean. In the rich Genevan élite in 1550–99, 26 per cent of marriages by men were re-marriages; in the village of Pedralba (Valencia) in the seventeenth century one marriage in three was a re-marriage. In Crulai (Normandy) a fifth of all male and a tenth of all female marriages were re-marriages; in this village one widower out of two, and one widow out of six, married again. In one French peasant parish in the seventeenth century, we are told by a contemporary,

when a husband loses his wife or a wife her husband, the surviving spouse at once invites everyone to a meal: this sometimes takes place in the house where the corpse is lying, and the guests laugh, drink, sing and make arrangements for remarrying their host or hostess. The widower or widow receives proposals, and gives reasons for acceptance or rejection: it is only rarely that the party comes to an end before the arrangement has been concluded.

The relative brevity of married life, and the very high infant mortality, meant that the balance of birth over death was very precariously maintained. Enormous importance must therefore be attached to the fertility rate at this period. In almost every town, deaths normally exceeded births, and population levels could only be maintained by continuous immigration. It may have been, as has been convincingly argued, that the newer immigrants in fact brought with them lower rates of survival; and that towns left to themselves might have had a healthy demographic balance with a need for only modest help from newcomers. Since in practice all large towns of early modern Europe experienced very considerable immigration, the objection is largely an academic one; though the birth rate among immigrants may have been lower, they contributed solidly in numbers to urban expansion.

Female fertility was radically affected by late marriage, which meant that girls started reproducing some ten years after they were able to. One historian has referred to this as preindustrial Europe's natural system of birth-control. When we bear in mind that most women had borne their last child by about 40 (the evidence for this across several countries is quite clear), it can be seen that the average reproductive period of women at the time was fifteen years, less than half the span of a woman's normal fertility. The inevitable result was few children. Age-specific fertility rates show that women marrying in the age-group 25 to 29 years tended to produce about four children; in older age groups the rate declined. In Spain, mothers conceived immediately after marriage; in England and France, on the other hand, they tended not to give birth until fourteen and sixteen months respectively after marriage. The interval between births grew longer with subsequent children: English averages suggest an interval of twenty-eight months between the births of the first and second child, where in France the interval was about twenty-three.

This fairly low reproductive rate, in a society where a high proportion of women never married, created a distinctive family pattern. In twentieth-century Europe the economically privileged classes and nations tend to have small families, the poorer communities tend to have large ones. In preindustrial Europe precisely the opposite held good: the poor had fewer children, the rich could afford to have more. In the sixteenth-century village of Villabañez (Old Castile) families seldom had more than four children; in Córdoba in 1683 58 per cent of families had no more than two children, 32 per cent had no more than four. In France the average number of children was just over four per family. In late sixteenth-century Norwich the poor had 2.3 children per family, the richer burgesses had 4.2. Europe was thus far from having the large families usually associated with preindustrial communities. The gentry and nobles, however, often exceeded the norm. The Genevan bourgeoisie, where girls habitually married younger, was capable of producing eleven and even fifteen children per family. The English aristocracy modestly limited itself to five per family, though the record was occasionally upset by the heroic few, such as the first Earl Ferrers (d. 1717), who had thirty bastards and twenty-seven legitimate children to his credit.

The absolute dependence of fertility on the age of the mother, is solid proof that birth-control was not widely practised. At the same time, however, there were mechanisms in existence that controlled fertility. It has been widely argued that late marriage in itself was a conscious method of control (though against this thesis one might cite the evidence of Spain, where a lower marriage age did not result in a different pattern of fertility). Breast-feeding, which delays a mother's possibility of conceiving, remained normal practice; but the evidence at least from French towns shows that a high proportion of mothers from the élite and artisan classes gave their infants out to be wet-nursed, and this increased their ability to conceive while reducing that of the wet-nurses. The most commonly practised method of controlling unwanted children was exposure after birth; most such abandoned infants were illegitimate, but several also were left by parents too poor to care for them. The practice of leaving babies on the steps of churches and hospitals grew regularly throughout the early modern period and led to the establishment of foundlings' hospitals in the major European cities. By the end of the seventeenth century the number of foundlings had attained alarming proportions: the hospital in Madrid had 1400 infants in its care in 1698, and in the same decade the hospital in Paris was taking in over 2000 a year.

The best documented cases of birth-control refer not to the rural but to the urban population and élites. Henri Estienne referred in 1566 to women who utilized 'preservatives that prevent them becoming pregnant'; and another French writer, Bourdeille, quotes the case of a servant-maid who, on being scolded by her master for becoming pregnant, claimed that it would not have happened 'if I had been as well instructed as most of my friends'. By the next century, according to a confessor's manual published in Paris in 1671, priests were instructed to inquire in the confessional whether the faithful had 'employed means to prevent generation', and whether 'women during their pregnancy had taken a drink or some other concoction to prevent conception'. At the same period contraceptive and abortive practices were known in Spain, to judge by confessors' manuals and the prosecutions undertaken by the Inquisition. A more scientific, though necessarily indirect, guide to contraceptive practices is the study of birth intervals: lengthy intervals, such as those of forty-nine months or more found in all social classes in early eighteenth-century Geneva, are clear testimony that controls were practised; but it is less certain that the practices involved anything more than careful abstention. Very gradually, the unspeakable came to be spoken, and birth-control was recognized to exist. In England in 1695 a book called *Populaidias, or a Discourse concerning the having many children, in which the prejudices against having a numerous offspring are removed*, defended the older values and attacked those 'who look upon the fruitfulness of wives to be less eligible than their barrenness; and had rather their families should be none, than large'.

Population trends

Although information about population can be found in tax and military censuses of the period, it is to parish records that we turn for reliable details. Fragmentary data on births, marriages and burials were kept in several countries prior to the Reformation. But even after such registrations became compulsory – in England after 1538 (not fully effective until 1653), in Catholic countries after the Council of Trent (1563) – it was rare for a parish priest to keep his records up to date.

Europe at the end of this period was still predominantly a rural, preindustrial society. The countryside dominated life: its open spaces, punctuated here and there by settlements, gave the traveller a feeling of immense loneliness. The largest area of dense population was northern Italy, but the most densely populated nation was the Netherlands. By contrast, Russia and the Ukraine were vast emptinesses: as one went farther east the towns disappeared and the spaces opened up. The countryside, with some 95 per cent of Europe's population, determined both society and politics, even though active leadership emanated from the towns.

From about 1450 Europe's population began to increase, but unevenly, given the now clearly identified differences in demographic structure between various countries. The highest rate of increase was in the north, where the Scandinavian countries by

1600 registered an advance of two-thirds on their 1500 levels, and Britain and the Netherlands over one-half. Central Europe, Spain and Italy increased by up to one-third, France by perhaps only one-eighth. The most notable increase was in the great cities: Antwerp and Seville, under the impetus of trade, doubled in size in the first two-thirds of the sixteenth century. Lyon quadrupled its population from 1450–1550, that of Rouen tripled during the early century. Where in 1500 there had been few towns of over 100,000 inhabitants (Paris, Naples, Venice and Milan), by 1600 there were at least nine (Antwerp, Seville, Rome, Lisbon, Palermo, Messina, Milan, Venice, Amsterdam), and three of over 200,000 (Naples, Paris, London). By 1700 these last three had half a million each, and Madrid, Vienna and Moscow had joined the ranks of those with over 100,000.

Both on a small and a large scale, both in town and country, the growth in population levels was unmistakable. In the village of La Chapelle-des-Fougerets (Ile-et-Vilaine) the records show an increase of 50 per cent between 1520 and 1610; in the Valladolid region, the village of Tudela de Duero increased by 81.7 per cent between 1530 and 1593, the village of Cigales by 53 per cent. In Provence the demographic level of 1540 was three times that of 1470, in Luxembourg population increased by 39 per cent between 1501 and 1554, in Leicestershire by 58 per cent between 1563 and 1603. The territory of Zürich (excluding the city) increased its population by 45 per cent between 1529 and 1585; Norway grew from 246,000 people in 1520 to 359,000 in 1590, an increase of 46 per cent in seventy years.

The causes of the demographic increase are not clear, though it is possible to point – for the early sixteenth century at least – to a relative absence of destructive wars and to a lull in the frequent attacks of epidemics. The consequences of the increase were momentous: a restless movement of migratory populations, settlement of overseas territories, growing pressure on land use, a rise in prices stimulated in part by higher demand, a crisis in the exploitation of labour and the level of wages. Population growth was not of course in itself the unique agent of change, and other economic and social factors must also be taken into account: but it helped to make possible changes that other factors may not by themselves have precipitated. There was a disproportionate increase in the town population, which probably doubled in England during the sixteenth century. In the province of Holland the rural population between 1514 and 1622 grew by 58 per cent, the urban by 471 per cent. Urbanization was thus a notable feature of the period. Towns grew principally, as we have seen above (p. 29), through immigration from the rural areas. As cities grew they generated demand and stimulated the economy; on the negative side, however, urbanization pushed up property and rent values, and worsened the material condition of the lower classes (see Chapter 8). In the rural areas population growth was an undeniable stimulus to higher output in agriculture (see Chapters 2 and 6).

The expansionist period that began in about 1450 came to an end after the 1580s. Throughout Mediterranean Europe the decades after this were marked by reverses, associated particularly with epidemics. In France and the Netherlands the major negative factor was war. By the early seventeenth century, much of Europe was entering a phase of demographic stagnation and, in some cases, decline. The significance of this for European development is discussed below in Chapter 9; in southern Europe the population levels of the early sixteenth century were not recovered for two hundred years.

Both in the sixteenth and seventeenth centuries, there were powerful negative influences on demography. The one great reality of life was death, readily accepted because always unavoidable, omnipresent not only in the ordinary course of living but also in the whole cultural environment: in the teaching and imagery of religion; in art, poetry and drama; in popular entertainment and public celebrations. Of the three scourges bewailed by the litany – *a peste, fame et bello, libera nos Domine* – the first two could be considered as natural, though already there were suggestions that public policy could remedy their worst effects.

Epidemics

Of the great bringers of mortality the most feared was epidemic disease. Though plague was the most virulent of all epidemics, the regular toll of other diseases such as influenza, typhus, typhoid and smallpox, may have in reality been responsible for more deaths. Influenza, for example, may have been responsible for the English report of 1558 that 'in the beginning of this year died many of the wealthiest men all England through, of a strange fever': it was a severe crisis (1557–9) during which possibly a tenth of the English population died. 'Fevers' were a regular phenomenon, whereas plague could be more easily identified by its savage impact. London's great plague years illustrate this: in 1603 plague victims were 77 per cent of all deaths, in 1625 they were 65 per cent and in 1665 some 70 per cent.

The proportion of people who succumbed to plague, especially in the cities, was staggering. Possibly one-quarter of the population of London perished in the plague of 1563, when the death rate was seven times higher than in normal years. Although 1665 became known as the year of the Great Plague, in fact proportionately more people died in the outbreaks of 1603 and 1625; together the epidemics of these three years caused the death in London of up to 200,000 people. The outbreaks in Amsterdam in 1624, 1636, 1655 and 1664 are estimated to have removed respectively one-ninth, one-seventh, one-eighth and one-sixth of the population. In Uelzen (Lower Saxony) the plague of 1597 carried off 33 per cent of the population, whereas a dysentery epidemic in 1599 killed only 14 per cent. Santander in Spain was virtually wiped off the map in 1599, losing 83 per cent of its 3000 inhabitants. The great 'Atlantic plague' of 1596–1603, which gnawed at the coasts of western Europe, possibly cost one million lives, two-thirds of them in Spain alone. In France between 1600 and 1670 plague carried off between 2.2 and 3.3 millions. Mantua in 1630 lost nearly 70 per cent of its population, Naples and Genoa in 1656 nearly half theirs. Barcelona lost 28.8 per cent of its population in the plague of 1589 and about 45 per cent in that of 1651. Marseille lost half its people in 1720.

There appeared to be no defence against the plague. Isolation was the commonest remedy adopted: during the 1563 epidemic in England the court moved to Windsor and (reports the annalist Stow) 'a gallows was set up in the market-place to hang all such as should come there from London'. The flea-infected rat was eventually recognized to be the principal carrier of the disease, though some recent theories suggest that human fleas were equally responsible, since the rapidity with which plague spread is more explicable by the mobility of humans than by the movements of the less mobile black rat. It was significant that plague followed trade routes, and was also spread by armies on the march. Isolation was fairly effective. In seventeenth-century Spain, for example, double military cordons were put around infected communities and commerce was cut; but it was always difficult to control inland epidemics. A ban on commerce by sea was, on the other hand, invariably successful: it saved the Netherlands from the English plague of 1563 (but not from its indirect impact through Germany in 1566, after being taken to the Baltic in English ships), and Spain from the Marseille plague of 1720. The latter was the last outbreak known in mainland Europe; the epidemic at Messina in 1743 ended the reign of plague in the west.

The social effects of plague have been imperfectly studied, but there can be no doubt that it discriminated among its victims. Thriving on filthy conditions, it struck first and foremost at the lower classes in the towns. In London, the Mortality Bills show epidemics taking their origin in the poorest suburbs. When an epidemic struck Lyon in 1628 a contemporary comforted himself with the thought that 'only seven or eight persons of quality died, and five or six hundred of lower condition'. We find a bourgeois of Toulouse observing in his journal in 1561: 'The contagion only ever hits the poor people. . . . God by his grace will have it so. The rich protect themselves against it.' The surest protection was in flight. When the plague hit Bilbao in the early autumn of 1598, 'only the totally impoverished remained' in the city. The bourgeoisie moved to other towns, the nobility to their country estates. Those rich who remained were aware that the plague discriminated in their favour. The banker Fabio Nelli, writing from Valladolid in July 1599 in a week when nearly a thousand people had died, commented that 'I don't intend to move from here . . . almost nobody of consideration has died'. Social tensions were aggravated. With the evidence plain before their eyes, the upper classes felt that the plague had been spread by the poor. The poor in their turn resented the fact that those who had never lacked material comforts should also be spared the vengeance of the scourge.

Poverty and poor nutrition were the two main features of epidemic victims. In Sepúlveda (Spain) in April 1599 'all those who have died in this town and its region were very poor and lacked all sustenance'. The connection between poverty and epidemics encouraged public authorities to improve conditions of hygiene in the towns, but it is doubtful if any of the measures taken by municipalities was really effective.

Famine

'This year', a Spanish correspondent wrote home from Naples in 1606, 'God has seen fit to visit this realm and Sicily and other parts of Italy with a ruinous harvest, and the one here is said to be the worst for forty years.' The report was an exaggeration, for there had been an even more severe famine only ten years previously; but inevitably each crisis seemed to be worse than its predecessor, and bad years were regular enough to have an adverse cumulative effect. In England between 1549 and 1556 there was not a single good harvest, and the Privy Council banned corn exports every year between 1546 and 1550; in 1549 grain prices were 84 per cent higher than in the preceding year, and in 1556 they were 240 per cent higher. The incidence of such crises must be put in perspective. Famines, in the sense of great natural disasters, were infrequent; far more significant was the threat from the common, daily inability to obtain enough food.

The availability of food was affected primarily by the weather, but it depended also on human factors such as adequate agricultural methods, the volume of demand from the population, good communication and transport, and the presence of war. In an era when in some countries customs barriers even separated one province from another, it was possible for one of two contiguous regions to starve while the other fed adequately. The significance of the 'subsistence crisis' for mortality has been much debated. Some scholars have argued that subsistence crises could have a devastating effect, and that people could die in big numbers in famine conditions. Others have maintained that few ever died from starvation or malnutrition in early modern Europe; and that though undernourishment may have weakened health the real killer in most cases was disease. The latter argument has been based principally on a study of price data: because in many cases high mortality has not coincided with high grain prices, it has been argued that lack of food could not have caused death.

The evidence for a link between food shortages and mortality seems, however, to be firm, to judge by the crises of the 1590s, of 1661, and of the 1690s. The years 1594–7 over most of Europe were ones of excessive rain and bad harvests, resulting in a steep rise in grain prices. In Spain, Italy and Germany in particular the disaster coincided with heavy mortality brought on by epidemics of plague. Discontent and unrest led to large-scale peasant revolts all over the continent (see Chapter 10). In England there were unsuccessful attempts at armed uprisings. The English government drew up a new Poor Law in 1597 to deal with widespread poverty and distress. The authorities at Bristol undertook relief measures whereby, they claimed with satisfaction, 'the poor of our city were all relieved and kept from starving or rising.' Newcastle was not so fortunate. An entry in the town accounts reads: 'October 1597. Paid for the charge of buringe 16 poore folks who died for wante in the strettes 6s. 8d.' In Aix-en-Provence in 1597 when 'the clergy of the church of Saint-Esprit were giving bread to succour the poor, of whom there were over twelve hundred, six or seven of them died, including little girls and a woman'. At Senlis in 1595 an observer saw 'men and women, young and old, shivering in the streets, skin hanging and stomachs swollen, others stretched out breathing their last sighs, the grass sticking out of their mouths'.

The crisis of 1659–62 created conditions that in many countries eased the way to absolute monarchy. The harvest failure of 1661 in north and eastern France helped to present the young Louis XIV to his people as a beneficent ruler. Colbert reported that the king 'not only distributed grain to individuals and communities in Paris and around, but even ordered thirty and forty thousand pounds of bread to be given out daily'. As in most subsistence crises, children were the most vulnerable: in the parish of Athis, south of Paris, 62 per cent of the deaths in 1660–2 were of those aged under 10. In the countryside, reported an eyewitness, 'the pasturage of wolves has become the food of Christians, for when they find horses, asses and other dead animals they feed off the rotting flesh'. 'In the thirty-two years that I have practised medicine in this province', reported a doctor in Blois, 'I have seen nothing to approach the desolation throughout the countryside. The famine is so great that the peasants go without bread and throw themselves on to carrion. As soon as a horse or other animal dies, they eat it.'

The years 1692–4 produced poor harvests in western Europe: in November 1693 the city of Alicante reported that 'there has been virtually no harvest because it has not rained for fourteen months'. In Galicia the city of Santiago reported that 'most of the people have died of hunger and most homes have been depopulated'. The exaggeration was not unfounded. In the district of Xallas, most of the conceptions of 1693–4 disappeared in the infant mortality of 1694–5; in 1691 there had been thirty-eight marriages in the parishes, in 1695 there were only twelve. For France 1693 was possibly the worst year of the century: at Meulan, north-east of Paris, the price of grain tripled and burials were nearly two and a half times those in a normal year. With associated attacks of epidemic, the mortality in France in 1693–4 may have exceeded two millions. Three years later, in 1696, Finland suffered a disastrous harvest failure which swept away possibly one-quarter of the country's population in the course of 1696–7.

Not all the people starved. 'Nothing new here', reported a Rome newsletter in February 1558, 'except that people are dying of hunger'. The same newsletter then went on to describe a great banquet given by the pope at which the chief wonders were 'statues made of sugar carrying real torches'. The rich were sometimes touched by the plague, but almost never by hunger. In Dijon in the great famine of 1694 the number of deaths in the wealthy parish of Notre Dame was ninety-nine, in the poor parish of St Philibert 266. Even in normal times the mortality rate was tipped heavily against the undernourished poor: in seventeenth-century Geneva, 38 per cent of children born to the upper bourgeoisie died before the age of 10, but 62.8 per cent of those born to working-class parents.

Among the lower classes, mortality was as a rule higher among the rural proletariat than in the towns, for while the townspeople could beg for relief the peasants had to find sustenance from their own inhospitable environment. When the soil had no grain to offer them they turned to carrion, roots, bark, straw and vermin. Of the famine in 1637 in Franche Comté a contemporary recorded that 'posterity will not believe it: people lived off the plants in gardens and fields; they even sought out the carcasses of dead animals. The roads were strewn with people. . . . Finally it came to cannibalism'.

It remains possible to maintain that death from hunger was rare in normal conditions, but it is not easy to define what 'normal conditions' were in a society that suffered frequently from crises of one sort or another. The common people were under no illusions about their susceptibility to starvation, and the regularity of bread riots in towns illustrates their refusal to accept their fate with resignation. In 1628 one of the pastors in Geneva explained to his congregation that the current food crisis (which was to last up to 1631) was brought upon them by their sins:

The people, who had been suffering for a very long time on a meagre diet, were outraged by this and left the church in great dissatisfaction, saying that they were more in need of consolation than of accusations . . . that they were very well aware of the true state of things; and that the pastor had no idea of the misery of the great number who passed whole days and weeks in their homes without a few loaves of bread; and that they had to go without that which others fattened themselves upon.

Undernourishment was common in Geneva in both normal and

abnormal times. In January 1630, during the subsistence crisis, silk-workers were earning only two *sols* a day, whereas the cost of bread was five *sols* a pound and two pounds was the minimum required for a reasonable daily diet. In these circumstances the city council had to order the payment of supplementary wages. In 1655, a normal year with normal prices, when bread was five *sols* a pound, and cheese and meat seven *sols*, a carpenter's daily wages were about twenty-two *sols*, which could barely have sufficed to support a family, yet carpenters were by no means the bottom layer of the urban working class.

Whole provinces and nations in early modern Europe lived at a parlous level of subsistence, and even in normal harvest years relied on food imports. The wheat fields of Sicily and of eastern Europe became the great suppliers. Spain in the sixteenth century was notoriously unable to meet its own needs, and became a regular importer from the Baltic, Sicily and north Africa. In the Netherlands there was not enough land available to feed the high density of population, and import was always necessary: it was logical that Amsterdam should become the great clearing-house for Baltic wheat.

On a smaller scale, rural communities and individual peasants constantly lived close to subsistence level, since the land they possessed did not suffice for their needs. In some areas, fragmentation of peasant estates further destroyed self-sufficiency. The village of Lespignan in Languedoc is evidence of this process (which is also discussed below, Chapter 6). In 1492 the great majority of peasant proprietors were able to produce a surplus which they sold in order to buy goods, so putting themselves above the minimum level of independence. By 1607 the majority were having to buy grain in order to feed themselves, and had to support their families by finding work elsewhere. In Beauvaisis the fragmentation of peasant holdings led to a situation where as many as nine-tenths of the peasant population were not economically independent and could not guarantee to feed their families adequately. The peasant who aspired to economic independence had to farm at least 12 hectares (30 acres) in years of plenty, 27 hectares (65 acres) in years of dearth; yet in the seventeenth century less than one-tenth of the peasants here owned 27 or more hectares.

Assessment of health at this period has sometimes been made on the basis of the calorie content of food. This has led to a number of disparate calculations. In modern diets 3000 calories a day is assumed to give a minimum level of adequate nourishment. A study of the food of building workers in Antwerp in the sixteenth century, with bread, vegetables, butter, cheese and meat in the diet, suggests a value of some 2000 calories a day. The average citizen of Valladolid in the same period apparently had a daily diet of some 1580 calories. Both these food levels have been assumed to be adequate for the time. On the other hand, a study of peasant diet on the Polish royal estates in the late sixteenth century arrives at a daily average of 3500 calories; Spanish seamen are supposed to have consumed up to 4000 calories a day in the period; and the Collegio Borromeo in Pavia supplied its indigent inmates with about 6000 calories a day. Since in all cases most (perhaps three-quarters) of these calories came from cereals, the bare figures may be misleading; an analysis of food and vitamin content would give a truer picture. On the grounds that among the peasants of the Beauvaisis meat was almost unknown, fruit rare, vegetables poor and the staple was normally bread, soup, gruel, peas and beans, it has been argued that undernourishment here was constant. The same might convincingly be said of many other peasantries, and it has been shown that armies of the time – notorious spreaders of epidemics – were also grossly underfed, meat and vegetables being largely absent from their diet.

War

All other scourges were subsumed in war. 'It has been impossible to collect any taxes', runs a report from Lorraine in the 1630s, 'because of the wars that have hit most of the villages, which are deserted through the flight of some of the inhabitants and the death of others from disease or from sickness arising out of starvation.' It was inevitable that war in itself could not cause extensive mortality: armies were relatively small until the end of the seventeenth century, mass mobilization did not exist, weapons were inefficient. Despite these limitations, the impact of warfare cannot be minimized: by their depredations the soldiery spread epidemics and aggravated famine, and sometimes committed horrifying atrocities. Summarizing the consequences of the great Cromwellian repression of Ireland, Sir William Petty, who had full access to state papers, estimated that 'about 504,000 of the Irish perished, and were wasted by the sword, plague, famine, hardship and banishment, between the 23 of October 1641 and the same day 1652'.

The early sixteenth century was relatively free from wars within Christian Europe, only Italy suffering to any extent (the sack of Rome in 1527 was a notorious example). By the late century war had become universal on both land and sea, whether in civil and religious conflicts or against the Turk, and armies began to grow in size, Philip II's army in Flanders rose to 85,000 men, in 1630 Wallenstein in Germany commanded about 100,000. By 1659 the French state had 125,000 under arms, the number doubling and tripling under Louis XIV. The following paragraphs touch on five areas where the army, as in most wars of the time, ruined the cornfields, drove civilians out of their homes, spread infection, and in the process aggravated mortality and retarded fertility.

The French civil wars (1562–98) were costly in terms of lives: the massacre of St Bartholomew's eve, for example, exterminated over 3000 Protestants in Paris and 20,000 throughout France. Many localities suffered an overall loss of population: Rouen lost one-quarter of its inhabitants between 1562 and 1594. The wars were not, however, a total disaster. A survey of parish registers reveals that the earlier period, up to the 1580s, coincided with the population expansion of the sixteenth century. In Burgundy births and marriages increased regularly during the wars, decreasing only in the 1590s, when famines rather than war were responsible for falling birth rates. There is little doubt that the civil wars were a principal reason why the total increase of population in France was smaller than in any other western European country, but the mortality was not so great as to reverse the period of positive growth up to the 1580s.

In the same years the Netherlands were going through a civil war. The Eighty Years War (1568–1648) split the country into a northern section (the United Provinces) and a southern (under Spanish rule). In the early years the north suffered substantially, but from the end of the sixteenth century it was the south that took the brunt of the war. Not until the 1630s, when the Dunkirk privateers successfully attacked northern shipping, did the United Provinces suffer serious reverses. A number of factors combined to produce disastrous effects on the south. The collapse of the country was to some extent a consequence of the collapse of Antwerp, which suffered from the blockade of the Scheldt after 1572 and from the rebellion of Spanish troops – the 'Spanish fury' – in 1576. From 1580 onwards a severe crisis developed in Belgian territory as the economy ground to a halt. In 1581 the linen industries of Courtrai and Oudenarde

· collapsed and nothing could be sown in the fields round Brussels because of the war. In 1582 the duke of Anjou's troops sacked several industrial towns. Mercenaries murdered farmers, farms were destroyed, fields were left untilled. In 1585 the Scheldt was firmly closed by the Dutch. Around Ghent for a while the area of cultivation fell by 92 per cent. In most villages of Brabant the population by 1586 had dropped to between 25 per cent and 50 per cent of 1575 levels. 'Trade has almost totally ceased', reported the duke of Saxony when he visited Antwerp in 1613. The outbreak of war in 1621, after the expiry of the Twelve Years Truce between Spain and the United Provinces, brought further problems. 'I have come to Amsterdam where I now am', reported a priest in 1627, 'and find all the towns as full of people as those held by Spain are empty.' The long struggle in fact had a less severe impact in the southern, Walloon, lands; and in many areas the survival of good land and other resources helped the people to recover rapidly from the war.

The earlier phase of the Dutch wars coincided with demographic expansion, so that there was only a moderate check to fertility. The wars of the seventeenth century, however, came at a time of demographic stagnation or decline, and had a more marked effect. In France the most serious reverses were associated with the Fronde (1648–53), which took place mainly in the north, around Paris. Angélique Arnauld in 1649 lamented 'the frightful state of this poor countryside; all is pillaged, ploughing has ceased, there are no horses, everything is stolen, the peasants are driven to sleeping in the woods'. A report of 1652 on the area speaks of 'villages and hamlets deserted, streets infected by stinking carrion and dead bodies lying exposed, everything reduced to cesspools and stables, and above all the sick and dying, with no bread, meat, medicine, heating, beds, linen or covering, and no priest, doctor or anyone to comfort them'. Harvests collapsed in the affected region. Though war was the cause of misery in these years, in fact the highest mortality was caused by epidemic disease spread by the soldiers. The population loss around Paris was about a fifth. In the summer of 1652, the year of highest mortality in the whole century in the south of Paris, the death rate was fifteen times higher than in the previous four crisis years.

The Thirty Years War (1618–48) is the most famous of the scourges of this period. Though literary accounts, notably Grimmelshausen's famous anti-war tract *Simplicissimus* (1668), have helped to exaggerate some of the effects of the war, detailed research has supported the traditional picture. At the same time there can be little doubt that epidemic disease, particularly the extensive plague of 1634–6, was the single most lethal killer. Nördlingen, for example, lost one-third of its population of 9000 in the plague of 1634. The human misery caused by military occupation that same year nevertheless caused a diarist to write that 'it was considered a blessing in these times to die of the plague'. The Rhineland, fought for by the troops of every nation in Europe, was reduced to ruins. 'From Cologne hither' (to Frankfurt), reported the English ambassador in 1635, 'all the towns, villages and castles be battered, pillaged and burnt.' 'I am leading my men', claimed the Bavarian general von Werth when crossing the Rhineland in 1637, 'through a country where many thousands of men have died of hunger and not a living soul can be seen for many miles along the way.' In the county of Lippe, a region only moderately hit by the war, the population fell by 35 per cent between 1618 and 1648. In the district of Lautern in the Rhineland, a more severely devastated region, of a total of sixty-two towns thirty were still deserted in 1656, and a population of 4200 (excluding the chief town Kaiserslautern) had sunk to about 500. Augsburg lost half its population and three-quarters of its wealth during the war; its richest taxpayers fell in number from 142 to eighteen. Over the German lands as a whole the urban centres lost one-third of their inhabitants, the rural areas about 40 per cent. The losses varied from under 10 per cent in Lower Saxony in the north-west to over 50 per cent in Württemberg in the south and Pomerania in the north. These figures must be treated with caution; there was an enormous refugee population, of whom many returned eventually to their homes, so that 'loss' may not necessarily mean death so much as displacement. Not only the German lands, but other adjacent countries, suffered badly: Franche Comté, devastated between 1635 and 1644, lost between a half and three-quarters of its population.

A long-forgotten war whose consequences persist down to today was that of 1640–68 between Spain and Portugal, which ended with Spain recognizing the latter's independence. Years of skirmishes and raids across the frontier turned every major town into a garrison-town, periodically ruined both livestock and agriculture, aggravated emigration and led to the collapse of both dwellings and population. The already poor province of Extremadura may have lost half its population in the quarter century that the war lasted; its capital, Badajoz, declined by 43 per cent between 1640 and 1691, at a time when most major cities in Spain were increasing in size.

Although some areas took as much as a generation to recover pre-crisis levels, many managed to do so with surprising speed. The virtual cessation of marriages and births in some communities was only temporary. As the crisis neared its end, households which had lost one parent would look around for a replacement, and the stock of unmarried women would become available for men seeking wives. Marriages and re-marriages would increase steeply. In Nördlingen during the four months of the plague and military crisis at the end of 1634, only three marriages took place. When the plague died away in December, a massive increase in weddings occurred: 121 were celebrated in the first four months of 1635. This wave of crisis marriages would then produce a big upsurge in births, as duly happened in Nördlingen. Helped additionally by an increase in immigration, the cities and eventually the countryside would recover steadily from the disastrous years of war.

2   Prices and change

The people are increased and ground for ploughs doth want, corn and all other victual is scant . . . and dear.
Alderman Box to Lord Burghley (1576)

Early modern Europe was a world in the process of change. The apparently fixed order of the past, in which men had lived and moved within a unified Christendom, a secure community and a recognized social role, was collapsing. The late medieval world had never, of course, been immobile: traders, pilgrims, artisans had ranged over the continent, explorers had looked to Africa and Asia in search of riches. In the sixteenth century, however, men began to be aware of new and profound changes in the quality of life. William Harrison, in his *Description of England* (1577), commented that the elders in his village 'have noted . . . things to be marvellously altered in England within their sound remembrance'. A generation later Thomas Wilson, in his *The State of England* (1600), said that 'I find great alterations almost every year, so mutable are worldly things and worldly men's affairs'. One of the most widely commented aspects of change was population increase.

Demographic movement

The demographic expansion of the early sixteenth century seems to have led commentators to exaggerate its impact. As early as 1518, Ulrich von Hutten claimed that 'there is a dearth of provisions and Germany is overcrowded'; while in the same year a commission of Jeronimite friars in Spain suggested that 'the surplus population of these realms go and colonise' America. In Germany in 1538 Sebastian Franck described the country as being 'full of people'; so great was the pressure on space in Swabia, according to a chronicler of 1550, that 'there was not a corner, even in the wildest woods and the highest mountains, that was not occupied'. 'France is full of people', reported the Venetian ambassador there in 1561, 'every spot is occupied to capacity'. Bodin in 1568 believed that 'an infinite number of people has multiplied in this realm'. Sir John Hawkins could speak of 'England, where no room remains, her dwellers to bestow'. 'The people are increased and ground for ploughs doth want', complained an English writer in 1576.

Over and above the exaggerations, there was the reality that men were more on the move than ever before, and it may have been the volume of movement, particularly towards the towns, that helped to give the impression of a swollen population. Many peasant societies, of course, remained immobile. Where peasants tended to have their own plot of land, or where they were tied down by feudal obligation and seigneurial control, they were very unlikely to move away. Geography – isolation in mountain areas or quite simply a fertile environment that gave self-sufficiency – sometimes froze communities into immobility. But there is ample evidence that the rural societies of early modern Europe were more on the move than has been thought. For England, a study of the tax-rolls in Northamptonshire shows that in some areas up to 60 per cent of the non-freeholders disappeared between 1597 and 1628, and about 27 per cent of the freeholders. About half the population of the village of Cogenhoe was replaced between 1618 and 1628. In eighteen villages in Nottinghamshire, only 16 per cent of the family names present in 1544 could be found in 1641. Evidence from Germany points the same way. A study of three towns in Brandenburg shows that in Beeskow only 15 per cent of the family names present in 1518 were still there in 1652; in Freienwalde between 1652 and 1704 only four family names survived; in Driesen between 1591 and 1718 only 9 per cent of names did so. A century and a half of rural emigration is illustrated by the villages around the town of Ratzeburg (near Hamburg), where between 1444 and 1618 about 90 per cent of peasant households changed their place of residence, a fifth of these as many as seven or eight times.

Most people did not move very far. In seventeenth-century Sussex they tended not to move farther than 20 miles away. In south and central England between 1660 and 1730, an analysis of over 7000 cases shows that more than half of those who changed their domicile did so within a range of 10 miles; only 3 per cent had moved more than 100 miles. By their nature, big urban centres encouraged a rapid turnover. A London clergyman at the end of the sixteenth century claimed that every twelve years or so 'the most part of the parish changeth, as I by experience know, some going and some coming'. In east London between 1580 and 1639 only 26 per cent of studied cases were born within the locality. In Cologne one-sixth of the population changed domicile between 1568 and 1574.

While many small towns and rural areas in Europe continued to experience stability of population, therefore, there is ample evidence that for most communities a high degree of movement was quite normal. Three main reasons for mobility are apparent: marriage, employment and distress. In an average small community blood relationships presented a problem. Marriages within the fourth degree of kinship were forbidden by canon law, and since a high proportion of the village's population might be interrelated it became necessary to seek outside the community for a partner. Consanguinity therefore became a barrier, but not always so in practice: in the seventeenth-century Spanish village of Pedralba (Valencia) about one-tenth of marriages were within the forbidden degrees. As a rule, however, in smaller settlements young people were obliged by kinship restrictions to go out to neighbouring villages, where they would be likely to meet prospective partners at local religious and harvest festivities. The search for partners would occasionally provoke inter-village strife, as young men tried to defend their women against outsiders and put pressure on the girls and their families or sought dispensations from consanguinity. Community pressures of this sort might result in a high level of endogamous marriages, though in general it can be concluded that the degree of endogamy was directly related to the size of the village: in the small village of Rouvray (216 inhabitants) in seventeenth-century Champagne 31 per cent of marriages were endogamous, while in Mussey (511 inhabitants) in the same area the figure was 68 per cent, presumably because of the larger choice available. Exogamy was always higher in the countryside than in the towns. In Altopascio (rural Tuscany) in the late seventeenth century about 60 per cent of marriages were with a partner from outside the parish; the outsider in most cases being male, suggesting that mobility for marriage was generally masculine except where there was positive discrimination against men.

Movement in the short distance between communities, and between communities and the city, accounted for the bulk of migration. The city was at all times the greatest magnet, offering all the prospects – freedom, fortune, marriage, work – not readily available in other communities: the increase in urban population in this period has already been noted. All classes moved cityward. In Dorset, reports that 'some of our welthie men and merchauntes be gone from us' suggest a move to the commercial attractions of London. London too was the setting of the play *The History of Richard Whittington* (1605), which showed how a penniless youth came to the big city, rose to the top of the social ladder and became thrice Lord Mayor of London. For the rural underprivileged, all cities had their streets paved with gold. In times of distress the drift to towns became a flood. In 1667, the residents of the villages of Palencia (Spain) claimed to have lost nine-tenths of their population in the preceding forty years, 'households and residents moving to the large towns such as Valladolid, Rioseco, Palencia and other nearby cities, deserting their houses and property through lack of capital'.

Mobility over longer distances was occasioned primarily by the search for employment. Some professions made it a rule to move about, as in France where apprentices were encouraged to train in different towns. Jean de la Mothe, a sixteenth-century cordwainer, left his home town of Tours at the age of 16 and ended up in Dijon four years later, after having trained in thirteen different localities. As a rule, migrants of good standing and with skills that were in ready demand did not need to move very far; whereas the lower and less skilled levels of the working population had to move farther and in greater numbers in order to find employment. The differences can be seen in Frankfurt: in the fifteenth century three-quarters of immigrants who were granted the privilege of citizenship came from less than 75 kilometres away, whereas of the locksmiths who came to train and work, 56 per cent came from over 150 kilometres away. Figures for the city of Zürich in 1637 are similar: only 4 per cent of new citizens came from distant foreign parts (mainly Germany), but one-third of apprentices did. In Oxford in 1538–57 some 45 per cent of apprentices came from distant areas of Wales and north-western England. Seasonal employment accounted for very large numbers of migrants, but only in specific areas of Europe, where, however, the available data – for the seventeenth century – coincide with a period of agrarian crisis which may exaggerate its extent. The best known example is of the peasants of Galicia (Spain), who because of their inadequate landholdings emigrated regularly to Castile and Andalucia to find supplementary work, returning only at harvest time. In the same way, thousands of French rural labourers crossed the Pyrenees each summer to help gather the Spanish harvest. Seasonal workers seem not to have been dissuaded by distance: the records of the hospital at Montpellier in 1696–9 show that hundreds of labourers came from as far away as northern France in search of a wage.

Distress, finally, was a regular precipitant of migration. Thousands of young men left the depressed countryside and went abroad to serve in the wars: 8000 Scots are estimated to have fought in the Thirty Years War; from Spain in the sixteenth century some 9000 men a year went overseas to fight. Inflation, enclosures and rising rents drove rural labourers from the villages; heavy taxation and the depredations of war forced many to leave and look for a new life elsewhere. The itinerant poor and vagabonds became a commonplace in every country in Europe.

Emigration abroad

From the sixteenth century attempts were made to expand the European frontier into the still unexplored reaches of the globe. The Russians had no difficulty in crossing the Urals, but their penetration of Siberia did not involve any significant movement of population: even as late as 1650 the outposts in Siberia were manned by no more than 10,000, and these were not settlers so much as mercenaries and Cossacks employed by the Tsar. The hero and pioneer of the eastern frontier was Yermak, the famous brigand turned mercenary soldier, who went to Siberia in 1582. The decades after him saw no heroes, only the remorseless push forward of troop-detachments and fur merchants. The south of Europe was even less promising a frontier, since the whole of the eastern and southern Mediterranean lay in the hands of the Muslim powers. Parallel with and contemporary to Yermak was Sebastian, king of Portugal, who like the Russian perished in an attempt to extend the frontier. Marching out to Morocco in 1578 at the head of his army, the young king was overwhelmed by Moorish forces at the battle of Alcazar-Kebir. The dream, initiated by Cardinal Cisneros's conquest of Oran in 1509 and continued by Charles V after him, of extending Christian rule into Africa, was subsequently abandoned.

There was no significant emigration eastward: the distances were too hazardous, and the advanced civilizations of the Arabs and the rulers of India and east Asia were too formidable a barrier.

Westward, on the other hand, there were new and apparently empty lands. 'Why then should we stand striving here for places of habitation', argued John Winthrop in 1629, 'and in the mean time suffer a whole continent [America] to be waste without any improvement?'

The sixteenth century opened with Spain's gradual advance into America. After the discoveries of 1492, settlement was restricted largely to the West Indies and in particular to the island of Hispaniola, where the New World's first city, Santo Domingo, was founded. Thanks to the dangers and the high death rate the number of settlers was at first fairly small, some thousand in 1499. In the first decade of the sixteenth century the principal islands and the early mainland settlements were colonized. The whole enterprise was conducted extremely slowly: nearly thirty years – a whole generation – elapsed between Columbus's landfall and the conquest of Mexico city by Cortés. At the end of that timespan, however, Spain had carried out two epoch-making feats: the circumnavigation of the globe (1519–22) and the overthrow of the Aztecs (1519–21).

These events opened up a new phase in Spanish expansion. Great rewards were seen to await even the humblest settler. Most of the conquistadors were social nonentities: Cortés was the son of a 'poor and humble' captain of infantry; Francisco Pizarro had been a swineherd; Valdivia and Alvarado did not even know where they were born. Yet many of them achieved an apotheosis. Cortés became a marquis in 1529, with the grant of an immense territory in Mexico comprising over twenty large towns and villages and some 23,000 Indian vassals. His case also illustrates the point that the Spanish frontier in America, for all its apparent initial freedom, rapidly began to reproduce the restrictive social patterns of old Spain. The earliest settlers had never wanted this: they consisted of small traders – shoemakers, blacksmiths, swordsmiths, cooks, plasterers, masons – who sought new opportunity in freedom. In Paraguay the governor asked that no lawyers be permitted, 'because in newly settled countries they encourage dissensions and litigation among the people'. In Mexico, according to Bernal Díaz, the Spaniards asked 'that His Majesty be pleased not to suffer any scholars or men of letters to come into this country, to throw us into confusion with their learning, quibbling and books'.

The ease in attaining wealth, however, helped bar the way to a democratic society. Wealth can be a spur to social mobility, but in America it made the white colonists into a leisured class exploiting the native population. As new reports of fabled riches trickled through, the settlers moved into the mainland. 'Being men fond of adventure', observed the historian Fernández de Oviedo, 'those who go to the Indies are for the most part unmarried and therefore do not feel obliged to reside in any one place. Since new lands are being discovered every day, those men believe that they will swell their purses more quickly in new territory.' A highly mobile settler class like this needed a secure source of labour to exploit the land and feed the population: this came from the Indians and later the negroes. 'In the Indies', reported a magistrate of Hispaniola in 1550, 'Spaniards do not work. All who go there immediately become gentlemen.' Spanish America certainly offered the underprivileged of the mother country a new perspective in life, but it did so at the cost of reproducing the inegalitarian structure of European society. The attempt to break away from the European pattern and create a new Utopian society (see Chapter 8) collapsed by the mid sixteenth century, by which time some 150,000 Spaniards had crossed to America.

English emigration westward began with Ireland. The plunder of the island by English soldiers and settlers precipitated the extensive depopulation observed by Sir William Petty. In America, however, the settlers began to construct a society quite distinct from the colonialist régimes in Ireland and Spanish America. In New England the relevant social feature of emigrants was their economic status rather than their religion. Consisting for the most part of small yeoman farmers and lesser traders, they were – unlike the Spaniards, and in default of a readily available labour force – content to till their own soil and trade their own produce. As a self-sufficient community they were from the beginning very close to being a one-class society, without any landlord or noble stratum above them or any depressed labour force below. There were several exceptions to this in the early days, notably in Virginia and the crown colonies, but the dominant trend, even in the proprietary colonies, was socially democratic and politically oligarchic. The attraction, then, was not so much the winning of great wealth, which could be got only through farming or energetic trading, as the winning of freedom from the social barriers in Old England.

The liberty sought by emigrants was complete. One could 'live freely there', a playwright informed his London audience in 1605, 'without sergeants or courtiers or lawyers or intelligencers'. Land was free, rents rare, opportunities unlimited. Sir Edwin Sandys naïvely hoped that this environment would produce in Virginia 'a form of government as may be to the greatest benefit and comfort of the people, and whereby all injustice, grievances and oppression may be prevented'. Some went to the land of promise involuntarily. From the beginning it was the practice (not however of the Spaniards) to transport penal offenders to the new lands, though there were few outright felons, less than 180 being sent to America prior to 1640. Among others forcibly transported were orphans, vagabonds, loose women and unemployed men; thereby, it was claimed with some truth, 'many men of excellent wits and of diverse singular gifts . . . that are not able to live in England, may be raised again'. Not without reason did Captain John Smith in 1624 call America 'the poor man's best country in the world'. Much of the optimism was misplaced, and not all the colonies were as comfortable as seventeenth-century Massachusetts, where poverty was almost unknown. The positive aspects of the American experience were, however, undoubted. Liberation from the feudal structure of Europe, its class conventions, its economic disabilities and religious oppression, opened up new horizons and helped to provoke change in Europe. 'I have lived in a country', the preacher Hugh Peter, recently back from America, told the Long Parliament in 1645, 'where in seven years I never saw beggar, nor heard an oath, nor looked upon a drunkard. Why should there be beggars in your Israel when there is so much work to do?'

The cost of living

In the Old World social relations were being subjected, from the end of the fifteenth century, to a new phenomenon that affected all classes and accelerated the rate of change: a rise in the cost of living. In Spain in 1513 Alonso de Herrera claimed that 'a pound of mutton now costs as much as a whole sheep used to'. In Germany in 1538 Sebastian Franck observed that 'everything costs more, and one deals now in groats rather than pennies'. In England in 1549 Sir Thomas Smith argued that 'sixpence a day will not now go as far as fourpence would aforetime; also where forty shillings a year was good honest wages for a yeoman afore this time, and twenty pence a week's wages was sufficient, now double as much will scant bear their charges'. Jean Bodin in France in 1568 testified that 'the price of things fifty or sixty years ago was ten times less than at present'. All classes suffered: the famous Italian engineer Antonelli, on contract to Philip II, claimed in 1581 that in Spain 'the prices of goods have risen so much that seigneurs, gentlemen, commoners and the clergy cannot live on their incomes'.

Nearly all the items that made up the ordinary stock of consumer goods rose appreciably in cost during the sixteenth century. Between 1500 and 1600 the price of wheat, a basic food for most of the population, rose by 425 per cent in England, 318 per cent in the United Provinces, 651 per cent in France, 271 per cent in Austria, 376 per cent in Castile, and 403 per cent in Poland. In most cases the price-rise was – as we shall see – smaller in manufactured goods, but even when these are taken into account and added to the prices of other basic commodities to construct a cost-of-living index, the picture is clear. An index constructed by Phelps Brown and Hopkins for the south of England shows that between 1450 and 1700 the cost of living there rose by over 700 per cent.

Some writers have questioned whether the term 'price revolution' is correct. The Brown–Hopkins index, for example, suggests that the annual average rate of price-rise in England between 1532 and 1660 was 0.86 per cent, and even in the more inflationary period under the Tudors, from 1532 to 1580, did not exceed 1.5 per cent. These figures seem derisory when compared with modern annual inflation rates of over 10 and 20 per cent. Was the sixteenth-century increase so revolutionary after all? Did Florence, where inflation between 1552 and 1600 did not exceed an annual average of 2 per cent, experience a 'price revolution'? With some qualifications, it seems reasonable to continue to use the term. In the first place the intensity of the price-rise varied; it was much slower in the late fifteenth and early sixteenth, and sharper only from the mid sixteenth to the early seventeenth century. This would seem to locate the real 'revolution' in the late sixteenth century, though it is also possible (as has been done for Spain) to plot prices on a different, logarithmic scale and show that the proportionate rate of inflation was higher in the early century. The second qualification is that the price-rise was unprecedented: it was this that most struck contemporaries and encouraged historians to speak of a 'revolution'. In the simple economy of the sixteenth century it was less easy to adapt to economic changes: if bread doubled in price, people starved; nowadays they can turn to alternative foods such as potatoes. Finally, the 'revolution' can no longer be discussed solely in terms of prices. It is necessary to bring into account other factors, such as wages and rents, which affected the standard of living quite as much as market prices.

Causes of the price-rise

Because the inflation was imperfectly understood, it was blamed in the first place on human greed. 'In the last few years', claimed the Cortes of Castile in 1548, 'the heavy purchases by foreigners of wool, silk, iron, steel, other merchandise and provisions', had pushed up price levels. In 1551 the Cortes said that 'the principal cause of the rise in prices is that aliens speculate in all kinds of provisions'. Monopoly interests in food and other goods were blamed by Bodin in the 1560s for much of the inflation and scarcity in France. In England the author of a tract of 1549 concluded that with high prices 'the principal cause is the engrossing of things into few men's hands'.

Such accusations were in a sense correct, since speculators and hoarders were undeniably active in these times of crisis. But speculation was a symptom not a cause. Speculators themselves had to find a defence against the financial instability caused by the devaluation of the coin of the realm. Between 1543 and 1551 the amount of silver in English coins was reduced by over two-thirds, and wage-earners found the purchasing power of their money greatly reduced. The very poor, who subsisted mainly on small change, found that much of it had now been made worthless; while traders raised prices so as to recoup their losses. Only in 1560 did Elizabeth finally attempt to stabilize the coinage and strengthen it against foreign speculation. Surprisingly enough, England after 1560 was the only major European country to have a currency that did not get devalued. All others, from Russia and Poland to France and Spain, suffered some degree of monetary inflation as a result of reducing the amount of silver in the coinage. In Spain small reductions in the silver content of coins occurred under Charles V and Philip II, but it was not until the reign of Philip III that silver began to disappear from the coinage entirely and the government resorted to extensive debasement. Similar debasements took place in other countries: in Poland the silver content of the *grosz* was reduced by two-thirds between 1578 and 1650.

Were the devaluations a cause of the price-rise? English monetary difficulties, like those of France, can be traced to the early sixteenth century at least; Spanish and Polish money, on the other hand, remained mostly stable until the end of the century. Yet, for all these countries a continuous rise in prices, whether or not accompanied by monetary devaluation, was a common experience. It appears that the price-rise was only partly to be blamed on the recoinages of the period. This fact struck Jean Bodin with peculiar force. In his *Discours . . . et Response aux Paradoxes de M. de Malestroict* (1568), an attack on a writer who denied that a price-rise even existed, the great political theorist pointed out the fallacy of relating price levels only to the silver or gold content of coins.

For Bodin 'the principal and almost the only' cause of the price-rise was '(a reason that no one has yet suggested) the abundance of gold and silver' from America. Bodin's argument was to become the classic exposition of the origins of the price revolution, particularly after a vast array of data accumulated by Earl J. Hamilton lent weighty support to it. The argument is that after the discovery of America bullion flowed not only into Spain but also into Europe, where it supplemented the flow of coin and began to push up prices. Any increase in bullion before the discovery of the American mines was attributed to increased output by the silver mines of central Europe. The connection between bullion imports and the rise in prices was firmly and convincingly argued by Hamilton in his study of silver shipments to Spain.

Not until the mid sixteenth century did European writers begin to look on American silver as a possible cause of inflation. Probably the first to connect the two phenomena was the Salamanca jurist Martin de Azpilcueta, who in 1556 argued that 'in Spain, in times when money was scarcer, goods and labour were given for very much less than after the discovery of the Indies, which flooded the country with gold and silver. The reason for this is that money is worth more where and when it is scarce than where and when it is abundant'. Francisco López de Gomara made a similar observation in 1558 in a work that remained unpublished until 1912. The author usually given the credit for the formulation and popularization of the argument is Jean Bodin. In France his ideas were taken up and reproduced by contemporaries, and in Spain he was read and popularized by the writer Sancho de Moncada. In England the author of the *Discourse of the Common Weal* (1581) accepted the role played by 'the great store and plenty of treasure, which is walking in these parts of the world, far more in these our days than ever our forefathers have seen in times past. Who doth not understand of the infinite sums of gold and silver which are gathered from the Indies and other countries and so yearly transported into these coasts?' Gerard Malynes, a prominent English merchant, argued in 1601 that 'the great store or abundance of money and bullion, which of late years is come from the West Indies into Christendom, hath made everything dearer'.

Historians have been wary of accepting the hypothesis fully. Just as inflation appears not to have been necessarily caused by debasement of coinage, so it seems that in some countries prices began to rise well before American silver made its impact. In Germany and parts of France price levels were already rising after 1470. Negligible amounts of bullion entered England in the early sixteenth century, yet already by 1550 the price level there had doubled: where the Brown–Hopkins index for 1510 is 103, in 1550 it is 262. In Italy bullion to finance the Spanish troops did not arrive in significant quantities until the 1570s, but already in the 1530s the price curve was moving sharply upward.

Difficulties arise even in the case of Spain, chief importer of New World treasure. Hamilton argued that 'beyond question the "abundant mines of America" were the principal cause of the price revolution in Spain'. There can be no doubt that bullion had a direct and stimulating effect on the economy of the peninsula, but three points require emphasis. First, despite Hamilton's excellent research his figures for bullion imports are often incomplete (because of the level of smuggling) for the period up to the early seventeenth century; and for the period after 1630 they are very unreliable. Second, much, if not most, of the bullion that theoretically entered Spain did not tarry there long and was rapidly extracted by foreign traders, so that there may in fact have been little bullion in circulation and its impact on prices may have been modest. As early as 1558 the writer Luis Ortiz petitioned the crown to stop exporting bullion because of its scarcity in the realm. In 1600 Martin González de Cellorigo argued that 'if Spain has no gold or silver coin it is because she has some; and what makes her poor is her wealth'. Third, prices were rising in Spain before bullion imports began, particularly in the south where the Granada wars were producing inflationary conditions, so that American silver was only one of many operative causes.

The argument relating inflation to bullion is based on the quantity theory of money. According to this, when demand is steady the level of commodity prices is determined by the amount of money available. Any increase in the amount of money (extra coinages, import of silver) would raise prices. This certainly happened in the sixteenth century, but interestingly enough not all prices rose at the same rate. In England in the early century, for example, grain prices more than trebled but non-agrarian prices only doubled. This suggests that demand for food outstripped that for manufactured goods. It also suggests changes in the relative quantity of agrarian and non-agrarian goods. On either count, consumer demand and the production of commodities must be considered to have played an important role in modifying price levels.

An increase in consumer demand followed from an increase in population. Demographic growth, indeed, had since the late fifteenth century begun to stimulate the European economy, which in turn stepped up its demand for more investment, so that the absorption of American bullion was almost a consequence rather than a cause of inflation. There was a regular and widespread increase in land values, a positive indication of land hunger on the part of an expanding population. There was also a pronounced fall in real wages, as labour became cheaper with the expansion of the labour force. The disparity between agrarian and non-agrarian prices is crucial evidence of the direct impact of population increase on prices. In Spain throughout the first three-quarters of the sixteenth century, agricultural prices rose considerably faster than the non-agricultural. The Brown–Hopkins estimates for three countries show that with the period 1451–75 represented by an index of 100, in 1601–20 the index stood as follows:

	Alsace	South England	France
Price index of foodstuffs	517	555	729
Price index of industrial goods	294	265	335

In each case food prices rose about twice as much as other commodities. This was clearly a selective inflation affecting the basic consumables most required by an expanding population, with demand outstripping production. It explains why prices began to rise even before the arrival of bullion from America. From the same premises it can be deduced that demand for non-essential industrial goods did not rise in the same proportion, though production continued to develop.

Incomes and the price-rise

In a less flexible economy than ours is today, with large sections of
the people, of all classes, subsisting on traditionally fixed incomes,
the impact of inflation, even at 2 per cent a year, could be
catastrophic. 'In times past', observed an English commentator in
1581, 'he hath been accounted rich and wealthy who was worth
thirty or forty pounds; but in our days the man of that estimation is
reputed next neighbour to a beggar.' The evidence shows that the
nominal wages of a labourer rose in the period of inflation: in Spain
from an index of 50 in 1511–20 to one of 165 in 1611–20, in Lwow
(Poland) from an index of 105 in 1521–30 to 144 in 1621–30, in
southern England from fourpence a day in 1548 to a shilling a day
in 1642. The doubling of wages, however, was insufficient to keep
pace with inflation; workers' incomes lagged way behind industrial
prices and even further behind food prices. Measured against the
cost of a group of consumer items, the real wages of building
craftsmen (as calculated by Brown–Hopkins for southern England,
Vienna and Valencia) declined by over a half between 1476–1500
and 1591–1600.

In the city of Speyer between 1520 and 1621 wages doubled and
sometimes trebled but over the same period the price of rye, a basic
staple food, increased by fifteen times, that of wheat thirteen times,
that of peas fourteen times, of meat sixfold, and of salt sixfold. Most
of the wages we have touched on have been industrial ones, but it
is not surprising to learn that agricultural wages also fell in real
terms. In Poitou a farmhand's wages in 1578 could purchase only 52
per cent of what they could have bought in 1470, and the income of
a mower had likewise declined to 58 per cent of its former value. In
Languedoc agricultural wages that stood at an index of 100 in 1500
fell to an index of 44 by 1600. All sections of the working class, in
all European countries, were severely hit.

A survey of wages alone does not, of course, give the full story.
The accounts of the chapter-house of the church of Notre-Dame in
Antwerp in the sixteenth century show that even workers in regular
employment were without work, and therefore unpaid, for about
one-sixth of the year. Their real income over the year would thus be
much less than the daily wage rate might indicate. There were
those, moreover, for whom a money wage formed only a small part
of income, since they were paid in kind – usually one or two meals
daily – and were consequently less dependent on ready cash. This

group often included the unskilled labourers in the towns, and over large areas of Europe formed an absolute majority of the rural working population. Many serfs, for example, were paid entirely in kind. The social problem in the sixteenth century was not, therefore, so much one of wages (since so few depended entirely on wages for a living) as one of rents, prices and debts, issues which affected both the skilled craftsman and the unskilled wage-earner. Thanks to being paid in kind, and perhaps enjoying fixed rents, some workers might even be cushioned against inflation.

There is no real doubt, however, that among the lower classes as a whole incomes were a serious casualty of the price revolution. A significant pointer to increased poverty was the gradual disappearance of meat from the working diet. In Sicily consumption of meat in rural areas declined from between 16 and 22 kg per person annually in the fifteenth century, to between 2 and 10 kg in 1594–6. In Swabia in 1550 a witness claimed that 'in the past they ate differently at the peasant's house. Then there was meat and food in profusion every day. . . . Today, everything has truly changed'.

Land and the price revolution

The basic unit of wealth in Europe was not bullion but land, and changes in the price and use of land made the sixteenth-century inflation memorable to contemporaries. The impact on the peasantry and on rural production is discussed below in Chapter 6. Landlords both gained and lost. Sir Thomas Smith in his *Discourse of the Common Weal* (1549) said that among those who profited were 'all such as have takings or farms at the old rent; they pay for their land good cheap and sell all things growing thereof dear'. The losers included 'all noble men and gentlemen that live by a stinted [i.e. fixed] rent or stipend, or do not maner [i.e. work] the ground, or do occupy no buying or selling'. Because of the decline in traditional incomes, 'therefore gentlemen do so much study the increase of their lands, enhancing of their rents, and so take farms and pastures into their own hands'.

Rent increases were universally condemned. The English writer Robert Crowley in 1550 denounced the rich landlords as 'men without conscience, men utterly void of God's fear, yea men that live as though there were no God at all. . . . They take our houses over our heads, they buy our grounds out of our hands, they raise our rents . . . '. Statesmen and churchmen joined in the chorus of denunciation. Yet, as Smith (himself a landlord) realized, inflation would have badly hit landlords if they had been unable to cover their rising costs with higher income.

In rural Languedoc land rents remained fairly stationary in the sixteenth century, and rose only in the early seventeenth. Many other regions, where population pressure was not excessive and where tenancies were guaranteed, likewise escaped the social tension engendered by rent rises. But the predominant trend was unmistakable. In the estate of Eiderstedt in Schleswig-Holstein a rent of 10.75 marks a hectare of arable in 1526–50 rose by 1576–1600 to 31 marks; and over the same period the market price of the hectare rose from an index of 100 to one of 662. In Poitou land which sold for a price index of 100 in 1531 was sold at an index of 520 in 1601. Bishop Latimer in England complained in the 1550s that his own father had a farm that had been leased to him originally at £3 whereas now the rent was £6. 'In my time', observed William Harrison in the 1580s, '£4 of rent be improved to £40, £50 or £100.' In East Anglia the rent of arable land rose sixfold between 1590 and 1650, a pointer both to the value of arable and to its importance over pasture, whose rental in the same period rose no more than two or three times.

English landowners were among the most proficient at increasing their returns. In the period 1619–51 the rents on the twelve Yorkshire manors belonging to the Saviles of Thornhill were raised by over 400 per cent. On new additions to the estates of the Herbert family in Wiltshire, rents rose from an index of 100 in 1510–19 to one of 829 in 1610–19. On new lands of the Seymour family in the same county, rents increased from an index 100 in 1510–19 to 951 in 1600–9. Such increases did not necessarily represent profit, nor did tenants always suffer. The gentry had heavy expenses that could only be met by higher rents. Assiduous tenants could make adequate profits when they worked their land well, and the rapid rise in the market price of cereals, meat and wool from their estates would readily compensate for having to pay more to a landlord. In the village of Wigston Magna in Leicestershire, the whole of the late sixteenth century was a time of profit for the small farmers because the steep rise in the price of foodstuffs they sold on the market more than compensated for any other expenses such as rents or taxes. This phenomenon of prices rising even higher than rents was commented upon in the East Frisian Chronicle (1545) of Beninga:

'When you consider how butter, cheese and everything that grows on the land and that a labourer has to buy, cost a great deal and have more than doubled in price in the last twenty years, taxes and rents cannot be said to have risen to the same extent.'

In addition to profiting from the price-rise, small farmers could be protected from rack-renting by the length of their tenancies. In Old Castile, and in Lwow (Poland), for much of the sixteenth century long-term contracts kept the peasant at least partly secure, and it was only in the seventeenth century that leases were revised for shorter periods. A long tenancy would encourage the peasant to invest in and improve his land, though in practice he could not profit fully from the price-rise if he had to pay rent in kind. By increasing the rent every time a new tenant took over, the hospital of the Holy Spirit in Biberach (South Germany) was able to raise its rental income from an index of 100 in 1500–9 to one of 1085 in 1620–9. Thus landlords found a way round the problem of long tenures and fixed rents.

Rent rises occurred in the town no less than in the country. Robert Crowley complained that urban landlords had bought 'whole streets and lanes, so that the rents be raised some double, some triple, and some fourfold'. The greed of landlords was not, however, always the explanation for higher rents. Demographic expansion and the movement of population to the towns, were sufficient in themselves to push prices up and open opportunities for speculators. When country gentry moved into the towns the same thing happened. In Valladolid in the mid sixteenth century, where the presence of the court helped to inflate prices, house rents within a decade increased by up to 80 per cent. In Lwow the rents of commercial premises increased between 1500 and 1550 by 150 per cent to 800 per cent. In Paris, rents increased tenfold between 1550 and 1670.

The 'land revolution' which followed the price-rise was for several reasons no less significant than the price revolution. First, the land protected the privileged. The holders of estates and manors in Germany, France, England, Italy, the noble lords whose soil produced corn, whose fields pastured sheep, whose peasants brought in dairy produce, kept their heads above the waves of inflation, raised their rents where possible or necessary, but most important of all began to exploit their resources to benefit from the favourable level of prices. One success story was the Seymour family, whose manorial holdings in Wiltshire produced receipts that rose from £475 in 1575–6 to £3204 in 1649–50. The aristocracy – at least the greater part of it – was not only saved but entrenched itself even more firmly into the political life of Europe. Second, the sure guarantee offered by land in a world where most other values seemed to be collapsing inspired those who had been successful in their own fragile enterprises – finance, commerce – to think of their families and to buy an estate or two on which to spend their declining days. Land was both the conserver and the solvent of society; while preserving the old forces, it also gave greater opportunities for wealth and mobility to those who had made their fortunes in professions frowned on by the upper classes. Finally, the process of change on the land produced a considerable number of casualties. In England the independent small farmer, the yeoman, tended to disappear (not only downwards, it should be emphasized, but also upwards). Everywhere, both in England and on the continent, even in lands which, like Sweden, had a relatively free peasantry, changes in land values and soil exploitation led to the expropriation of a section of the peasant class and to the growth of unemployment, both urban and rural. Landlessness became a prime consequence of the rise in land values (in Myddle in Shropshire only 7 per cent of the population were without land in 1541–70; in 1631–60 the proportion was 31.2 per cent). At the same time vagrancy increased and agrarian conflict intensified.

Governments and the price revolution

Inflation inevitably preoccupied the state: it affected the stability of the coinage, and made the waging of war (the primary activity of governments at this time) more expensive. Governments had been debasing money well before the impact of the price-rise, mainly in order to profit from the debasement. The inflow of silver created further difficulties by aggravating inflation, which in turn led to a fall in the real value of money.

On the continent the struggle to stabilize the coinage in the sixteenth century is closely connected with the American silver sent abroad in great waves by Spain to finance its troops. Spain became the international pace-setter. Already in 1557 the collapse of its credit and the declaration of bankruptcy brought with it a universal declaration of bankruptcy in France, the Netherlands, Naples and Milan, making necessary the peace of Cateau-Cambrésis in 1559. To recover its fiscal stability and imperial position, Spain had to divert large resources of silver to Italy and the Netherlands. France, too, received a large volume of silver, not only indirectly through trade but also directly through the subsidies paid by Spain to the Catholic League in the 1580s. In all these countries silver began to exercise an inflationary role, aggravated quite naturally by the uncertainties of constant war. In Italy the silver began to be issued by the mints as coin: in Naples alone, between 1548 and 1587, 10.5 million ducats were put into circulation in this way. Yet by 1587 only 700,000 of this remained in circulation. The rest had fallen into the hands of speculators and hoarders, ordinary people who were insuring themselves against bad money. In France the same phenomenon occurred. First there was an inflation of the silver coinage, then when attempts were made (as in 1602) to limit the face value of the coins, they began to disappear from circulation. Counterfeit or debased coin flowed in to take its place. Foreign speculators were active, as a report from Lyon in 1601 claimed: 'the German and Swiss traders in this city, under the shelter of their privileges, are amassing coin to carry out of the realm'.

Spain, the source of silver, was the greatest sufferer. Philip II had fought against the rise in prices without ever allowing himself to debase either the silver or the vellon coinage. Philip III, however, opened his reign by allowing (in 1599) the issue of vellon without any silver content. The government made a profit out of this, as it also did in 1602 when it ordered a reduction in size of the copper coins. The coining of more copper in subsequent years was supposed to cure the scarcity of money; instead it had two main adverse effects. It led to severe inflation, and it all but eliminated silver from circulation. The price level in Spain achieved heights paralleled almost nowhere else in Europe; and copper, rather than silver, came to represent over 98 per cent of the coin being used in Spain in 1650.

England was the only country to maintain a relatively stable coinage in this period, thanks to the recoinage undertaken by Elizabeth in 1560–1, an exercise that took several years to complete, restored public confidence in the currency, and brought in a small profit to the crown. Elsewhere in Europe the intrinsic value of the coinage fell repeatedly, almost from year to year. Just as regularly prices and the costs of the state tended to spiral upwards.

A lower real return from taxation, and higher costs of war, were the unhappy lot of all governments in the age of the price revolution. The plight of the early Stuarts in England is reflected in the plaint of Lord Treasurer Cranfield in 1623: 'you cannot easily conceive into what straits I am daily driven for supply of money for His Majesty's occasions, which the exchequer is not able to support, they are so infinite and of so many pressing natures'. In France the wars of the late sixteenth century crippled the monarchy, which repeatedly suspended payment of interest on the *rentes* and repudiated its debts. When Sully came to power his first act was not to pay the debts of the crown but to repudiate them and in effect declare a bankruptcy. In Spain, the worst hit of all, the government repudiated its debts regularly every twenty years: in 1557, 1575, 1596, 1607, 1627, 1647.

'War is extremely expensive to him', wrote a Frenchman in 1597 about Philip II, 'and costs him more than it does any other prince.' The statement was a truism, in view of the fact that Spain – or rather, Castile – had to finance the largest empire in the world. A memorandum of April 1574 drawn up by Juan de Ovando put the crown's income for the coming year at a presumed 5,642,304 ducats, of which only 1 million was expected from America in the form of bullion. The crown's total debts at that date (as distinct from its current obligations) amounted to 73,908,271 ducats, of which 4 millions were owing in the Netherlands. Other estimates made at the same time differed slightly, but the proportion of the debt appears all too credible.

Since the real value of taxes declined, governments were forced to look for new ways to pay for their obligations. In their search for more money, they clashed with the privileged orders and with constitutional bodies. The years of political crisis in France after 1630, and the Eleven Years' Tyranny in England, were both connected with problems of royal finance. The revolutionary 1640s, when popular uprisings throughout Europe chose taxation as their primary grievance, showed that the problem remained unsolved. Those who favoured a freer hand for the state in fiscal matters, defended the 'absolute' rights of the crown. The struggle over 'absolutism', which occupied much of the seventeenth century, was thus at heart a struggle over public finance. The burden on taxpayers in some areas can be approximately assessed. In Castile the level of indirect taxation doubled between 1556 and 1584, outpacing the price-rise, and by the early seventeenth century stood at unprecedented heights. In Montpellier the *taille* doubled between about 1550 and 1580, and had quadrupled by 1640. Incomes also rose, but not enough to offset the people's impression that they were being crippled by taxes.

Inflation continued as a major problem of the seventeenth century. It continued to be fed by American treasure, the imports of which amounted in the ten years 1591–1600 to nearly 3 billion grams of silver and 19 million of gold. Thereafter, according to Earl Hamilton, bullion imports fell. In fact, as recent research makes clear, the amount of silver reaching Europe stayed for the rest of the century at about the same level attained in the early 1600s. Much less of it came directly to Spain: most of it was channelled out into the trade routes across Europe, and a considerable proportion went to Asia.

As silver went into the hands of traders, however, it disappeared from the hands of governments. Spain, the world's chief importer of silver, was so short of the metal that the government had to issue its first pure copper coinage in 1599. Other states were likewise driven to issue debased or non-silver coinages. After 1602, France began to issue copper coins in the absence of enough silver. The copper mines of Sweden began at this time to pour out their produce, and the metal was adopted for coinage in several countries, with predictable results. In Moscow, Lwow and Gdansk the value of the coinage was dislocated. In Germany a pamphleteer of 1632 complained that 'for the last few years the minting of copper has caused great confusion in Germany and Spain'. In southern Germany around 1620, speculation, profiteering by mints, and coin-clipping produced the Kipperzeit (a Kipper was a coin-clipper). Monetary inflation was rife in Alsace and Brandenburg between 1619 and 1622. In Leipzig prices in 1621–2 rose to levels never surpassed even in the worst years of war. Shrinking markets and the collapse of credit made the burgomaster complain that in 1603–20 the rate of interest had risen to 'unchristian heights never known since the world began'.

The crisis (see also Chapter 9) was international, affecting finance, production and trade. From about 1610–20 the volume of Spanish trade with America began to decline. England suffered a trade slump from 1616, caused partly by an incompetent attempt to reorganize the cloth export trade, partly by currency manipulation abroad and heavy competition from the Dutch. The crisis of the 1620s saw a parting of the ways between northern and southern Europe. In the north recovery was slow. Of the eastern Baltic ports the only one to expand markedly was Riga; others such as Gdansk remained in relative decline until mid century. In England a series of crises in the first half of the century depressed trade periodically and led the Venetian ambassador to write from London in 1640 that 'the trade of this city and kingdom is stopping altogether'. Though the crisis can be viewed as a prelude to the mid century crisis, in the north of Europe at least the difficult years led to a readjustment in trade patterns and did not involve any decline in commercial strength. In the Mediterranean, on the other hand, the 1620s initiated a decline from which there was no real recovery, and both Spain and Italy suffered a prolonged depression for much of the seventeenth century.

The invasion of the Mediterranean by foreign interests was irreversible. Already in the sixteenth century the problem of feeding the expanding population of the area had led to imports of grain from the north and the Baltic. After the great hunger of the late 1590s northern grain implanted itself firmly in southern markets. It is possible that in the seventeenth century the Mediterranean, aided, for example, by Sicilian grain exports, managed to feed itself. But by then the foreign ships had found other articles in which to trade: tin and lead, timber and textiles. The Spanish market in particular was firmly within foreign hands at the end of the sixteenth century. As inflation soared in the peninsula, domestic costs increased and foreign goods, produced in northern Europe where inflation was well under control, could be sold very competitively.

English traders entered the Mediterranean: in 1582 they had already gained the right to trade freely in Malta; in Livorno there were six English vessels in 1590–1 and sixteen in 1592–3. The English Levant Company had fifteen vessels trading in 1595. The Dutch expanded their trade remarkably during the Twelve Years Truce (1609–21) with Spain. In 1611 the States General named their first consul for the Levant and the next year their first consulate in Italy was opened, at Livorno. After the trade crisis of the 1620s there was a further expansion of Dutch shipping in the Mediterranean. In fiscality, as in the terms of trade, inflation undermined the weak economies of southern Europe and paved the way to the dominance of the northern, mainly Protestant, powers.

3 Economic structures

It is faith that brings salvation. Faith in money-value as the immanent spirit of commodities, faith in the mode of production and its predestined order, faith in the individual agents of production as mere personifications of self-expanding capital.
    Karl Marx, *Capital*, vol. III

The sixteenth and seventeenth centuries were the bridge between the feudal world and the modern world of capitalism; though they facilitated passage from the one to the other they represented no fixed dividing line, and Europeans lived both in one world and in the other.

Money and capitalism

Money played a relatively small part in the lives of the people of Europe. Barter and exchange still had inordinate importance in some regions, and in entire areas (such as in Sweden) metallic money was not used as a medium of exchange. The principal reason for this was that agricultural communities continued to be domestically self-sufficient. It was only when the town economy became bound up with the rural areas, and when external trade had become necessary, that the need for money as a unit of exchange became felt. Even then the common people rarely saw or held in their hands a coin made of gold or silver; and for the most part they traded in small change, in units of copper or other baser metals of which small coins tended to be made. The circulation of gold and silver was severely restricted, and tended to be concentrated in the hands of a small number of traders. Moreover, credit may well have played a larger part than cash transactions in the ordinary activities of agricultural producers. On either count, there was the *form* of a money or cash economy, but it was still quite far from the reality.

In the primitive economies of the Baltic littoral, in the Balkans, in large areas of western Europe, a money economy was still in the process of formation. It was not until its copper mines began to pour out their wealth that Sweden even began to be supplied with enough metal to form a coinage. Meanwhile the peasantry paid their dues in the shape of labour services, and received their wages in kind rather than cash. The proportion of income received in cash either by peasants or by landlords was very small in most agrarian areas in Europe. The bishopric of Olomouc in Bohemia in 1636, for example, drew its income almost exclusively from three sources: agricultural output, labour services, and taxes in kind (only occasionally in cash). In the Beauvaisis in France in the seventeenth century, harvesters and vineyard workers were given their meals and a small monetary payment: no question here of gold or silver coin. Textile workers in rural areas sometimes had to be content merely with a piece of cloth they had woven. Peasant debts in Beauvais were repaid either in kind or in labour. Elsewhere in rural sixteenth-century France even the upper classes were not over-conversant with cash. Cases of traders in Poitou, in Lyon and in Toulouse, show that it was exceptional to turn fortunes into cash. What mattered was land, or the accumulation of credit, and it was there that energies appear to have been directed. It is in the Beauvaisis, too, that we can see the operation of agricultural credit. Indebted peasants would sign sworn recognizances of debts on slips of paper, and the slips would serve to represent capital, to be sold or transferred according to demand.

Coexisting with this still primitive world was an increasingly sophisticated apparatus of financial capitalism. The commutation of feudal dues to cash, the expansion of industry, trade and markets, the collapse of the ban on usury, meant that money was assuming a more important part in the affairs of the community. The volume of money in Europe also increased appreciably in this period: as a result of growing population, greater demand and greater velocity of circulation; but also in the form of bullion imports into Europe from America, imported not only through the official channels so carefully listed by Earl Hamilton, but also through unofficial means – smuggling and privateering. The several coinages, re-coinages and debasements of the period all aimed to get more cash into circulation. The distribution of this money was, as we have seen, confined largely to the urban and the upper, trading classes, and was excluded in general from the lives of the common people and the countryside.

The most interesting development in the money economy of the sixteenth century was the manipulation of capital by means of credit. Credit as such was not new, nor did it obtain its greatest triumphs until well after this period, but it was now that the activities of financiers brought a new perspective into the utilization of capital. In Marx's words, 'the two characteristics immanent in the credit system are, on the one hand to develop the incentive of capitalist production . . . , on the other hand, to constitute the form of transition to a new mode of production'. Marx was referring to the modern credit system, but his remarks have equal value in the context of our period, where credit provided an essential instrument for the move to capitalism. It did this first by making capital more mobile and facilitating investment, and second, by enabling the chief manipulators of credit, the bourgeoisie, to accumulate property in their hands at the expense of both of the rural and the noble classes.

The machinery of credit varied immensely from country to country. At the lowest level it rested on the activities of moneylenders. In sixteenth-century England, as Tawney has observed, 'the vast majority of lenders were, in the rural districts, farmers, yeomen or gentlemen, and in the towns, merchants, shopkeepers, mercers, tailors, drapers, haberdashers, grocers and similar tradesmen'. The handling of money remained principally in the hands of those who, like goldsmiths or textile merchants, were primarily connected with individual trades. In time, however, it was these very goldsmiths and merchants who abandoned their actual trades as the volume of purely monetary transactions grew. A profession that became very important in the world of finance by the late sixteenth century was that of the notaries, clerks whose original task had been the management of business and legal affairs but who, by their indispensability at a time of increasing turnover in landed property and expansion of trade, drew a great deal of financial business to themselves and became leading money-brokers. The several trades engaged in this sort of finance tended to deal with actual coin, and of those interested in coin none was more prominent than the goldsmiths, who are usually credited in English history with being the predecessors of modern banking. In the sixteenth century, however, all money-brokers, not merely the goldsmiths, took part in coin transactions. The brokers not only made loans, they also accepted deposits of cash. By 1660 a contemporary could report that 'the goldsmiths in Lombard

street . . . are just in the nature of bankers at Amsterdam . . . ,
keeping at this day many great merchants of London cashes'. This
system of deposit with private brokers had been practised through
much of western Europe well before 1550, and gave rise to two
important developments. The taking of deposits clearly meant that
brokers had now become private bankers. Moreover, where
bankers did not charge for the deposit service, they tended to lend
the money out in the modern way. A depositor who called for his
capital might get it in cash or, as often happened, in credit. He
might even be granted an overdraft in order to increase his
confidence in the deposit banker. The extension of deposit and of
credit services were an essential feature of the private banks which
flourished more in their traditional home, the Mediterranean lands,
than in northern Europe.

The very nature of private banks bred insecurity. Their capital
was small, and deposits were often put into very risky ventures. The
practice of credit was shaky, since it needed only a few persistent
rumours to cause a run on the bank and hence its collapse. For a
banker who dealt in international exchange a crisis anywhere, in
Antwerp, in Spain, could bring several private firms collapsing in
ruin. This happened in continental Europe when the Spanish
monarchy renounced its debts in 1557 and in subsequent years. The
uncertainty of credit hit not only the big financiers but also the
smaller men in France, Germany, the Netherlands and Italy, who
could not protect themselves. In Venice alone, the statesman
Contarini claimed in 1584 that of 103 private banks that had once
existed in the city, ninety-six had come to an unhappy end. In
France the Wars of Religion precipitated disaster. In 1575 there
were still forty-one banks at Lyon, in 1580 there were a score, in
1592 only four. The years 1587–9 seem to have been particularly
fatal, for in Spain and Italy alone there were then twenty
bankruptcies among the large bankers.

Financial uncertainty in the face of these collapses was one of the
main pressures behind the growing demand for public banks. Early
sixteenth-century firms had been called 'public', but this meant only
that they were licensed by public authority. In the late sixteenth
century several old banking foundations put themselves on a more
truly public footing. In 1586 the Casa di San Giorgio of Genoa
opened public deposit facilities; other banks did the same in 1587 in
Venice and Messina, in 1597 at Milan, in 1605 at Rome. In the
territories of the crown of Aragon, public bank facilities had existed

since the early fifteenth century, notably in Barcelona and Valencia: these institutions were now given new life. The essential feature of a public bank was that it was open to both private and governmental clients, but the bulk of the capital supporting it was in fact 'public' or municipal. In Valencia, for example, the *Taula* or bank was both treasurer and administrator of the city's finances. Since financial security rather than enterprise was the watchword of these public banks, credit was seldom allowed. Despite this, the evolution was a promising one, and led in 1609 to the foundation of a public exchange bank in Amsterdam.

The weakness of private banks and the lack of credit offered by public banks meant that speculative finance had to look elsewhere for a profit. This was where the merchant-bankers (already well-established in medieval times) came in. Although referred to almost universally at the time as 'bankers', they were properly speaking *financiers*, since their commerce was with money, merchandise and credit, and they seldom operated along deposit and banking lines. They began as small capitalists, dealers in merchandise, and branched out into international exchange of money that was necessary to promote trade. Since cash could not be transferred internationally, credit was, and the principal instrument used for this was the bill of exchange.

The bill of exchange was the most important of the means of credit with which we are concerned. Originating and widely used in an earlier epoch, it had by the mid sixteenth century become firmly accepted in the financial world. As the Antwerp financier Jan Impyn observed in 1543, 'One can no more trade without bills of exchange than sail without water.' The bills of the sixteenth century, however, often had little connection with trade. In Tawney's words, the bill 'had been used in the Middle Ages mainly as an instrument for paying international debts and had been drawn against tangible goods. What puzzled and enraged moralists and statesmen in the sixteenth century was that its use was being extended from paying for imports to the making of advances and the raising of loans, without goods passing at all'. A bill advanced in Antwerp, for example, to be paid at Lyon within three months, would be simply a financial transaction, a loan. In two important respects, however, this would be more significant than an ordinary loan. The period of time involved meant that credit was being extended. Moreover, though the payment in Lyon was of exactly the sum loaned, the costs of the transaction as well as the difference in exchange rates would be added to the bill, and these costs would accumulate until the bill was redeemed. This plainly created a capital market, in which both credit and usury (the 'costs') were being practised, but under disguise. Financiers could in this way lend and borrow money anywhere in Europe, and profit from it as well. 'In other words', to quote Tawney again, 'the exchanges kept capital fluid throughout the whole world of commerce, put the reserves, not merely of the national but of the European market at the disposal of any firm of good standing, and supplied a convenient channel of investment to merchants and bankers who desired to earn a high rate of interest on short loans.'

The great fillip to the money market, and the principal reason for the emergence in the sixteenth century of great firms such as Fugger, Grimaldi and Herwarth, was the insatiable demand for cash made by the national monarchies of western Europe. The intervention of the state in finance encouraged financiers to group together in combines in order to meet its demands: the trend in finance, no less than in commerce and industry, was towards concentration and monopoly. Great firms like the Fuggers and Welsers were, as Ehrenberg has shown, not family enterprises so much as combinations of capitalists who put their money into the firm in return for a fixed rate of interest.

This pooling of capital brought in record returns. The Genoese financier Niccolò Grimaldi, who began his career in 1515 with 80 thousand ducats, had by 1575 increased this capital sum to over 5 millions; the Fuggers, whose assets in 1511 came to 196,761 florins, had 2,021,202 in 1527, an annual profit of over 54 per cent. To be a creditor of the state was clearly an advantage, particularly when this favoured position allowed one some control over government income and over commercial policy. Moreover, the financiers as individuals could and did rise in the social ladder: the Fuggers, for instance became princes of the Empire. But the disadvantages of involvement with the state were to become all too apparent after the international crash of 1557. The bankruptcies of the Spanish crown in particular were fatal for financiers.

In the sixteenth century most governments tended to be behind in the payment of debts. They invariably spent their income one, two or more years in advance. Although this was common practice, it was never looked on with favour, and ministers like Sully were concerned above all with retrenchment, with balancing the books. By the seventeenth century the economically most progressive countries had come to realize that a large debt was not necessarily a liability. We find a Venetian ambassador to the United Provinces reporting in 1620 that 'the province of Holland alone has a debt of forty million florins, for which it pays six and a quarter per cent interest. It could easily get rid of its debts by raising taxes, but the creditors of the state will not have it so. I have heard it said that the merchants have so much capital available that the state can obtain from them all that it requires'. The debt in this case was looked upon as a sound investment by the creditors of the state. Writing in 1673, Sir William Temple observed that increases to the debt in Holland were so popular that 'whoever is admitted to bring in his money takes it for a great deal of honour; and when they pay off any part of the principal, those it belongs to receive it with tears, not knowing how to dispose of it to interest with such safety and ease'.

The growth of a public debt had two important consequences. It brought into existence in the sixteenth century a large *rentier* class, drawn principally from the bourgeoisie. It also reinforced the financial and political stability of the government, by postponing any settlement of fiscal arrears and by tying creditors more closely to the régime. In Spain, which thanks to its expensive imperial programme had become committed to deficit finance, the public annuities or *juros* became the mainstay of the social order. As the years went on, the public debt accumulated, with the possibility of full repayment receding further than ever into the future.

While the growth of a public debt is an example of the extension of credit, the ultimate effect of credit facilities of this sort was non-productive and anti-capitalistic. Money became immobile, was tied up in institutions, and served only to support a *rentier* class. When the volume of financial business required it, the establishment of a public bank of the new type was seen to be far more advantageous. The result was the foundation in 1609 of the Exchange Bank of Amsterdam, with exchange and deposit facilities and, from 1614, lending facilities. The Amsterdam Bank, which was to be cited thereafter as a model for all other nations, became prized by its investors for its security, but its principal function was the promotion of commerce, industry and the money market. It had 708 depositors in 1611, and 2698 in 1701. Deposits rose from 925,562 florins in 1611 to 16,284,849 in 1700. The greatest capitalists of Amsterdam, in particular those with international interests, were among this number. The great machine to which the Bank was geared was that of commercial capitalism, and in order to serve this world of commerce a vast volume of credit was made available. Bullion holdings in both gold and silver certainly existed to support any credit, but the amount of monetary transactions, their international scope, and the speed with which they were carried out, enabled a fund of credit to be built up which made dependence on hard cash less essential than in other trading centres of Europe.

Trade and capitalism

The formation of capital depended principally on commerce, which fed its profits into financial activity and banking. Amsterdam's wealth was founded not on financial speculation but on trade. The new forms of trading that developed in the sixteenth and seventeenth centuries faced a formidable number of obstacles. Transport, whether by land or sea, was slow, and perishable goods, therefore, had their market restricted by the time factor. With poor roads and especially in time of war, land transport was risky. Sea or river transport was the most reliable for bulk goods, but natural disaster and piracy made this method equally vulnerable. 'It's not usually good business to transport wheat by sea', complained the merchant Simon Ruiz of Medina del Campo, in 1591. 'I have seen those who have lost a great deal that way.' Time was no less vital a concern: when wheat from the Baltic reached its destinations in the Mediterranean in the 1590s, it was already a year old. The difficulty of taking goods any great distance by land was caused not only by stubborn terrain and poor roads, but also by the lack of effective motive power, horses or mules being the principal draught animals. Even when roads were improved (as much for military as for commercial purposes) and canals built, markets were not appreciably enlarged. There were few technological innovations to overcome the old barriers of space and time.

The human barriers were no less noteworthy. Politically and fiscally, *ancien régime* Europe was an enormous mass of small independent jurisdictions which interfered constantly with the free passage of trade. A road or a river which passed over several jurisdictions was likely to have a separate toll post at each territory. Travelling from his home town to Cologne in the late sixteenth century, the Basel merchant Andreas Ryff counted no less than thirty-one customs barriers which goods would have had to negotiate in this way. The river Elbe at the same period had thirty-five customs posts, while the Danube in Lower Austria alone had seventy-seven. In 1567 the river Loire and its tributaries had 200 tolls, collected in 120 different spots. On the Rhône in the seventeenth century the short stretch from the Savoy frontier to Arles alone had forty tolls. The cumulative effect of all this on costs and distribution is obvious.

The result of these hindrances to internal trade was that the great leap in the volume of transactions came in coastal and international traffic; in, that is, external sea transport. The profits to be gained from sea trade were comfortable, even in European waters. Sending hops from the Netherlands to England incurred only a 5 per cent capital expense in the late sixteenth century; shipping flax from Reval to Lübeck in the same period cost only 6 per cent. Over longer journeys the expense was higher, but few traders undertook these unless the returns were commensurate. The Antwerp firm of Della Faille traded to Seville with regular profits of 100 per cent, ample reward for the initial outlay. In colonial ventures to America and Asia, the returns were so large as to seem staggering to modern eyes. Early expeditions to India brought back goods worth as much as sixty times the original costs. By the seventeenth century profits of 100 per cent were being marked up regularly by the English East India Company (in 1617 it made a profit of 500 per cent), and Sir Walter Ralegh referred to a 100 per cent profit from one colonial enterprise as 'a small return'.

The overseas discoveries created a marketing system which the Portuguese and Spaniards (and the Dutch and English in their earlier period) laboured to develop. It was, simply, a primitive system of exploitation, in which highly valued overseas goods were secured in exchange for items that Europeans valued less. Shipping figures bear witness to expansion: the tonnage sent from Spain to America rose from about 10,000 tons in the 1520s to over 40,000 in the first decade of the seventeenth century; likewise, though Portuguese shipping to Asia declined from 150 vessels in the first decade of the sixteenth century to twenty-three in the last decade of the seventeenth, the contribution of the Dutch and English helped to increase the overall number of vessels sent to Asia from about fifty a decade in the mid sixteenth century to over 400 a decade in the late seventeenth.

In America the system for most of the early modern period centred around bullion, which as we have seen did not remain in the Iberian peninsula but went out into the mainstream of European trade, where it helped to push up price levels and boost the trading capacity of other states. A proportion went out of Europe to the Levant (in 1595 Venice alone sent 29,400 pounds weight of silver to Syria to pay for trade) and to Asia. Piracy against Spain and Spanish America accounted for another channel for bullion: the Venetian ambassador in 1617 commented that 'nothing is thought to have enriched the English more or done so much to allow many individuals to amass the wealth they are known to possess, as the wars with the Spaniards'. In return for bullion, however, the Spaniards had little to offer America. Though Spain initially sent out its own limited produce (textiles, wine, olive oil, ironware) the Spanish Americans rapidly became self-sufficient in these and there was no Indian demand. Moreover, the Spanish supply system was poor: in 1555 the clergy of Hispaniola complained that 'provisions arrive only at intervals of years, and we are without bread, wine, soap, oil, cloth, linens'. To establish a proper bilateral trade Spain was driven into becoming an entrepôt for European manufactured goods (from England, the Netherlands, France) which poured into the peninsula, destroying Spanish industry in the process, and thence into America. The bullion that came back thus went to European suppliers rather than to Spaniards, and did not appreciably stimulate capitalism in the peninsula. Far from 'declining', Spain actually failed to 'take off', thanks to its inability to develop anything more than an exploitative system of marketing.

The nations trading to Asia faced a similar problem, since they too had little to offer in return for spices and silks. The Venetians, Portuguese and their successors were obliged, therefore, to reverse the Spanish procedure: instead of importing bullion, they exported it. Even Spain did so: in Manila in the Spanish Philippines, Mexican silver was paid for Chinese silk, which found its way back to America and Spain. Both the Dutch and the English in Asia paid for up to four-fifths of their purchases with gold and silver. In the first ten years of its existence the English East India Company (1600) exported £170,673, of which 70 per cent was bullion. In order to cut down on bullion exports the Dutch during the early seventeenth century built up a profitable carrying trade within Asia: by the 1640s the Dutch East India Company had eighty-five vessels devoted exclusively to trade in Asian waters.

Because they were merely exploitative the early colonial trading ventures did little to stimulate European capitalism. The notable increase in shipping, however, provided the raw material for further developments by the English and Dutch. The merchant tonnage of England expanded from some 67,000 tons in 1582 to 115,000 in 1629 and 340,000 in 1686. Dutch sea power quickly outpaced all competitors: by the 1670s the Dutch merchant fleet probably exceeded the combined tonnage of all other west European fleets, including England. One index to this expansion was the trade of Amsterdam, where the income from port charges, measured against the year 1589, had increased in 1620 by 310 per cent and in 1700 by 805 per cent. Three-quarters of the capital active on the Amsterdam exchange was geared to the Baltic trade, 'the source and root of the most notable commerce and navigation of these lands', according to De Witt.

What had made the great expansion of commercial activity possible? On the whole we can point to four main internal causes: the ease of credit; the growth of insurance; technical improvements in shipbuilding; and the creation of joint-stock companies. The necessity for credit was widespread, particularly since without it there was little possibility of the one great stimulant – the willingness to take commercial risks – developing. Small merchants could in this way commit themselves to enterprises on which the returns were wholly speculative, and long-distance trade could replace the certainties of local trade. There was also the consideration that the turnover from any large capital investment was slow in materializing, as for instance with the Seville shipments of the Antwerp firm of Della Faille, whose operations lasted between nine and thirteen months. An extension of credit while capital was tied up in one enterprise would allow the next to be put into operation. The use of the bill of exchange in matters like this speeded up the mobility of capital and simplified the task of the merchant. The development of marine insurance was of comparable importance, since it guaranteed against security risks.

Improvements in shipbuilding were a logical consequence rather than a cause of expanding trade. The initial problem was simply that of building a vessel with a large enough freightage to make long-distance trade profitable. The problem was complicated by the fact that merchant vessels would have to vary according to the sea in which they sailed, and allowance might have to be made for armament. The most successful of all merchant ships that evolved in this period under the Dutch, who were always the pace-setters in shipbuilding techniques, was the *fluyt* (1595). Designed especially for the Baltic trade, with few or no guns, this vessel was unsuitable for use in the Atlantic or the Mediterranean, and had a restricted sphere of operations. It became symbolic none the less of the supremacy in European waters of the capitalists of the United Provinces.

None of the factors we have touched on involved any radical innovation in technique. The same cannot be said of the joint-stock company, which marked a significant departure from previous practice. Trading companies, or regulated companies, had consisted of a number of merchants trading together with joint capital for the duration of an operation. At the end of each operation the proceeds were shared and the enterprise wound up, after which the merchants were theoretically free to depart with their capital. The joint-stock company, properly so called, consisted not so much in the co-operation of merchants as in the permanent funding of capital, which existed continuously and was not split up after each operation. The restricted world of personal participation and private partnerships in trade was superseded by a framework in which merchants did not need to participate at all: they purchased stock in the company, which traded on their behalf. By drawing on investments from different sources, not merely from merchants, a company's directors could build up a considerable stock of ready capital which enabled them to pursue long-term projects. At the same time merchants could take part by proxy in several enterprises at once, without prejudice to those that might require personal attention. For the first time, then, the joint-stock company created the possibility of large-scale, long-term commercial enterprises of a monopolistic nature, the tendency to monopoly lying in the fact that there could be little competition with the resources controlled by the company. (Regulated companies, it is true, also tended to become monopolies, but in theory there could be limited competition among members of the company.)

The first big firm in England to adopt a joint-stock (of lesser firms, the Muscovy Company had been first with a joint-stock in 1553) was the East India Company, which began in 1600 as a regulated company and changed in 1612 to a common fund; not until 1657 was this fund treated as permanent. At the same time the Dutch East India Company (the VOC or Verenigde Oostindische Compagnie, 1602) came into being, with a joint-stock ten times bigger than that of the English company. Both companies, and other organizations that followed their example, increased in size. By 1703 the capital of English joint-stock companies had reached 8 million pounds. The concentration of mercantile capital promoted the wealth and position of the trading classes, stimulated industry, and enhanced the power and prestige of the state.

Industrial organization and proto-industry

Industry occupied a minor part of capital and of labour in the sixteenth and seventeenth centuries, and though output increased phenomenally in some sectors (coal production in England, for example, rose by 1400 per cent between the 1550s and the 1680s) it affected the economy only marginally and lacked the qualitative advance that was to make the Industrial Revolution possible. Technological change was of course not absent, since man was always capable of innovation: significant improvements were made in mining methods, in metal extraction (such as the mercury amalgam process to extract silver, used in America from the mid sixteenth century), in textiles (the mechanical or 'Dutch' loom, 1604), in armaments, and several other industries.

Large-scale enterprise was limited to textiles and mining. Though textiles was the biggest of all industries, and occupied a huge labour force, most of the work was done in rural homes rather than in factories. Perhaps the largest textile factory of the time was the Gobelins mill managed by the Van Robais in France, which kept as many as 1700 workers together in one enterprise, divided into departments. In coal-mining the big collieries averaged 100 workers: the biggest Liège mine of the early sixteenth century had 120, Kincardine colliery in Scotland in 1679 had seventy-one, and the Grand Lease colliery near Newcastle in the early seventeenth century had 500 working below and above the surface. A unique position among mining concerns was held by the alum mines at Tolfa (near Rome), which in 1557 employed 711 labourers, making it one of the biggest industrial enterprises of its time. Other industries using irregular labour could of course be much bigger, such as the Venetian Arsenal which in 1560 employed some 2346 shipbuilding workers.

Traditional restrictions on product size and quality, and working hours, were among the chief obstacles that prospective investors and capitalists faced. The 'Dutch' loom met with bitter opposition from both guilds and working people. By medieval precedent the guilds, which represented individual crafts or groups of crafts, regulated conditions of employment, training and production. The rules laid down at Liège for the cloth industry were typical. In 1589 the corporations allowed only single-frame looms 'so that the poor as well as the rich can live, and not be oppressed by the rich'; production was limited to 'only two pieces of cloth a week', and no more than 12 pounds of wool could be bought at any one time. In 1618 they determined that the length of an apprentice's training should be eight years. These few rules, taken together, would if obeyed have meant a severe restriction in the number of skilled workers, the volume of production, the speed of production and the variety of technique. The rules were totally anti-capitalist, and would have restricted textile production to being a cottage industry. Admirable as the aims of the guilds may have been in trying to protect their small producers, they were an open hindrance to a developing industry.

Several factors combined to out-manœuvre the corporations. Immigration of foreign workers was a powerful solvent, as we can see from the protest drawn up by English guilds in 1616 against alien immigrants on the grounds that they 'keepe their misteries to themselves, which hath made them bould of late to devise engines for workinge of tape, lace, ribbin and such, wherein one man doth more amongst them than seven Englishemen can doe'. No longer would the native guilds have a monopoly of technical knowledge. The rules of the guilds, moreover, applied only to the old sections of the economy and to established trades. They found it difficult to extend their restrictions to cover new industries and new methods of work. In addition, though the state sympathized strongly with the guilds and made every effort to reinforce their control, it allowed so many individual exceptions that the system was slowly undermined. New, independent and wealthy capitalists, for instance, were given extensive concessions by the crown for fiscal or other reasons. Finally, the various factors operative in an age such as this, where change was universal and where old rules ceased to apply to new situations, made the demise of the old guild organization inevitable.

The gradual decay of the old industrial system brought about a restructuring of method, investment and labour. Industry began to move out of the towns, for two reasons: the agrarian problems of the sixteenth century offered, in the countryside, an unemployed and cheap source of labour; and various urban problems, ranging from excessive guild control to high production costs and economic crisis caused by wars, encouraged manufacturers to move out. Once outside the restrictions of the urban sector, manufacturing could expand freely and adjust itself to its own preferred markets. The process has been called 'proto-industrialization' (a term that has recently been subjected to penetrating criticism). In 'proto-industrialization', it is argued, capitalist producers began to industrialize the rural sector while profiting from the surplus obtainable from lower production costs. From the seventeenth century, rural industries began to expand on this basis. In textiles, the process took the form of a 'putting-out system', in which rural domestic units, some of them quite large (it has been estimated for England that twenty-five workers, including at least six spinners, were needed for each loom), sent in their produce to a central clothier, who would use his own outlets to sell the cloth. The cotton industry of Lancashire, first introduced by Belgian immigrants, controlled a rapidly expanding putting-out system which employed large numbers of poor rural workers, so that by 1696 it was reported that 'the number of poor that are employed in the manufactures of Manchester by a modest computation are above fourtie thousand'.

Proto-industrialization proceeded further in some areas than in others. In Italy, it has been suggested, the commercial problems of the big centres encouraged manufacturers to move out into the rural areas, bringing about a shift of investment rather than simply a decline. In Germany the disruption of the Thirty Years War accelerated the process of taking industry out of the towns: by 1748, 81 per cent of the linen production of Silesia was located in the countryside. Putting-out brought money and work to the rural areas, and allowed labourers to cease having to rely only on the land for survival. Economic security in its turn stabilized the family, checked emigration and encouraged marriages. The results could be seen in Electoral Saxony, where the cottagers who operated most rural industry expanded between the sixteenth and eighteenth centuries from 5 to 30 per cent of the total population. The reverse side of this picture was that cottage industry was heavily dependent on outside capital, which could be easily withdrawn or could set unfavourable terms of employment leading to a further pauperization of rural areas.

Low wages in both town and country were cause for protest. In 1597 in Holland a decree condemned child slave-labour, and in Delft in 1636 the courts condemned it again; but in the Leiden textile boom of 1638–48 the city's employees imported 4000 orphans from Liège to work the looms. In 1646 an edict was passed to prohibit children working more than fourteen hours a day.

Labour conflicts occurred most frequently in the printers' trade.

In Paris and Lyon in 1567 and 1571 there were riots involving printers who, in addition to complaints about working hours, demanded unions and arbitration machinery. A strike in 1571–2 in both cities was followed in 1577 by a demonstration, with placards, through the streets of Paris. In the Netherlands in 1572 the famous printer Christophe Plantin complained of 'malice and conspiracy among all our workers', who were striking for better conditions. Plantin operated a lock-out and told his workers that he would shut down the press. Fearing for their jobs the men came back after a few weeks, and as Plantin observed later in triumph, 'all of them now show themselves as willing to be of good service to me, as previously they showed themselves to be rebellious and discontented'.

Many workers formed secret trades societies. In France these societies (*compagnonnages*) involved oaths, initiation ceremonies and other quasi-religious paraphernalia. They flourished among French workers in this period, despite hostile legislation, and adopted exotic names (Children of Solomon, Wolves, Children of Master Jacques). In 1655 the faculty of theology at Paris condemned the *compagnonnages*.

Leiden had regular strikes, in 1637, 1643 and 1648, with a dangerous one in 1638. At Amiens there were regular disputes among textile workers in 1620–35; in 1623 a union was formed and 'they all simultaneously quit their work, and those who did not wish to do so freely were forced to do so by the chief strikers, who numbered about twenty or thirty and were known as "big brothers" '. Strikes and riots could be particularly dangerous in big industrial cities such as Lyon, where the labouring population was almost two-thirds of the urban total.

Refugees and the diffusion of capitalist technique

The unique role of refugees in the diffusion of capitalist skills and methods requires emphasis. It has been argued that the stranger from a developed community is an ideal vehicle for economic enterprise, and most fitted to prosper in his host country because he is not bound by the country's ethical standards. It is also true that in Europe any large number of emigrants includes a core of those who emigrate precisely because they can take their skills with them, and who hope to redevelop the skills elsewhere. Invariably the refugees maintain links with their homeland or with other refugees, and a ready chain of commercial contacts is created.

Virtually all large-scale emigration in early modern Europe was caused by religious persecution (see Chapter 7). Because Catholicism began as the established religion, most refugees were Protestants. The most notable contributions to capitalism were made by refugees from the two most economically advanced regions of Europe: Italy and the southern Netherlands.

The Italian émigrés went initially to German-speaking Switzerland. They came principally from Vicenza, Cremona, Locarno and Lucca, and their chief contribution was in textiles. Zürich's economic success came to be founded on the work of the Locarno entrepreneur, Evangelista Zanino (d. 1603), who established the first large-scale textile industry in German Switzerland. The Pellizzari, who came from Vicenza in 1553, flourished in both Basel and Geneva. The most important of the Lucca refugees was Francesco Turrettini (d. 1628), who came to Geneva in 1575, and in 1593 founded the Grande Boutique, the biggest Genevan silk company of its time. The capital of the Grande Boutique grew in twenty years from 18,000 to 120,000 crowns, and Turrettini died leaving a fortune of over 200,000 crowns. In Switzerland the Italians were responsible for the introduction of new production methods and new fabrics (they brought in mulberry culture). They initiated large-scale enterprise in the area, and freed Switzerland to some extent from dependence on its neighbours. Although capitalist methods had already existed in the country, the Italians made further advances by breaking through the guild system, establishing a new industrial organization and forming trading companies.

A few Italians went to other countries, but their work was hardly new. Since the Middle Ages Italian financiers had been prominent as commercial capitalists: men such as the Florentine Lodovico Diaceto, active during the French Wars of Religion; the Lucca firm of Bonvisi, who flourished everywhere in the sixteenth century, but mainly at Antwerp and Lyon; Zametti, also of Lucca, who became chief banker to Henri IV and whose son became a bishop of France.

The contribution of the Italians was overshadowed by the astonishing role of the Netherlanders, who unlike the former dispersed themselves throughout Europe. The decay of Antwerp was the major reason for their emigration, though several had left even before the Dutch revolt. By the end of the sixteenth century all the major west German cities had a strong representation of Flemish and Walloon capitalists. Of foreign firms in Cologne at this time, up to twenty-five were Portuguese, forty Italian and sixty Netherlandish.

The impact of Belgians (we may call them such, since they came almost exclusively from the southern Netherlands) may be seen in the case of Frankfurt, where the refugees were so numerous – an annual 2000 in 1560 and 1561 and in 1554–61 they were 38.4 per cent of all new citizens – that the city council passed laws in 1583 and 1586 restricting the rights of immigrants to buy houses and become citizens. The production of silk was introduced by the newcomers, and they became the biggest dealers in nearly all the principal commodities, primarily in the textile industry. Everywhere in Germany they made their mark. They founded the town of Frankenthal in 1562, Neuhanau in 1597, Mannheim in 1607. In Leipzig in 1551–1650 only ten Netherlands merchants obtained citizenship, but these ten came to be the richest and most prominent traders of Leipzig, and to them Saxony owed the beginnings of its industrial expansion.

When, in the 1620s, Wallenstein began his military career he had a Netherlander, Hans de Witte, as his financial director. Born in Antwerp, Witte came to Prague in about 1600. His activities were facilitated by contacts with other refugees scattered through central Europe, from Antwerp to Nuremberg. From about 1550 the refugees began to seek shelter in England. London by 1568 is said to have had up to 7000 refugees, nearly 80 per cent of them from the southern Netherlands. Textile traders and workers formed over 35 per cent of the refugee total in London in the late sixteenth century; by 1635 the proportion had risen to 68 per cent. In Norwich the refugee contribution was summed up as follows:

In primis, they brought a great commodity thither, viz. the making of bays (etc.) . . . item – by their means our city is well inhabited, and decayed houses reedified and repaired . . . item – they dig and delve a number of acres of ground and do sow flax, and do make it out in linen cloth, which sets many on work . . . item – they dig and delve a great quantity of ground for roots which is a great succour and sustenance for the poor . . . item – they live wholly of themselves without charge, and do beg of no man, and do sustain all their own poor people. . . .

The immigrants introduced their skills in glass-engraving, pottery and lacemaking. They were commonly known as 'Dutch', but most were Belgians, despite references to the 'Dutch' multiple loom, introduced by southerners; the 'Dutch' merchants, like John Carré (of Antwerp), who brought in glass-workers to England; the eighteen 'Dutch' financiers (nearly all from the south) who were arrested on currency charges and initiated the part played by 'Dutch' bankers in London finance; and the 'Dutch' churches set up by Flemish immigrants. Immigrants were not all Protestants: a survey of 1573 suggested that just over half the foreigners entering London that year did so for economic rather than religious reasons.

Finally, the contribution of the Antwerp exiles to the growth of Amsterdam and the economy of the Dutch Republic was transcendent. Numerically the refugees from the southern Netherlands were very significant indeed, but it was in their quality and function that their principal importance lay. Amsterdam became inevitably their chief goal. Over 30 per cent of those obtaining citizenship in Amsterdam in the years 1575–1606 were from the south, and of the southern immigrants to the city in this period over 50 per cent came from Antwerp alone. The immigrants included names that were soon to rank among the most prominent in the north: Johan de Brauw and François Fagel from Flanders, Frans van Aerssen from Brussels, Daniel Heinsius from Ghent, Louis Elsevier from Antwerp, Gomarus from Bruges, Justus Lipsius from Overijssche. But it was the financiers and the magnates of commerce and industry whose presence really helped to transform the potential of the United Provinces: men such as Louis de Geer from Liège, Isaac Lemaire from Tournai, Balthasar de Moucheron from Louvain, Willem Usselincx from Antwerp, and scores of others from Liège (like Trip and De Besche), Antwerp (like Heldewier, Della Faille, Dirck van Os and Balthasar Coymans) and elsewhere in the south.

Their contribution lay, first and most obviously, in the sphere of merchant capital. Of the 320 biggest account-holders in the Amsterdam Exchange Bank in 1610, over half came from the south. By 1631 it was estimated that one-third of the wealthiest Amsterdammers were southern by origin. A comparable picture might be drawn of Rotterdam, where one of the wealthiest and most influential merchant citizens was Johan van der Veken, a Catholic from Malines. Southerners took the lead in all the great enterprises of Dutch commercial and imperial expansion. It was, for instance, Olivier Brunel from Brussels who laid the basis for Dutch trade to the White Sea; Balthasar Moucheron who became the first and most eminent projector of the expeditions to the North Pole and Novaya Zemlya; Lemaire and von Os who were the two

biggest stockholders in the East India Company, that cornerstone of
Dutch prosperity; Usselincx who founded the West India Company,
which nearly won Brazil for the Dutch. Some 27 per cent of the
shareholders of the Amsterdam chamber of the East India Company
in 1602 were from the south, and they provided 40 per cent of the
total capital. In the West India Company, at least half of the sixty-six
directors in 1622–36 were from the south.

Equally notable was the influence on Dutch industrial prosperity.
Antwerp and the south became the power-house for the rapid
expansion of those manufactures that were needed for commercial
success. The textile industry was the main beneficiary as émigrés
came from Hainault and Flanders to Haarlem, Leiden and
Middleburg. They fled not solely for religious reasons, but because
war and the stoppage of trade in the south had hit at industries and
at their own livelihood. Whole communities and industries
transported themselves northwards. Almost overnight, great
industrial centres of the south became depopulated. Haarlem won
its bleaching industry from the southern provinces, Leiden its
prolific textile industry. New handicrafts, such as the working of
gold and silver, were introduced: of the thirty-eight goldsmiths who
became citizens of Amsterdam in 1585, twenty-eight came from the
south. If we take the principal trades represented in accessions to
citizenship in Amsterdam over the period 1575–1606, we find that 22
per cent of the clothiers came from Belgium, 37 per cent of the
textile manufacturers, and nearly 35 per cent of the merchants.
These figures give us some indication of the great loss suffered by
Belgium as a result of the war in the Netherlands, and of the great
gain made by the United Provinces.

The work of Antwerp did not stop there. From their new homes
in the northern provinces the Belgians extended their influence
throughout western Europe. In France the 'Dutch' established
themselves prominently at Paris as well as in the citadel of French
Protestantism, La Rochelle. The French historian Mathorez has no
hesitation in claiming that 'the seventeenth century [i.e. 1598–1685]
was the great period of Dutch penetration into France'. How Dutch
were these Dutchmen? The most prominent of them, used
repeatedly by Richelieu as a financial agent, was Jan Hoeufft, no
Dutchman but a southerner, a Brabanter who had fled his home and
become naturalized in France in 1601. His brother Mattheus settled
in Amsterdam as a financier, and helped France thereby to draw on
credit in the Dutch capital. The task of draining marshes in France

was entrusted in 1599 to another Brabanter, Humphrey Bradley, without whose large capital investment the task could never have commenced.

It is interesting to note that one of the immigrants to France in these troubled times was an artist, almost certainly from Belgium, called Noël Bernard, whose grandson Samuel refused to follow the vocations of his father and grandfather, and instead turned to capital enterprise, which made him eventually the greatest and wealthiest of all the financiers of Louis XIV. Samuel Bernard's success symbolizes the great importance of Belgian finance in the history of France.

Nor France alone, but all Europe, was open to the Belgian entrepreneurs. As an example we may take the Marcelis family. Gabriel Marcelis fled from Antwerp during the wars, settled down in Hamburg, and built up business connections in Amsterdam and Copenhagen. His three sons Gabriel, Celio and Pieter each became based on Amsterdam, from where they extended their interests to northern Europe with a particular commitment to the munitions industry. The younger Gabriel became in the 1640s a leading financier to the Danish government, and in 1645 helped to raise a fleet for Denmark against the Swedes. Celio served as entrepreneur and arms contractor to the Danish government, while Pieter had interests in the ironworks of Muscovy. Of the total of fifty-seven manufactories built in Russia in the sixteenth and seventeenth centuries, foreigners – in particular Pieter Marcelis – were responsible for thirty-three. Across the sea in Sweden, even their extensive activities were outdone by those of another southern Netherlander: Louis de Geer of Liège.

De Geer (d. 1652) was one of the outstanding capitalists of the century. Though born in Liège he was brought up in the United Provinces after 1596 and moved to Amsterdam in 1615. De Geer began his career as a military financier: he made loans to Sweden, England and France, and helped pay the armies of Gustav Adolf and Mansfeld in Germany. In the 1620s he moved to Sweden where he continued to finance Gustav Adolf, and at the same time began to develop the Swedish mining industry, for which he imported Walloon workers. Finance, mining and munitions were the three mainstays of de Geer's vast empire. In 1645, when Sweden went to war with Denmark it was he who went to Holland to collect and equip a fleet under the Swedish flag. Sailing to the Baltic, the fleet after an initial reverse defeated the Danish fleet, which had itself been partly equipped by Marcelis's Dutch resources.

Huguenot emigration was likewise seen as a spur to progress. The persecution of the mid sixteenth century drove many to Geneva, where the *Livre des Habitants* reveals the great transference of skills from France to Switzerland, with textile-workers and artisans as by far the biggest professional group among them. Three trades in particular benefited: watchmaking was introduced into Geneva at this period by Huguenot craftsmen; textiles were boosted; the Genevan book industry received a stimulus from the many printers and booksellers who fled. Other parts of Switzerland also benefited: the lace industry was brought to Basel in 1573 by a refugee from Lorraine. The persecution that culminated in the Revocation of the Edict of Nantes had a significant impact on the Protestant countries to which the refugees went. Huguenot financiers in exile continued to maintain links with their converted brethren in France (among them Louis XIV's banker Samuel Bernard) and helped promote the growth of international finance. In England, Huguenot artisans did not make any new contribution to industry but they helped develop many existing ones; in Ireland, on the other hand, they boosted the development of linens. In Brandenburg-Prussia their skills aided economic recovery after the wars of the earlier period.

By contrast with the foregoing refugees, Jews had little to contribute to capitalism. Expelled notably from Spain in 1492, they settled in Christian Europe where they could worship freely, principally in Italy and central and northern Europe. By 1600 some of the most prosperous commercial centres of the west – Amsterdam, Hamburg, Frankfurt – were also the cities with the largest Jewish communities. There were, however, serious political and social pressures against Jews which explain their inability to contribute actively to capitalism. In many parts of the continent, as in Rome (where in 1592 there were about 3500 Jews), they were legally restricted to their medieval role as lenders of money. In the Spanish-controlled territories, such as Belgium, they were free to operate as converts (*conversos*), but the watchful eye of the Church authorities (and, in Spain, of the Inquisition) was always on them. When Jews or *conversos* fled from Spanish control, they were accepted elsewhere reluctantly and subjected to civil disabilities. In both Hamburg and Frankfurt they were confined to ghettoes.

Once they accepted their restricted role, Jews could prosper. In Frankfurt they became an active part of the city's commercial life until the Fettmilch uprising (1612), when the ghetto was sacked. In

Hamburg and Amsterdam the wealthiest Jews were of Portuguese origin; exploiting their links with the peninsula, they were able to break into the trade of Spain and of Brazil. The Amsterdam Jews were less prominent than often asserted: as late as 1630 there were only 1000 in the city, many of them active in printing, which made Amsterdam the centre of the Jewish book-trade. In England Jews had been forbidden since their expulsion in 1290, but by 1550 there was a community of 100 in London and in 1625 a pamphleteer claimed that 'a store of Jews we have in England; a few in Court; many in the city; more in the country'. Hoping to gain financially from their presence, and encouraged by those who believed that their conversion would speed the Second Coming of Christ, Cromwell in 1655 officially allowed Jews back into England.

Persecution of racial and religious minorities had an effect out of all proportion to the number of refugees involved. From the industrial centres of northern Italy, the rich metropolis of Antwerp, the ghettoes of Spain and Portugal, the artisan homesteads of France, a stream of self-made men, tried by long adversity and deprived finally of their homes, went out to live among strangers and to develop among them their very considerable talents. In this movement of people we can see visibly represented the passing of capitalist leadership from Catholic to Protestant Europe.

Capitalism and economic growth

So few data are available on capital in early modern Europe that attention has tended to be focused less on capital and more on the means through which it came into existence and was developed. Most historians have discussed capital growth in the context of the population increase of the early sixteenth century, which set in motion various sectors of the economy and created a pool of demand that also boosted overseas trade, which in turn fed wealth back into Europe. In general terms, this presentation has been given above (Chapter 2) and there is no reason to doubt its accuracy. The conditions of growth, however, did not lead to expansion everywhere, and indeed produced contradictory effects in various countries.

Because of this, it has recently been argued by a few (mostly Marxist) historians that demographic and commercial factors were not the generators of change, which they argue was caused exclusively by the structure of class relations. For such historians, the central theme of early modern Europe is 'the transition from feudalism to capitalism', and the key to explanation is the nature of agrarian class relationships, since agriculture was the basis of the economy and of most social obligations. All other causes of change are taken to be secondary to 'class structure'. The inability of a sector of the economy to produce innovations or capital growth, for example, is to be explained by the nature of relations between lord and peasant, in which either the lord denies to the peasant the means to expand output, or the lord misuses any surplus he gains by frittering it away on unproductive luxuries. On a broader level, such historians argue that a principal reason for capitalist development in western Europe and particularly in England, was that the expropriation of the small peasantry concentrated land and wealth in the hands of landlords, who reinvested their surplus in agrarian improvement, encouraged proto-industry in the countryside, and improved landlord–tenant relations so as to give tenants more financial independence, which in turn encouraged the latter not to revolt and also helpfully turned them into consumers for the expanding market.

It is, or course, true that capital cannot grow if the social system is hostile to it (as in the medieval prejudice against usury), and if the relationship between classes retards the creation of market forces (as in eastern Europe, where serfdom made it impossible for a class of consumers to emerge). It is, therefore, little more than a truism to maintain that no account of social change should omit consideration of social structure. However, a crude attempt to explain all aspects of capital in terms of landlord–peasant relationships is very difficult to sustain. The relation between lord and peasant was always crucial (see Chapter 6), but it was only one of several relationships in society, and in any case did not affect the validity of the universal factors – such as population increase – that historians have been trying to study.

The growth of capital can also be examined through the nature of investment, and the nature of demand. Investment from the agrarian sector was inevitably fundamental in a preindustrial economy. It is true that agricultural profits and qualitative change in methods of land exploitation only became important in the eighteenth century, so that only then was surplus capital accumulated from the land and reinvested in industry. But already in the earlier epoch there was change. In England new crops and grasses were introduced; the production of fodder, corn, meat and dairy goods was increased; enclosures, prohibited by royal policy before 1640, went on apace after that date. A basis was being laid for the reallocation (through enclosures, for example) of labour from the land to the clothing industry (proto-industrialization), and for higher production of food which would help to free England from dependence on imports. Even in eastern Europe, the use of capitalist methods in agriculture has led historians to refer to the system of great estates worked by serf labour as 'feudal capitalism'.

Investment by the moneyed sectors can be illustrated by Holland. Profits there could not be put easily into land, since there was little available; nor did the purchase of public office occupy as large a part in social priorities as elsewhere. Savings therefore went into *rentes* (municipal loans), shipping, fishing and drainage enterprises. The important part played by the concept of savings among the Dutch was emphasized by Sir William Temple when he observed that 'their common Riches lye in every Man's having more than he spends; or, to say it properly, in every Man's spending less than he has coming in, be that what it will'. The willingness of small investors to use their savings to good purpose must have contributed substantially to the ready availability of money, a direct cause of the low interest rates in Holland. It was upon low interest (in the early seventeenth century a merchant in good standing could borrow at from 3 per cent to 4½ per cent interest) that the successes of Dutch capitalism rested.

Demand was in effect little more than the other face of investment, but it is difficult to identify demand in the preindustrial economy. Since the real income of wage-earners declined in the early modern period, it is not possible to state without qualification that they created a growing market, given the fall in purchasing power; on the other hand, the increase in numbers in urban centres certainly boosted consumer demand. Since the bulk of goods entering international trade, particularly in textiles, were luxury items catering for the needs of the élite, the expansion of trade was itself a guide to demand; few traded where consumers could not buy. Extending this argument, it is possible to consider a great many of the material and cultural improvements of the time – the growth in housebuilding, the use of glass in windows, the beginning of street lighting (in Paris from 1667) – as real indexes of demand. There is also no doubt that the state was the biggest of all spenders (on armaments, ships, uniforms) and therefore the biggest single generator of demand, which could be measured by the escalating size of armies and navies in early modern Europe.

The expansion of European capitalism has recently led to interesting suggestions that a capitalist 'world system' was being created. According to this view, during the period 1500–1750 international developments (in the economy and in social classes, within individual countries as well as between countries) brought about a world-economy centred on north-west Europe. The 'core' of this system was made up of the maritime and capitalist states (Holland, England, Belgium), supported by a dependent 'periphery' of other European nations, which together exercised hegemony over the world economy. The schema is implausible for the sixteenth century, when capital growth was limited and a world-economy barely identifiable, but more convincing for the seventeenth, when the Dutch and then the English began to subordinate production and trade in several countries to their own demands. Among the virtues of the schema (which inevitably also has weaknesses) is that it presents the process of world economic growth in terms of interlocking relationships rather than simply in terms of the linear progress made by individual countries. The lack of good data for capital growth must, however, render such presentations highly speculative; it was a pre-statistical age, and it will continue to be difficult to measure or analyse that which, in the absence of reliable records, cannot be satisfactorily measured.

4   Nobles and gentlemen

In so far as we are born of good lineage, we are the best.
  Stefano Guazzo, *La civil conversatione* (1584)

We live in a moving reality to which we try to adapt ourselves like
algae that follow the thrust of the sea. The Church has been given
the promise of immortality; we, as a social class, have not.
  Don Fabrizio, in Lampedusa, *The Leopard*

When Sir William Segar wrote his *Honour military and civil* (1602)
he used the word 'gentleman' to describe the uppermost social
category as follows: 'Of gentlemen, the first and principal is the
King, Prince, Dukes, Marquesses, Earls, Viscounts and Barons.
These are the Nobility, and be called Lords or Noblemen. Next to
these be Knights, Esquires and simple Gentlemen, which last
number may be called Nobilitas minor.' The one word 'nobility' –
noblesse, *nobleza*, *szlachta* – referred to the entire status élite and
was notoriously imprecise. As new men rose into the élite, it
became necessary to define terms. The abstract word 'gentleman'
(*gentilhomme* in France, *hidalgo* in Spain) was accepted as referring
to a 'true' noble, one that is who was born such and not created. In
the rural provinces of western Europe a knight, *caballero* or
chevalier was likewise normally a representative of the old nobility.
Titles were rare, a mark of state favour rather than a guarantee of
old nobility.

  Wars of the late fifteenth century brought about an increase in the
number of those rewarded with noble titles. At this time it was still
common to repeat the medieval division of society into three grades
– those who fight, those who work, those who pray – and to identify
nobles with 'those who fight'. At least for the sixteenth century, the
military ideal continued to be a noble monopoly. At the same time
nobles tended to be in possession of land, their primary source of
wealth, and – more crucially – to exercise jurisdiction, feudal or

otherwise, over it. War, land, jurisdiction, were three basic and traditional aspects of nobility; though none of them was in fact essential to the *quality* of nobility. Because the medieval ideal had been that a noble should serve his prince, he was also conceded various privileges which were largely upheld in the sixteenth and seventeenth centuries: the exclusive right to carry weapons, to have a coat of arms, exemption from direct taxation, the right to trial by one's peers, were among the more important.

Changing fortunes and social mobility brought controversy into the ranks of the élite. Problems centred on three points: the role of the state, of new wealth, and of old blood. The role of the state had been clear since medieval times: only the king could create new nobles. By the sixteenth century, however, many kings had, whether to raise money or simply to build up political support, multiplied the ranks of the nobility. There were two main methods: royal letters would grant noble status (Louis XIV in the 1690s issued up to 1000 letters in an attempt to raise money); or status would be granted as an automatic corollary of service to the state (particularly in administration and the judiciary). Though the nobility of the newcomers was never in doubt, critics maintained, in a phrase that rapidly gained currency, that 'the king could make a nobleman, but not a gentleman'. The true quality of nobility, in other words, could not be conferred but only inherited. In the 1500s all monarchies, from England to Russia, attempted to reorganize their élite in order to obtain security for the state. Charles V in Spain in 1525 divided the aristocracy into two: an élite core of (twenty) grandees, and a large group of titled nobles (*títulos*): together with the thousands of *caballeros* and *hidalgos*, these made up Spain's noble class.

Doubts about a state-created nobility were aggravated by the number of those who were rising in the social scale through riches. In the sixteenth century a number of writers in Flanders, France and Italy reacted against the parvenus and reaffirmed that the hereditary élite were the true aristocrats (in the original Greek sense of *aristos*, the best). The Monferrat noble Stefano Guazzo claimed in 1584 that 'in so far as we are born of good lineage, we are the best'. Alessandro Sardo in his *Discorsi* (1587) maintained that nobility was conferred not by virtue or service but by birth and lineage, and could not be destroyed even by evil acts. This created a new emphasis, which was to last into the eighteenth century, on origins and 'race'. Nobility could only be transmitted by heredity: nobility, it has been commented, was seminal fluid. The racialistic view of status brought with it an extreme concern over marriage and the dangers of *mésalliances*, marrying below one's rank. At the same time a broad range of social attitudes was created around the concepts of 'reputation' and 'honour', which grew to become the exaggerated ideals of the nobility. In order to project the image of a 'race' backwards into the past, myths were created according to which the aristocracy were descended from the Franks (in France and Germany), the Goths (in Spain), and other warlike tribes.

The racialistic outlook exercised a powerful influence and was inevitably accepted even by the newer nobles, who took care to draw up genealogies proving that they were of ancient stock. Many writers none the less pointed out that nobility must also be based on merit. Guillaume de la Perrière in his *Le miroir politique* (1567) claimed that 'stock and lineage maketh not a man noble or ignoble, but use, education, instruction and bringing up maketh him so'. The Renaissance emphasis was on virtue, education and service to the state; the last of these came to be basic to the new ethic. Girolamo Muzio in his *Il Gentilhuomo* (Venice 1575) begins by saying that 'nobility is a splendour which proceeds from virtue'; he finds that the noble class has long since lost its honour, and turns his attention from a degraded traditional nobility to a new civic nobility created by the state because of its virtue (i.e. its services). The government must still be aristocratic, though entrusted not to the old militarist nobles but to an aristocracy that has distinguished itself in letters and in laws.

The differing views of nobility were evidence of a significant change in both the habits and the social composition of the élite, whose overall numbers, however, probably did not vary in the early modern period. The titled aristocracy were always a tiny group, but when we add the large number of lesser nobles and gentry it is possible to estimate that in Spain nobles (*hidalgos*) were as much as 10 per cent of the population, in Poland (the *szlachta*) 15 per cent, as against 1 per cent for France and even less for the nations of north-west and northern Europe.

War and violence

The military significance of the nobles lay in their own private armed retinues as well as in the troops which they called out in the service of the king. Both attributes were feudal, and on both counts the nobility controlled most of the fighting forces within the realm. The privilege which made them the only class allowed to bear arms, confirmed the fact that they had a near monopoly of violence in early modern Europe. In the Russia of Ivan the Terrible even more power for violence was put into the hands of the so-called 'service nobility' so as to enable them to extend the authority of the crown through terror. But in the nation states of western Europe private violence was becoming more and more of an anachronism, because it openly contravened public order, the order maintained by the crown.

Arbitrary personal violence by the nobles arose out of community tensions, clan rivalry and simple gangsterism. Broader ideals such as those present in religious wars, were superimposed on this local pattern. 'The nobility today is so unbridled and unlicensed', complained the town of Epernay in 1560, 'that it devotes itself solely to the sword and to killings.' François de la Noue, a veteran of many wars, in 1585 condemned gentry who believed that 'the marks of nobility were to make oneself feared, to beat and to hang at will'. During the French civil wars many felt that the nobles were using religion as an excuse for plunder. Was there not ample evidence, claimed a writer in Dauphiné, that the nobles seldom attacked each other's property, even if they were on opposite sides, and only sacked the houses of commoners? The Huguenot and Catholic nobility, it was reported from Languedoc, 'openly help each other; the one group holds the lamb while the other cuts its throat'. The wars bred noble banditry: Claude Haton in 1578 reported the activities in Champagne of a group of seigneurs 'perpetrating unmentionable and incredible beatings, robberies, rapes, thefts, murders, arson and every kind of crime, without any respect of persons'. Supported by local ties of kinship, powers of jurisdiction, and feudal followings (*fidélités*), many nobles were strongly ensconced in their localities. The duc de la Rochefoucauld raised 1500 gentlemen within four days for the siege of La Rochelle (1627), and said proudly to the uneasy king, 'Sire, there is not one who is not related to me'. Some local seigneurs were tyrants, like Gabriel Foucault, vicomte de Daugnon, governor of La Marche, described by Tallemant des Réaux as 'a great robber, a great borrower who never returned, and a great distributor of blows with a club', who rewarded his retainers by granting them other people's daughters whom he had carried off.

The state tried to harness this violence by absorbing it into the national army, but was hindered by the fact that up to the early seventeenth century most armies were still feudal musters. Under

Henry VIII in 1523, one-third of the total English army was directly contributed by the titular aristocracy. When Philip II invaded Portugal in 1580, nearly half his army consisted of the troops raised by the aristocracy. Up to the reign of Louis XIV, France was still employing the *ban et arrière-ban* (feudal muster); the forces raised by the nobles during the Fronde outnumbered those of the crown. It was not surprising in these circumstances that all rulers feared the power of the aristocracy, in rebellions such as that of the northern earls in England in 1569 and of Montmorency in Languedoc in 1632. Not until the early seventeenth century was a serious move made (by Maurice of Nassau in Holland, by Gustav Adolf in Sweden) to form a national army free of feudal allegiances; and only with Cromwell's New Model Army was a modern national force created. Even then it was inevitable that the nobles and gentry should become the officer class. In the late seventeenth century, with the professional armies of Louvois and the Great Elector, nobles and Junkers monopolized all officers' posts, though this time as servants of the state rather than as commanders of their own forces.

By the mid 1600s, then, the state was successfully beginning to lay claim to a monopoly of violence. It was more difficult to deal with the limited violence associated with feuds, duels and straightforward crime. The exaggerated concepts of 'honour' which obtained in France and Italy, and to a lesser extent in other countries, encouraged duelling. Every state outlawed the practice, but to little effect. In the Duchy of Lorraine formal and solemn prohibitions of duelling can be found in 1586, 1591, 1603, 1609, 1614, 1617, 1626 and so on almost indefinitely. In late seventeenth-century Madrid challenges (*desafíos*) occasioned about a tenth of all prosecutions for crime. In France Sully was bitterly opposed to duelling and Richelieu in 1632 ordered the execution of Montmorency-Bouteville because 'the king needs to make examples'. But though there were numerous French edicts against it between 1609 and 1711, none was ever seriously enforced. The state was, of course, primarily concerned to stop the ruling class destroying itself; 'nothing being dearer to me', as Louis XIII observed, 'than to do all I can to preserve my nobles'. According to the marshal duke of Gramont, duelling alone cost the lives of 900 gentlemen during the Regency of Anne of Austria. By contrast, according to Saint-Simon, under Louis XIV 'duels were extremely rare'.

The aristocracy were tamed in three main ways: by the deliberate policy of law enforcement adopted by western monarchies, by the gradual impoverishment of many noble families and subsequent economies in retinue, and by a growing preference for litigation rather than brigandage. In 1592 an English judge warned the earl of Shrewsbury that 'when in the country you dwell in you will needs enter in a war with the inferiors therein, we think it both justice, equity and wisdom to take care that the weaker part be not put down by the mightier'. In 1597, six years after Philip II had ordered the execution without trial of Aragon's chief dignitary and the life imprisonment of that realm's two biggest nobles, his chief judge, Castillo de Bobadilla, claimed that the king had humiliated the nobles and 'did not pardon them with his usual clemency, nor did he respect their estates, and there is no judge now who cannot act against them and take their silver and horses'. By the early seventeenth century the old aristocracy was beginning to lose its taste for the military ideals it had once cherished. In England the armaments as well as the retainers kept by leading aristocrats dwindled sharply. In Spain Olivares complained of a lack of nobles to serve as officers in the army. Only in France, with the Fronde, did the nobles reassert their old habits, and that too was a final gesture.

The nobility in business

Just as they had monopolized warfare, so the nobles dominated the sources of wealth. They owned estates, forests, coastlines, sections of rivers. In theory their economic power was very great, and it can be seriously misleading to emphasize only one negative aspect of their position, namely the hostility to earned wealth. The Ferrarese noble Sardo had observed that 'inherited wealth is more honest than earned wealth, in view of the vile gain needed to obtain the latter'. This was the economic dimension of the sixteenth-century reaction in favour of principles of heredity and lineage. The prejudice was also directed in part against the ascent of rich self-made men into the nobility. Since the new concepts of a 'nobility of race' were largely confined to the Latin countries, it is no surprise to find that the prejudice against earned wealth was also strong only in the Latin countries, and even there it was not shared by everybody. For a time in the late sixteenth century the opinion of most Latin jurists appeared to be that nobles must not engage in business, but in the course of the seventeenth century attitudes changed.

Among the writers in the late sixteenth century who argued in favour of trade was the French jurist André Tiraqueu, whose *Commentarii de nobilitate* (Commentary on nobility) (Basel 1561) claimed that commerce did not derogate from nobility when it was the only way to make ends meet. In Italy the jurist Benvenuto Stracca, representing it is true a more conservative view than had formerly prevailed in Venice, made it clear in his *Tractatus de mercatura* (Treatise on trade) (1575) that a noble could take part in large-scale trading but not in petty commerce, nor must he participate in person but only as a director. These distinctions were standard ones that came to be widely accepted. Prevailing views were summed up by the jurist Loyseau in his *Traité des Ordres* (1613): 'it is gain, whether vile or sordid, that derogates from nobility, whose proper role is to live off rents'. 'Derogation' (*dérogeance*), a concept which was strongest in France, meant loss of noble status for those who participated in money-making or manual labour; wholesale but not retail trade was allowed. Agricultural labour on one's own land was, by contrast, never viewed as derogatory, being considered 'no less worthy for a gentleman in peacetime than that of bearing arms in wartime is glorious'. Like other jurists, Loyseau admitted that to take part in commerce did not result in a loss, but merely a suspension, of noble status: 'all that is necessary for rehabilitation are letters signed by the king'.

Two main influences helped to break down prejudices against nobles in business: the first and most important was the strong wish of the self-made élite to continue in commerce even after they had gained status; the second was the wish of the state to divert the considerable wealth of nobles into trade and industry. In France as early as 1566 the élite of Marseille had been allowed to be both noble and merchant; in 1607 the royal council informed the merchant-nobles of Lyon that 'the king wishes them to enjoy fully and freely the privileges of nobility, as though they were nobles of ancient lineage, and they may continue to do business and trade, both in money and banking as in any other large-scale trading'; and in the Code Michau (1629), drawn up by Richelieu and Marillac, it was declared that 'all nobles who directly or indirectly take shares in ships and their merchandise, shall not lose their noble status', terms repeated in an edict of 1669. In Spain there was far less opposition than in France to nobles in trade. A Castilian writer of the sixteenth century maintained that 'to labour and sweat in order to acquire riches in order to maintain one's honour', was reconcilable with the noble ethic; and in 1558 the royal official Luis Ortiz argued in a petition to the crown that all sons of the nobility should be trained in commerce or a profession. In Aragon declarations by the Cortes in 1626 and 1677 stated that there was no incompatibility between manufactures and nobility; and in 1682 the crown, responding to a petition from the textile manufacturers of Segovia, issued a decree that manufacturing 'has not been and is not against the quality of nobility', an important measure that removed all legal obstacles to the social ascent of the new nobility.

Elsewhere in Europe there was so little objection to aristocratic entrepreneurship that we find everywhere nobles involved in industrial and commercial activity. It is sometimes said that, in western Europe at least, the nobles seldom traded and were more concerned with industry. In England Dudley Digges in 1604 claimed that 'to play the merchant was only for gentlemen of Florence, Venice or the like'. If nobles preferred industry to trade, however, there were very good reasons for it: they tended to be landed, and the land produced ore, coal, metals, wood and many similar items which it was only logical for the landowner himself to invest in. Trade, particularly overseas trade, was not always a priority for a man with a rich industry in his own back garden. This did not mean that a noble industrialist was prejudiced against commerce, for very many industrialists also took an interest in exchanging and exporting.

The attempt to alter established attitudes is shown by the existence at this period in both Lorraine and France of the terms *gentilshommes-verriers* and *gentilshommes-mineurs*, which referred to those who enjoyed noble privileges as a result of their participation in the industries concerned, glass manufacture and mining. In England there was little need to break down the barriers. There the nobles distinguished themselves by the exploitation of mines on their estates and by their promotion of mercantile enterprises. In the Elizabethan period the most active entrepreneur in the country was George Talbot, ninth earl of Shrewsbury. He was a large-scale farmer, a shipowner, an iron-master, and the master of a steelworks, coal-mines and glassworks; in addition he had interests in trading companies. The most prominent aristocratic names in the realm, among them Norfolk, Devonshire and Arundel, were associated with industrial enterprises. The scale of their commitment was not very large. Not all the nobles were direct entrepreneurs: a few merely lent their names. No aristocrat relied on industry alone for his income. The biggest profits were still in land, and it was to urban development and to fen drainage that nobles tended to turn after about 1600. When all allowances are made, however, noble participation in business was still highly significant. The peerage fulfilled a role that no other class, neither the gentry nor the merchants, was able to rival. They risked their money in industrial and trading endeavours to an extent that certainly brought ruin to many, but also helped to pave the way for the later injection of capital by other classes.

In Scotland, the earl of Wemyss told Cromwell in 1658 that the estate of many Scottish 'noblemen, gentlemen and others doth consist very much in coalworks'. Significantly, the noble entrepreneurs of Scotland relied on a depressed labour force in their coalworks. This combination of feudalism and capitalism was common on the continent, where the wealthy noble merchants and industrialists of Holstein, Prussia, Bohemia, Poland and Russia benefited from the availability of cheap labour that followed changes in the agrarian economy. Heinrich Rantzau, the first and greatest of the sixteenth-century Holstein aristocratic entrepreneurs, made huge profits from demesne farming and ploughed much of this back into industries on his estates. He established thirty-nine mills for the production of lumber, flour and oil, and for the manufacture of articles from copper, brass and iron. Both landed and industrial produce was traded abroad, so that the richest merchants in Kiel, for example, were nobles. After the crisis years of the early seventeenth century the Holstein nobility tended to withdraw from business and turn to their estates. We even find one aristocrat, Duke Johann Adolph of Holstein-Gottorf, claiming in 1615 that 'trade is not proper for noblemen'.

In the early seventeenth century we find the biggest capitalist concern in central Europe being brought into existence in the duchy of Friedland by Wallenstein. There were, it is true, special features connected with Friedland: it was both financed by, and geared to, war; and its industries, among them munitions, were not primarily concerned with peaceful trade. But Friedland illustrates the common situation that only the nobles had the means of raising capital and putting it to work. In areas where the bourgeoisie was weak, or in the process of decline, it was the nobility who took control of both trade and industry. If we take the whole of Europe into consideration, it is clear that a significant part of the nobility were active in business, not excluding trade.

In Sweden the nobles were prominent as entrepreneurs from the sixteenth century. They tended to work the mines on their own estates – principally in iron ore – and from mining they moved to trade. Trading profits allowed them to accumulate capital which they invested in forges and manufactories, and also lent out at interest. Their investment in trade was assured by a guaranteed privilege that they could export the produce of their own estates free of duty. Many of the wealthiest nobles consequently purchased ships. The nobility of the German lands varied in their application. In Brandenburg they tended to monopolize both industry and trade. In Lower Saxony Duke Anton I von Oldenburg encouraged his nobles to take a personal interest in market procedures, from which came a class of noble capitalists. One of these was Stats von Münchhausen, who based his enterprise on land, but then invested his agricultural profits in ironmongery and timber. His fortune grew to be immense: by 1618 he was said to possess over ten tons of gold and over 1 million *thaler*. Some of this money went into building himself the castle of Bevern on the river Weser. On the Baltic coast, in Pomerania, the family of Loytze, from the city of Stettin, made themselves into the 'Fuggers of the north' through reinvesting the profits they made from land. When their firm collapsed in 1572 a large number of the nobility fell into difficulties and the chancellor of Pomerania committed suicide because of his losses.

Hungary may be taken as a brief example of the situation in the eastern countries. Since the economy was in no sense industrialized, Hungarian foreign trade consisted in the export of agricultural goods and the import of industrial goods. The nobles were lords of the soil and by extension dominated the trade in its produce. Hungarian seigneurs were consequently both farmers and merchants. In his autobiography the seventeenth-century Transylvanian nobleman Bethlen Miklos tells us that he took part in the trade of wheat and of wine. Moreover, 'I have traded in salt without losing anything; on the contrary it is by these three items [wheat, wine and salt] that I have gained nearly all my goods, for the revenue from my lands alone would never have met all the expenses I had to make'. Bethlen traded in cattle, sheep, honey and wax.

In Russia, conditions differed so radically from those in western Europe that a shocked Austrian ambassador reported in 1661 that 'all the people of quality and even the ambassadors sent to foreign princes, trade publicly. They buy, they sell, and they exchange without a qualm, thereby making their elevated rank, venerable that it is, subservient to their avarice'. The tsar himself was the biggest of Russian businessmen, with profitable interests in both trade and industry. Industrial enterprise of every sort existed on the estates of tsars, monasteries and boyars. Among the biggest noble merchants of the sixteenth century were the Stroganov family, whose members had international trade connections. To serve the producing and trading interests of the élite, a labour force of 'state serfs' was brought into existence.

The nobility in business were not necessarily fulfilling a progressive function. In central and eastern Europe the entry of aristocrats into business checked the growth of an independent merchant class (see Chapter 5) and in some cities destroyed an existing trading sector. The manipulation of capital by the feudal classes hindered the development of a strong bourgeoisie, and the rise of landed noble traders led to the decay of urban centres. Only in those countries where the moneyed classes – both noble and bourgeois – co-operated in creative development, can the contribution of the nobility be seen as a beneficial step. In any case, the positive aspects of noble investment must not be exaggerated: especially in western Europe the bulk of noble wealth was tied up in a single immobile asset – the land – and dedication to other activities could not have absorbed more than a small proportion of capital.

Aristocratic wealth and changing fortunes

The one essential mark of nobility was wealth: the aristocracy were the rich. Although sixteenth-century theorists of a 'nobility of race' would have liked to argue that blood was more fundamental, common opinion was against them. As a Spanish writer, Arce Otalora, observed: 'It is the law and custom in all Italy, Germany and France, that those who do not live nobly do not enjoy the privilege of nobility.' In Spain, too, the ancient laws of Castile declared that 'if any nobleman falls into poverty and cannot maintain his noble status, he shall become a commoner and all his children with him'. In an age when many men of noble rank were becoming impoverished, it was not surprising that they should cling to the belief that a blood élite did not cease to be an élite simply because it had fallen on hard times.

Certainly, when the noble class was as big as it was in Spain and Poland, poor *hidalgos* and *szlachta* were commonplace; in the former, the theme of an impoverished gentry became standard in literature. In France the census returns for the *arrière-ban* under Louis XIII show that the provincial aristocracy at its base consisted of a vast number of penniless gentlemen. Despite these cases, the nobles were on the whole wealthy, their resources coming directly from the land. In western Europe the aristocracy were drifting away from their estates and becoming absentee landlords rather than agrarian producers; in the east they were being drawn further into exploitation of the soil. In west and central Europe the sale of land, which received its greatest impetus from the Reformation spoliation of the Church, changed the character of aristocratic income and also facilitated the rise of a new class of nobles. In England before 1600 the receipts of the earl of Rutland from demesne farming came to about one-fifth of his income; after 1613, when leasing of land had begun, they fell to about one-twentieth. The decay of demesne farming, however, did not mean that nobles lost their grip on the land, merely that they were turning to cash rather than agricultural income. In the seventeenth century two-thirds of the fortunes of the dukes and peers of France were still in land.

The growing role of cash can be seen in some random examples: in 1617 the marshal d'Ancre, the royal favourite, drew six-sevenths of his income from office; in 1640 the duc d'Epernon, a member of the old aristocracy, drew half his income from office, and the rest from his twenty-three estates; in the 1690s Colbert de Croissy, France's foreign secretary, drew 98 per cent of his income from office. In Spain the duke of Lerma in 1622 drew two-thirds of his income from land; in 1630 the duke of Béjar drew 35 per cent from demesne and 45 per cent from rents; in 1681 the marquis of Leganés drew 14 per cent from demesne, 39.8 per cent from rents and cash dues, 45.5 per cent from state annuities.

Cash came from two main sources: rents (of land and houses), and court pensions. The growth of courts was a logical development from the rise of centralized monarchies. The archetype was Rome: staffed by wealthy aristocrats such as the Colonna and Orsini, dispenser of patronage to the largest bureaucracy in the world, that of the Church. By the early seventeenth century Europe's other principal courts were in London, Vienna, Madrid and Paris. Each court (Madrid was referred to simply as *la Corte*) was a combination of city and monarch's residence, of political and social life, and above all the heart of the state bureaucracy. The system was based on patronage. Royal patronage encouraged the rise of men like d'Ancre, Buckingham and Lerma. In addition, kings sold or gave away lucrative pensions and offices. From 1611 to 1617 the French court paid out 14 million livres in pensions to nine nobles. In England the gentry received lands in gift or on lease, from dissolved monasteries and from Ireland; they obtained cash (James I in the peak year 1611 gave away £43,600 to Scots favourites) or annuities, and secured trade privileges, tax-farms and monopolies to such an extent that the merchant class began to direct its resentment over economic policy against the crown. In Madrid the nobles were given *mercedes* (favours), lucrative offices in Spain and the Indies, annuities and land. The most famous of courts began to be constructed by Louis XIV in the 1670s at Versailles; in 1682 he took up permanent residence. Thereafter, Versailles became the scintillating centre of patronage, government and culture; an astonishing, indeed unique, example of showmanship in the early modern state.

As courts rose, however, aristocrats seemed to decline. 'The lords in former times', observed Sir Walter Ralegh in the early seventeenth century, 'were far stronger, more warlike, better followed, living in their countries, than now they are.' 'There have been in ages past', claimed Bacon in 1592, 'noblemen both of greater possessions and of greater commandment and sway than any are at this day.' In the United Provinces the aristocracy had lost many estates during the war of independence. In France the civil wars helped to bring ruin. 'How many gentlemen', wrote La Noue, 'are shorn of the riches that their houses were once adorned with under Louis XII and Francis I!' The city of Seville in 1627 claimed that the nobility 'have to keep themselves on incomes that will not buy today what could be bought previously with one-fourth of the same'. 'The greater part of the grandees of Spain', observed a French visitor under Philip IV, 'are ruined even though they possess large revenues.'

These comments need to be set in context. Though some great lords disappeared, others took their place; many lesser nobles decayed, but were quickly replaced by rising newcomers. In no European country was there an absolute decline of the aristocracy. Their economic problems, however, were real. We may summarize them in terms of conspicuous expenditure, declining estate income, and rising expenses aggravated by inflation.

Conspicuous expenditure rose from the need to be seen to live like a noble. The Spanish duke of Béjar confessed in 1626: 'everyone judges me to be rich, and I do not wish outsiders to know differently because it would not be to my credit for them to understand that I am poor'. The system of keeping a large household of retainers and servants was a typical problem. In England in 1521 the earl of Pembroke had 210 men wearing his livery, in 1612 the earl of Rutland had 200. Retaining encouraged violence between rival households, kept up the trappings of feudalism, made idleness fashionable and impoverished the nobility. Governments consequently tried to limit it. Bacon commented that the beneficial effect of the English Statute of Retainers (1504) was that 'men now depend upon the prince and the laws'. In Spain a law of 1623 limited personal households to only eighteen persons, yet half a century later the chief minister Oropesa had one of seventy-four. In Rome the size of households ran into the hundreds. In Poland the French ambassador reported that 'many of the nobles are followed by five to six hundred retainers'. Entertainment was, likewise, a standard item of conspicuous expenditure. The English Lord Hay in 1621 gave a feast to the French ambassador, in the preparation of which 100 cooks were employed eight days to cook 1600 dishes. When in 1643 the Admiral of Castile gave a great dinner to the ambassadors of the Grisons, 'the other seigneurs', reported a Jesuit, 'who had also been asked to entertain, were fearful of the event because they could not do more than he. The times were not propitious for such excessive expenditure; but if they spent less it would be observed'. Nobles also tried to outdo each other in keeping luxury coaches, which were consequently legislated against in sumptuary laws.

A major item of expenditure was the building of residences. The late sixteenth and early seventeenth centuries were a peak period for investment in houses. 'What has been created in the past is small in comparison with our own time', observed La Noue in 1585, 'since we see the quality of buildings and the number of those who build them far exceed any yet known, particularly among the nobility.' French gentlemen returning home from the wars yearned to build houses as they had seen them built in Italy. In Paris the rebuilding was given a stimulus by Henry IV, who altered the royal palaces and laid out spacious new squares like the Place Dauphine. The nobles built large town houses (*hôtels*), for which Sully set the style with his Hôtel Sully just as Richelieu did later with his Palais-Cardinal. In England the great rural reconstruction of this epoch (several country houses were rebuilt and new ones begun in a process that began in the 1560s, but reached its peak in the 1690s) was paralleled by the work of the nobility: it was the age when Chatsworth, Hardwick and Longleat made their appearance in the world. 'There was never the like number of fair and stately houses', wrote Bacon in 1592. 'No kingdom in the world spent so much in building as we did', reflected another. European courts and capitals blossomed: in London Somerset House and the Banqueting House at Whitehall were constructed, in Counter-Reformation Rome Pius IV and Sixtus V attempted to create the most beautiful urban centre in Europe (the sixteenth century saw the building in Rome of fifty-four churches, sixty new palaces – including the Vatican – twenty new aristocratic villas, two new suburbs and thirty new streets), in Valladolid some 400 seigneurial houses and palaces filled the city.

Estate income varied widely. Many lords profited from the favourable market conditions of the sixteenth century. In Piedmont the nobles invested in the soil, since other outlets offered limited scope; in the early seventeenth century their annual returns came to over 5 per cent of invested capital. Thomas Wilson testified that in England in 1600 the gentry 'know as well how to improve their lands to the uttermost as the farmer or countryman'. The well-administered estates of the Percy family produced an income that rose from £3602 in 1582 to £12,978 in 1636. Both in England and on the continent, however, there was a strong move to lease out land rather than cultivate it. The leasing of demesne was an old practice, but it was done so extensively in the early modern period that it is possible to consider most of the nobility of western Europe as a *rentier* rather than a producing class. Where rents could be increased this was done: on the Welsh estates of the Somerset family, rents doubled between 1549 and 1583, and a sample from the estates of seventeen English noble families shows that their rents doubled between 1590 and 1640. On this basis, landlords could keep pace with inflation and even make a profit. However, many rents were settled by feudal custom and written agreement and could not be raised without mutual consent. If, in addition, a tenant of this sort had a long lease, the landlord would be receiving only a fraction of the real rental value. In 1624, for instance, the customary tenants of the earl of Southampton were paying him a total rent of £272, when the real market value of their tenancies was £2372. In 1688 the duke of Infantado's tenants in Jadraque (Guadalajara) were paying him exactly the same cash dues as 100 years before, in 1581. In such cases a lord's income was bound to be severely affected. A powerful lord could use threats to change the terms of tenancy. But equally powerful forces could block such moves: the right of tenants to hold to their customary rent, the danger of rebellion, the social pressures that demanded good relations between landlord and tenant.

Rising expenses could be blamed in most cases on inflation: the cost of food, building, clothes and luxuries was rising, and could have catastrophic results if there was no proportionate increase in the revenue from rents and demesne. There were, however, also other expenses: service to the crown in the army and in ambassadorships could involve unforeseen costs; the state repeatedly – in France under Richelieu, in Spain under Olivares – tried to get cash sums from the nobility in order to pay war debts; payment of dowries could be crippling (41 per cent of the duke of Infantado's debts in 1637 arose from the dowries of his daughters); litigation could absorb money and drag on for years.

By the seventeenth century, complaints of aristocratic poverty were universal. In 1591 the Danish historian Vedel deplored seeing gentlemen begging in the street of Kiel. In 1604 the Danish royal council informed King Christian IV that 'an important section of the nobility already has enormous monetary debts'. Richelieu in 1614 described the French nobles as 'poor in money but rich in honour'. In Venice the nobles had had their fortunes tied to commerce; when that decayed they found it difficult to reinvest. Their numbers declined from a total of 2090 in 1609 to 1660 in 1631; as they shrank, they became exclusive, caste-ridden and yet more aristocratic. The English ambassador in 1612 observed them 'buieng house and lands, furnishing themselfs with coch and horses, and giving themselves the good time'. In the United Provinces, likewise, the remnant of the nobility had shrunk to a small group who, according to Sir William Temple in 1673, protected their élitism by refusing to marry below their rank, and affecting an exclusiveness which showed itself in the adoption of French dress, manners and speech.

The lesser nobility everywhere were the most prominent casualties. In Denmark, where of the 500 or so noble landowners in 1625 one-third held over three-fourths of all land, it was inevitable that many should have few means. In France the country gentry (*hobereaux*) were notoriously held to be poor, but in many cases their poverty was, perhaps, only relative. The rise and rapid fall of one French family can be traced in the case of Nicolas de Brichanteau, seigneur of Beauvais-Nangis, captain of a troop of fifty men, who died in 1563. His son Antoine rose to prominence in the army, won royal favour and ended up as admiral of France and colonel of the guard. Excessive expenditure in this exalted position began his ruin. His son Nicolas tried to make his way at court but the family's debts caught up with him. In 1610 the estate of Nangis was covered with debts, accumulated at court, of up to four times its value. Nicolas was thereupon forced to retire to his estates in poverty.

In Spain 'the grandees, títulos and individual caballeros who own lands and other rents today', wrote an observer in 1660, 'are completely deprived of any revenue because of the decline in population and in the number of farm labourers, and because prices have risen so disproportionately'. 'Many of the Castilian títulos', reported a Jesuit in 1640, 'have excused themselves from court because of the great want in their finances.' Indebtedness since the late sixteenth century is shown by the number of great lords of Castile – the dukes of Alburquerque and Osuna, the counts of Benavente and Lemos, the marquises of Santa Cruz and Aguilar – who feature among debtors to the money lenders of Valladolid in the 1590s: Alburquerque borrowed to pay for litigation, Aguilar in order to pay a tax, Benavente to pay a dowry. By the mid seventeenth century the Spanish nobility, including the titles of Alba, Osuna, Infantado and Medina Sidonia, were overwhelmed by debt.

In Naples by the end of the sixteenth century, of 148 noble families as many as fifty were too poor to maintain their rank and position. The prince of Bisignano, who possessed sixty-five estates in Calabria and other regions, was so burdened by debt that by 1636 all his holdings were sold up. Of twenty-five estates held by the princes of Molfetta in 1551, fifteen were sold by the early seventeenth century. Between 1610 and 1640 alone, in eight of the twelve provinces of the kingdom of Naples at least 215 towns were alienated, by families with names as distinguished as Carrafa, Pignatelli and Orsini.

'How many noble families have there been whose memory is utterly abolished!' wrote an Englishman in 1603. 'How many flourishing houses have we seen which oblivion hath now obfuscated!' In so far as the principal item of wealth passing out of noble hands was land, it was often the bourgeoisie who benefited. In Naples the space vacated by the old aristocracy was filled by Genoese, Tuscan and Venetian merchants, and by Neapolitan bourgeois and office-holders. In Spain the creditors of the nobility were bourgeois and government officials. A Norman noble expressed his hatred of the urban bourgeoisie in 1656 by claiming that

Three things have ruined the nobility: the facility in finding money, luxury, and war. In peace they are consumed by luxury; in war, since they have no money in reserve, the most comfortable gentleman can go only by mortgaging his field and his mill. So true is this that it can be proved that since 1492, when money became more common, men from the towns have acquired more than six million gold *livres* of revenues from noble lands owned by gentlemen rendering service in war according to the nature and quality of their fiefs. . . . Men from the towns lend money (and as a result) all the proprietors are chased from the countryside.

But in some parts of Europe it was the lesser provincial nobility – the gentry in England, the *szlachta* in Poland – who profited from the difficulties of the aristocracy. Many of the lesser nobles had originally risen from the trading bourgeoisie and were firmly settled in their new status and life-style: in Italy and Spain they formed the élite in most provincial towns.

The English gentry were not for the most part men of a bourgeois cast of mind. 'I scorn base getting and unworthy penurious saving', wrote one of them, Sir John Oglander, in 1647, thereby disavowing two of the main hallmarks of the bourgeoisie. Their fortunes followed much the same lines as those of the higher aristocracy. Some of them fell on hard times, were unable to meet their debts, sold their property; others prospered from mistakes, invested in land or business at a time when the returns were promising, and founded great fortunes. The gentry increased in numbers and wealth, due principally to the high turnover of land in the property market. How this worked may be illustrated by the sales of land made by Lord Henry Berkeley between 1561 and 1613. Of a total sales value of about £42,000, over £39,000 in land was sold to thirteen members of the higher gentry, the balance being purchased by twenty-five other persons of unspecified rank. Building their fortunes in this way, by purchase of property, many new families made their way up the social ladder. In Wiltshire between 1565 and 1602 no less than 109 new gentry names had been added to the original total of 203. This swelling in their numbers and wealth gave the gentry a new significance in the eyes of contemporaries. The political theorist James Harrington went so far as to claim in his *Oceana* (1656) that the gentry had become the richest estate in the realm: 'in our days, the clergy being destroyed, the lands in possession of the people overbalance those held by the nobility, at least nine in ten'. Another contemporary claimed in 1600 that the richer gentry had the incomes of an earl, and it was said in 1628 that the House of Commons could buy the House of Lords three times over. Like many contemporary claims, these statements have little proof to support them. It is true that the number of gentry increased, and most likely that as a group they held more wealth in their hands by 1660 than a century previously. But there was no radical transfer of power or of wealth from the aristocracy to the gentry.

The emergence of the gentry cannot in any case be measured merely in terms of wealth, for there were still few of them who could compete with the great aristocratic landlords, and even the sales of royalist lands during the republican period did not create a new much-landed gentry class. If their significance is to be gauged, it must be in terms of a steady accumulation of power in the countryside (rather than at court, where few gentry prospered), based largely on land, it is true, but precipitated by the events of the 1640s and by the devolution of authority, in those years of crisis and beyond 1688, upon the one class which had maintained its hold on the people of England.

The changing balance between old and new wealth can be seen in Italy, where the rising class of industrialists and traders eventually transformed themselves into the patriciate of the cities, reinvesting their money in public office and land. With a few exceptions (Lucca was one) the north Italian cities became re-aristocratized (or 're-feudalized', the term used by Italian historians). In Milan families that had made their fortune in munitions in the early sixteenth century had moved out into country estates by the end of the century. Some claimed to exercise feudal authority over their peasantry. The economic difficulties of the seventeenth century, however, began to hit even the new nobility. In one noble estate in Lombardy, state annuities in the period, at 4 per cent, promised a higher rate of return than the land, which gave only a 1 per cent annual profit. The restricted social world of the city state limited the intake of new blood, and gradually old and new élites alike began to decay, as in Venice and Holland. In Siena between 1560 and 1760 the size of the élite shrank by 58 per cent. Although the city was nominally a republic it had become an aristocratic state, where noble incomes were drawn from land, not from trade, and where by the early eighteenth century the Loggia della Mercanzia ceased to be a meeting-place for the business community and became the place where on a summer's day the Sienese nobles might meet to chat.

Most of the observations we have made about the economic difficulties of the aristocracy, do not apply to the greater part of eastern Europe. Thanks to the more feudal landed structure in the east (see Chapter 6), the nobles there faced different problems. Nevertheless, in the east as well there was a change in fortunes: the root cause in most cases was political rather than economic. The rise of the Russian gentry is associated above all with the struggle of the boyars and magnates against the absolutism of Ivan IV (the Terrible). Ivan's attempts in 1564–72 to crush the aristocratic opposition ruthlessly by confiscating their lands and destroying their persons, was from the political point of view a complete success. His two principal demands were for a reliable military force and adequate revenue. He obtained both by introducing the basic features of the 'service state', in which the state offered protection in return for services performed. In 1556, for instance, the tsar decreed that landlords were to supply one fully equipped horse-soldier for each quantity of land held; alternatively, this service could be commuted into a money payment. This was to introduce feudal principles that were falling into disuse in western Europe. Ivan, however, went further. He arbitrarily divided his kingdom up into a vast demesne territory controlled by a court called an *oprichnina* (comprising half of Muscovy and particularly the area around Moscow), and a territory in which boyar landownership was conceded, the *zemshchina*. Within the *oprichnina* area boyar power was abolished, estates destroyed and opponents executed. To enable this revolution to succeed, Ivan gathered to him the gentry class, the *dvoryanstvo*, who were liberally rewarded out of the lands confiscated from the boyars. Writing to the tsar in 1573 of the excesses committed by the *oprichniki*, who carried out Ivan's policies in the *oprichnina*, the opposition boyar prince Kurbsky denounced 'the laying waste of your land, both by you yourself and by your children of darkness [the *oprichniki*]'. Kurbsky's rhetoric mirrored the very great immediate evils brought about by the *oprichnina*: political and social discontent was wide-spread, agriculture was ruined, depopulation common, and the military defences of Muscovy were shattered.

On the ruins of this old order, the gentry rose into prominence as the new noble class. The process was continued into the early seventeenth century under the Romanovs. In 1566 Ivan had summoned an assembly called the Zemsky Sobor, consisting mainly of gentry in the service of the crown, to serve as a counterbalance to the boyar assembly. The gentry were also granted estates, but on new terms of tenure; whereas the old magnates had held their lands freely, as *votchina*, the new landowners held it on terms of service, as *pomestye*, and were known as *pomeshchiki*.

As the Russian gentry established their predominance through the land, so too the Polish gentry, the *szlachta*, became the noble class of Poland by extending their control over the soil and over agricultural production. In the early fifteenth century the noble estate was composed, on the one hand, of the great magnates with vast demesnes – families such as the Ostorogs, the Leszczynskis and the Radziwills – and, on the other, of the numerous company of knights and gentry. The latter increased their political power primarily by acting as a body to secure constitutional guarantees of their rights and status, and by establishing their authority at a local level through county committees or *sejms*. By the late fifteenth century the local *sejms* had given rise to a national Sejm or parliament composed of three orders: the king, a senate (consisting of bishops and senior nobles in the administration), and a chamber of deputies (consisting almost entirely of *szlachta*). The constitution of this parliament was officially confirmed by the king in 1505, when he promised not to act on any important issue without its consent. Numerically superior in the Sejm, the gentry inevitably came to dominate its councils and used it to promulgate legislation that served their own interests. By the late sixteenth century, despite the continuing influence of the great magnates, it was the *szlachta* who represented the nobility of Poland.

Like the gentry elsewhere, the *szlachta* were not an economically homogeneous group. Throughout the Polish territories (essentially, Poland and the Grand Duchy of Lithuania) the noble class made up about 15 per cent of the population. But over half of this number were very minor gentry indeed, enjoying noble rights and status, but possessing little more land than an ordinary peasant. Despite this, it was the land that was the basis of *szlachta* power, and to defend their interests they took care to limit the powers both of the clergy and of the townships. Clerical posts were infiltrated by gentry, and the Church was deprived in 1562 of its disciplinary powers over heresy. In 1565 the Sejm restricted the activities of the merchant class. In this way the so-called 'republic of nobles' came into being, where all gentry, of high and low degree, shared equally in the government of Poland.

In other lands of central and eastern Europe it is also possible to talk of a rise of the gentry, associated with a change in the exploitation of the soil. Perhaps the most outstanding example is East Prussia, where the new nobles, the Junkers, made their appearance in the fifteenth century from the knights, soldiers and adventurers of the German frontier. The process of recruitment of this new landed estate, which must be looked upon essentially as a squirearchy or gentry, since it possessed little of the élitist ethic of the nobility of western Europe, continued throughout the sixteenth and early seventeenth centuries.

Political crisis of the aristocracy in western Europe

Though large numbers of the old peerage declined in fortune, the class in western Europe did not lose its wealth. The political fortunes of the aristocracy, by contrast, changed fundamentally. As the Venetian ambassador observed in 1622 of the English aristocracy, 'the magnates are mostly hated for their vain ostentation, better suited to their ancient power than their present condition'.

The principal reason for the decay in noble power was the increase in strength of the crown. Aristocrats were affected in three main ways: by the reduction of military power, by exclusion from high office, and by greater subordination to the law.

The growth of absolutist theory served to support the state, but monarchs were not in principle hostile to the interests of the aristocracy. On the contrary, kings recognized the nobles as the natural and traditional rulers of the people, and the only foundation of the state. Though impatient with the proven incapacity of sections of the élite – 'their contempt of the various branches of knowledge and the little trouble they take to fit themselves for various posts', as the duke of Sully put it – the absolute monarchy never proposed to supersede the nobles in posts of influence: the whole mentality of absolutism was too aristocratic for that. As the state grew in power, therefore, it found itself in an increasingly illogical position; on one hand it relied upon and fostered the hereditary ruling class, and on the other it was obliged to look outside the ranks of that class for the necessary co-operation in setting up a strong administration. This created an internal contradiction within absolutism, one that would be resolved by radical, even violent, methods in the course of the seventeenth century.

The first and greatest danger facing the monarchies was the armed might of the nobles, as we have seen above. Much of the success in controlling noble bellicosity must be attributed, first, to the fostering of a strong sense of personal loyalty to the crown, and second, to the gradual absorption of noble forces into those of the state. The results varied from country to country. In England, observed Raleigh, 'the force by which our kings in former times were troubled is vanished away'. Strong crown pressure to keep the peace, the inability of nobles to afford private armies, the relative absence of foreign wars (while three-quarters of the titled peerage before mid century had done some service, by 1576 only one in four had had military experience), all helped the English monarchy. In Spain Philip II drew the nobles into a partnership in which they were given control over all local militia, with each grandee taking command in his own province, while the crown independently recruited the armies serving abroad. Ironically, therefore, in Spain the grandees became militarily more powerful: a notable case was that of the dukes of Medina Sidonia, whose authority over south-west Spain was extended. The state had no other provincial officials it could use; the peace, therefore, was kept in Spain, but at a price. In France it was the power of the nobles to raise troops in the provinces (the Montmorency rebellion in Languedoc 1632, the noble Fronde 1650) that committed Louis XIV to follow a policy different from that of Spain.

Armed rebellions arose in part from noble complaints that they were excluded from high office. In medieval times it had been the right of magnates to give advice to the king, usually through the council, and to hold the chief posts in their provinces. From the late fifteenth century, the crown was forced to exclude over-powerful or unreliable nobles from positions of authority. It was normally impossible to diminish their power in their home provinces; only time would attenuate this. At the centre of the administration, however, the state could build up a bureaucracy consisting of lesser men whom it could trust and who did not rely on any great lord for preferment. With few exceptions, this bureaucracy was drawn from university graduates trained in law (see Chapter 8). Though few of the new administrators had titles, by the time they reached the upper echelons of the state and judicial apparatus they were already of confirmed noble rank. All the western monarchies quickly replaced aristocrats with the new trained bureaucrats, but in no sense was this a resort to low class officials: the administrators were of noble status, necessarily so in virtue of the authority that they exercised over others, and many founded dynasties.

Subordination to the rule of law was seldom a matter of law-enforcement, despite the executions of the duke of Norfolk, the duke of Montmorency and the Justiciar of Aragon. The state could legislate through the sumptuary laws, could prohibit duelling, could restrict the competence of seigneurial courts; but in practice the rule of law could only operate if the nobles adjusted themselves psychologically to the growing authority of the crown. Governments were aware of the delicate situation and trod carefully. The law of treason, for example, seems to have been applied rigorously only in England. In France, as late as the mid seventeenth century the state refused to act with severity against the open treason of the cities of Bordeaux and Marseille (both tried to ally with Spain), and the prince of Condé, who led a Spanish army against his own country, was eventually pardoned and allowed back into his estates.

The aristocracy began to be tamed, though their power base was never seriously undermined. A census of New Castile in 1597 showed that the lords controlled nearly 40 per cent of the towns and had jurisdiction over 34 per cent of the population. In Old Castile by the eighteenth century 47 per cent of the population lived under seigneurial jurisdiction; in the province of Salamanca as many as 60 per cent. Great nobles such as the Constable of Castile and the duke of Infantado were seigneurs in over 500 towns each. While continuing to exercise extensive authority, however, the Castilian nobility accepted the role of the crown. The partnership between crown and nobles initiated by Ferdinand and Isabella, created a political stability almost unique in western Europe: there was not a single noble rebellion between 1516 and 1705.

In England the Tudor monarchy (1485–1603) introduced administrative changes that completely altered the balance of power in the realm. The extensive authority assumed by the royal council in London and in the provinces was wielded by nobles and prelates who had adopted the cause of the crown. But the men on whom the real task of administration fell more and more were the gentry, the class from whom sheriffs and Justices of the Peace tended to be chosen. The gentry were, in addition, the group that formed the bulk of the membership of the House of Commons, whose constitutional importance grew enormously in the late sixteenth century. Cut off for the most part from participation in local and central government, a task for which they never had much taste anyway, the aristocracy depended for advancement on the great offices of state that lay within the gift of the king – lord-lieutenantcies of counties, posts and sinecures in the royal household and in the military and diplomatic services. The traditional loyalty and deference to peers in their country seats still continued to a very great extent, but even this link was dissolving as feudal tenures disappeared and tenants became less dependent on their lords. Inevitably, then, the peers gravitated towards the court, and it remained for the crown to decide among which groups favours should be divided. Official policy welcomed the opportunity to have nobles serve usefully under the crown. 'Gratify your nobility', Burghley advised Elizabeth in 1579, 'and the principal persons of your realm, to bind them fast to you.'

The efforts of the French monarchy to tame its nobles were constant, from the time of Catherine de Medici through Richelieu's ministry to the reign of Louis XIV. Under Richelieu plotters were executed: Chalais in 1626, Montmorency in 1632, Cinq-Mars in 1642. Great military commands were taken away from the grandees: the offices of admiral and constable of France were abolished in 1627, and great nobles removed from the governorship of frontier provinces. In part because of the great size and population of France, the crown was unable to control noble separatism, support for popular rebels, and illegal activity; all this made the Fronde possible. Beginning with the introduction of intendants in the 1630s, and the reform of judicial administration in the 1660s, a more stable régime began to be created, in which the nobles were guaranteed all their privileges but effectively excluded from day-to-day government. The absolutism of Louis XIV brought peace not by eliminating the aristocracy but by redefining their function.

Nobles in former times had earned their social ascent through distinction in warfare. The western monarchies now played down the emphasis on war, and preferred to reward on their own terms, which included service to the state in administration, diplomacy and commerce. Thus loyalty to the crown became the major road to preferment. Both old and new nobles benefited. In Spain there had been 124 titled nobles in 1597, by 1631 there were 241, and under Philip IV alone nearly 100 new titles were created. Philip IV in 1625 explained: 'Without reward and punishment no monarchy can be preserved. We have no money, so we have thought it right and necessary to increase the number of honours.' Between 1551 and 1575, 354 new members of the Order of Santiago had been created; from 1621 to 1645 the total shot up to 2288. Charles II (1665–1700) created during his reign as many new honours for the élite as all his predecessors had done in the preceding two centuries. In Spanish-ruled Naples the number of titled barons increased threefold between 1590 and 1669.

Before the accession of James I to the English throne in 1603 the realm had about 500 knights. In the first four months of his reign he created no fewer than 906 new ones; by the end of 1604 the total of new creations was 1161. The titled aristocracy were also affected: in the thirteen years 1615–28 James and later Charles I increased their numbers from eighty-one to 126. This increase pales before that achieved in Sweden, where Queen Christina within the space of ten years doubled the number of noble families and sextupled the number of counts and barons.

In nearly all cases the noble titles were sold: the creations aimed to raise cash and did not form part of a deliberate policy of social advancement. Louis XIV, as we have seen, resorted to selling titles on a large scale in the 1690s in order to raise money. The flood of new creations, or 'inflation of honours' as it has been called, did not necessarily placate the already discontented peerage. 'It may be doubted', wrote an Englishman of the next generation, Sir Edward Walker, 'whether the dispensing of honours with so liberal a hand was not one of the beginnings of general discontents, especially among persons of great extraction.' In England and in Sweden the resentment led to the overthrow of the ruler, and in France helped to provoke the Fronde. The consequences, however, were not all negative. In both France and Spain the creations helped to raise up a newer class of administrators: the families of Phélypeaux in France and of Ronquillo in Castile were typical of the rising élite of state nobles who served the crown with distinction for over two centuries.

The capacity of the aristocracy to survive economic decline and political and military decay is to some extent illusory. Though the crown appeared to be chiefly responsible for their difficulties, it was also the most reliable ally of the nobles. In the first place, the state guaranteed the integrity and status of the noble class. In France from 1555 to 1632 several edicts legislated a fine of 1000 livres against any commoner usurping nobility. In 1666 and throughout the reign of Louis XIV a thorough inquiry into all noble titles was undertaken, and rigorous proofs demanded; intendants were ordered to impose heavy fines. In Spain the inflation of honours led in practice to a more rigid application of the criteria for nobility. Second, the crown extended its system of pensions so as to save aristocrats about to topple into penury: both in Versailles and in Madrid the scale of hand-outs gave visitors the impression of an impoverished aristocracy. Poor relief for nobles was in fact of long standing: in 1614 the French treasury was giving out sums of ten livres to 'poor gentlemen . . . to help them live'; and in 1639 Louis reminded his judges 'not to imprison nobles for debt, nor to sell their goods'. Third, the crown gave legal protection to noble property. Several countries had laws allowing only nobles to buy noble land. In Denmark this had the effect of preserving within the class the large amount of land that might have been sold to pay noble debts, estimated in 1660 as equivalent to the value of one-third of all their land. A more rigorous form of control was the entail, a legal device disallowing any alienation of property. Known as *mayorazgo* in Spain, the crown from Ferdinand the Catholic (1505) onwards made it obligatory on the grandees. This preserved noble assets and thus allowed the ruling class to serve the state decently. However, precisely because land could not be sold to meet expenses, many lords fell deeply into debt. This made them more dependent on the crown, which in return took exceptional measures to save them. In 1606 the duke of Sessa died 'out of melancholy at being ruined and because the king did not give him a *merced* to pay his debts'. In fact, Philip II met one-quarter of the dead duke's debts, and settled an income on his widow and son. Entails were common in Italy in the sixteenth century, and in France, Germany and England in the seventeenth. Because of the problems caused by entails (they provoked indebtedness and depressed the land market) primogeniture was preferred in some states. Piedmont attempted in 1598 to limit the period of entails, and in 1648 Charles Emmanuel II issued an edict encouraging the practice of primogeniture, 'since it so concerns us to maintain and develop the splendour of the nobility'.

Thanks to state protection, the aristocracy survived. Their estates were favoured by law, their pockets were often flattered by pensions, they were exempted from most taxation, their persons were frequently immune from criminal proceedings. By the late seventeenth century their life-style and political role had changed, but they remained as powerful as ever.

5 The bourgeoisie

> Another kind of person has risen among us, born to bring about
> the ruin of others. . . . It is they who have chased the two pillars
> of the state, the gentry and the peasantry, from their ancient
> holdings.
>
> Memoir by a Norman noble (*c.* 1656)

In his *Traité des Ordres* (1613) the jurist Loyseau defined a
bourgeois simply as the inhabitant of a town or *bourg*. More
commonly the term referred to the urban élite, and it was in this
sense that it was used in Germany (*bürger*) and England (burgher).
When referring to the middle section of society, Loyseau talked of
'the Third Estate', which again signified the urban classes, since, of
the three estates normally represented in parliaments of the time,
the third was drawn from representatives of the towns. For present
purposes we shall broaden our terminology to cover all the middle
sectors of society under the word 'bourgeoisie', but it should be
made clear that contemporary use varied. In particular, the
bourgeoisie will be assumed here to be the people of the towns
(even though in the south of France, for example, rich farmers were
sometimes called 'bourgeois').

In general the bourgeoisie were thought of as sandwiched
between two other classes, those at the bottom who had to toil for
their living, and those who lived off unearned income at the top. At
the lowest level the bourgeoisie consisted of petty traders, minor
officials, prosperous craftsmen and others who tended to have
independent means and were not in the employ of another.
Contemporary usage, however, tended to ignore these and to lay
stress on the bourgeois as being, to cite a statement of the
Parlement of Paris in 1560, 'good citizens living in the cities,
whether royal officials, merchants, people who live off their rents,
or others'. All these terms imply the possession of property, leading

to the conclusion that though there were different types and status levels among the bourgeoisie, possession of substantial property was always an essential trait. 'Good citizens': in many towns the citizen (bourgeois, *bürger*) was one who had been formally accepted into the 'book of citizens', which bestowed several privileges of residence and taxation. In seventeenth-century Lille, the inhabitants were divided into 'citizens' (bourgeois) and 'commoners'; the former made up one-fifth of the population. 'Royal officials': as the bureaucracy of state grew, royal officials became more prominent in the towns; Loyseau in his *Traité* placed financial officials and lawyers at the apex of his 'Third Estate'. 'Merchants' were likewise an integral part: Loyseau wrote that 'the merchants are the lowest of the people enjoying an honourable status, and are described as *honorables hommes* or *honnêtes personnes* and *bourgeois des villes*, titles not given to farmers or artisans and even less to labourers, who are all regarded as commoners'.

None of these categories was in any sense fixed or stagnant, and there was considerable mobility through the middle ranks of society. Some rose into the bourgeoisie from the shop, some from the plough. In upper Poitou in the sixteenth century, rich peasants put their sons through university, managed to buy them a minor office, and so initiated their rise into the bourgeoisie. In Burgundy in 1515 the Ramillon family was still practising agriculture in the town of Charlay. By the seventeenth century some members of the family had moved to Varzy: there they took up small trading, as a butcher or a baker. By 1671 Etienne Ramillon had become a merchant draper. In 1712 a grandson of his became an *avocat* to the parlement.

The bourgeoisie in trade

Because of imprecision about status, it is difficult to determine the size of the bourgeoisie. Where figures are available (usually tax-figures) they tend to describe a town oligarchy rather than an economic class. In Venice in the late sixteenth century the *cittadini* were 6 per cent of the city's population. In Norwich in the early century the upper middle class numbered about 6 per cent of the population and owned about 60 per cent of the lands and goods for which taxes were paid to the city. A further 14 per cent could be included as coming within the definition of 'middle class', but these were somewhat poorer. In Coventry at the same period 45 per cent of the property was owned by only 2 per cent of the people, among them the grocer Richard Marler, who paid one-ninth of the town's subsidy contributions. In late seventeenth-century Beauvais some 300 out of a total of 3250 tax-paying families constituted the upper bourgeoisie, but even within these 300 there was a smaller élite of 100 families.

Most of the bourgeoisie achieved status through one of three principal channels: trade, finance, and office. By these means they obtained the capital which most came to invest in land. The trading bourgeois was a type that had been known in the Middle Ages and was to be captured perfectly in Dutch seventeenth-century portraits. He could be found in all the major sea-ports, industrial centres and market towns of Europe: in cities such as Antwerp, Liège and Medina del Campo. Unlike the 'citizen' bourgeois, who was firmly rooted in the confines of his own region, the trading bourgeois had universal horizons, carrying on negotiations with financiers and merchants throughout the country and overseas. He had to be capable of handling large sources of capital which for him were little pieces of paper (bills of exchange), and of taking risks with his own money and that of his associates. The trading community was already internationalized at the beginning of the sixteenth century, with Genoese merchants in Seville, Spanish merchants in Nantes and Antwerp, Netherlands merchants in the Baltic. The chief trading nations were all Catholic, with Antwerp at the heart of the system.

The Reformation, by taking over many of the trading routes of the older system, helped to give Protestant enterprise a great stimulus in northern Europe. The growth of Amsterdam was particularly remarkable. Sir William Temple, as we have seen, testified to the bourgeois ethic of the Hollanders, 'every man spending less than he has coming in'. Trade, however, was not an assured and permanent source of profits; and as merchants made money they tended to diversify their investments in order to gain security.

In Amsterdam the commercial classes became more exclusive in structure as they grew more wealthy. In part this was because of business marriages, in part because of a wish to conserve control over political life. In 1615 a burgomaster of Amsterdam reported that the élite – the regent class – were still active in trade; by 1652 it was said that the regents were no longer in trade 'but derived their income from houses, lands and money at interest'. Examples from the rest of western Europe show that it is wrong to see the merchant bourgeoisie as one single-mindedly devoted to reinvesting in commerce. All who made fortunes were concerned to diversify their income. In Liège, most big bourgeois in 1577–8 drew their money from both trade and finance. In 1595 a foreigner, Jean Curtius (from Den Bosch), had the biggest single income in Liège, drawn from munitions. During his most active period of capital accumulation, in 1595–1603, Curtius invested in precisely the things that attracted the merchants of Amsterdam: land and rents. In Spain the financier Simon Ruiz, of Medina del Campo, belonged to a family specializing in trade with France. He grew rich and founded a hospital for his home town. But from 1576, when the trading world began to get shaky in part because of the Dutch revolt, Ruiz moved his money into public financing. The next generation of his family began to dissipate his wealth and preferred to abandon the money market for the desirable honours of noble status.

These illustrations of a general phenomenon help to place in context Jacques Savary's *Le Parfait Négociant* (1675), where an exaggerated contrast is drawn between the merchants of France and Holland:

From the moment that a merchant in France has acquired great wealth in trade, his children, far from following him in this profession, on the contrary enter public office . . . whereas in Holland the children of merchants ordinarily follow the profession and the trade of their fathers. Money is not withdrawn from trade but continues in it constantly from father to son, and from family to family as a result of the alliances which merchants make with one another. . . .

Savary's view was in part anticipated by a report to Richelieu in 1626: 'What has hurt trade is that all the merchants, when they become rich, do not remain in commerce but spend their goods on offices for their children.' It was realized at the time that alternative investments (offices, *rentes*) were attracting money away from commerce. In 1560 the Chancellor L'Hospital had complained that 'trade has decayed greatly because of the issue of *rentes*'. Among the merchant bourgeoisie of Amiens twenty-seven had been principally active in the textile industry in 1589–90; only six of them were still active thirty-five years later. Of thirty-eight merchant surnames active in the industry in 1625, only seven remained by 1711. A Lyon merchant of the time protested that 'trade creates wealth; and nearly all the best families of Paris, Lyon, Rouen,

Orleans and Bordeaux originate not only from lawyers, notaries and attorneys, but also from merchants. . . . The merchant acquires, the office-holder keeps, the nobleman dissipates . . .'.

The complaints about France, if taken literally, would point to a decay of the merchant classes by the early eighteenth century: a manifestly absurd conclusion. What happened was a steady move towards securing the future of one's family in terms of tangible wealth and social position. The fortune left by the Beauvais merchant Lucien Motte in 1650 shows the beginnings of this diversification: 4 per cent of his assets were now in land; and 27 per cent in *rentes* and other assets external to commerce.

The bourgeois as *rentier* and financier

Rentes were loans made by the public to the state, in return for annual payment of interest. They existed in Italy in the Middle Ages, and most other states began to issue them in the fifteenth and sixteenth centuries. In France the *rentes*, though technically a loan to the crown, were issued by the Hôtel-de-Ville at Paris. In Spain state loans were called *juros*, private and municipal loans *censos*. In Italy the *monti*, as the public debts were called, had long played a part in municipal finance.

Annuities were a tempting form of investment, particularly when the state offered both security and a high rate of interest (about 7 per cent in the late sixteenth century). In an age when banking was relatively unknown, the authorities became bankers, borrowing from citizens and paying them their interest out of taxation. In late fifteenth-century Florence it led to the emergence of a *rentier* mentality among the wealthier bourgeoisie, and to the concentration of financial wealth in the hands of the upper rank of citizens since it was these who controlled the machinery of state. It is possible that investment in the *monti* diverted capital from entrepreneurial activities. A comparable situation prevailed in other parts of Italy at a later period. In the Como region near the duchy of Milan, a vigorous and wealthy middle class existed. In addition to their other interests, the citizens of Como devoted themselves to money lending. Their clients were both peasant communities and the government, and from these the bourgeoisie drew their annuities, their *censi*. In 1663 the rural community of Gravedona, one among others, complained that it was crippled by debts because of the *censi* it had to pay to former councillors and officials of the city.

By itself, investment in *rentes* was not open to criticism. What was important was the priority given to it. The Amsterdam bourgeoisie was as large a *rentier* class as any in western Europe (Louis Trip, for instance, at his death in 1684 left something like 157,000 florins in *rentes* alone), but Dutch investment in this sort of commodity took place only after the capital demands of commerce and industry had been met, so that *rentes* tended to eat up only a proportion of working capital. In Germany, France and Spain, on the other hand, the devotion to *rentes* amounted to a passion.

For many investors in Spain, the *juros* represented quite simply their principal source of income. The nobles invested no less than the bourgeois, and examples of nobles who in 1680 depended on the *juros* alone for their cash income are revealing: the viscount of Ambite 'whose whole income consisted in them'; the viscount de la Frontera 'who had no other income to live on'. Innumerable families, particularly widows, drew on *juros* as though they were a pension scheme. Those who lived off the interest from annuities were in effect living off the state, without making any productive contribution to it. Striking examples of this are the city of Valladolid, where 232 citizens in 1597 drew more money from the government by way of *juros* than was paid by the whole city in taxes; and Ciudad Rodrigo, where in 1667 the holders of *juros* drew 160 per cent more from their annuities than the whole city paid in taxes.

The peasantry and the village communities of Europe tended to depend exclusively on the bourgeois money lenders of the towns for the capital they needed in order to improve their landholdings. The cash available to the peasant was never very considerable; in times of deflation or disaster, when credit was most needed for improvement and survival, the situation became critical. The peasantry inevitably became the largest class of borrowers. The accounts of the Valladolid notary Antonio de Cigales show, for example, that in the years 1576–7 over 51 per cent of his debtors were peasants. The sums were invariably small, but certainly helped the peasant to make ends meet and to develop his holdings when necessary.

It was when the question of payment of annuities and redemption of the loan arose that difficulties occurred. A peasant who did not manage to repay the loan when a good harvest came, often lost the chance forever. A bad year could bring with it the beginnings of an inability to pay; this in turn could lead to permanent indebtedness and final bankruptcy. The *rentier* could step in and confiscate the landholding that had been the guarantee of the loan. In the long periods of agrarian depression which recurred in the rural economy, thousands of peasant holdings passed out of the hands of their owners into those of the urban bourgeoisie. Castile in the seventeenth century was amply populated with towns and villages labouring under the burden of *censos*: one such was Aldeanueva de Figueroa, which in the years 1664 to 1686 alone alienated over one-third of its land to the bourgeoisie of Salamanca.

The transference of land from the peasantry is relatively easy to understand, but there were other sections of society that also became indebted to the *rentiers*. In the number of Antonio de Cigales's debtors for 1576–7, about 10 per cent were artisans and 13 per cent were holders of offices, while nearly 3 per cent were nobles. All of these did not necessarily lose their property, but the cross-section of society that did tend to lose land was surprisingly wide. In one of the parishes in the Rouen area in 1521, of a total of 288 people selling their plots of land, 183 were peasant farmers, fifty-two were artisans, twenty were labourers, nineteen were bourgeois, and fourteen were priests. The purchasers were almost without exception bourgeois.

Loans, therefore, became an instrument for the deterioration and expropriation of an independent peasantry, and promoted the conquest of the soil by the urban classes. The transfer of land from peasant to bourgeois was not, of course, caused exclusively or directly by *rentes*. The economic circumstances of the early sixteenth century had already given a firm impetus to the process. But peasant indebtedness to *rentiers* certainly played a large part in it. By the mid sixteenth century over half the land around Montpellier was said to belong to the city's inhabitants. Whereas tax officials held only 6 hectares of Montpellier territory in 1547, by 1680 they held 220.

The nobility also were prey to the activities of the town moneylenders. The scale of indebtedness of the Castilian nobility was so alarming (the count of Benavente in the early seventeenth century paid out 45 per cent of his annual income for *censos*) that towards the end of his reign Philip II stepped in to save his ruling class. By royal decrees, individual noble debtors were allowed to seek reductions in the rate of interest they paid; if this was refused by creditors, the nobles were allowed to redeem their *censos* – by creating new debts elsewhere in order to repay the old debts. So great was the demand for income from *censos* that reductions were readily conceded by the bourgeoisie.

Thanks to the debts contracted by the nobility, the urban classes proceeded to take over the ownership of the soil from the nobles no less than from peasants. An extraordinary premium was set on land, as the fortune of Toussaint Foy shows. A tax officer for one region of Beauvais, his fortune at his death in 1660 was made up as follows: lands 55.8 per cent, cash and goods 14.1 per cent, office 5.8 per cent, *rentes* 13.5 per cent, houses 10.8 per cent. The most valued lands were those which carried lordship and seigneurial rights with them; although purchase of these did not confer nobility, it certainly enhanced status. Throughout western Europe the bourgeoisie and urban élites put their money into soil.

In seventeenth-century Dijon the middle class made up a third of the population. Though the core consisted of officials and members of the parlement, there were also several gentry who had moved in from the countryside in search of income from office. In their turn the bourgeoisie moved their interests into the countryside, buying land which would give them the mark of *qualité* that bestowed status. By mid century, the city of Dijon had obtained a firm grip on the surrounding land. In Amiens at the same period the upper bourgeoisie drew nearly 60 per cent of income from land and rents. A survey in Amiens in 1634 showed that 351 citizens, all commoners, held land ranging from small plots to large seigneurial estates. Of these estates, twenty-eight had feudal jurisdiction, eighteen belonged to the *noblesse de robe*, five to bourgeois citizens, and four to lawyers. From Alsace in 1587 comes the complaint that 'more and more from day to day grows the unheard-of pace at which houses and holdings pass into the hands of the Strassburgers'. Soon many bourgeois became the new seigneurs of the soil. One example was Pierre Cécile, a counsellor of the parlement at Dôle (Franche Comté). By the time of his death in 1587, he was the owner of 250 plots of land and meadow, three town houses, three small country houses, and fourteen vineyards scattered through the territory of over twenty-five different towns and villages.

The indebtedness of the rural nobility may be studied in the accounts of a leading judge of the Beauvais region. Of those who held *rentes* from Maître Tristan in 1647, nearly three-quarters were noblemen, all with distinguished names, including that of the family Rouvroy de Saint-Simon. Nearly all the lands, houses and *seigneuries* that fell into Maître Tristan's hands as a result of his activities as a *rentier* came from noble debtors. From the illustrious

Gouffier family, descendants of two Admirals of France, a family, moreover, that was now overwhelmed by debts and had sold all its possessions in Picardy to bourgeois, Tristan bought the estates and fiefs of Juvignies and Verderel, which remained in his family for over a century. By the end of the seventeenth century, the Tristans had climbed to wealth over the decayed fortunes of impoverished noblemen, and in the early eighteenth century they obtained noble status through the purchase of an office at court. Their example, one among many even in the confines of Beauvaisis, illustrates the extraordinary extent to which *rentes* served to transfer land and property from the aristocracy to the rising middle classes, and helped eventually to create a new nobility in France.

The acquisition of land by the bourgeoisie has often been looked upon without qualification as a retrogressive, anti-capitalist development, above all since it took money out of commerce. In fact, few bourgeois invested only in land; and the investment of bourgeois money was in any case highly beneficial when put into land. In many regions, only the bourgeoisie had the capital necessary to revive agriculture, so long neglected by aristocrats who had seen their estates as property to be exploited, or by peasant-farmers who had been struggling against debts. In the estates which the merchant classes acquired around Toulouse in the mid sixteenth century, a rationalization of labour was introduced: the number of tenants was reduced to a working minimum; rents were asked for in kind rather than in cash; and share-cropping (*métayage*) was substituted for less profitable types of tenancy. After the 1630s in Alsace, it was the urban bourgeoisie of Strassburg and other towns who helped to restore villages destroyed by war. In the 1650s in the Dijonnais, it was thanks to bourgeois seigneurs that the villages were repopulated, the fields restored, the vineyards replanted and extended, the cattle brought back. In many areas of Germany after the Thirty Years War it was the urban merchants who advanced the capital without which rural reconstruction was impossible.

The leading part played by bourgeois in handling money is reflected in their activity as tax collectors and financiers. Since the Middle Ages kings and prelates had employed commoners to direct their estates and collect their rents. These administrators were officials of rank and standing, and not modest functionaries; many were already moving into the ranks of the titled nobility. The state preferred to rely on men who could draw upon large reserves of credit rather than on those whose wealth was (like noble wealth) tied up in land: it therefore turned to traders with international connections, which explains the regular appearance of foreigners and Jews in the tax systems of western Europe. In sixteenth-century France Italians (like Zamet) were prominent in finance, in the seventeenth century Belgians and Germans (like Herwart) became prominent; the Spanish crown relied in the sixteenth century on Germans (the Fuggers) and Italians, in the seventeenth on Italians and Portuguese Jews.

The function of office

Public position was, at some stage, always necessary to the process of social mobility. By the fifteenth century local élites in all towns had secured a firm hold on administrative posts; where they failed to secure a monopoly, it was because the local aristocracy were powerful or because the older system of open elections was still adhered to. Élite control of local offices created oligarchic rule but also usually brought continuity and stability into local politics.

Over most of Europe, money was not normally the key to office in the localities, where family influence and other forms of status were more decisive factors. Most local office-holders were untitled and probably commoners, but important sectors (like the gentry in England, the *caballeros* in Spain) were of noble status. The greater the extent of oligarchic rule, the less likely it was that money would play a part in the path to office, whether locally or at government level. In England, posts in Parliament or in county administration, all unpaid, were the reward of status and did not confer status, so that money played only an indirect role. In Venice and the United Provinces, senior posts were controlled by an oligarchy into which it was almost impossible to rise other than by marriage or favour. Sir William Temple observed of the Dutch merchants that 'when they attain great wealth, [they] chuse to breed up their sons in the way, and marry their daughters into the families of those others most generally credited in their towns, and thereby introduce their families into the way of government and honour, which consists not here in titles but in public employments'.

The phenomenon of a 'sale of offices' began when the central government, in search of money, began to extend its patronage system. In Venice this resulted in minor offices being put up for sale. In Spain the regular sale of offices was begun in 1540 and pursued by Philip II, principally in towns where the crown controlled nominations to posts. By 1600 in Spain, municipal offices represented three-fourths by value of all offices sold. Although such sales appeared at first to be a threat to local oligarchies, in the end they merely reinforced oligarchic control, since it was the local élites who purchased the offices. A typical case was that of Josep Orti, secretary to the Estates of Valencia, who in 1696 reported that his family had held the post for over 200 years and that he was about to transfer it to his nephew. In Spain and in most countries, however, sales were limited in number; the big exception was France.

The initial purpose of the French crown in selling offices was to raise money, but by the sixteenth century this had created major problems. In 1546 the Venetian ambassador reported that 'there is an infinite number of offices, and they increase every day'. Loyseau estimated that in the second half of the sixteenth century about 50 thousand new offices had been created. The profession most represented in this spectacular growth was the law, this 'amazing flood of lawyers' as Noël du Fail put it. It was they who thronged the administrative bodies of the state at virtually every level – but only on paper. In practice many of the new officials were absentees, who had acquired the office for social position and a salary. The threat to the state came more from absenteeism than from over-bureaucratization. Heavy demand provoked an inflation in prices. A judgeship in the Parlement of Paris, officially valued in 1605 at 18,000 livres, was worth 70,000 under Louis XIII and 140,000 in 1660.

For many rising bourgeois, the purchase of office was the first step to nobility. They might then go on to buy land, and the process would be completed by taking up noble pursuits such as military service. These stages might occur in a different order (in Dijon, purchase of land normally preceded purchase of office), or all together. Offices were obviously valued most if they could be passed on from father to son. In 1604 the French government allowed offices to be inherited on payment of an annual tax, the *Paulette*. Prior to this there had been informal ways of making offices hereditary; the new tax legalized hereditary tenure and inevitably provoked an inflation in prices. The part that office might play in incomes can be seen from two examples: in 1589 the fortune of Nicolas Caillot, *conseiller* of the parlement of Rouen and son of a goldsmith, consisted 22 per cent in *rentes*, 33 per cent in rentals and 45 per cent in the fruits of office; in 1629 the Norman official Jacques d'Amfreville left a fortune of which offices made up 30 per cent, land 49 per cent. More generally, offices played a smaller role; Loyseau wrote that the bourgeoisie put 'inheritances [i.e. land] in the first place, as being the most solid and secure property, of which the family fortune should chiefly consist; offices next, for in addition to the profit they gave rank, authority and employment to the head of the family and helped him to maintain the other property; and left *rentes* to the last since they merely brought extra revenue'.

Through venality of office the bourgeoisie rose to govern France, producing administrators such as Jeannin, de Thou, Seguier, Molé and Talon. They formed the *noblesse de robe*, whom the duke de Saint Simon castigated under Louis XIV as 'vile bourgeois' but who were in every sense noble. Before 1600 the thirty-strong Royal council had consisted largely of the traditional sword nobility (*noblesse d'épée*); by 1624, twenty-four were nobles of the robe.

The rise of the bourgeoisie

The rise of the middle classes was an unquestionable phenomenon of sixteenth-century Europe. Those who had made their way in trade, office and land were now concerned to consolidate the gains, in social status as well as in political influence, made by their class. Together with the increase in importance of the urban bourgeoisie went the growing importance of towns in the national economy. It was the moneyed urban classes that began to set the pace, not only in England and Holland but also in other countries where working capital was obtainable only from this group. Their aspirations were widely resented as being subversive of the natural order of ranks. 'Who ever saw so many discontented persons', complained an English observer in 1578, 'so many irked with their own degrees, so few contented with their own calling, and such numbers desirous and greedy of change and novelties?' Even by that date, the process of bourgeois advancement was well under way in countries like France, and a new 'nobility' had come into existence in the form of the *noblesse de robe*. The early modern period was one of rapid social mobility during which serious inroads were made into the privileged position held by the partly impoverished aristocracy. In Denmark in 1560 the merchant classes still described themselves in a petition as 'lowly branches shadowing under Your Majesty and the nobility of Denmark'. In 1658, however, the bourgeoisie of Copenhagen were openly calling for 'admission to offices and privileges on the same terms as the nobles'.

The evidence, clearly observed by many contemporaries, of new blood, *parvenu* blood, in the ranks of the gentry, was enough to arouse condemnation. In October 1560 at a meeting of the provincial estates at Angers, a lawyer named Grimaudet poured his scorn on 'the infinity of false noblemen, whose fathers and ancestors wielded arms and performed acts of chivalry in grain-shops, wine-shops, draperies, mills and farmsteads; and yet when they speak of their lineage they are descended from the crown, their roots spring from Charlemagne, Pompey and Caesar'. In 1581 the author of the *Miroir des Français*, Nicolas de Montaud, denounced 'certain gentlemen who have taken the title of nobility as soon as they emerge from their apprenticeships as shoemakers, weavers and cobblers'.

These malicious claims had more than a grain of truth. Some bourgeois could work their way up in society in as little as a generation, as with the sixteenth-century Lyon grocer, Jean Camus, whose investments and purchases of land left him at the end of his life in possession of eight noble estates, some of which included villages and towns. In Amiens the rise into nobility took one or two generations. Among the city's *noblesse de robe* in the mid seventeenth century, office counted for between 30 and 40 per cent of income, but the major part of the remainder came from land and *rentes*. Office or wealth were not in themselves enough: only 21.5 per cent of the 544 patents of nobility granted in Normandy between 1589 and 1643 were to office-holders. In the end the decisive criterion was whether a man was 'living nobly'. Those who could prove that their noble style of life had made them accepted as noble in their communities, found little difficulty in being granted status.

The coexistence of old and new nobility was an uneasy one. New nobles and members of the *noblesse de robe* were in all juridical respects fully nobles, equals of the aristocracy; in some cities, such as seventeenth-century Amiens, they intermarried and were virtually indistinguishable. Yet in the 1690s, it was still possible for Saint Simon to sneer at the ministers of Louis XIV as bourgeois, and in Madrid in the same decade the *corregidor*, Ronquillo, was despised as a *parvenu* by the grandees even though his family had been noble for nearly two centuries. In France, intermarriage between old and new was deceptive: because inheritance was in the male line, male sword nobles were happy to marry robe daughters, but robe males very seldom married sword daughters, proof that there was active but discreet discrimination.

The nobility in England, though an élite, was not a caste, and it required little effort to become part of its lower ranks. 'Who can live idly and without manual labour, and will bear the port, charge and countenance of a gentleman', claimed Sir Thomas Smith at the time, 'he shall be called master, for that is the title men give to esquires and other gentlemen, and shall be taken for a gentleman.' One could become a gentleman simply by living as one, and without necessarily having any landed property. This was one of several ways in which the landed and mercantile classes became confused, making it difficult to distinguish origins. The confusion was increased by the tendency of gentry sons to engage themselves as apprentices to trade: by the 1630s nearly a fifth of the London Stationers' Company apprentices came from gentry stock.

The middle classes in town and country also supplemented the ranks of the gentry proper. There were two main streams that contributed to this, the successful yeomen of the country and the rising town merchants who purchased land. With the yeoman it was certainly the mobility of land that facilitated social mobility. Independent landholders (though not necessarily freeholders), they benefited from the increased value of the soil, and as a class their average wealth probably doubled in the period 1600 to 1640. Living in the same environment as the country gentry, often more prosperous than many gentry, they rose almost imperceptibly into the higher status group. 'From thence in time', observed a contemporary in 1618, 'are derived many noble and worthy families.' Of the fifty-seven Yorkshire families granted arms between 1603 and 1642, over half were wealthy yeomen. Of a total of 335 gentry in the county of Northamptonshire in the mid seventeenth century, the great majority were newcomers not only to the county but also to the squirearchy, and at least three-quarters of them had only very recently arrived in their new status.

Land was important: by the early seventeenth century it was difficult to find a prominent London capitalist who was not also a substantial landowner. The contemporary Stow remarked that 'merchants and rich men (being satisfied with gain) do for the most part marry their children into the country, and convey themselves, after Cicero's counsel, *veluti ex portu in agros et possessiones*'. But though land was clearly a spur to mobility it was often (unlike the situation in France) no more than the last stage in the progress to status, nor did families who obtained land cease to trade. A study of the wealth of seventy-eight gentry families in Elizabethan Sussex shows that among the twenty-five wealthiest families only four were supported chiefly by land, while the majority had heads who were still – what they had been before emerging as 'gentry' – ironmasters, managers of forges and furnaces, merchants and lawyers. If we look at the greater merchants of the city of London in the early seventeenth century, we find them living in the style of the gentry, with country estates and stewards to manage them, parks and gamekeepers to patrol them, and country houses which regularly dispensed hospitality. But three-quarters of them, despite this formal commitment to the country, never moved their roots from London, and maintained both their business and their friends in the city throughout their career.

Many merchants must have hesitated between the choice of profession or status. Claude Darc, merchant of Amance (Franche Comté), who died in 1597, solved his difficulties in a particularly appealing way. His daughters were married off to legal officials, so that their status was guaranteed. Of his two sons he chose the elder, Guillaume, to remain in the business; but he trained the younger, Simon, to become a doctor of laws. In this way, one branch of the family would continue to accumulate wealth while the other sought position. In his will he spoke of Simon 'and all the expense he has caused me, both for the pursuit of his studies and for his upkeep these twenty-five years past, and at Paris, Freiburg, Cologne, Rome, Naples, Dôle and elsewhere that he has been up to now, for the eight years that it takes to become a doctor; all this has cost (God help me!) more than twelve thousand francs'. He also spoke of Guillaume, who had 'exposed the best years of his youth, and risked his person many times, to the peril and danger of the long journeys he made to distant and strange countries, and in those twenty years he has, by his work and labours, added to and increased the family fortune by much more than the said doctor has spent'. Two widely differing paths, but to each the father gave his wholehearted support.

In the United Provinces the achievement of national independence left the bourgeoisie firmly in control. The change in Amsterdam may be dated from the year 1578, when a coup or *Alteratie* led to the overthrow of the old régime, with its officials and clergy, and the staffing of the ruling council of the city with new bourgeois Calvinist members. In historical terms, the bourgeoisie continued to dominate the United Provinces because their trading interests had made them support the struggle against Spain. In geographical terms, it was the west and north-western half of the country that had profited from the war of independence. 'Whereas it is generally the nature of war to ruin land and people', observed a burgomaster of Amsterdam, C. P. Hooft, 'these countries on the contrary have been noticeably improved thereby.' Protected by their rivers and with the open sea before them, the bourgeoisie of Holland and Zeeland had since the 1570s enjoyed virtual immunity from the war, so that while Spain was expending its strength against them in the south, they built up in the north-west a flourishing base on which the Dutch economy was to rest.

The eastern half of the country was, on the other hand, underdeveloped, primarily agricultural and dominated by the noble class. It was the nobles of Guelderland and Overijssel, in particular, who were the main support of the House of Orange in its differences with the bourgeoisie of the west. Their relative weakness in the country as a whole gave control of administration to the bourgeois élite of the cities, the regent class. Senior administrative officers of the towns, the regents were drawn originally either from active merchants or from those who had recently retired from business. Their tenure of office inevitably became a comfortable monopoly, and tended to make them withdraw from active trade. The old clash between commerce and office-holding worked to the detriment of the former. By 1652 the Amsterdam merchants were complaining that the regents had ceased to support trade and were drawing their income 'from houses, lands, and money at interest'. The traders of the late sixteenth century had become a *rentier* class in the seventeenth. The de Witts are an obvious example of the drift. Cornelis de Witt, born in 1545, was burgomaster of Dordrecht and a successful trader in timber. The most prominent of his sons, Jacob, continued his father's business, but his growing involvement in public affairs (notably his opposition to William II of Orange in 1650) obliged him to dispose of the family business between 1632 and 1651. Jacob's son Johan, a distinguished member of the regent class, concentrated entirely on the duties of political office.

The Dutch bourgeoisie lived unpretentiously. Sir William Temple testified that 'of the two chief officers in my time, Vice-Admiral de Ruyter and the Pensioner de Witt . . . I never saw the first in clothes better than the commonest sea-captain . . . and in his own house neither was the size, building, furniture or entertainment at all exceeding the use of every common merchant and tradesman'. As for de Witt, 'he was seen usually in the streets on foot and alone, like the commonest burgher of the town'. 'Nor was this manner of life', adds Temple, 'used only by these particular men, but was the general fashion or mode among all the magistrates of the State.' This apparent austerity was only the prelude to the adoption of a neo-aristocratic way of life. Social mobility in the usual sense was an irrelevancy, since in practice the regent class by the seventeenth century ranked above the old nobility. In this position, the upper bourgeoisie adopted distinctly conservative habits. 'Their youths', reported Temple, 'after the course of their studies at home, travel for some years, as the sons of our gentry use to do.' When they went to university, they usually read civil law. Johan de Witt was one who read law at Leiden, and did the grand tour with his brother in 1645–7. A patrician class arose, and its rise was accompanied by the abandonment of frugality. 'The old severe and frugal way of living is now almost quite out of date in Holland', Temple was to complain, having in mind the bourgeoisie of Amsterdam and the Hague. The trend towards luxury was illustrated by a pamphleteer of 1662 who called for the passing of sumptuary laws on the grounds that people were beginning to dress and live above their station.

Sumptuary laws were the standard method of attempting to preserve rank and check mobility, but the Dutch were relatively free of them. Elsewhere in Europe the pretensions of the middle classes were subject to both legislation and comment. 'I doubt not but it is lawfull for the nobilitie, the gentrie and magisterie, to weare rich attire', said Philip Stubbs in his *Anatomie of Abuses* (1583). 'As for private subiectes, it is not at any hand lawful that they should weare silkes, velvets, satens, damaskes, gold, silver and what they list.' The abundant sumptuary legislation in Europe at this period is proof that the authorities shared Stubbs's views, though legislation was invariably a failure. The French crown was obliged to issue thirteen sumptuary edicts between 1540 and 1615, but with little success. After 1604, when it repealed all existing sumptuary laws, the English government did not bother to dictate the rules of apparel to its subjects. As Bodin observed of France: 'Fine edicts have been passed, but to no purpose. For since people at court wear what is forbidden, everyone wears it, so that the officials are intimidated by the former and corrupted by the latter. Besides, in matters of dress he is always considered a fool and bore who does not dress according to the current fashion.'

Betrayal by the bourgeoisie?

The bourgeoisie had an essential role to play in the development of capitalism. They were the sector in which wealth was created and mobilized; by contrast, the lower classes were unable to accumulate wealth and the upper classes had already acquired and invested theirs. The commercial and financial life of states was therefore closely related to the activities of the middle class. The commercial success of England and Holland was based on a steady investment of capital by gentry and mercantile bourgeoisie. Out of over 5000 Englishmen who invested in their country's overseas trading companies in the period 1575–1630, 73.5 per cent were bourgeois merchants, 2.4 per cent were merchants who had been knighted, 9.9 per cent were knights, 9.3 per cent were gentry, 3.5 per cent were nobles and 1.4 per cent were yeomen and men in the professions. Gentry and nobles were prominently active, representing 44.7 per cent of membership of the Virginia Company and 78.9 per cent of that of the Africa Company; in these fifty-six years, moreover, they invested something like £1.5 million in the companies. But it was the bourgeois merchants who were beyond all doubt the foundation of England's commercial greatness. At no time in the seventeenth century did any other European nations match the success of the English and Dutch in mobilizing the resources of the middle and upper classes.

Why was this? In his study of *The Mediterranean*, Braudel argued that a conscious 'betrayal by the bourgeoisie' had been a root cause of the decline of the trade of Spain and Italy. Other writers have extended this argument to the bourgeoisie of France and northern Europe. Even in seventeenth-century England, Thomas Mun had complained that 'the son, being left rich, scorns the profession of his father, conceiving more honour to be a gentleman than to follow the steps of his father as an industrious merchant'. In reality, the evolution of the bourgeoisie was more complex than the concept of 'betrayal' suggests. First, most traders and bourgeois were powerless to control the conditions of trade under which they worked; they were not free to make a choice. Second, many – particularly in eastern Europe – were restricted by political environment and social prejudice. Third, many who withdrew from commerce in order to invest elsewhere, did so because it seemed a rational course to adopt. These points will be touched on in referring to specific parts of Europe, and go far towards explaining the depletion of bourgeois capital resources.

Spain

By the fifteenth century there were active trading links between Aragon and Italy, and between Castile and Flanders. The chief export was raw wool, negotiated by colonies of Spanish merchants in Bordeaux, Antwerp and other cities. Under Charles V and Philip II the fairs at Medina del Campo made Old Castile an integral part of the west European market, and successful merchants like Simon Ruiz represented the most enterprising section of the Castilian bourgeoisie. The expulsion of the Jews in 1492 had done nothing to weaken the middle classes, since *conversos* (Christians of Jewish origin) continued effectively to carry out the roles Jews had fulfilled. The energy of the Spanish bourgeoisie, however, was deceptive. Spain around 1500 was a poor country with inadequate grain output, no significant industry, and with exports consisting almost exclusively of raw materials (wool, agricultural produce). This was too weak an economic base to nourish a bourgeoisie or to foster investment, and the import of foreign manufactures (mainly textiles) to balance raw material exports quickly gave foreign capitalists a big say in the direction of the economy. 'The foreigners do with us what they will', complained Simon Ruiz. The discovery of America temporarily stimulated the Spanish economy but did not improve the industrial situation, and foreign manufactures rapidly took over the American market.

Unable to invest in an economy that did not expand, the bourgeoisie entered the money market, lending both to the government (*juros*) and to individuals (*censos*). With interest rates at up to 7 per cent in the sixteenth century, it was an attractive outlay. Moreover, *censos* to the peasantry were a form of investment in agriculture, and benefited the rural economy. But writers on economic affairs, the *arbitristas*, were critical of the extent to which the moneyed classes were willing to live off unearned interest rather than invest their money in productivity. Contemplating with dismay the effects of a *rentier* mentality, the Valladolid bourgeois Martín González de Cellorigo in 1600 condemned *censos* as 'a plague which has reduced these realms to utter poverty, since a majority of people have taken to living off them, and off the interest from money'. In a sharply-worded passage, he claimed that

Censos are the plague and ruin of Spain. For the sweetness of the sure profit from *censos* the merchant leaves his trading, the artisan his employment, the peasant-farmer his farming, the shepherd his flock; and the noble sells his lands so as to exchange the one hundred they bring him for the five hundred the *juro* brings. . . . Through *censos* flourishing houses have perished, and common people have risen from their employment, trade and farming, into indolence; so that the kingdom has become a nation of idleness and vice.

Price inflation, aggravated later by debasement and monetary inflation, added to the problems of a country where trade was largely in the hands of foreign interests. Spanish bourgeois were active both in commerce and industry, but the scanty resources of their environment and the fact that most American bullion went to pay for foreign imports (hence the continual petitions by the Cortes against the export of bullion), deprived them of investment capital. Inflation periodically wiped out trading profits and made the interest rate on *juros* and *censos* all the more attractive as an alternative outlay. Despite its aggressive imperial role, Spain remained underdeveloped and an economic colony of other nations; it did not decline because there was no level of achievement against which 'decline' could be measured. Not until the late seventeenth century did the bourgeoisie begin to find favourable conditions for investment in trade and industry.

Italy

The slowing down of the Venetian textile industry in the late sixteenth century, and its decline after the opening of the seventeenth, could not fail to lead to a redistribution of investment. Increasing difficulties in the Levant trade, and growing commercial rivalry from other Italian cities and from northern countries, made the comparative security of land and rentals more desirable. Nobles, citizens and people of Venice purchased property and estates on the mainland, the Terraferma, particularly at the end of the sixteenth and the beginning of the seventeenth century. At the same time, in Venice as in other cities, opportunities to live as a *rentier* were readily available. The decline of commerce, no less than success in business, encouraged the merchant classes to leave their traditional occupations in favour of security and status. Gradually the mercantile oligarchy became a patriciate, as in the city of Lucca; and in the city of Como, while maintaining hold on its business interests, it extended itself into the collecting of interest from loans it had made to the government or to rural communities. In Milan, many of the great merchants and industrialists of the fifteenth century had, by the seventeenth, joined the ruling feudal classes. The Missaglia family, prominent armament manufacturers of the fifteenth century, obtained a noble title at the end of their period of greatest success, and withdrew their capital from the business. Sixteenth-century merchants like the Cusani diverted their money from trade to the purchase of land. Bourgeois who had spent their career in the public service (families like the Borromeos, patricians like the Moroni), members of the professions, and office-holders, all committed their fortunes to the land, from which they derived a noble title and feudal rents.

The evolution of one family, the Riccardi of Florence, is instructive. Starting in the mid fifteenth century the family began to buy land: between 1480 and 1517 the output from their holdings increased 3½ times in grain, 1½ times in wine; between 1517 and 1568 their landholdings increased by 250 per cent. From the 1560s they began investing their profits from the land in wool and textiles in Florence, and from 1577 they set up a bank devoted to lending money and investing in trade. In the 1580s the Riccardi were trading both to the Levant and to Spain. In 1600 their business investments – excluding land – were 69 per cent in banking, 16 per cent in wool, 15 per cent in silk. They continued to buy more land and to invest the profits in commerce: clear evidence that there was no formal contradiction between one and the other. By the early seventeenth century, as business declined (Florence had 152 wool producers in 1561, only eighty-four in 1616) the Riccardi shifted their emphasis to land and the security of social position. In the village of Villa Saletta in 1563 they owned 36 per cent of the land, the Church held 28 per cent, and others 36 per cent; by 1620 the Riccardi held 90 per cent, the Church 4 per cent, and others 6 per cent. A member of the family became a senator in Florence in 1596; in 1598 they bought a palace in the city. When Riccardo Riccardi, the head of the family, died in 1612, his fortune consisted 63 per cent in land, 24 per cent in business, 10 per cent in loans, 3 per cent in *rentes*.

Germany

Tenure of office characterized the bourgeoisie in most central

German cities. An imperial decree of 1530 described the urban middle classes as falling into roughly three categories: the common citizens (including retail shopkeepers and journeymen), then above them the merchants and master craftsmen, and finally the patrician class of office-holders. In smaller towns the last two groups tended to merge, in line with the fact that even self-made men allowed themselves to be attracted by office and by 'living off investments and rents' (to quote the 1530 decree). Merchant families supplied recruits to the class of officials, but the vast majority of them came from the body of university graduates (who here as everywhere else in western Europe tended to study law in order to enter the administration), drawn from patrician families and therefore assured of a place in the élite after graduating. In Württemberg in the mid sixteenth century this group occupied nearly three-quarters of the places in public administration. Here was a flourishing middle class, a rising bourgeoisie, yet one which had divorced itself from any part in the production of wealth, and had committed itself to the ideals of office and *rentes*, ideals which in a monarchical régime were a prelude to the attainment of noble status.

The trading bourgeoisie flourished in the early sixteenth century, and are best represented by the financial firm of the Fuggers, whose leading members became nobles of the Empire and bought estates in Swabia, where by the end of the century they had 100 villages covering about 93 square miles. Good exploitation of these resources brought the Fuggers an annual average 6 per cent return on the capital invested in the land, showing the application of good business acumen. Changing patterns of trade affected the German bourgeoisie no less than those of Spain and Italy: the south German towns decayed at the same time as the trade of Italy and Antwerp.

Central and east Europe

The fate of the central and east European bourgeoisie was linked to one fundamental fact: in a part of the continent with a lower density of population than western Europe, the towns were smaller and weaker, and so more likely to be dominated by the rural areas. The long struggle between the traders of the towns and the producers in the countryside (a struggle which in Russia lay behind the great urban revolts of 1648) was eventually resolved in favour of the producers. The feudal structure of Russian society repressed the growth of an autonomous urban bourgeoisie. There was no field that the traders and merchants could specifically call their own. We have already seen that the nobility and monasteries dominated large-scale trade and industry. The chief minister Morozov, who fell from power in 1648, traded in grain, mined and produced potash, possessed distilleries and mills, exploited iron mines and ran a metallurgical industry. He was at once a great landowner, a merchant, an industrialist, entrepreneur and usurer. When princes of both state and Church promoted capitalism to this extent, what function could be nascent bourgeoisie possibly have?

What gave the conflict between traders and producers elsewhere in Europe its peculiar importance was that the latter, owners of the soil and of the peasantry, were the noble class. Strengthened in their possession of land by the seizure of Church property after the Reformation, the nobility gradually came to exercise within the state a political preponderance that no ruler could dispute. At the political level this had a serious effect upon the bourgeoisie, since the rulers repeatedly took the side of the nobles in constitutional disputes with the towns, so that the voice of the towns in the Estates of each realm was progressively weakened. But it was the economic factor that was decisive. The fate of urban privileges in Brandenburg provides an example. As elsewhere in central Europe, brewing was a leading industry of the towns. The nobility enjoyed some exemption from taxes on this commodity, and consequently were able to produce cheaper beer than the urban breweries, in open violation of the law that equalized beer prices. They soon took over much of the rural market and brought depression to the towns: in 1595 the authorities counted 891 ruined breweries in the towns of Brandenburg, while new ones continued to spring up in the countryside. Commerce, long an activity of the town bourgeoisie, suffered similarly. When the nobles began to develop production of corn from their estates, they also began to find ways of transporting it themselves in order to avoid the middlemen in the towns. Despite some attempt to restrict this, by the mid sixteenth century the nobility were exporting their corn freely. By the early seventeenth century the Brandenburg gentry were claiming that they were entitled to export freely by both land and water, and that they were exempt from tolls and duties.

The result was the decline of the towns and their trading population. At times the towns even had to suffer famine because of the way in which the producers held back supplies in order to speculate in prices. It was not corn and beer only, but all the other produce of the land, in which the gentry began to deal on the basis of the unequal privileges they were accorded. The towns lost their privileged trading and industrial position, and the noble class rose at the expense of the bourgeoisie. The picture was the same throughout the north-east. In Prussia and in Pomerania, too, exemption from taxes gave the gentry a clear field in the sphere of corn and beer. After a century of complaints the great port of Königsberg in 1634 claimed that nothing had been done to remedy the situation. The economic and commercial decay of the towns, and the weakening of the bourgeoisie, continued in the course of the seventeenth century, and the trend was consolidated in the 1650s and 1660s by the various measures of state control adopted by the rulers of Brandenburg-Prussia.

In the east, the case of Hungary presents a similar picture. Suffering from the burden of the long wars against the Turks, Hungary underwent both a political crisis and a crisis of production. Anxious to rescue their fortunes, the nobles, as agrarian producers, laid claims to control over distribution as well as over production. Some concessions were made when, in 1563, the kingdom passed a law permitting nobles who were refugees from the Turks to buy houses in the towns and to import wine from the countryside free, provided this was for their own use only. Once granted to a section of the nobility, these privileges opened the way to the nobles as a whole to establish themselves in the towns and, what is more, through marriage with the urban patriciate to take part in the government of the towns. It was in vain in 1574 that the cities presented a demand that landlords should not be allowed to trade in agricultural produce. The diet ruled that provided the customs duty was paid they could trade both internally and externally in all goods. Inevitably the towns and the bourgeoisie collapsed before the economic domination of the gentry.

This glance at different areas of Europe suggests that if sectors of the bourgeoisie failed it was because external conditions, rather than a conscious defection, determined their situation. When they changed their investment pattern, it was because developments presented them with a logical alternative. In Antwerp merchants bought houses and lands (Jacob della Faille in the 1570s owned 800 acres and eleven houses) because these represented tangible wealth as against the intangible wealth of overseas trade and credit. In 1661 the Venetian merchant Alberto Gozzi had 200,000 ducats invested in commerce and industry, but he also had 174,000 invested in land; at this period the percentage return from land was higher than that from trade, so that land was a rational purchase.

At the root of the notion of a 'bourgeois betrayal' is the premise that the bourgeois had ideals or an ethic to which he should have held. In some regions the bourgeoisie certainly showed a clear identity. In Franche Comté they were the most active social group: as traders, they devoted themselves to work, travelling throughout Europe on commercial missions; as landowners, they developed the soil, and went riding and hunting; the men did military service; their libraries showed a high level of culture; and their sons were educated abroad. The *group* identity of the bourgeois, however, never gave rise to a coherent *class* indentity in pre-industrial Europe. The private records and wills of merchants and capitalists give only fragmentary hints of their outlook, hopes and ideals. Unlike the nobles, who knew and recognized the ideals of their status, the bourgeoisie felt that they belonged ultimately not to their present condition but to the rank towards which they aspired. Social mobility encouraged them to adopt the ideals of the traditional upper orders. This did not necessarily involve the withdrawal of capital from wealth formation.

The aristocratization of the middle classes was inevitable. In the Italian state of Lucca the commercial ruling oligarchy which had formerly described itself as *patres, patricii senatoresque*, altered its description by the end of the sixteenth century to *nobilitas*; while the group formerly dignified as *plebs et populus* was downgraded to the rank of *ignobilitas*. The function and status of the new nobility of Lucca were discussed for the first time by the writer Pompeo Rocchi in his *Il gentilhuomo* (1568). In Holland the social change was commented upon by an English observer in the early eighteenth century: 'their government is aristocratical; so that the so much boasted liberty of the Dutch is not to be understood in the general and absolute sense, but *cum grano salis*'. In France, according to a seventeenth-century robe president of the Parlement of Paris, 'there is only one kind of nobility, and it is acquired through service either in the army or in the judiciary, but the rights and prerogatives are the same'. The notion of service likewise formed the basis of the theories of the Huguenot writer Louis Turquet de Mayerne in his *De la monarchie aristodémocratique* (written 1591, publ. 1611). He claimed that 'birth is neither the origin nor the basis of nobility', and that 'the common people are the seed-ground of the nobility'. 'True nobility has its basis only in good acts; in the work, I mean, of men who deserve well of the state.' 'Proper fulfilment of one's public office ennobles a man.' In a frank justification of bourgeois mobility, Mayerne argued that only the merchant deserved nobility, for he proved it by his worldly success; moreover, he benefited the realm through trade, which enriched the country and also gave him a knowledge of public affairs that no other profession did. Arms and war, then, were an ignoble profession; what was noble was trade, finance and agriculture.

6   The peasantry

Whosoever doth not maintain the plough destroys this Kingdom.
  Sir Robert Cecil (1601)

By far the most important sector of the economy before the era of industrial capitalism was the land; by far the largest and most essential sector of the population was the peasantry. Agriculture was the mainstay of economy, society and state. The peasant classes were correspondingly the mainstay of all three. In a well-known German print of the sixteenth century, the tree of society is illustrated with peasants as the roots and – after the ascent branch by branch through the lower and upper classes, king and pope – perhaps even more significantly, as the crown of the tree.

By the seventeenth century artists began to represent peasants as drunken, boorish louts, a sign, no doubt, of a growing lack of comprehension among the expanding urban population. But the respect attached to the status of peasant still retained a powerful influence over social attitudes and political policy. Adam was the first peasant: all men and all nobles were therefore descended from peasants. Far from being a revolutionary assertion, this claim was commonplace. It can be found in the literature of most countries in Europe. In the peasant was to be found those virtues of labour, patience, subordination, duty and piety that every Christian priest praised from his pulpit. The peasant was not sullied by the sins of the townsmen, by the search for profit. He represented a self-contained unit, who lived off no other man, and who trusted in God. Such at least was the myth, and it was by no means a harmless one, for it determined the prejudices of many centuries of Christian civilization. In economic life the acceptance of subsistence agriculture as natural and good and of trade, particularly in trade for profit, as bad, had a persistently regressive effect. Social groups which did not engage in agriculture to any appreciable extent were ostracized as economic parasites who would not soil their hands with true work: hence the popular basis of anti-Semitism, since Jews tended to be an urban minority, and were devoted to the unnatural vice of usury.

In an age when land values were changing rapidly and the function of rural labourers was being disturbed, those who were concerned for social justice were alarmed most of all by the depressed state of the peasant classes. In England in particular, the sixteenth century witnessed an effort by numerous writers to preserve the position of the independent labourer in rural society. In the process, the virtues of the English yeomanry were highly idealized, as though the fate of the kingdom virtually depended on their freedom. On the whole, the English managed to keep a class of free tillers of the soil. On the continent, the trend was quite different.

The agrarian economy

The dominant feature of sixteenth-century agriculture was the extension of arable to meet the food needs of a growing population. Claude de Seyssel in his *Grande Monarchie de France* (1519) observed that 'the abundance of population could be observed from the fields, for many places and regions which used to be untilled or wooded are at present all cultivated and peopled with villages and houses'. Attractively high cereal prices encouraged farmers to make profits by putting their land under the plough. There were three main features of the boom: the advance of the plough into forest land, the conversion of common and pasture land to arable, the reclamation of land from the sea.

The erosion of forest was the least significant of these. Though woodland was continually disappearing, causes included not simply conversion to arable but also sales of trees by impecunious owners (including the crown), levelling of woods to lay out parks (a frequent habit of aristocrats), and thefts of timber by peasants. In France and Spain there was continuous legislation to protect forests; in France the crown made its legislation apply to all feudal and private woods, claiming that these were within the scope of its sovereignty. Trees were a major public concern because they supplied fuel, were used in shipbuilding, and helped to prevent soil erosion. Charles I of England seems to have appreciated forests less for these reasons than because they were a useful source of income in sales of trees (the French crown also broke its own laws in this way), and were perfect for hunting. Where woods were destroyed arable crept in: 'the countryside is being deforested', the estates of Languedoc exaggerated in 1546. In England the argument that arable was of more benefit to the nation than forests began to gather force in the seventeenth century, and found parliamentary expression in the 1653 Act for the Sale of Royal Forests.

Conversion of pasture to arable depended on the needs of other agrarian sectors: livestock, for example, was essential for meat, milk, hides and wool, and would have been prejudiced by reduction in pasture. Indeed, herding increased. Cattle figured as 55 per cent of the exports of Hungary to Vienna in 1500 and 93.6 per cent in 1542; the Danish trade in cattle tripled between 1500 and 1600; in Spain the sheep in the Mesta attained their peak numbers in 1550. The emphasis, however, was on grain (though it should be noted that an extension of arable always implied some extension of pasture, since in fallow years the fields were turned from tillage to grass). In East Anglia the rent of arable rose sixfold between 1590 and 1650 while that of pasture rose by only two or three times. Villages and feudal seigneurs extended the plough into common lands: in Spain this occurred in the Tierra de Campos, for example, and around Valladolid. Farmers wishing to extend arable instigated lawsuits against the Mesta, which was very likely more sinned against than (as often supposed) sinning. At the same time, in the Mediterranean the culture of supplementary foods was intensified. Vine- and olive-growing areas were extended: at Gignac in Languedoc, olives in 1519 occupied 15 per cent of the tilled soil, in 1534 as much as 42 per cent. In the Basque country wine output trebled during the seventeenth century. The famous wines of Italy and Hungary developed in this period. In the north of Beaujolais vines in 1580 covered 5 per cent of the soil, by 1680 they covered 20 per cent.

Land reclamation was striking evidence of the demand for arable. In the United Provinces between 1565 and 1590 some 8046 hectares were won back from the sea; from 1590 to 1615 the total was 36,213 hectares, the largest area to have been reclaimed for two centuries. In Schleswig Holstein by 1650 about 25,000 hectares of coast marshland had been drained. Henry IV invited a distinguished team of Netherlanders under Humphrey Bradley to supervise drainage of marshes in France, and it was Netherlanders, profiting from their long experience, who played a leading part in most reclamation schemes elsewhere on the continent, in Italy and Germany. At Aigues-Mortes in France, revenue from reclaimed land trebled between 1500 and 1560. In England under the early Stuarts, Cornelius Vermuyden undertook to drain the Fens, and some 160,000 hectares were eventually reclaimed.

The emphasis on agriculture was accompanied by a spate of farming manuals. In Spain Pérez de Herrera's *Agricultura General* (1515) held the field for two centuries. In England the outstanding writers were Walter Blith and Richard Weston, both writing in the 1640s. In France the works of Estienne and others were followed by the best-selling Olivier de Serres's *Théatre de l'Agriculture* (1600). In Germany Heresbach's *De re rustica* (1570) was followed at the turn of the century by Coler's *Oeconomia ruralis*. Gostomski published the popular Polish work *Notaty gospodarskie* (Notes on the rural economy) in 1588.

At least up to the 1570s there was a steady rise in agrarian output. In the villages of Bureba (northern Spain), production in grain between the 1550s and 1580s rose by 26 per cent, in wine by 51 per cent. In Calabria on the lands of the prince of Bisignano, harvest output rose 75 per cent between the 1520s and 1540s. Output of wheat measured in yield ratios (ratio of grain reaped to grain sown) was fairly high in western Europe, ranging from over 10:1 in Berkshire and Friesland to 6.8:1 in Bureba and 5:1 in Poitou. In eastern Europe yields were lower, as much as 6.5:1 in Masovia (Poland) but below 4:1 in Hungary.

Despite the boom conditions up to the late sixteenth century, no real technical advance in production was achieved. As much as one-half of the arable soil in Europe might be vacant in any year, because of adherence to the old methods of leaving fields fallow. Manure was scarce and the rotation of root crops did not begin to spread until the end of the seventeenth century; agricultural implements remained primitive and peasant communities resisted innovative techniques. Thus, although two important developments occurred in the early modern period – an extension of cultivated land, involving in some areas (such as land reclamation) a greater investment of capital; and a change in social relationships, which in western Europe meant the decline of feudalism and in eastern Europe the onset of a new feudalism – no substantial changes occurred in the character of the agrarian economy.

There were, however, regional variations in this picture. Whereas France appears to have experienced no significant agricultural innovation before the nineteenth century, further north in the Netherlands new methods had been creeping in since the fifteenth century. Population increase and greater urbanization facilitated the use of manpower in labour-intensive industries. Since the land was not capable of producing an adequate amount of cereals, these were imported in bulk from the Baltic. Available soil could thus be put to alternative use, for intensive dairy farming and other industries such as hops and flax. Where land remained in arable, use was made of convertible husbandry (i.e. alternating crops and grasses), with clover or peas grown in fallow years; turnips were grown as fodder, with turnips, clover and grain sown in rotation in the early seventeenth century in Flanders; and a wide range of manures was applied, including both dung and compost. While the overall output of grain did not apparently increase (and this was never an objective, since the nation relied on imports), yield per hectare was possibly the highest in Europe. For England, likewise, it has been argued that the period witnessed an agricultural revolution, most of whose achievements occurred before the 1670s. Changes included the floating of water-meadows, the introduction of new fallow crops and grasses, marsh drainage, manuring and stock-breeding: crop yields rose, and in areas the food production apparently doubled between 1540 and 1700.

Peasant obligations

The soil of Europe was largely in the hands of peasants and peasant communities. In France it has been estimated that about half the land was held by peasants, varying from a fifth in Brittany and Normandy to over half in Dauphiné. In Brunswick (Germany) the nobles held only 8 per cent, and the peasants 67.5 per cent of all agricultural land. Such figures are, however, deceptive; and the single word 'peasant' is quite unsatisfactory when used to describe the broad variations in tenure and income among the rural classes.

The peasantry, as the largest social class, were too numerous for the land available, and their holdings were usually inadequate. The average peasant plot was only in exceptional circumstances capable of supporting a rural family comfortably. The division of the soil was normally unfavourable, as at Roquevaire in Lower Provence in 1663, where the clergy owned 1 per cent, the bourgeoisie 19 per cent, the nobles 23 per cent and the peasants 57 per cent. The peasantry, on the face of it, got the lion's share; but the landholding community at Roquevaire was made up of nine nobles, twelve bourgeois and over 150 peasant proprietors, so that in reality each noble family held nine times, and each bourgeois family three times as much as the average peasant landed family.

In any case, few peasants actually 'held' land. Peasants might be personally free, as in most of western Europe, but their land was, for the most part, not held outright, and had to fulfil various obligations to a lord; in effect this meant a tenancy, not an ownership. The average peasant in Europe was not a freeholder. Where the feudal system and related contractual systems were operative, peasants had to perform services both in kind and in labour for their lord, a duty which restricted their own effective freedom. All peasants, whether free or not, were in any case finding that the basis of their independence and prosperity was being steadily eroded by developments (such as taxation) that were beyond their control. Last, and by no means least, a huge proportion of the rural population held no land at all.

Thanks to the administrative and legal structure of feudalism in England, where the forms of Roman law never took root, the English peasant farmer was almost totally free by the sixteenth century. The landed peasants in some areas continued to pay traditional dues to manorial lords, but the proportion was not numerically or socially significant. Those who did not farm their own land made up a rural labouring sector which formed as much as a third of the total country population. As in any period of change, the peasant farmers developed both upwards and downwards: in the former case, they improved their lot and moved into the yeomanry or gentry; in the latter, they augmented what was, in an age of expanding population, a growing rural proletariat. Generalizations like these become more comprehensible if we look at one detailed example.

The village of Wigston Magna in Leicestershire doubled its numbers from about seventy to 140 households in the course of the century 1525–1625, thereby becoming one of the most thriving villages in the English Midlands. A breakdown of the occupations of the villagers in the late seventeenth century shows that 36 per cent depended on agriculture for a living, 30 per cent on crafts and trades connected with the land, 17 per cent on framework-knitting. In addition 16 per cent were simply described as 'poor'. The peasant farmers benefited from the rise in food prices during the century of inflation, and accumulated a comfortable surplus, which in the

years up to the early seventeenth century was largely untouched by
taxation. The forms of feudal organization vanished here in 1606
when the last manor was sold by its lord, and the villagers refused
to continue to pay the feudal dues to the new occupants. The end of
manorial control also meant the end of tenure by copyhold, for the
rolls which proved tenure used to be kept by the lord. All tenure now
became freehold. As the village developed, its economic life became
more diversified. The peasant farmers grew wealthier, because of
the demand for their food produce; but the smaller peasants were
unable to compete with the larger producers, and as population
increased the landholdings of the smaller peasantry became even
more inadequate. Beside the prosperous farmer there now
appeared the beginnings of the rural proletariat. The village world
of subsistence economy was also being invaded more and more, in
proportion to the growth of commerce for the market, by money.
Cash transactions became more common, and a ready example can
be found in the giving of marriage settlements in cash rather than in
kind.

The growth of rural poverty was a notable feature of the period.
In the Midlands the cost of living for a farm labourer rose sixfold
between 1500 and 1640, while his real wages over the same period
fell by about 50 per cent. Not surprisingly, economic distress among
the rural population was widespread, and contributed primarily to
the growing numbers of vagrants, who were often no more than
landless labourers seeking employment. The situation did, of
course, vary widely in other parts of England, and there were even
a few patriarchal figures such as Sir George Sondes of Lees Court
in Kent who for thirty years spent, in his own words, 'at least a
thousand pounds a year' in giving economic help to his farm-
labourers.

An independent and free community like Wigston Magna might
be representative in that it illustrates the end of feudal control and
the increase of both wealth and poverty; but it is not a clear example
of one of the dominant trends of the period, the redistribution of
landed income in favour of the landed class. Small farmers and farm-
labourers had an increasingly difficult time; the former, because it
was a constant struggle to make output exceed the level of rents, the
latter, because wages fell rather than rose. A small landowner might
profit, but he had to compete with the greater marketing power of
the larger producers. The lesser tenants had to cope with high rents
(the rents at Stoneleigh manor in 1599 came to £418 and in 1640 to

£1440), and enclosures (which incurred opposition mainly in the Midlands, where the acreage enclosed in Leicestershire rose from 5870 in 1599 to 12,280 in 1607, and in Lincolnshire from 4866 to 13,420).

It was no less difficult a time for the peasantry of continental western Europe. While production expanded, the social condition of the peasant deteriorated. Unless land was held outright (as 'allodial' or non-feudal land), the peasant had to pay dues to a seigneur (these varied, and might include a nominal cash sum, payment in kind such as a proportion of harvest, and taxes on fishing and using the lord's mill to grind corn), to the Church (tithes, not always a strict tenth), and to the state (in France, for example, the *taille*). Three brief regional glimpses will illustrate this.

In the Beauvaisis (northern France) in the seventeenth century a typical village community of 100 families might have two rich peasant farmers (*laboureurs*), five or six middling farmers, about twenty middling peasants (here called *haricotiers*), and a large class of up to fifty farm-workers and day-labourers (*manouvriers*). In the Dijonnais in Burgundy these workers were the vast majority of the male adults in the countryside, and totally out-numbered the peasant farmers, who were usually fixed in their residence while the rural workers had no means of their own and were often on the move, particularly into the towns. The average *haricotier* of the Beauvaisis worked about 5 hectares of land. The payment of taxes to the crown would take up about one-fifth of his output (the *taille* accounted for most of this), leaving him with 80 per cent of his harvest. The tithe and Church taxes would take up another 8 per cent of his revenue, and other taxes would account for 4 per cent more, so that eventually the peasant would be left with 68 per cent of his harvest. Another fifth, however, would have to be set aside for running costs and for seed to be sown the following year. This left 48 per cent, and still the outgoings were not at an end, for the landlord's rent remained to be paid. This varied widely, depending on the system of tenure. What the peasant received eventually might be only a small fraction of his original harvest. This, of course, was in a normal year, and takes no account of the possibility that the peasant might have debts to be repaid. If the year had been a bad one, or if his debts were many, the peasant faced disaster.

If, when he sowed his ground [observed a French lawyer, La Barre, in 1622] the peasant really realised for whom he was doing it, he would not sow. For he is the one to profit least from his labour. The first handful of grain he casts on the soil is for God, so he throws it freely. The second goes to the birds; the third for ground-rents; the fourth for tithes; the fifth for *tailles*, taxes and impositions. And all that goes even before he has anything for himself.

In New Castile the landholding peasant was in a minority, up to 70 per cent of the rural male population consisting of landless agricultural labourers (*jornaleros*). In many villages there were no landholding peasants at all. A census of New Castile drawn up for Philip II in 1575 confirms the plight of the peasant producer, who was obliged on average to consign well over half his harvest to the payment of taxes and dues. The lightest of his burdens tended to be traditional dues payable to the seigneur. Tithes, which were usually assessed at a strict tenth, came to ten times the value of seigneurial dues. One contemporary commentator, Lope de Deza, asserted in 1618 that the tithes in Toledo province equalled all other taxes in value, but (such was the nature of loyalty to the Church that all writers shared) rather than recommend an end to tithes he suggested that all the other taxes be suppressed. After tithes the peasant had to pay his taxes to the crown; these came to about the same value as the tithes. Finally, and most important of all, came the land rents. In New Castile these took up between one-third and one-half of a peasant's harvest, and quite often would amount to three or four times the value of the tithes. Adding up the rent and the taxes, little could have remained to the producer, as we gather from one village near Toledo which complained in 1580 that 'after paying the rent, nothing was left them'. Nor was this an end to the sorrows of the peasantry for, as we have already seen, those who fell into difficulties borrowed money and found themselves bound by *censos*. 'In short', complained the cortes of Castile in 1598 when presenting a petition against *censos*, 'everything tends towards the destruction of the poor peasantry and the increase in property, authority and power of the rich.'

In the west German lands labour services formed part of the system of estate economy known as *Grundherrschaft* (some demesne exploitation, but most land leased out). In Brunswick the labour dues were formalized by a law of 1597. According to this the peasantry in that state owed weekly services: an *Ackermann* (peasant farmer) was to give two days' statute-labour with his plough-team; a *Halbspänner* (or holder of half a hide of land) was to give one day. When it came to purely manual labour, the peasants owed services varying from two days to half a day a week. By any standards these were fairly heavy demands, yet they occurred in a system which is usually described as free, in contrast to the serfdom of the east. Labour services with a plough, for example, were onerous, since the team was required to supply two persons and four horses, with a cart. The enormous utility of these services to the landlords is shown by the fact that in the demesne of Gandersheim in the fifty years 1610–60 no work-horses at all were kept, since all the ploughing was done by labour teams. In the year 1639 the demesne obtained 248 ploughing days from labour teams, more than enough for its needs.

The basic problem of peasant obligations was everywhere aggravated by weather and war (see Chapter 1), fiscality (see Chapter 2), and debt. In Spain the burden of rural *censos* provoked depopulation; in France, Loyseau in 1601 observed that 'debts are swollen by interest charges, creditors are more pressing, debtors poorer'. A combination of many factors is shown in the case of the village of Noiron-les-Cîteaux in Burgundy, which suffered badly from the Thirty Years War and had to sell common lands to meet debts. In 1557 it had been a free community with a rich domain and paid only a small *taille*. By 1666 the domain had vanished in alienations, and to the *taille* had been added a heavier *taille*, payments in kind, *corvées* and a tithe. As economic difficulties grew for both rural labourers and smallholders, a depression of the peasantry set in. Three major consequences followed.

First, there was a greater polarization between rich and poor among the rural classes. A rural bourgeoisie grew up side by side with a rural proletariat; many middle peasants disappeared. At Chippenham (Cambridge) between 1544 and 1712, the smallholder all but vanished; farmers with over 90 acres increased from 3 to 14 per cent of residents, landless families increased from 32 to 63 per cent. It was a process common to all countries on the continent. A 1667 report on Burgundy observed that 'formerly all or nearly all inhabitants were proprietors of land which they worked, now there are only share-croppers [*métayers*] and labourers'. Second, the concentration of estates took place as part of the process of expropriation of the peasantry. In the village of Manguio in Languedoc, in 1595 there was only one estate exceeding 100 hectares, by 1653 there were three and in 1770 eight. Third, as we have seen above (Chapter 5), the urban bourgeois appropriated rural holdings. At Avrainville (a village near Paris) the proportion

of land held by Paris townspeople rose from 53 per cent in 1550 to
83 per cent in 1688; by 1680 around Toulouse only one-fifth of the
land was in local peasant hands. In the Como region (Italy) the
expropriation of the peasantry reached its height in the crisis years
1620–50, with most of the land falling into the hands of the
bourgeoisie and the Church.

It is evident that these developments must have created a major
crisis for the European village community. Internally, the
community was threatened by the polarization of wealth and by the
consequent social tensions and loss of the neighbour-ethic known in
more democratic times. Families drifted away, and within the
village there were growing conflicts, leading frequently to riots,
between tax-exempt property owners and those poor who had to
pay taxes. Externally, there were severe financial problems: the
communal debt was always the heaviest burden, sharply intensified
in this period by the frequency of war and by the soaring fiscality of
the state (in Castile between 1570 and 1670 the tax burden probably
quadrupled). Common lands and other assets had to be sold to meet
the debts, further weakening the economic position of the village.
Finally, in this weakened condition the community was ill-equipped
to resist continuous encroachments on its privileges by seigneurs,
urban landlords, and the government. The view, therefore, that the
peasant community remained strong in continental Europe and by
its conservatism blocked the agrarian change that eventually
became restricted mainly to England (see Chapter 3 in the section on
Capitalism and economic growth) is not tenable.

Seigneurs and serfs in eastern Europe

Why should eastern Europe (east, that is, of the Elbe) be discussed
separately from the west? The sparsity of population (varying from
a density of fourteen persons per square kilometre in Poland to three
in the Ukraine) meant that with less manpower there were special
problems of labour availability. The near-subsistence economy of
the region was, moreover, balanced by an extraordinary capacity to
supply grain in vast quantities to the west European market. Finally,
the machinery of a centralized state had not come into existence in
the east, leaving the nobility with far greater autonomy than in the
west and allowing them to acquire great wealth and power.

The predominance of the noble class was a striking feature of
eastern Europe. The sixteenth century saw the emergence of the

Junkers in East Prussia, the *szlachta* in Poland, the *pomeshchiki* in Muscovy; these gentry now took their place beside the older noble class. The paucity of large towns (of the 700 towns in Poland in 1600 only eight had a population exceeding 10,000), the corresponding lack of a vigorous bourgeoisie, and the constitutional weakness of the Third Estate, gave the nobles an inestimable advantage.

Since the fifteenth century the eastern ports had been grain suppliers to western Europe. The produce of eastern estates and the activity of ports like Königsberg and Gdansk were closely tied to the market demands of the west. With the important exception of Russia, most eastern countries were to some extent part of the European market. This was true even of landlocked territories such as Hungary, since thanks to its political status as a Habsburg sphere of influence western Hungary exported agricultural goods through Vienna and south Germany. The close commercial link between east and west, despite their dissimilar economic development, is reflected in the prices of grain and food. Though the level of prices remained lower in the east (over the fifty years 1551–1600 prices at Gdansk were only 53 per cent of those at Amsterdam, and those at Warsaw only 46 per cent), the order of inflation was comparable to that in the west. In Poland wheat prices quadrupled in the sixteenth century.

The rise in cereal and food prices, caused in part by foreign demand, supplied the incentive required by landowners of the east. Moreover, the different price levels between east and west guaranteed a profit for all, both exporters in the east and importers in the west, concerned in the grain traffic. While demesne farming declined in western Europe and the nobles attempted to secure incomes from sources other than agricultural production, in much of central and eastern Europe they went back to the land as a source of wealth. On an estate of the Rantzau family in Holstein in 1600, of an annual income of 5000 marks only 250 came from peasant rents; the rest came from livestock, grain and dairy produce.

Peasant and waste lands were absorbed into demesne, and the production of grain for a lucrative market became a primary occupation. In countries without access to the sea, grain did not necessarily dominate the economy of the great estates. On the contrary, in Bohemia the principal item of production for both the internal and the external market was beer; and in Hungary wine was by far the most important source of income and capital. Both ecclesiastical and secular lords shared in this expansion of production, which increased their capital earnings and allowed them to operate a virtual monopoly over economic activity. The price-rise, fatal to seigneurs in the west, consolidated their power in the east.

Noble entrepreneurship took a great step forward. 'The nobles in past years', commented a Pomeranian official in the late sixteenth century, 'have not been very industrious and keen to make their living. But now in recent years they have become better at it, and since the country existed the nobility has never been so rich and powerful as nowadays.' The progress of the gentry in Hungary was comparable. A royal decree of 1618 in Hungary confirmed the freedom of the gentry from excise and taxes. In 1625 controls over prices and wages were removed. In 1630 the Diet decreed that the nobles could take part in foreign trade without paying taxes or customs duties. By 1655 a memoir of the time could claim that 'the nobles deal in all kinds of trade', in corn, wine, cattle, honey and so on. How this affected other classes was described by the memoir: 'The seigneurs and nobles take over trading; they seize for themselves whatever they think profitable; they exclude the common people and the merchants; they confiscate everything indiscriminately from the poor, and hold it as their own private property.'

The economic progress of the great nobility was accompanied by the growth of serfdom. The recourse to demesne farming stepped up demand for labour, but peasants were not available in adequate numbers nor were they all obliged to perform regular labour services. When existing burdens were increased the peasants fled, aggravating the labour problem. Noble influence, therefore, brought in the power of the state. The legislation passed by various governments from the sixteenth century onwards had one aim: to make the peasant's labour available by binding him to the soil and depriving him of freedom of movement.

In Prussia, ordinances of 1526, 1540, 1577, 1612, and 1633 progressively limited the right of a peasant to move from his land, or to inherit property. Labour burdens were increased and lords were given the right to exploit the labour of a peasant's children. In Brandenburg, laws of 1518, 1536, and subsequent years likewise tied peasants to the soil, and the question of labour was settled in the early seventeenth century when the High Court ruled that all peasants were liable to unlimited services unless they could prove the contrary. In the Habsburg lands the trend was the same, but the particular problem of these frontier provinces – proximity to the

Turks – caused shifts in policy. The general picture can be illustrated by the case of Hungary. Laws of 1514 and 1548 fixed official limits for the labour service (*robot*), but in practice peasants were exploited well above the authorized level of fifty-two days a year. This situation led to the flight of peasants, which in its turn provoked legislation tying the worker to the soil, as measures of 1556 and 1608 stipulated.

Unlike the west, where hired labour was common, many central European estates had to survive largely off feudal services. As in the west, peasant obligations also consisted of tribute in cash and in kind. Since labour rather than tribute was required on the great estates, it became the universal rule in eastern Europe to commute services in cash and in kind into labour services. This can be seen, for example, in Brandenburg, where in 1608 the Von Arnim family, in the Uckermark, was granted a general permit to use the services of its subjects instead of their rents. Extension of labour services became general in this region. By the end of the sixteenth century most of the villages owned by the cathedral chapter of Havelberg had to render about ninety days' labour in the year. Peasants belonging to the Margrave in the vicinity of Wittstock in 1601 had to serve as much as three days in the week normally, and had to give unlimited service during harvest-time. This process was accompanied by attempts to tie the peasants to the soil. At the end of the fifteenth century a law had declared that any peasant leaving a domain must find a replacement before he could leave. In the sixteenth century this law was made a general rule. In 1536 no peasant was allowed to be admitted to any town or domain unless he could produce a letter from his lord showing he had left with his consent.

The expropriation of the peasantry followed inevitably from any intensification of tax or labour dues. The number of free peasants had never been high. In Bavaria, even by the liberating eighteenth century they numbered only 4 per cent of the peasant population. A community of free and independent peasantry like the *Cölmer* of Prussia was exceptional. In Bohemia by 1654 no more than about 500 peasants out of a total of 64,000 were personally free. The vast majority was economically underprivileged and heavily dependent. In a time of crisis they fell easily into debt and so into the hands of the principal moneylender – the landlord himself. Indebtedness of an impoverished peasantry became one of the essential factors in the evolution of serfdom. There were several categories of peasant, ranging from the relatively free to the wholly servile, but all were reduced by poverty to a common level of existence. The deterioration in status can be seen in Brandenburg, where in 1552 a local writer said in his description of the New Mark: '*Rustici omnes in libertate educati sunt: tota enim Marchia neminem habet servili conditione natum.*' Fifty years later the jurist Scheplitz commented on the same passage: '*vix dici potest*'. In 1632, for the first time, some peasants of the Ucker and the New Mark were classified simply as *leibeigen*, serfs.

It was in Russia that the reduction in status was most marked. Before the final legalization of serfdom there had been varying grades of peasants, from slaves and villeins, who were found usually on noble demesnes, to completely free peasants and independent landholders. Between these extremes there were the normal categories of tenants, with different degrees of obligations. The second half of the sixteenth century witnessed a severe dislocation of the Russian state, caused principally by wars and by the *oprichnina*. In the depression and depopulation that followed these events, the landlords found it very difficult to secure an adequate labour force. Thousands of peasants had emigrated beyond Muscovy, and the attempt by the landlords (the *pomeshchiki*) to exploit those who remained served only to aggravate the flight from the land. As feudatories of the crown, the *pomeshchiki* appealed to it for help. In the spate of legislation that emerged between the late sixteenth and the mid seventeenth centuries, all categories of peasants suffered, both dependent and free. As usual, the laws concentrated on restricting the peasants' ability to move. The first of these laws was in 1580. Its effectiveness can be seen in the monastery of Volokolamsk where in 1579–80 as many as seventy-six peasants fled and twenty were attracted in; in 1581 not a single peasant moved. But it was difficult to obtain satisfactory observance of the law everywhere, as shown by the need for decrees in subsequent years. Of these, the most important were passed in 1597 and 1607. It is important to observe that these laws, unlike similar ones elsewhere, bound the peasants not to the soil but to their lord: the dependence was wholly personal. While this was going on, the liability of the peasants to taxes and to labour services (*barshchina*) was being increased. Labour services were a major obligation not only in central Russia, for as landlords elsewhere found it more profitable than ordinary dues in kind, they began to extend it to their peasants. The mounting difficulties faced by free peasants obliged very many to borrow and hence to fall into debt. A combination of several factors had by the early seventeenth century reduced the Russian peasants to the common status of serfs. Finally, in 1649, this was constitutionally legalized.

In the course of these developments, many of the peasants of eastern Europe lost their land. For the nobles appropriation of land was nothing new. The spoils obtained from the Church during the Reformation gave them the basis for new extensions to their territory. In 1540 in Brandenburg the Margrave granted the nobles of the Old Mark, and later those of the whole country, the right to buy out their peasants and to replace peasant holdings by demesne. With the active support of the rulers, who themselves bought land, the nobles replaced smallholdings by large estates. Between about 1575 and 1624, according to a survey of the latter year, 441 peasants out of a total of 7988 were bought out in the Middle Mark. The result was an increase of demesne lands in this area by over 50 per cent and a decrease in peasant lands by about 8 per cent. In north-east Estonia, where the landlords likewise took over peasant lands, the number of estates increased from about forty-five in the early seventeenth century to 135 in 1696.

The new estates were of considerable size, and big estates remained a feature of the trans-Elbe economy. In Mecklenburg, Pomerania and the central area of East Prussia, over half the estates extended to more than 100 hectares of agricultural land each. In Prussia and Brandenburg between a third and a half were of this size. West of the Elbe estates were usually much smaller. The process of alienation of peasant property is shown in the table below, which gives details for holdings in the Russian district of Varzuga, by the White Sea. The unit of land is the *luk*, which tended to consist of about 3 hectares of agricultural and woodland.

While the rise of the manorial estate was at the expense of the peasants, the degree of expropriation must not be exaggerated.

Owners of lands (in luki)	1563	1575	1586	1614	1622
Peasants	830⅓	726⅓	429	266½	—
Monasteries	36	128	415	549	549
Patriarchate	—	—	—	—	266½
Other	—	12	21½	21½	21½
	866⅓	866⅓	865½	837	837

Even by 1624 in the Middle Mark of Brandenburg the peasants still technically held four hides of land to every one held in demesne. Of the land in Prussia, according to an estimate of the early seventeenth century, the free Cölmer held 15 per cent, the nobles 36 per cent, and the peasants 49 per cent. Yet these were among the regions which suffered most from the coming of serfdom. In some areas the peasant losses were small. In Saxony the overall loss of peasant land up to the eighteenth century did not exceed 5 per cent of peasant holdings. The peasantry possibly suffered more through deterioration of status than outright loss of land.

What opposition, if any, was there to these developments? The towns and their burghers resented the economic power which the introduction of serfdom granted the nobility. In certain areas of Germany and western Europe the bourgeoisie themselves shared in the expropriation of the peasantry; but in the east this was almost unknown, and indeed there the nobles actually began to expropriate the burghers as well. The towns were, therefore, fighting for their lives when they attempted to resist the encroachments of the landed classes. This explains the bitter struggle between the Baltic ports and the noble estate. Among the cities to resist most strongly was Reval, which carried on a long but ultimately hopeless fight against the nobility of Estonia. The burghers objected in particular to the fact that the nobles traded directly with the Dutch, and in 1594 obtained an order prohibiting this, but the order was repealed later in the same year. In the same way the city of Riga was engaged in a struggle with the nobles of Livonia. Königsberg committed itself even more directly to protest against the legalization of serfdom in Prussia. The city refused to observe the terms of edicts which restricted the privileges of peasants, and maintained firmly that all peasants fleeing to it were beyond the jurisdiction of their masters. In 1634 the city authorities in a joint statement claimed that all peasants in Prussia were free and not serfs, and that they and their children were entitled to freedom of movement. After denouncing exploitation by the Junkers, Königsberg went on to reject totally the practice of serfdom. Many burghers from other towns also had the courage to denounce serfdom. Among them was the Stralsund alderman Balthasar Prutze, a member of one of the town's leading families. In 1614 he described Pomeranian serfdom as 'this barbaric and Egyptian servitude', saying that 'in our territory serfdom did not exist fifty or a hundred years ago, but latterly, it has been brought in on a large scale, with the help of the authorities'.

The state did not always support serfdom. In Electoral Saxony the rulers preferred to 'protect' the peasants, since land passing into seigneurial control became tax-exempt and strengthened the nobles. The Electors therefore bought up land for themselves, both from peasants and lords: between 1590 and 1626 Elector John George I bought up four towns and 108 villages. Meanwhile, successive laws – in 1563, 1609, 1623 and 1669, in particular – restricted the burdens of Saxon peasants and the alienation of their land. In Bavaria there was only a limited move towards serfdom, since the principal landowners were the state and the Church, and neither had any interest in changing the methods of exploitation already in existence.

The Church was among the biggest landowners and in the eastern countries it contributed as much as any other landlord to the growth of serfdom. The territory held by the Russian monasteries in the 1580s was very considerable: in the Moscow district they held 36 per cent of all arable land; in the Pskov district 52 per cent. Some of this had been donated during the *oprichnina*, when the nobles, fearing confiscation, handed their estates over to the Church in return for a life tenancy. In 1570–1 alone, ninety-nine such estates went to monasteries in Muscovy. In Poland, the see of Gniezno possessed (by the eighteenth century) scattered holdings that included no less than 426 villages and towns. In Poland and Russia production on Church estates was directed towards an external market, so that the Church had an interest in controlling mobility of labour.

By the beginning of the seventeenth century a combination of economic and political factors had reduced the peasantry of much of central and eastern Europe to a state approaching servitude. Friedrich Engels once described this state as 'second serfdom' (*zweite Leibeigenschaft*) since it differed both in time and nature from the early period of European serfdom. There were two distinctive features that created the new serfdom and were essential to its growth: the consolidation of landed power in the hands of the noble class; and the dedication of the manorial economy to the produce of grain for a (usually external) market. On these terms, did serfdom justify itself economically?

The surplus value reaped by the landlords from the labour of the depressed peasantry, and the imbalance in grain prices between eastern and western Europe, assured steady profits and an expansion of the export trade. The exports of grain from the ports of the eastern Baltic increased in volume steadily from the sixteenth tó the seventeenth century. For the whole of this period the principal grain to be exported was rye, whose volume was often ten times as great as that of the wheat exported. Poland's exports of rye grew from about 20,000 tons a year in the early sixteenth century to about 170,000 tons in 1618. The biggest import area was Amsterdam, which in 1600, for example, took over 80 per cent of Gdansk's rye exports. Of this, Amsterdam itself used only 25 per cent, so that substantial profits were made in the west through re-exports.

Though exports rose, however, this did not necessarily mean that serfdom was efficient. The growth in production seems to have occurred more because acreage under the plough increased than because serfdom was raising output. In seventeenth-century Hungary, the yield-ratios for serf-produced grain varied from 2.5 to 3.5; independent peasants managed to double these figures. In viticulture, when wage-labour was used instead of labour services, productivity in the same century tripled. Though yield-ratios can vary widely and are not always reliable evidence, a run of figures for Polish estates suggests that the level of output probably fell between 1550 and 1700. What is certain is that, even at their most efficient, the demesnes of eastern Europe never managed to produce as much as those in the west, where yield-ratios were consistently twice as high.

As in western Europe, the crises of the seventeenth century produced a further severe depression in the condition of the serf peasantry. Two aspects predominated: falling west European demand for grain; and the negative impact of wars. As the west European economy adapted to a falling birth-rate and growing sufficiency in wheat, demand for Baltic grain diminished. In Gdansk the prices of cereals fell sharply, while that of meat rose. Between the 1630s and the 1670s the quantity of grain exported out of the Baltic through the Sound fell from an index of 250 to one of 100. To make up for declining income, eastern landlords increased their demands on the peasantry. Dues were increased, and labour obligations made more onerous.

The wars were particularly ruinous. Swedish forces were campaigning throughout the early 1600s against Russia and Poland. The latter suffered severely from the Swedish invasions of 1626–9 and 1655–60, when the region of Masovia lost 64 per cent of its population, suffered the destruction of a tenth of its villages, and had 85 per cent of its cultivated land put out of use. The Thirty

Years War in the Germanic lands was notoriously destructive. The decline in population owing to death or emigration had serious repercussions on the agrarian economy. Wartime disruption had forced many independent peasants to leave the countryside for the cities; and dependent peasants, long smarting under labour obligations, drifted willingly from the land. In these circumstances it was possible to buy up deserted land at bargain prices. Nobles and landlords with the necessary capital accumulated property formerly belonging to independent villages and free peasants. The restoration of agriculture was consequently carried out in accordance with the wishes of the landlord class. Only as many peasant dwellings were restored, for example, as was consonant with the needs of the new owners of the soil. Manors replaced villages. In one case near Stralsund, fourteen peasant holdings were replaced by one large estate. The peasant communities were unable to resist the process, since many of them were heavily in debt and saw little alternative to selling out. Both individually and communally the peasantry were ushered into a period of economic ruin. The worst areas for estate consolidation appear to have been Mecklenburg and Pomerania: in the district of Stargard in Mecklenburg, where the war virtually annihilated the peasantry, three-quarters of peasant holdings fell into noble hands.

At the same time, the need to have a reliable source of labour continued to be urgent. Earlier attitudes to legislation had been casual and unhurried. When, in 1616, regulations for the peasants of Pomerania-Stettin were drawn up, these were described as '*homines proprii et coloni glebae adscripti*', a major change in their status no doubt, but one that was not formalized in an official code. In subsequent years the authorities made every attempt to give formal legal validity to serfdom. In Estonia a law of 1632 began combating peasant flights, and by mid century stability of the labour force had been obtained. A system of contractual serfdom, based on that practised by the Swedish estates of the De La Gardie family on the island of Osel, was introduced. In Russia a major social and political crisis preceded the passing of the Code of Laws, the *Ulozhenie*, of 1649. As a result of the crisis, in which the victory of the landed nobility was confirmed, the Russian peasantry were fully enserfed. All peasants and their families were declared bound to their masters, with no right of departure, and no right to asylum in the cities. No distinction was made between peasants and villeins: both had to serve on the same terms and with the same obligations and lack of freedom. Like the *Ulozhenie*, the *Recess* (or Code) granted by the Elector of Brandenburg in 1653 was influenced by the nobility. For the first time, this edict assumed that the peasants were serfs, and laid the onus on the peasant to prove that he was not one. In the Swedish-occupied territories, such as Pomerania-Wolgast, energetic opposition to serfdom was shown by the Swedish authorities. But the situation proved uncontrollable, and in 1645 and 1670 laws issued by them gave additional legislative confirmation to the existence of serfdom in Pomerania.

Did the establishment of serfdom take eastern Europe back into the Middle Ages? On the face of it, it looks as if the imposition of the forms of feudalism – demesne economy (*Gutherrschaft*), labour services, the *pomestie* – was a step backwards. The similarities are none the less outweighed by the differences. The 'second serfdom' was directed firmly towards production for the external and overseas market, a major departure from the limited commercial range of the medieval manorial economy. The 'second serfdom', moreover, lacked any free labour, and its peasant institutions were backward; both differed from the rich diversity of medieval peasant structures. Finally, the 'second serfdom' lacked any significant amount of money-capital in its system. This last point makes it impossible to accept the term 'feudal capitalism' which has sometimes been applied to the east European economy of this period. There was no significant accumulation of money capital in the systems operative in Poland and Russia, and cash earned by the noble producers was spent instead on luxuries imported from the west. A few nobles may have shown hints of being capitalist-minded. One such was the Hungarian Gy. Hedervary, who wrote in 1542: 'My one aim is to buy a ship, and to transport thousands of bushels of barley and wheat.' A century later, in 1642, one of his descendants had developed different habits, and scorned the frugal life-style: 'I am my father's son, and cannot live the way others do.' In the long run the serf economy harmed the internal economy by undue emphasis on export; hindered the expansion of urban enterprise; made social change impossible by fixing status barriers; and concentrated wealth in the hands of a feudal aristocracy. Eastern Europe and its peasantry developed in a direction opposite to that of the west. In the west the bourgeoisie and commercial capital developed hand in hand; in the east they did not merge until the nineteenth century. In the west the peasants were developing towards greater freedom and mobility; in the east it was the reverse.

7   The marginal population

> Though the number of the poore do dailie encrease, all things
> yet worketh for the worst in their behalfe.
>
>   Thomas Dekker, *Greevous Grones for the Poore* (1622)

No century had been so conscious of the poor as the sixteenth. Commentators agreed that the numbers of poor and the problem of poverty were both of unprecedented size. In Rome, Sixtus V in 1587 complained of vagrants who 'fill with their groans and cries not only public places and private houses but the churches themselves; they provoke alarms and incidents; they roam like brute beasts with no other care than the search for food'. Juan Luis Vives denounced poor who entered churches while the faithful were at prayer: 'they push through the congregation, deformed by sores, exuding an unbearable smell from their bodies'. Pierre de l'Estoile reported of Paris in 1596 that 'the crowds of poor in the street were so great that one could not pass through'.

In western Europe at least one-fifth of a town's population might consist of the wholly poor. In Troyes in 1551, 17 per cent of the population were classified as beggars and vagabonds, a figure that excluded the settled poor; in Louvain at the same date the poor constituted 21.7 per cent, and in Leyden about 40 per cent. In Brussels the proportion was 21 per cent, and in Segovia in 1561 one-sixth were registered as poor, without counting vagrants. In Bergamo in 1575, 35 per cent of a population of 20,000 were registered as poor, a minimum figure that included only 'the aged, the sick and children aged fifteen or below'. While poverty was an undeniable feature of the towns, with their large numbers of unemployed, it would be wrong to think of it only as an urban phenomenon. Many of the poor came originally from the countryside. In Normandy in the early 1500s a contemporary census of forty-six rural parishes described 24 per cent of the families as 'poor and beggars'. An estimate for eighteen villages in Lower Saxony suggests that the poor were nearly 30 per cent of the population.

For both town and country poverty was a normal experience. In the villages around Valladolid up to one-fifth of the rural population was poor. Gregory King estimated in 1688 that one-quarter of the total English population consisted of paupers. A pamphleteer of 1641 estimated that 'the fourth part of the inhabitants of most of the parishes of England are miserable poor people and (harvest-time excepted) without any subsistence'. In both Leicester and Exeter, half the population lived below the poverty line.

As towns grew, classes became economically segregated. In Exeter there was a nucleus of wealthy residential areas in the city centre, in the parish of St Petrock, surrounded by a ring of poorer districts, some outside the city walls. In Valladolid and in Amiens, the centre was held by the propertied classes and the poor lived in the outer parishes. When poor relief was handed out, women and children featured as the majority among the registered poor. Of the 765 people qualifying for relief in the parish of St Gertrude in Louvain in 1541, over half were children. In 1561 in Segovia women were 60 per cent of the adult poor and in Medina del Campo 83 per cent. Of the poor registered in Norwich in 1570, nearly half were children; in Huddersfield in 1622 children were 54 per cent.

There had always been poor, but contemporaries agreed that mass beggary was new; and there had always been vagrants, but mass vagabondage was apparently recent. The publication in Germany in 1510 of the *Liber Vagatorum* (Beggars Book), which till then had circulated in manuscript; the expulsion of vagabonds from Paris by the Parlement in 1516; the beginning of urban poor relief in the 1520s; all seem to point to a specific period. Harrison in his *Description of England* (1577) identified the period of origin precisely when he claimed of organized beggary that 'it is not yet full threescore yeares since this trade began'.

The dates – the end of the fifteenth and opening of the sixteenth century – coincide with major social and economic changes. The epoch of price revolution, demographic increase, social change and political crisis, contributed to greater polarization between rich and poor. The economic position of the lower classes worsened. Industrial advance had its casualties: John Hales said that in the cloth industry 'a few men had in their hands a great many men's livings'. The Reformation and other religious changes played their part: Robert Aske, leader of the Pilgrimage of Grace, claimed that 'in the north parts much of the relief of the commons was by succour of abbeys', but this had vanished at the dissolution of the monasteries.

The most striking aspect of the new poverty was its mobility. The drift from the land to the towns was aggravated by enclosures, higher seigneurial dues, and expropriation, creating a drifting and workless proletariat. Labourers crowded into the towns, where they aggravated social problems and helped to depress wages. Poor living conditions encouraged crime.

Vagrancy

The mobile poor were always looked upon with fear and suspicion. Even if their numbers were not always so high as those given above for Troyes in 1551, they were drawn to the population centres for three main reasons: work, shelter and charity. Poor relief in London had, it was claimed in 1569, 'drawn into this citie great numbers of vagabondes, roges, masterless men and idle persons, as also poore, lame and sick persons'. Indiscriminate poor relief thus fell into rapid disrepute. The vagrants were resented not merely as idlers but as a threat to the ordered society: they were rootless, unemployed, strangers in the host community, aliens. William Lambard, a Kent magistrate, spoke harshly in 1582 of 'vagrant and flying beggars who . . . infect and stain the earth with pilfery, drunkenness, whoredom, bastardy, murder and infinite like mischiefs'.

Many of the wandering poor were of course simply looking to earn their living. Subsistence migration, on the increase in the sixteenth century, was tied closely to the agrarian cycle: evidence for England in the 1570s suggests that movement was at its highest in August and September, at the end of the harvest, and then in April and March, at sowing time. In contrast with traditional seasonal migration, where workers moved to harvest areas in summer and then back to their villages in autumn, the new migrants were often rootless, like Nicholas Lawrence of Thanet who explained that 'he is a poor labouring man and is sometime in one place and sometime in another'.

The most readily identifiable group among the vagrants were the ex-soldiers, back from the wars and far from inclined to settle down to steady employment. They brought their habits of violence with them, and contributed greatly to the general fear that the population felt of beggars. Typical is the French complaint in 1537, of ex-soldiers 'in company with other vagabonds, people of slothful and evil life, who are to be found in groups and companies in various places in the kingdom'. To protect themselves against vagrants the cities of Franconia in 1559 bound themselves into a league against their 'outrages, murders and robberies'. Legislation assumed that the workless were idle by choice, and dealt harshly with them, as in the 1554 Netherlands decree ordering to the galleys all 'brigands and vagabonds who do nothing but oppress poor people, going from village to village and one farmhouse to another demanding alms and often using threats, and at night retiring to taverns, barns and similar places, without their poverty resulting from the mischance of war or other honest causes, but solely from waywardness and pure sloth, through not wishing to work or toil to earn their bread and living'.

Migrants and vagrants were astonishingly mobile, travelling across nations and across seas. In the sixteenth century Valladolid received migrants from Galicia, Exeter had migrants from London. Of a sample of vagrants who passed through Amiens in the early seventeenth century a fifth came from Normandy, 4 per cent from Franche Comté. The Irish, all too often involuntary migrants from their homeland, fled for economic relief to the land of their oppressors, England. There they met draconian poor laws. 'Philip Maicroft and his wife', says a record from Kent, 'were whipped the 8th March 1602, and had granted unto them six dayes to be conveyed from officer to officer out of the country of Kent, and then to be conveyed to Bristol, the place (as they say) wher they landed, from thence to be conveyed to Dungarvan in Munster in Ireland, the place (as they say) of their birth.' The emigration from Ireland, especially in times of famine, could not be stemmed. In 1629 the mayor of Bristol reported that 'the scarcity of corn in Ireland is such that the poor people of that realm are enforced . . . to come over into this kingdom'. Again in 1633 the Somerset justices complained of a 'troop of Irish, that begin again to swarm out of that country'.

In western Europe the direction of movement was north to south, towards the Mediterranean. Between France and Spain the movement was almost exclusively southwards, dominated by the host of seasonal workers, often indistinguishable from vagrants. Fernández de Navarrete in the 1620s claimed that 'all the scum of

Europe have come to Spain, so that there is hardly a deaf, dumb, lame or blind man in France, Germany, Italy or Flanders, who has not been to Castile'. It was reported of the hospital in Burgos that 'every year, in conformity with its rules, it takes in, cares for and feeds for two or three days, from eight to ten thousand people from France, Gascony and other places'.

The vagrant problem was also in part a gypsy problem. Gypsies appeared in eastern Europe in the fourteenth century and in west and central Europe in the early fifteenth. Their coming coincided with the rise of organized begging and with the persecution of witches, and they were often identified with both. They were repeatedly arrested and accused of sorcery because of the way in which they dabbled in magical cures and fortune-telling. In Hungary and Transylvania they were enslaved from the fifteenth century. In Moldavia they were sold at slave markets. In Germany in 1540 Agrippa denounced them because they 'lead a vagabond existence everywhere on earth, they camp outside town, in fields and at crossroads, and there set up their huts and tents, depending for a living on highway robbery, stealing, deceiving and barter, amusing people with fortune-telling and other impostures'. In 1560 the Estates General at Orléans called on 'all those impostors known by the name of Bohemians or Egyptians to leave the kingdom under penalty of the galleys'. In Spain the harsh legislation included a 1633 decree ordering them 'no longer to dress as they do, and to forget their language', with bans on public assembly.

The dangerous classes

Two widely differing views of the poor were held in this period. One, of an old humanist and Christian ancestry, felt that the poor deserved well of society since society had not done them well. The other, which obtained greater currency after the Reformation, was that the poor needed reforming, since their own incapacity had put them where they were. Martin Bucer declared that 'such as give themselves wilfully to the trade of begging be given and bent to all mischief'. Poor relief encouraged 'the greatest pestilences and destructions of a commonwealth'. This opposition to charity, based on a concern for social order, was elsewhere reflected in a strong belief that class distinctions had been created by God, and that the poor must stay in their place. 'God hath made the pore', observed Sir John Cheke to the rebels in Kett's revolt, 'and hath made them to be pore that he myght shew his might and set them aloft when he listeth, for such cause as to hym seemeth, and pluck down the riche to hys state of povertie, to shew his power.' Others felt that rebellion was proof of the unwillingness of the poor to turn their hands to any useful thing. In England some Puritans, notably William Perkins, felt strongly that to be poor was to be wicked, in conformity with a general belief that idleness was evil and bred further evils. For Perkins vagrants were 'a cursed generation', and begging was 'a very seminarie of vagabonds, rogues, and stragly persons that have no calling, nor are of any Corporation, Church or Commonwealth'. Others in this tradition expressed themselves even more harshly: Cotton Mather in New England asserted that 'for those who indulge themselves in idleness, the express command of God unto us is that we should let them starve'.

The hostility to 'idleness' was moral rather than economic. In the preindustrial economy most labour was seasonal and even full-time workers might be 'idle' for much of the year. The hostility was likewise based on the political fear that 'idleness' bred mischief. The Elizabethan annalist Strype condemned vagabonds as 'lewd idle fellows . . . who run from Place to Place . . . to stir up Rumours, raise up Tales, . . . devising slanderous Tales and divulging to the People such kind of News as they thought might most readily move them to Uproars and Tumults'. The fear of rumour, common to Elizabethan England and discernible in Shakespeare's plays, was fed by the conviction that the poor and simple were easily stirred to rebellion. The bishop of Vance (France), proposing in 1657 that beggars be banned from the streets, said that 'in the recent disturbances in Paris, they were the people most inclined to sedition and pillage of the houses of the rich'. Archbishop Whitgift observed under Elizabeth that 'the people are commonly bent to novelties and to factions, and most ready to receive that doctrine that seemeth to be contrary to the present state and that inclineth to liberty'.

Despite this picture of a constantly rebellious populace, there seems to be little evidence of an endemic state of insurrection. However, in the bigger towns a high level of unemployment among the proletariat provided good reason for revolt. Amiens in 1578, a city of perhaps 30,000 people, was stated to have had as many as 6000 workers 'supported by the alms of the well-to-do'. In these circumstances charity was no more than an attempt to stave off social unrest. In Troyes in 1574, poor who came from outside the city were, according to a common practice, given leave to stay no more than twenty-four hours. The reason given was illuminating. It was said that 'the richest citizens began to live in fear of a disturbance and of a popular riot by the said poor against them'. Unemployment and poverty explains what happened in the city of Tours at Pentecost in May 1640. About 800 to 900 silkworkers who were dissatisfied with their wages staged an uprising. Soldiers were called in, and when these were found to be inadequate some royal troops were called in. To penalize the people a tax was imposed on them. This led to another rising in September, when several tax-officials had their throats cut, and the rioters threatened to put the city to the torch, a threat which eventually brought a temporary compromise solution. The situation in Lyon, probably the biggest industrial city in Europe, must have been extremely worrying. Of its population of 100,000, as many as two-thirds consisted of workers; a large proportion of them lived in extreme poverty, many were regularly unemployed. In 1619 about 6000 of the workers were in receipt of poor relief of some sort; in 1642 the figure was 10,000. The lesson that unemployment bred insurrection was not forgotten in Spain. In 1679, the authorities in Granada, Spain's largest industrial centre, which had a population of over 100,000, estimated that the number of poor who depended on labour in the silk industry for their daily wage exceeded 20,000. Mindful of the 1648 uprising, steps were taken to relieve the distress occasioned this time by the plague. At a later date, 1699, when unemployment in Toledo threatened their livelihood, the silkworkers of that city protested that although over 3000 were out of work no steps had been taken to come to their aid. If this situation were to continue, they threatened,

it would not be surprising if in order to obtain bread they were to resort to all the means permitted by natural law, and even to those not so permitted. The people have no wish to be angered nor to cause riots or a scandal; all they desire is that, since God has brought better weather, their lot should also be bettered.

The social tension brought about by unemployment was well described by an English writer in 1619: 'The poor hate the rich because they will not set them on work; and the rich hate the poor, because they seem burdenous.'

If the common people were looked upon as the source of all disaffection, they were also looked upon as the source of crime.

Surviving records give the impression that violence and disorder originated exclusively among the lower classes. This picture is obviously misleading. Nobles, by their violence and oppression, were also responsible for a high proportion of crime, but the law was biased in their favour. 'You will see no one but poor and humble thieves being hanged', comments the bandit Oliver in Grimmelshausen's *Simplicissimus* (1668). 'Where have you ever seen a person of high quality punished by the courts?' Early modern Europe was a mass of conflicting jurisdictions, with state, Church and seigneurial courts sometimes overlapping in authority. In many regions nobility still had the power to pass death sentences. The confusion of jurisdictions often caused prolonged quarrels over competence. As the centralized state attempted to impose an acceptable system of law and order, it began to phase out the confusions, introduce its own norms, and reserve powers of punishment to itself alone. In the process it partly superseded community systems of law, which, however, continued to exist throughout Europe in many forms. Since law officials were, even by 1700, few and normally non-resident, rural communities were often left to police themselves. This meant that, for lack of a law-enforcement machinery, many 'crimes' were never punished or prosecuted, and apparently tranquil communities may well have experienced more lawlessness than the records show.

Moreover, even where offences were prosecuted, the local community might well block official penalties that it considered inappropriate. In Spain, though rape was officially punishable with death it was more common to force the rapist to make restitution, such as marriage. In England, local magistrates and juries conspired to make the harsh laws inoperative. Of nearly 1000 cases coming before the Maidstone Quarter Sessions in the late sixteenth and early seventeenth centuries, in none was the death penalty applied when it should have been. Faced with the letter of the law, juries preferred to acquit rather than condemn. The attitude of both witnesses and jurymen in Somerset in 1596 was described by a local magistrate, Edward Hext:

Most commonly the simple Countryman and woman, lokynge no farther then ynto the losse of ther owne goods, are of opynyon that they wold not procure a mans death for all the goods yn the world, others uppon promyse to have ther goods agayne wyll gyve faynt evidence yf they be not stryctly loked ynto by the Justyce.

In countries where there was little chance of popular attitudes influencing the courts, hostility to the harsh laws intensified opposition, as we can see by the actions of the rioters in Seville in 1648:

They went to the offices of the secretaries of the criminal courts, broke them open, seized all the papers and burned them in the middle of the square, in full view of all the judges. They did the same with the gallows and ladder in the same square, and with the torture-rack and all the instruments of the executioner. They also burned at the same time the committal records which contain the names of all those imprisoned in all the gaols. But great care was taken not to burn the civil records.

The real level of crime in preindustrial Europe is impossible to establish with any confidence. The apparent absence of violence in the countryside was probably, as we have mentioned, deceptive; and in any case prosecutions tended to be directed against outsiders rather than members of the local community. In the Kentish countryside most of the crimes (principally theft) appear to have been committed not by local people but by outsiders and travellers, by soldiers in transit to and from Dover, and by gangs operating from London. Yet records from other regions give a different picture. Two-thirds of the 3129 indictments presented at Essex assizes in 1559–1603 were for theft; it was the same in Wiltshire, where twenty-three out of eighty-two indictments in 1615, and forty-two out of 103 in 1619, were drawn up against local people for this offence. Second only to theft in Essex came prosecutions for witchcraft; some violence occurred, but tended to be mostly among kin groups within the villages. The level of violence in rural England can appear to be deceptively low if only the higher courts are consulted. Between 1615 and 1660, for example, only twenty-three cases of violence from the village of Preston turned up at the local Quarter Sessions; but there happened also to be a manorial court at Preston, and of the 4758 cases with which it dealt over the same period over 26 per cent involved assault, a far surer guide to the degree of village conflict.

In rural France, of 400 cases tried before the courts in Angoulême in 1643–4, 23 per cent concerned trespass and other property offences, a further 22 per cent involved personal wrongs such as marital infidelity, drunkenness and sorcery; thefts answered for 16 per cent, and violence occurred in 18 per cent of cases. In Spain, violence seems to have been more common. In the mountainous region known as the *montes* of Toledo, of 1988 cases covering the period 1550–1700, over 42 per cent concerned violence in various forms, and only 10 per cent involved petty theft. Partial evidence for the late seventeenth century in Valencian and Catalan villages shows a similarly high level of violence within the rural community, aggravated by the widespread possession of firearms: in 1676 the viceroy of Catalonia deplored 'the many great and enormous crimes perpetrated in the principality'.

A possibly moderate level of crime in the countryside must be contrasted with the situation in the large towns, where problems of housing, food and employment were severe. The figures are, again, possibly misleading. Police officials were particularly harsh to off-duty soldiers and to outsiders, two categories that consequently appear with frequency in the records. Of those condemned to corporal punishment by the municipal court at Bordeaux from 1600 to 1650, nearly 52 per cent were vagabonds and other outsiders. Urban crime was violent, at least in Spain. In 1578 the municipality of Valladolid had to appoint two extra law officers to deal with the increase in theft and murder. For Madrid the reports present a frightening picture. 'Not a day passes but people are found killed or wounded by brigands or soldiers; houses burgled; young girls and widows weeping because they have been assaulted and robbed', writes a witness in 1639. 'From Christmas till now', wrote another in June 1658, 'there have been over 150 deaths and no one has been punished.' An analysis of Madrid crime in the late seventeenth century gives some support to these accounts. In 1693, one of the peak years for violence in the period, repeated street-brawls led to the arrest of over 300 persons for disturbing public order; there were twenty-nine recorded murders and fourteen cases of rape. The municipal police were unafraid to act against nobility, who that year were implicated in incidents of assault, rape, brawling, theft, wife-beating and murder. The authorities initiated 382 criminal prosecutions during the year but 212 of these could not be proceeded with because they had fled the city. Over the period 1665–1700 crimes of violence represented about half of all detected crimes, sexual incidents came next (rape, sex-crimes and marriage quarrels), and cases of theft last of all.

Criminal activity was popularly associated with two groups: vagabonds (and *pícaros*), and beggars. The vagabond *pícaro* was a literary type rather than a historical figure. He emerges as one of the preponderant themes in the literature of Spain's Golden Age.

Mateo Alemán's *Guzmán de Alfarache* (1599) is commonly regarded as the earliest novel to describe the amoral vagabond life of the *pícaro*, but already in the *Lazarillo de Tormes*, which appeared half a century earlier in 1554, the main features of the picaresque life were described, though without actually using the word *pícaro*. The next famous work of this genre was Quevedo's *Buscón* (1626). The picaresque world of thieves, vagabonds, prostitutes and swindlers was not confined exclusively to Spanish society. Italy, Germany and France were no less afflicted by the same social type, and translations of the Spanish novels found a ready market in those countries. The *Lazarillo*, for instance, was translated into German in 1617, *Guzmán* two years earlier in 1615. To say that the *pícaro* was essentially a literary type is not to deny that *pícaros*, social delinquents, actually existed. But in literature the features of the delinquent were romanticized and his basic criminality glossed over.

The literature on beggars was even more exotic than that on *pícaros*. From the late fifteenth century written sources speak of a strange and mysterious organization called the Beggars' Brotherhood, with vagabonds and professional criminals under its sway. Romantic and imaginative literature on the Brotherhood, which appears to have been little more than a myth based on the late medieval predilection for the vagabond life, ranges from the anonymous *Liber Vagatorum* in Germany, to the *Vie généreuse des Mercelots, Gueuz et Boesmiens* (1596) of Pechon de Ruby in France, and *Il Vagabondo* (1621) by the Italian, Rafaele Frianoro (a Dominican friar whose name in religion was Giacinto de Nobili). Many other writings, including several in English and Spanish, were also published on the same theme.

Beggars had their folklore, their methods, their impostures. In Rome in 1595 when a youth was arrested for begging he informed the papal police that 'among us poor beggars there are many secret companies, and they are different because each has a distinctive activity'. He went on to name nineteen different types of imposture: the *famigotti*, for example, were beggars who pretended to be invalid soldiers; the *bistolfi* wore cassocks; the *gonsi* pretended to be rustic idiots. By 1621, when Frianoro was writing his book, the Italians had twenty-three categories of imposture; there were similar categories in other nations. Not all the details given by contemporaries about the beggars can be written off as romanticism. The world of the Brotherhood was a recognizable 'underworld'. Groups of beggars might have their leaders: in France the 'king of the beggars' was called the '*grand Coesre*'. The seventeenth-century historian Henri Sauval testified that the beggars did not practise marriage nor did they frequent the sacraments, and if they entered a church it was only to cut purses. They were an anti-society, organized against it, disbelieving in its ethics and religion. They were also separated from it by their jargon, called cant in English, Rotwälsch in German, argot in French, jerga de la germanía in Spanish. Cant had a virtually international vocabulary. The first comprehensive account of it in English was Harman's *Caveat for common Cursetors* (1567). In France *Le Jargon de l'Argot réformé* (1628) summarized both the language and the customs of the beggars. The beggars were not, for all this, an organized society: they were essentially vagabonds, tied to no locale, with their home in any nation they chose to reside in, true citizens of the world.

In each major city they had a regular place of assembly, the so-called 'Court of Miracles'. Most frequently it was in the heart of the slum quarter. In Paris, Sauval tells us, 'it was in a very large square at the end of a large, stinking, noisome, unpaved cul de sac'. There, according to one legend from which the Court derived its name, all the poor and maimed who entered in emerged healthy and upright. But, according to another, the true miracle was that there 'the poorest among them is deemed the richest'. The resort of the beggars to trickery and crime was explained by Robert Greene in his *Defence of Conny Catching* (1592): 'This is the Iron Age, wherein iniquitie hath the upper hande, and all conditions and estates of men seeke to live by their wittes, and he is counted the wisest that hath the deepest insight into the getting of gaines.'

Poor relief

Feared and despised by their betters, the poor were still essential to their spiritual welfare for, as Catholic tradition proclaimed, to succour them was a major act of charity. It was this that made Guzmán de Alfarache cynically defend the impostures of false beggars. Since charity was given, he argued, less for the material welfare of the recipient than for the spiritual welfare of the donor, it might as well be given to the false poor as to the real. This perverse view is a good reflection of the weaknesses in the old medieval attitude to poverty. Since poverty could never be eradicated ('the poor you have always with you', Christ had said) it was seldom seriously attacked, and tended to be exploited as a source for conferring spiritual graces on oneself. Thus, outdoor relief, which later writers were to attack as a positive encouragement to mendicancy, became a corporal work of mercy. Rich men, who in their lives had shown no solicitude for the needy, prepared their way to heaven by leaving sums to the poor in their wills. In Valladolid the consciences of the rich were eased by the unusual practice of arranging to have an entourage of paupers to bear the candles at the funeral; some even had themselves interred as paupers.

Only in the sixteenth century, with the extraordinary increase in the scale of poverty and vagabondage, did writers, both Catholic and Protestant, adopt a more constructive attitude towards the problem. Luis Vives quite rightly has the honour of being the first to outline a methodical approach to poor relief, in his *De subventione pauperum* (On the relief of the poor) (1526). Vives's concept of charity was the classic Christian one: the poor have a right to aid, and the propertied have an absolute moral obligation to help them. Where Vives went beyond the poor relief of medieval times was in his firm opposition to begging and his rejection of the view that charity was mere material relief. Hospitals must be set up to take the poor off the streets, and relief must consist 'not in mere almsgiving, but in all the ways by which a poor man can be uplifted'. Implicit in this approach was the conviction that the Christian state had a duty to maintain its less fortunate citizens and that the task should not be left to private charity. Other Spanish writers besides Vives were among the most prominent students of the task of poor relief. Juan de Medina, in his *Plan of poor relief practised in some Spanish towns* (1545), outlined a scheme to abolish begging and to hospitalize the sick and needy. His plans were apparently already being practised in Valladolid, and seem to have been partially successful, for 'the police testify that, in contrast to former times, they find hardly anyone now to hang or flog for robbery'. Domingo de Soto in the same year produced his *Considerations on the poor*, and in 1598 came Cristóbal Pérez de Herrera's *Discourse on the assistance of the poor*. It was Juan de Mariana, in his *De rege et regis institutione* (1599), who confirmed the new emphasis on state intervention by urging that 'piety and justice necessitate relieving the poverty of invalids and the needy, caring for orphans and aiding those in want. Among all the duties of the Sovereign, this is the chief and most sublime. This too is the true purpose of riches, which should not be directed to the enjoyment of one person only, but to that of many; not to the satisfaction of our personal and transient interests, but to the attainment of justice, which is eternal'. Mariana goes on to say: 'the state is bound to compel us to this, by organising poor relief in each locality as one of the public tasks'.

This evolution of Spanish thought towards secular relief is interesting for it contradicts a common assumption that it was the Reformation that was responsible for the laicization of charity and for the substitution of municipal for clerical relief. Secularization was, in fact, common to Catholic and Protestant alike, and was a logical response to the need for control.

The early years of the sixteenth century experienced a worsening of social crisis: 'the poor', announced a German decree of Charles V in 1531, 'abound in this country in far greater numbers than they used to'. A Vicenza noble wrote in 1528: 'you cannot walk down the street or stop in a square or church without multitudes surrounding you to beg for charity'. There was a surprising unanimity about the measures taken to control the problem. Augsburg in 1522 banned street-begging and appointed six poor-guardians to supervise relief. Nuremberg followed suit, so did Strassburg and Breslau in 1523, Regensburg and Magdeburg in 1524. Luis Vives was the direct inspiration for a scheme put into practice at Ypres in 1525. Between 1522 and 1545 some sixty towns on the continent (about thirty in Germany, fourteen in the Netherlands) reformed their poor relief system. Luther in 1523 helped to reorganize the system in Saxony, Zwingli did so in 1526 in Zürich, in 1541 Calvin passed an ordinance on relief in Geneva. All these schemes, both Catholic and Protestant, stressed three new principles: a ban on begging, centralization of relief in civic hands, compulsory work for the able-bodied. In 1528 Venice, where previously the religious fraternities (Scuole Grandi) had supervised charity, began a system of hospitals for the poor. In 1531 the civic authorities in Lyon, terrified by the urban riots of April 1529 (the Grande Rebeyne), started to establish the famous Aumône Générale, which centralized relief and laid particular emphasis on the creation of jobs for the workless.

Many traditionalists deplored the new attitude. The Sorbonne in 1531 declared the ban on begging to be 'uncatholic', the mendicant orders were inevitably hostile, and the Anglican annalist John Stow lamented the passing of the 'ancient and charitable custom' of outdoor relief. On the other hand, Ignatius Loyola was so impressed by what he saw of the new system that when he returned to his Basque hometown of Azpeitia in 1535 he helped introduce it there. By the mid sixteenth century, the Counter Reformation was giving its support to a revision of the medieval attitude. While not denying the ideal of poverty, much Catholic thought was concerned to eliminate the evils arising from poverty. Relief was in future intended to secure the spiritual welfare of the recipient; his bodily welfare was only secondary, as was the spiritual benefit obtained by the donor. The recipient was required to mend his ways, resume his religious duties, and seek employment in order to help his dependents; hospitalization was meant to help him achieve all this, through giving him a bed, proximity to a chapel, and access to job-training schemes. Though the Church co-operated closely in all the new relief projects, in principle they were controlled and financed by the municipality or state: charity was not therefore 'secularized', but it was largely taken out of private hands.

One initial problem was to stem the flow of vagrants and localize the problem of the poor. The earliest control measures consisted in granting beggars a licence to beg within a certain area only, usually the place of their origin. In London in the 1520s genuine local paupers were given licences and identification discs: all others were to be whipped out of town. The purpose of this was to dissociate begging from vagrancy. As the poor realized they could only beg in their own localities they would cease to drift, and vagrancy would soon cease. Charles V in Spain restricted beggars to an area within six leagues' radius from their home towns. Under Philip II this method of control was centred on the parish: the parish priest alone issued begging licences, each parish created officials to superintend the poor, and an attempt was made to register all vagrants. The licénce system failed completely, partly because it was so easy to counterfeit licences. In Scotland the laws restricting beggars to their native parishes were passed in 1535, 1551 and 1555 and not renewed thereafter. In 1556 the Cambridgeshire authorities banned all begging whatsoever and suspended the licence system. Norwich followed this example. By mid century, then, the licence system was being discarded.

At about the same time the local authorities resorted to the dual system of institutional care and outdoor relief. Institutional care was provided through hospitals: in 1544 the great pre-Reformation

London hospital of Saint Bartholomew's was re-founded, and by 1557 there were four 'royal' hospitals in the city – Saint Bartholomew's, Christ's, Bridewell and Saint Thomas'. In order to help pay for such institutions, a compulsory tax for poor relief was decreed in London. Other local authorities followed suit. In order to maintain its workhouses of 'houses of correction', Norwich in 1557 issued regulations for compulsory taxation. In France a similar procedure was followed. The Paris authorities in 1554 set up their first poor hospital, at Saint-Germain; this was subsequently called the Hôpital des Petites Maisons and lasted till the end of the *ancien régime*. Hospitals were meant almost exclusively for the invalid poor; for the able-bodied, workhouses were set up in all the major towns of England and France. They offered refuge and employment, neither in a very appealing form, to those who had no other way of earning their living. Like England, France delegated control of poor relief to the localities. The ordinances of Moulins (1566) and Blois (1579) stipulated that local authorities should raise money through parish collections and tax levies. Lyon was perhaps the earliest of all French cities to provide for the unemployed, and seems to have been the first to set up workhouses: the Aumône Générale was in existence as early as 1533 and was replaced in 1614 by the much larger Hôpital Général de la Charité.

The English poor relief system mirrored those on the continent. Harsh laws were passed against vagrants; a pamphleteer of 1580 denounced 'that loathsome monster idleness'. In 1547 a statute specified slavery as one penalty for vagrancy. Two years later the slavery clauses were repealed but in 1572 another harsh proposal became law. By this act a vagrant could be whipped and bored through the ear on the first offence, adjudged a felon on the second, and be punished by death on the third. All these penalties were repealed in 1593.

To preserve public order and to keep the poor honest, work must be made available. 'This is the best charity', wrote a seventeenth-century Puritan, 'so to relieve the poor as we keep them in labour. It benefits the giver to have them labour; it benefits the commonweal to suffer no drones, nor to nourish any in idleness; it benefits the poor themselves.' The famous statute of Artificers (1563) was an elaborate scheme to put the able-bodied to work. Then at the end of the reign of Queen Elizabeth a comprehensive act to regulate poor relief was passed. This, the act of 1597–8, was amended and re-enacted in 1601. Together, the legislation of these years formed the basis of poor relief in England for the next two centuries. Poor relief was localized: it was placed in the control of churchwardens of the parish and four overseers of the poor appointed every Easter by the Justices of the Peace. The poor were divided into categories, each of which was to receive particular treatment. The able-bodied poor were either to be put to work or confined in houses of correction; children were likewise either to be set to work or apprenticed; and the sick and maimed poor were to be housed and cared for 'at the general charges of the parish, or otherwise of the hundred or the county'. Begging and vagrancy were prohibited. To finance the work of the Act, a compulsory poor rate was to be raised in each locality. This legislation was devised to meet a severe emergency, for these were years of great economic distress throughout Europe. Predictably, the success was only partial. The harsh régime of the workhouses or houses of correction resembled prison life, and were hated more than prison: their purpose clearly was to make life so unbearable that inmates would prefer to seek work outside. A Somerset Justice of the Peace, Edward Hext, cited some vagrants who 'confessed felony unto me; by which they hazarded their lives; to the end they would not be sent to the House of Correction, where they should be forced to work'. The machinery to run the Poor Law was not always adequate. An observer of the situation in south-east England in 1622, Thomas Dekker, reported that 'though the number of the Poore do dailie increase, all things worketh for the worst in their behalfe. For there hath beene no collection for them, no not these seven yeares in many parishes of this land especiallie in countrie townes'.

Institutionalization of relief was only one of the many solutions used to tackle the problems of poverty and mass unemployment. Regulation of wages and prices was also necessary. Outdoor relief and food subsidies continued: in 1623 the bailiffs of Derby reported that 'wee have at the charge of the cheife and ablest inhabitants of this Burrowe provided 140 quarters of corne which wee weekely afford to the poore as their necessities require under the common price of the markett'. Sometimes the drastic measure of forced emigration was proposed. In 1617 one London parish contributed 'towards the transportation of a hundred children to Virginia by the Lord Mayor's appointment'. Vagrants were occasionally transported, and on one occasion during the Protectorate it was suggested that prostitutes be expelled to America. Numerically, however, compulsory emigration was not significant. Instead, further changes were introduced into the poor relief system. At Bristol in 1696, for example, John Cary modified the organization of workhouses.

French practice followed the same general lines, but lacked the important central direction provided in England by Privy Council and Parliament. Compulsory hospitalization of the poor was ordered in a decree of 1611, but discontinued as general policy after 1616, though there were subsequent efforts (as in the 1629 Code Michaud) to impose the principle on municipalities. Each region and city continued local practice. In Aix-en-Provence, for example, a general hospital or Misericorde was founded in 1590 and designed to help both disabled and able-bodied poor. In 1640 alone three important charities were founded in the city: the Charité (a general hospital), the Refuge (for prostitutes) and the Providence (for homeless women). Large general hospitals were established in Paris in 1612 (the Pitié) and in Lyon in 1614 (the Charité).

No significant progress towards change was made in France until mid century, when the religious grouping known as the Company of the Blessed Sacrament turned its considerable energy and wealth to the problem of poverty. The Company was firmly committed to hospitalization. The establishment of a branch at Aix in 1638 was primarily responsible for the hospitals set up there in 1640. Other hospitals were set up at Marseille in 1639, Orléans in 1642, Grenoble in 1661, and in other major cities. The plan for the Company's Aumône at Toulouse revealed its hostility to traditional almsgiving, which was regarded as useless to protect 'the poor, who by birth should serve the rich'. In 1656 the Company founded the Hôpital Général des Pauvres at Paris. The institution was made deliberately unpleasant. The inmates could be punished by the directors of the hospital, all their activities were timetabled, and they were to be 'clothed in grey robes and caps and have each on their robes a general mark and a particular number'.

A collaborator of the Company, St Vincent de Paul, became the best known of all Christian servants of the poor. Combining both a devotion to the medieval ideal of poverty and a commitment to the reforming concepts of the Counter Reformation, he distributed outdoor relief on one hand and founded hospitals on the other. His hospital for beggars, the Nom-de-Jésus (1653), provided both shelter and obligatory work. Throughout the north of France in the worst years of the Thirty Years War and the Fronde, St Vincent and his helpers were everywhere present to save lives as well as souls. 'For the last two years', states a letter of 1653 to Vincent, 'the whole of Champagne and this town in particular have lived only from your charity. All the countryside would have been deserted and all the inhabitants dead from hunger if you had not sent someone to relieve them from poverty and give them life.'

From the 1650s, when better times returned to France, the government turned to a policy of hospitalization. Colbert later stated that 'nothing is so detrimental to the state as the begging of able men'. An edict of 1662 prescribed the establishment of a general hospital in every city and large town. The policy was reaffirmed in a 1676 circular letter to all bishops and intendants, and after 1680 hospitals were founded with more frequency. The trend to shut the poor away has been, with some exaggeration, referred to as 'the great confinement'. Certainly, the hospitalization of the disabled was an impressive move: in 1666 the Salpétrière hospital in Paris housed 1900 inmates, of whom 110 were blind and paralysed, eighty-five were imbeciles, ninety were infirm aged, sixty were epileptics, and 380 were aged over 60. But only a fraction of the poor could be accommodated; moreover, the milder régime of 'hospitals' was reserved mainly for women and younger persons; the few men who accepted charity were put into the harsher 'workhouses', from which they escaped if they could.

In Catholic and Protestant countries alike, it was the élite and the bourgeoisie that gave to charity. In the United Provinces, where workhouses were established from 1589 after the publication of Dirck Coornhert's *Discipline of Knaves* (1567, publ. 1587), an English traveller observed in 1685 that 'there is nothing shows more the charitable inclination of the Hollanders than their great care in relieving, maintaining and educating their poor, for there are no beggars to be seen anywhere in the streets'. In England the London merchants distinguished themselves in giving to charity. Both before and after the Reformation the greater merchants gave a substantial part of their personal fortunes to charity: in the century before the Reformation the proportion reached 29 per cent of their estates, in the Elizabethan age about one-quarter. One of the most significant aspects of the gifts made by London burghers was the 'secularization' of their donations, a trend which may have worked in favour of the poor. Over the period 1480–1540, for example, the lesser merchants of London gave 61 per cent of their gifts to religious purposes and only 18 per cent directly to the poor. From

1601 to 1640, on the other hand, religion was given no more than 9.8 per cent, while the poor were given 52.4 per cent. The figures may be somewhat misleading (in the earlier period money donated to religion often found its way to the poor, while in the later period it seldom reached the poor directly and went to institutions), but in absolute terms they reflect a growing concern with a grave social problem. In seventeenth-century Milan private donations were by far the most important source of income for the poor. Milanese merchants gave large sums to the hospitals; among them was Giulio Cesare Lampugnani who, besides giving 90,000 lire in legacies to two charitable institutions, left, in his will in 1630, 196,000 lire in goods and 63,500 in capital for supplying the poor with bread, rice, coal and clothing. In Spain lay donations appear to have played a smaller part in financing poor relief. On the other hand, in the seventeenth century in Madrid several lay brotherhoods came into existence, devoted to caring for the poor, paying for their education and feeding, clothing and burying the indigent: the most active was the Brotherhood of the Refuge, which was founded in 1618 and went through its most flourishing period in the 1670s.

Slavery

There were, broadly, two types of slavery in Christian Europe: the 'colonial' and the 'feudal'. The 'colonial' type of slavery was the predominant one in western Europe, and owed most of its vigour to practice in the Iberian peninsula. There the *Reconquista* – the reconquest of Muslim territory – had since the later Middle Ages led the Christian races to dominate and exploit the defeated Moors. So-called 'Saracen' slaves were a commonplace in central and southern Portugal and Spain in medieval times. The struggle between Christian and Muslim extended beyond the peninsula, and it was through sea warfare that the institution of slavery continued to perpetuate itself. Muslim corsairs were operative throughout the Mediterranean in the sixteenth century, and collected Christian slaves from as far afield as Russia and England. The Christian powers, in turn, did not scruple to enslave any Moors they could lay their hands upon. With this experience behind them, the Iberian powers accepted slavery as a standard feature of their public life. The medieval laws of both Spain and Portugal sanctioned the holding of slaves.

Spanish slavery had been firmly Moorish, and continued to be so even after the expulsion of the Moriscos in 1609. The only Moriscos not expelled from Spain were those being held as slaves, and these must have numbered several thousand. After each Morisco rebellion in the sixteenth century, and particularly after the rising in the Alpujarra mountains in 1569, large numbers of rebels, reportedly running into thousands, had been sold into slavery. This native source of labour (used mainly for domestic work, but also for the galleys and for forced labour in the mercury mines at Almadén) was supplemented from abroad. The battle of Lepanto brought many Turks into Spanish households; slave raids were also fruitful, as with the expedition made in 1611 by the marquis of Santa Cruz to the island of Querquenes, when he captured 400 slaves.

When the age of discovery began, Iberian slavery took on a new texture. From being a Mediterranean institution it became an Atlantic one. The geographical change also implied a racial one: in the place of Moors, black Africans were traded. In both quantity and quality a new era had commenced, for not only were the negroes enslaved in numbers that exceeded any previous practice, but they were employed primarily to serve the needs of the colonial economy in America and elsewhere. The logic of this was that those countries which resorted to slavery in their colonies – Portugal, Spain and, later, France and England – tended to accept the extension of slavery in their own metropolitan territories, thus introducing into Europe the colonial pattern of race relations.

Portugal, the first of European countries to develop the new type of slavery abroad, was the first to be inundated at home. By 1553 a Belgian humanist, writing from Evora, could report that 'there are slaves everywhere here, consisting of negroes and of Moorish captives. Portugal is so full of slaves that I could almost believe Lisbon to have more slaves, of both sexes, than free Portuguese'. In 1551 Lisbon was calculated to have one slave for every ten free Portuguese; by 1633 the estimate was of 15,000 slaves in a city population of 100,000, with a further 2 per cent consisting of free coloureds. In the whole of Portugal, which had a population of just over a million, slaves and blacks constituted about 3 per cent of the population, the largest ratio of any European nation.

The development of negro slavery in America had a direct effect on Spain. A Flemish observer reported in 1655 that 'the American trade has given new life to the institution of slavery in this country, so that in Andalucia one sees few servants other than slaves, mostly Moors as well as blacks'. The slave population tended, as elsewhere in the Mediterranean, to concentrate on the sea-ports. Seville in 1565 had 6327 slaves (7.4 per cent of the population), most of them black; Cadiz in 1616 had 300 Moorish and 500 black slaves. In Spain slaves were normally domestic servants. There was initially very little racial prejudice against coloureds or blacks, as shown by the case of Juan Latino, whose parents were both black slaves. He began his career as page to the duke of Sessa, managed to enter the university of Granada, graduated there in 1557, finally obtained a chair in Latin and married the daughter of a noble family.

Outside the Iberian peninsula, Mediterranean slavery could not rely on the colonial system and owed its continued existence almost exclusively to piracy. In France the ports of Marseille and Toulon inevitably had to harbour the booty of slave-hunters. Beyond these Mediterranean ports slavery was very rare in the country. There were recorded cases of slaves in Roussillon (which became French in 1659) but they were nearly all Moorish, an overspill from Spain. In theory slavery was illegal. In 1571 the parlement of Bordeaux, ruling against a slave-trader, declared that 'France, the mother of liberty, does not permit slavery'. 'All persons in this realm are free', wrote the jurist Loisel in 1608, 'and if a slave reaches these shores and gets baptised, he becomes free.' The growth of the overseas empire, however, militated against statements like this, and as colonial slavery grew so did its acceptance by metropolitan France, which imported coloured labour mainly through La Rochelle and Nantes.

Piracy made Venice, Genoa and other Italian ports into leading slave centres. A slave cargo brought back from the Levant by four Florentine galleys in June 1574 had a total of 300, made up of 238 Turks, thirty-two 'Moors', seven negroes, two Greeks, five Arabs, five Jews, five Russians and six Christians. They were taken to the market at Messina, where 116 were sold and most of the Christians freed. Slaves were purchased for galley and domestic service. The navies of the Italian states and of Spain were heavily dependent on slaves for rowers. An agent for the Spanish royal galleys shopping for slaves in Genoa in 1573 bought 100 slaves in February and another thirty-two (these last from Hungary) in April. At this period the cost of each slave was about 100 ducats. Their places of origin – Aleppo, Salonika, Istanbul, Algiers – point to the overwhelmingly Muslim character of slavery in the Christian Mediterranean. In the Arab Mediterranean, of course, Christians were the slaves. In 1588 it was estimated that over 2500 Venetian subjects were scattered throughout the Mediterranean '*in misera captività*'.

In Italy, as in Spain, domestic slavery predominated. A prince of the Church like Cardinal d'Este was said in 1584 to have had fifty Turkish slaves in his villa in Tivoli. But though slavery was accepted in practice, the laws were equivocal, and a fugitive slave (and, in particular, a baptized slave) was legally entitled to be free. Servitude was looked upon as a temporary condition, a result of adverse fortune such as being captured in war. Being temporary, it could not be inherited. It was in those very Mediterranean countries were slavery was most in use – Spain, Italy, France – that Catholic theology and public law conspired to guarantee the dispossessed their right, both as men and as Christians, to manumission and social equality. In normal circumstances this would have meant the gradual disappearance of slavery from Europe. But new life was given to the institution by the growth of colonial economies dependent on cheap labour.

'Feudal' slavery in Europe was associated with the availability of labour. Scotland's most capitalized industry, mining, was introduced to the profits of slavery in this period. Colliers had been personally free up to 1605. Then in July 1606 an act of parliament forbade them moving their labour elsewhere and also in effect froze their wages. The 1606 act applied to coal-mines, another in 1607 applied to metal mines, and in 1641 a statute extended these terms to factory workers.

In Russia slavery was a standard feature of the rural scene. The slaves (*kholopi*) performed essentially the same function as serfs, their distinctive feature being the loss of personal freedom. One could become enslaved by contract for a limited or unlimited period, or be enslaved through war, or fall into servitude because of debt. Non-Russians were also enslaved: Polish slaves rose to positions of responsibility in noble households, and there was a brisk trade in Tatars captured on the frontier. In the steppe, where many estates had no peasants, slave labour was common; the proportion of slaves to free peasants in some districts was as high as 50 per cent. The importance of slavery in the Russian state is shown by the fact that 200 of the 940 clauses in the Ulozhenie of 1649 were concerned specifically with it. Paradoxically, slavery disappeared as it intensified. The distinction between a slave and a serf had always been slight, and as both categories became depressed in the course of the seventeenth century they tended to be legally merged into one. The last great distinction between the two was the exemption of slaves from taxation. Laws of 1680 and 1724 made the landless slave as liable to taxation as the landed serf, and with these measures slavery became merged into the larger institution of serfdom.

Emigrants and refugees

Major population movements took place during the early modern period, but since it was a pre-statistical age none of them can be measured with any accuracy. The movement out of Europe was certainly impressive. From Portugal about 2400 men a year are believed to have emigrated to India in the first quarter of the sixteenth century. In mid century the emigration to Brazil and the Atlantic took over 3000 men a year. Since Portugal had a population of only just over a million, the drain was serious. Spain's loss was also severe. In the half century between the discovery of America and 1550, some 150,000 Spaniards probably crossed the Atlantic; in the whole sixteenth century the total was possibly around 250,000. The northern nations did not begin to lose emigrants on any considerable scale until the early seventeenth century. Between 1620 and 1640, about 80,000 English emigrated to North America and the West Indies.

Europe was, as we have already seen (Chapter 2), not an immobile continent. Even after the Reformation, pilgrimages caused large movements of people. Holy Year 1575 brought 400,000 visitors to papal Rome; in 1600 the number was 536,000, and this to a city whose resident population that year was only 100,000. Major cities elsewhere housed permanent foreign communities: Antwerp in 1568 had over 16 per cent of its inhabitants listed as 'foreigners', Zürich in 1637 had 14.7 per cent, London in 1587 had 4.5 per cent. To emigrate knowing that one could return home was one thing; to know that return was impossible was quite another. For hundreds of thousands, their native land became no more than a memory.

Both the Reformation and the Counter Reformation created refugees. Fugitives from the Catholic states first became numerous in the 1540s with the creation of the Chambre Ardente in France in 1547 and the establishment of the Roman Inquisition in Italy in 1542. The Italian Protestants fled principally to Switzerland. In 1555 emigration from England began, as a result of the Catholic restoration there. Of the 800 or so English refugees who fled to the continent, most went to the Rhineland. Emigration from France was numerically the most important. Originating in the repression of the 1540s, it reached its peak after the massacre of Saint Bartholomew's. The chief centre of refuge was Switzerland and Geneva. From 1549 to 1587 Geneva probably received as many as 12,000 French refugees, most of them in 1572. Plans were also made at this period for Protestants to emigrate to America. Admiral Coligny made efforts to set up a Huguenot colony in Brazil, and some emigrants did leave France for the New World. In the seventeenth century these efforts continued: in 1627 600 Huguenots went to colonize the island of Saint-Christophe.

The bulk of refugees from the southern Netherlands (see also Chapter 3) went to the north. To Middelburg alone in 1584–5 over 1900 southern families came. Southern immigration to Leiden was so heavy that it came to be looked on as a Flemish city, though the Flemings (most came from Bruges) in fact amounted to only 10 per cent of the population. From 1500 to 1574 only 7.2 per cent of new citizens (*bourgeois*) had come from the south; from 1575 to 1619 the figure rose to 38.4 per cent. In Amsterdam from 1575 to 1606 southerners made up 31 per cent, in Middelburg from 1580 to 1591 three-quarters, of all new citizens. Netherlanders also went abroad in large numbers. In London up to the end of the sixteenth century they always formed about five-sixths of the foreign population. In western Europe they lived chiefly in west Germany and notably in Frankfurt, where from 1554 to 1561 as many as 38.4 per cent of those obtaining citizenship were Netherlanders. By the late 1580s the refugees made up nearly a third of Frankfurt's population.

Emigration from the Celtic nations of Britain was in some measure provoked by English hegemony. Scots went to the Baltic countries and, according to an estimate of 1620, there were about 30,000 of them in Poland alone. The Irish were, of course, the most direct victims of English rule. Writing in 1596 the poet Edmund Spenser described the province of Munster as 'a most populous and plentiful country suddenly made void of man and beast'. Irish nobles, soldiers, clergy and scholars all felt obliged to emigrate. Every Catholic university on the continent had its contingent of Irishmen. Typical of these wandering scholars was young Christopher Roche of Wexford who in 1583 at the age of 22 took passage to Bordeaux, worked and taught for his living then went on to study in Toulouse, Paris, Lorraine (for three years), Antwerp,

Brussels, Douai and St Ouen, a long tour of eight years, during which he both worked for his food and studied when his circumstances allowed. Sir William Petty, as we have seen (above, p. 40), estimated Irish population losses in mid century alone at over half a million. This total included deportees, of whom 'there were transported into Spain, Flanders, France, 34,000 soldiers; and of boys, women, priests etc no less than 6,000 more, where not half are returned'; and those transported to the Barbados and elsewhere as slaves (estimated at about ten thousand).

The largest mass deportation in early modern history was that of the Moriscos from Spain. In 1569, as the result of a rebellion, Moriscos had been expelled from Granada and exiled to Castile. Attempts to Christianize these, as well as the older Morisco communities of Valencia and Aragon, were unsuccessful. When the expulsion was eventually decided upon, it was in the conviction that the Moriscos were an alien minority; yet many informed Spaniards, including nobles, clergy, intellectuals and government ministers, were opposed in principle to the measure. The expulsions began in April 1609 and, with various intervals, continued up to 1614. In all, some 300,000 Moriscos were deported, representing a third of the population of Valencia and a fifth of that of Aragon, with smaller proportions from other parts of Spain. The great majority went to north Africa: in some towns, such as Algiers, they were well received; in others, they were hated as foreigners. Perhaps as many as 50,000 were received in France, but most decided to travel on to the Levant because of hostility from the French government.

The Thirty Years War was responsible for another great migration, from the Czech nation. The battle of the White Mountain (1620) marked the end of Czech independence. The first refugees were the élite who had served the Winter King, Frederick of the Palatinate. Early in 1621 the arrests and expulsions began. Fifty of the Czech leaders were arrested and their estates confiscated: in June twenty-five of them, both Catholic and Protestant, were executed. Religious persecution was not immediately put into effect, and not until 1624 were the last Protestant clergy ordered out of the country. By 1627 about 36,000 families had fled Bohemia. Voluntary and involuntary evacuation reduced the population of some towns by as much as a third. By the end of the Thirty Years War the population of Bohemia had sunk by 45 per cent, that of Moravia by a quarter.

The most notorious refugee problem of the late seventeenth century was that created by Louis XIV's revocation of the Edict of

Nantes. Some two million people, or one-tenth of France's population, were Huguenots, living principally in the south-west of the country. As religious persecution gathered momentum in the 1680s, many resolved to emigrate, though the bulk of refugees left only after the Edict of Nantes (which had theoretically granted toleration since 1598) was officially revoked in October 1685. The Calvinist clergy were expelled, but Huguenots in general were discouraged from leaving. Despite this, some 200,000 French people fled their country between about 1680 and 1720. The largest numbers (70,000) went to the United Provinces, the rest to England, Brandenburg, and other Protestant countries. The refugees were mainly from the professional and artisan classes, who could rebuild their careers in a strange land; but even members of the highest élite chose to go abroad, among them two of France's most prominent generals, Schomberg and Ruvigny. The revocation and emigration were inevitably condemned by Protestant nations, and many Frenchmen both then and later doubted the wisdom of the measure. In 1716 the council of Commerce claimed that of the many reasons for France's declining trade position, 'the first is the flight of our Religionists who have transplanted our industry to foreign soil'. In fact, the revocation varied in its impact, and was not uniformly disastrous. Business and industrial centres like Paris and Lyon, where there had been few Huguenots, were barely affected. France's problems at the end of the century were due to a number of factors, among which the revocation was not always the most important.

Refugees, as we have seen (Chapter 3), helped to transfer technical skills from one country to another. Emigration also extended national culture. In Alsace-Lorraine, the frontier of the German language was extended several kilometres as a result of emigration after the Thirty Years War. The same happened to a significant extent in both Switzerland and Bohemia. Culture was likewise transplanted, but usually to the detriment of the country of origin: of some 10,000 Czech exiles in Saxony in the mid seventeenth century as many as 22 per cent were nobles or intellectuals, a proportion that must have helped to impoverish intellectual life in Bohemia after the White Mountain.

Rich and poor suffered dispossession equally. Like the Moriscos, few saw their native homes again. 'If I forget thee, Jerusalem, let my tongue cleave to the roof of my mouth. . . . How shall we sing the Lord's song in a strange land?'

8   Culture and communication

There were neither witches nor bewitched until they were talked and written about.

Inquisitor Alonso Salazar de Frias (1612)

The art of Printing will so spread knowledge that the common people, knowing their own rights and liberties, will not be governed by way of oppression.

Samuel Hartlib, *A description of the famous kingdom of Macaria* (1641)

It is likely that the culture of Europeans changed significantly during early modern times. A simple, popular, universal culture, which (it has been argued) included in its upper strata the intellectual achievements of the élite, was gradually fragmented into a culture for the élite – what has been called the 'great tradition' – and another for the masses – a 'little tradition'. The former consisted of the arts and sciences, the recorded and the memorable, and the latter of entertainments such as folksongs, plays and festivals; the former persists in our manuals, the latter has been largely forgotten. Traditions are not easy to measure or to pursue through time, particularly when oral and undocumented as most popular culture was. The present chapter will look briefly at some aspects of the changing culture of both common people and élite, their religious beliefs and attitudes, their access to information and knowledge, their aspirations.

The Reformation and Counter Reformation, movements that amply cover the entire period we are concerned with, have seemed to be two great theological systems locked in conflict, struggling for the soul of European man. The conflict was real enough (tens of thousands died in the religious wars) but the arena of conflict is still imprecisely defined. The movements had much in common: both were heirs to the same reforming, humanist tradition; both shared a wish to extirpate superstition and inculcate a new morality. The early and heady days of the Reformation, when urban masses in Germany and France gave their allegiance to the new cult, were paralleled on the Catholic side in the wind-swept hills of Mexico where massed villagers likewise accepted the new faith offered by Franciscan friars. The friar Mendieta, looking back on that period, felt that souls being lost to Satan by Luther were being balanced by those gained for Christ in the New World. The enthusiasm of the 1530s, however, could be seen more in perspective a generation later; it was then that the task of missionaries both Catholic and Protestant seemed to have much in common. The Franciscans and Jesuits inveighed in America against superstition, animism, idolatry and other ineradicable obstacles to the faith; but in the same generation the theologian Alfonso de Castro pointed out that these defects existed also in Spain: in the Basque mountains, he had heard, they even worshipped a goat. From this decade the Jesuits in their correspondence recognized that Europe, too, remained to be converted: there were 'Indies' at home no less than in the New World. The Protestants for their part realized that it was not enough to persuade the people to give up popery.

The environment into which zealots of Reform and Counter-Reform thrust their dogmatic certainties, was overwhelmingly rural. It was a largely unlettered world, often isolated from the culture of the great cities; the dominant realities were the precariousness of harvests and the insecurity of life. Food and survival, as in primitive rural communities today, dictated social, moral and religious attitudes. Poor diet, frequent crop failures, a high mortality rate: these, as we have seen, were not mere hazards but part of the very fabric of existence. They were therefore accepted as inevitable: the response to them was not necessarily one of fear or of profound anxiety, as is sometimes suggested, but of determination to overcome the obstacles to survival. Then as now, men took out insurance against what they could not foresee or control: religion became a major protective force, and where official religion seemed inadequate other rites were used. Life was not, for all that, a pessimistic attempt to ward off disaster. Given that some things were inevitable, there was every reason to abandon oneself to joy and celebration: in a rural Europe, there could never be the full-time labour of post-industrial society, and the Christian Church obliged by turning at least one-third of the days in the year into obligatory feasts.

Festivities – plays, carnivals, processions – were thus not incidental but a major, integral and regular aspect of life. They were essential to the life of the community, which normally dictated their form and content; and they were pleasing to the Church, with whose great festivals (Christmas, pre-Lenten carnival) they coincided. The mixture of communal and religious elements in popular festivities had always caused problems and friction, but long use tended to hallow the ceremonies; some customs, though outrightly non-religious, were even performed within the ambit of a church service. One feature of community festivities was the deliberate inversion of authority roles at a time of celebration: wise men and fools, princes and beggars, old age and youth, were exchanged, reversed and stood upside down, in a brief mockery of the world and its ways. At carnivals, similarly, there was an informal licence to gluttonize (as a prelude to Lent, when no meat could be eaten), be lascivious, and misbehave. Role reversal occurred in the English custom of the 'lords of misrule', and in the west European custom of the 'boy bishop' (who was placed in the bishop's chair at some Christmas celebrations). Partly as a role reversal, partly also as a gesture to sexual fecundity, young people were given a leading part in carnivals, festivities and harvest ceremonies; in some areas they were organized into 'abbeys of misrule' headed by an 'abbot' (in Provence) or other symbolic personage. They also directed 'charivaris', a curious custom of making a noise and a nuisance at second weddings and other occasions, which was common all over western and central Europe. During the great religious feasts, such as Corpus Christi was in southern Europe, all the ingenuity of the community was directed to organizing processions (with giant statues), dances and music; some of the celebration might be incorporated into the church service, as in Artois where sheep were brought into midnight mass or in Besançon where the labourers did a dance in the church to mark the end of the wine harvest.

Well before the Reformation, critics had pointed to the low cultural level of the country areas and the superficial Christianity of those who participated in the festivals but who otherwise came seldom to church or communion and sought remedies for their daily ills in superstitious practices. Many of these ignorant simple folk were in later years singled out as witches. The Protestant reformers were faced with a dual problem: the survival of Catholic practices and the continuation of popular rites. The former survived for a remarkably long time: 'three parts at least of the people', it was claimed of England with some exaggeration in 1584, 'are wedded to their old superstition still'. As late as 1604 the people of Lancashire were said to be in the habit of crossing themselves 'in all their actions'. In seventeenth-century Languedoc the sign of the cross was still used among Calvinists, and the cult of the saints continued for a long time in the Lutheran Rhineland. More ineradicable than Catholic practice, however, were the popular customs: the agrarian festivals, maypoles and Morris dances in England; the 'maypoles, garlands, carnal songs and choruses' condemned by Dutch Calvinists in 1591. After persistent legislation and prohibition, it proved possible to do away with most Catholic as well as popular rites; but that was no guarantee that the people were being Christianized. Lutherans could complain in Wolfenbüttel in the 1570s that 'people do not go to church on Sundays. . . . Even if one finds a man or woman who remembers the words, ask him who Christ is, or what sin is, and he won't be able to give you an answer'. From Wiesbaden in 1594 it was reported that 'all the people hereabout engage in superstitious practices with familiar and unfamiliar words, names and rhymes . . . they also make strange signs, they do things with herbs, roots, branches . . . '. Criticisms of this sort were invariably made by men with high and exacting theological standards, and may not fully reflect the real situation.

The evidence does suggest, however, that Protestant reformers were up against more than mere survival of Catholic or communal rituals: in a real sense, they were beginning to penetrate into regions where Christianity had never shown its face. This situation was worst in isolated and mountainous areas, but there were also large patches of ignorance close to civilization. In Essex as late as 1656 there were apparently people as ignorant of Christianity as the Red Indians, and Hampshire was said to have 'ignorant heathenish people'. In many parts of Europe, then, the Protestants were attempting to convert people not just from Catholicism but in effect from paganism. In the process, they were trying to change generations of popular culture at all levels and replace it with a new outlook.

The Catholics started from the same point: Erasmus, for example, condemned a carnival he had witnessed in Siena in 1509 as 'unchristian'. Church legislators were trying to stamp out disorder, licentiousness and superstition long before the Reformation commenced. The Protestant movement gave a timely stimulus to ineffective and half-hearted Catholic efforts, which picked up energy only from the mid sixteenth century and after the closure of the Council of Trent (1563). Although the Counter Reformation may appear to have had a simpler task, merely to defend what existed and to purify it, in reality the obstacles facing it were no less daunting, because the Catholic reformers were committed to changes as revolutionary as those proposed by the Protestants. Their early missionaries quickly realized that much of Catholic Europe was still pagan. 'Near Bordeaux', reported an appalled Jesuit in 1553, 'stretch about thirty leagues of forest, whose inhabitants live like rude beasts, without any concern for heavenly things. You can find persons fifty years old who have never heard a mass or learnt one word of religion.' There were similar reports from Spain and Italy. Another Jesuit in Brittany in 1610 was horrified to see women beating and drowning images of saints who had not answered prayers.

Where the Protestant effort had been split into distinct areas and confessional loyalties, the Catholic effort became from the 1560s a vast co-ordinated campaign backed by pope, bishops, councils and missionary clergy. Literature was examined and purified, plays were banned, popular participation in carnivals and feasts was regulated, a whole range of liturgical customs (like the boy bishop, or dancing in church, or seasonal rites such as the song of the Sibyl in the Christmas service) was rapidly done away with, statues and paintings were censored. Religious practice was thoroughly revised. We can see the impact in Catalonia, where the bishops and the religious orders eliminated popular religious practices, enforced the new ritual (Catalonia, like England, had had a distinct rite of mass), ordered sabbath observance, set up Sunday schools, changed the imagery in the churches, and stopped the custom of 'playing guitars and singing profane songs before the Sacrament' (1610).

The effect of all this in both Catholic and Protestant Europe was comparable: the forms of religious and popular culture were extensively modified within a couple of generations. At the level of the 'great tradition', Protestant religious music came to dominate and even replace other forms of melody, filtering down into the everyday singing of ordinary folk. Catholic hymnology was never so successful; on the other hand, Catholics were offered brilliant new music, brighter churches, new devotions, new saints. Even in traditionalist Spain, the new Catholicism was recognizably different, and therefore not easily accepted by either people or clergy. Missionaries of both faiths were concerned to replace a defective culture with a new one. This had an immediate effect on sexual customs. In Spain during the sixteenth century the Inquisition of Toledo investigated more people for sexual sins than for any other single offence. The moral laxity of a past age was gradually undermined. It would be an exaggeration to describe the changes as repressive: popular culture was flexible and not easily extirpated, ordinary people by their mere passivity made it difficult for new morality and attitudes to be enforced. After a constant campaign of preaching in a village in Cambridgeshire the preacher Richard Greenham in 1591 gave up and left, blaming 'the unteachableness of that people'; in 1611 the parish priest of Sant Feliu de Recho in Catalonia explained to his bishop that he did not hold catechism classes because nobody came to them. Despite such failures the frontiers of Christianity were certainly extended: in the mountains of Languedoc, Bohemia, Asturias and Wales a people who had not been instructed were slowly introduced to Christianity. In the Western Isles of Scotland, where Presbyterian preachers did not venture, intrepid Catholic missionaries implanted for the first time a Christianity that endures down to today. Reformation and Counter Reformation merged into each other: overtly hostile, they were in practice part of a single great movement to transform the habits and attitudes of old Europe. The process has been presented as the imposition of an élite culture on a popular culture, resulting in the transformation and sometimes disappearance of the latter. This undoubtedly happened in some regions of Europe, but for much of the continent the evidence is still unclear. The argument is perhaps more plausible when applied to religion (post-Reformation Catholicism, for example, differed strikingly from the late medieval variety), but again it is important to take account of the continuity in much religious practice. The primitivism of rural peoples in early nineteenth-century Europe remained as proof that the 'great tradition', whether in belief or in culture, had not convincingly succeeded in swamping the 'little tradition'.

The kingdom of darkness: witchcraft

A possible distinction between élite and popular traditions can be observed in the question of witchcraft. Popular belief in the villages had always assumed that there were unofficial solutions to common problems. A loved one who did not reciprocate, a recurrent illness, a cow that would not give milk, all these could be attended to by the local wise woman (or man), who would offer lotions, unguents or verbal spells. Fortune-telling, love-potions, divination for lost goods, were 'white' magic, serving where religion and medicine were unable to. By extension, evil effects could be brought about, such as putting a curse on someone or making their cattle sick: this was *maleficium* (evil-doing), sometimes called 'black' magic. Though both black and white magic had a recognizable function at the popular level, the belief was also firmly rooted in the uppermost levels of society: princes and prelates were known to be interested in the possibilities of supernatural power.

At various times in the medieval period people were tried and condemned for practising *maleficia*. When this involved using alien, diabolic, help the crime was also called sorcery (*sortilegium*). Nobody seriously questioned that diabolic intervention was possible, since medieval theology and imagery had continually emphasized the reality of the devil. It is more doubtful if the devil played any part in everyday village magic, which was more preoccupied with finding answers to the anxieties and insecurity that ordinary people encountered in their normal activities. From the fifteenth century, for reasons that are still obscure, commentators began to take the notion of diabolic interference seriously. The authors of the German handbook, the *Malleus maleficarum* (Hammer of Witches) (1486), claimed that witches worked harm 'by the help of the devil, on account of a compact which they have entered into with him'. More than this, witches acted communally, by attending midnight meetings called Sabbaths at which they worshipped the devil and performed unspeakable rites. The act of fealty to Satan immediately transformed witchcraft into heresy. As evidence from witch trials became available, learned jurists and theologians analysed and identified the problem. Distinguished manuals were written by men such as Jean Bodin (1580); the coadjutor bishop of Trier, Peter Binsfield (1589); the chief justice of Burgundy, Henri Boguet (1591); the procurator-general of Lorraine, Nicolas Rémy (1595); the Belgian Jesuit Martín del Río (1599). Their works were cited as authority by subsequent witch-finders, and gradually the notion of the Sabbath worked its way into general recognition, except in England where the Roman Law of the continent was not current and its concepts consequently not used.

In early modern Europe tens of thousands of people were executed for sorcery: the persecution began around 1500 and ended shortly before 1700. What peculiarity of this period gave rise to the phenomenon? Some have described it as a witch-craze (*Hexenwahn*), as though it were an irrational occurrence. Every country seems to have experienced it, though there were important differences in each. A glance at the areas and types of people affected will help us get closer to an answer.

The German historian Hansen pointed out that mountainous areas were particularly affected, notably the Alps and Pyrenees; the name applied to one group of Alpine heretics, the Vaudois, was in the fifteenth century applied also to witches in France and Belgium (in Arras in 1459–61, thirty-two 'Vaudois' were tried and eighteen of them executed). The biggest Spanish outbreak, in 1610, was in the Pyrenees; the most sizeable French outbreak, as recorded by Pierre Delancre, in Toulouse and the French Pyrenees. The great witchhunter Henri Boguet operated in the mountains of Franche Comté in the late sixteenth century. An analysis of some of the afflicted regions shows that for the most part the victims came from remote and relatively inaccessible regions with a low cultural level and a poor record of practising Christianity. Where Christ had not reached, the old folk superstitions were still strong. Perhaps the most intensively affected area was central Europe, both by the borders of and within Switzerland. The Valtelline was a hotbed of witchcraft, and so too was Geneva in the time of Calvin. The theory that victims of witchcraft prosecution were mainly unlettered mountaineers out of reach of civilization is, however, not easy to reconcile with the fact that they were also drawn from lowland areas such as Essex and the Netherlands. Even these might be fitted into a pattern if we accept the view that witchcraft flourished in all marginal, outlying areas, whether mountain or lowland; but this cannot apply to southern Germany, where the phenomenon was frequently urban.

People accused of witchcraft were generally from the lower levels of rural society. 'It is amazing', commented the Italian humanist Galateo when the witch-fear began seeping through southern Italy in the early sixteenth century, 'how this fantasy has seized on everyone through being spread by the poorer classes.' The Italian friar Samuele de Cassinis, the first person to denounce the persecution, pointed out that 'witches' were usually the old and weak-minded (*quaedam ignobiles vetulae, aut personae idiotae atque simplices, grossae et rurales*). An analysis of 366 cases in the county of Namur in 1509–1646 shows that the accused came from the less privileged sectors; and in the Jura region the aged and sick made up most of the victims. It would appear that those least able to defend themselves were singled out. Enclosed and isolated communities were particularly vulnerable, as the cases of 'diabolic possession' at the convent of Notre-Dame du Verger at Oisy (Artois) in 1613–15, and at the convent of the Ursulines at Loudun in France (1634), demonstrate.

It was these people, poor, outcast, maimed and afflicted, who were accused of conjurations and crimes so terrible that judges, bishops and even kings bestirred themselves to take part in the work of extermination. *Maleficia* were the most common offence: all but eleven of 513 people prosecuted in the courts of Essex for witchcraft in 1560–1680 were accused of injuring or killing humans or their property. Accused tended to be women: only one-fifth of those accused throughout the modern period (1351–1790) in northern France were men. The testimonies show that many witches really believed in their own magical powers, and were convinced that they had been transported to Sabbaths and had had sexual intercourse with the devil. At the level of folk superstition there was nothing surprising about this. The Italian peasants of this period (from Friule) who believed in the cult of the *benandanti* were convinced that they had the power to leave their bodies at night and go out and battle against the powers of darkness. The beliefs of the *benandanti*, however, were a purely local agrarian cult with no associations of *maleficia*. What staggered the courts trying witchcraft was that in case after case the accused came up with virtually identical stories, and that these varied very little from country to country, so that right across Europe there emerged the terrifying vision of hundreds of thousands of formerly Christian souls dedicated to the service of Satan. Sex played little or no part in witchcraft, whose whole spirit was against fertility. The alleged orgies of the Sabbath, far from being fertility rites, were in fact infertility rites: congress with the devil, it was well known, froze the womb.

Denunciations of witches arose out of antipathies and grievances within the local community. Petty suspicions, jealousies and gossip led to the victimization of individuals and eventually to their prosecution. Reginald Scot, who argued in his *Discoverie of Witchcraft* (1584) that the phenomenon was a delusion, described the process of accusations:

May it please you to waie what accusations and crimes they laie to their charge, namelie: She was at my house of late, she would have had a pot of milke, she departed in a chafe bicause she had it not, she railed, she

curssed, she mumbled and whispered, and finallie she said she would be
even with me: and soon after my child, my cow, my sow or my pullet died,
or was strangelie taken. Naie (if it please your Worship) I have further
proofe: I was with a wise woman, and she told me I had an ill neighbour,
and that she would come to my house yer it were long, and so did she; and
that she had a marke above hir waste, and so had she: and God forgive me,
my stomach hath gone against hir a great while.

In a changing society, the disappearance of traditional
neighbourly charity and mutual help gave rise to resentments. The
fear of retaliation by witchcraft forced villagers to keep dispensing
favours to those who were suspected of being witches or who, to
exploit the situation, claimed to be witches. In times of crisis such
persons were persecuted and denounced to the courts. Community
tensions might go beyond the victimization of individuals: it has
been argued that the outbreak in Salem, Massachusetts, in 1692,
was provoked by dissensions that went through the entire town.

A curious feature of many cases was the role of children. There
were cases in Valenciennes in 1590 and 1662 of children denouncing
their own parents; an outbreak at Chelmsford (Essex) in 1579
started with a sick child's accusations, and in the Warboys case the
evidence for the prosecution rested principally on the evidence of
three children. The important outbreak in Sweden in 1669 revolved
entirely round a group of children accused of witchcraft (eighty-five
people were executed), and children initiated the Salem trials which
ultimately cost twenty-two lives. Perhaps the most bizarre case
occurred in Spain, when the inquisitor Salazar in 1611 visited
Navarre; 1802 people came forward as self-confessed witches, and
of them 1384 were children aged under 14. At Quingey (Franche
Comté) in 1657, as two boys of 13 and 11 were being taken out to
execution one of them, dimly aware of the horror into which his
statements had led him, cried out to the examining officer, 'You
made me say things I didn't understand!' The problems involved in
the investigation of such cases go far beyond the merely
sociological.

The cost of the witch-craze in terms of human lives was
impressive, though contemporaries, especially the great
witchhunters, often exaggerated their figures. Nicolas Rémy of
Lorraine claimed to have gathered the materials for his study of
demonology from the trials of 900 people he had sentenced to
death; the court records suggest that death sentences were really

about one-seventh of this figure. Boguet claimed to be responsible for 600 executions in 1598–1616; the records reveal perhaps twenty-five executions for that period. Delancre is credited with 600 executions in the pays de Labourd in 1609; the true figure is closer to eighty. Despite exaggerations, the reality was grim. In south-west Germany between 1560 and 1670 some 2953 people were executed for witchcraft, four-fifths of them between 1570 and 1630; in the Jura over 500 were executed between 1570 and 1670; at the Essex assizes some 110 people were condemned between 1560 and 1680. The figures are probably small when set beside regular criminal executions; their significance lies not in numbers but in the interesting origins and character of the witchcraft phenomenon.

If witchcraft was in reality little more than folk superstition, why was it heavily prosecuted in the early modern period alone? Did the increase in prosecutions reflect a real increase in witchcraft? It has been argued that 'witchcraft' was primarily a delusion foisted on to the people by theologians and lawyers. In the early Middle Ages many scholars had rejected the belief in witchcraft, which as unofficial magic threatened the monopoly of the Church. By the fifteenth century, in a trend that culminated in the *Malleus Maleficarum*, writers accepted the possibility of diabolism and then of the Sabbath. Sorcery became part of élite culture; political opponents habitually accused each other of conspiring with the aid of the black arts. Scotland's first great outbreak of witch mania coincided with the crisis in 1590–7, when the earl of Bothwell was accused of 'consulting with witches . . . to conspire the king's death'. In England in 1568–71 plots involving Mary Queen of Scots had important witchcraft complications. In France the wife of the royal favourite Concini was condemned as a witch, and Cardinal Richelieu accused another favourite, Luynes, of plotting 'with two magicians who gave him herbs to put in the king's slippers'. In Russia witchcraft was a regular accusation in political struggles.

Sorcery was not, of course, simply a delusion foisted from above, since magical beliefs and practices had always been common. What were new were the notions of a Sabbath and a compact with the devil, to which the treatises of the great jurists helped give credence. The learned tradition now intruded into the popular tradition of folk magic, and so produced the offence of diabolic witchcraft. The notion of a pact with the devil also seemed to proliferate wherever torture was used in trials, because learned interrogators tried to elicit answers that accorded with their own beliefs; in England, where torture was not used in such cases, no doctrine of the Sabbath emerged in witch trials. What brought about the merging of the learned and popular beliefs? There seems little doubt that it was largely precipitated by the same intellectual ferment that gave rise to Renaissance humanism and the Reformation. Élite intellectuals dabbled in sorcery and the occult because they presented paths to knowledge; others reacted against this and felt that the faith should be protected against the intervention of the devil. It was therefore no coincidence that the high tide of prosecutions occurred precisely during the epoch of Reform and Counter-Reform: in destroying witches the zealots were also destroying superstition and heresy.

Though these comments may clarify the part played by the élite tradition, they are no proof that the witch crisis was provoked exclusively by learned men. Sorcery was a direct product of social tensions, and the origins of the witch-craze must be sought within society. 'Whence comes the witch?' asked Michelet in his study of *La Sorcière*. 'I say unhesitatingly: from times of despair.' Sorcery, he argued, arose in times of depression, war, famine, economic and social crisis, loss of faith, of certainty and of orientation. Hence the great witchhunts during the civil wars in France, the Thirty Years War in Germany, the Civil War in England. In rural areas ravaged by war and food shortage the population victimized those in whom they saw their ills personified. In every country the most intensive outbreaks of persecution were in times of disaster.

To this general picture there were inevitably numerous exceptions, of which the most striking is Spain. Though secular tribunals there periodically condemned people for witchcraft, the Inquisition from 1526 onwards systematically refused to prosecute, on the grounds that witches were self-deluded. In 1610, as a consequence of the frenzied witchhunt being conducted just across the border inside France by Pierre Delancre, a wave of hysteria swept into Spanish Navarre and led to a number of executions at an *auto de fe*. The inquisitor Alonso Salazar de Frias was sent to inquire into the circumstances and came to the conclusion that 'there were neither witches nor bewitched until they were talked and written about'. Witchcraft only existed, he felt, if it were prosecuted. As a result, the Inquisition never again tried witches. The learned tradition here therefore refrained from imposing itself on the popular belief in folk magic, which, of course, continued long after. In 1665 a Catalan widow of Mataró, Isabel Amada, went begging for alms one day where some peasants were tending two mules and a flock of sheep, but was refused any. 'Within three days', testified a witness, 'the two mules died and also thirty sheep. The accused claimed that she had caused the deaths among the herd with the help of the demon.' Isabel told the inquisitors that she had been set upon and beaten by the peasants and had only mentioned the demon to save her life. She was set free.

As in Spain, so in Europe there was an alternative tradition that refused to accept the reality of the Sabbath or the devil's role. Opponents of the witch-craze included scholars from all faiths: Catholics such as de Cassinis (in a work of 1505), Adam Tanner, and Friedrich von Spee (1631); Lutherans such as Johann Weyer, physician to the duke of Cleve. In his *De praestigiis daemonum (The deceptions of demons)* of 1563, Weyer explained that 'I fight with natural reason against the deceptions which proceed from Satan and the crazed imagination of the so-called witches. My object is also medical, in that I show that illnesses which are attributed to witches come from natural causes.' One vital factor began to change learned opinion: lawyers and judges became sceptical about the evidence adduced in witchcraft cases. The Parlement of Paris in the late sixteenth century rejected a majority of the prosecutions which reached it, and in the period 1564–1640 confirmed only just over a tenth of the 1094 death sentences for witchcraft which came before it as a court of appeal. In 1624 it ruled that all witchcraft sentences involving the death penalty must be appealed. In 1644 the archbishop of Reims protested to Chancellor Séguier against persecution of 'witches' by local magistrates: 'the abuse is so widespread that one finds up to thirty or forty falsely accused within a single parish'. By the 1670s Colbert was intervening to stop the passing of death sentences, and in July 1682 a royal decree forbade further prosecutions. In the late seventeenth century scepticism grew also among English lawyers: the last witch condemned to death in England was Jane Wenham in 1712, but she was reprieved; and in 1736 an Act of Parliament stopped further prosecutions.

Religious scepticism

The Protestant and Catholic reform movements were directed towards the rural frontiers of Europe. It was some time before the missionaries turned their efforts to the core of unbelief in the urban centres. Yet lack of belief, or at least ignorance of the faith, there certainly was. In 1595 when the police arrested a young beggar in

Rome he informed them that they (the beggars) were not well-disposed to the Faith: 'among us few practise it, because most of us are worse than Lutherans'. The Spanish writer Pedro Ordóñez observed (1672) of the urban vagabonds that 'they live like barbarians, for they are not known to, nor have they been seen to, go to mass or confession or communion'.

Many minority groups still remained marginal to Christianity. The gypsies, even when nominally Christian, were unable because of their nomadic way of life to have normal recourse to the sacraments. The nomadic Cossacks were likewise barely Christianized: some stages of Razin's revolt in 1670 were openly anti-Christian. In Spain and Portugal many *conversos* nurtured hostility to the official faith. In regions where the Moriscos lived the traveller could pause and wonder as, on the eve of a Muslim fast, every dwelling in sight remained shuttered and closed and no living man could be seen: this among a people nominally Christian.

While ignorance was deep-rooted in popular religion, and considerable sections of the population remained unchristianized, in the upper levels of society inquiring minds rejected dogmatism, and scepticism became fashionable. Intellectual curiosity impelled the learned to resort to alchemy, astrology and magic. The link with witchcraft may be seen in the art and iconography of the age, most notably in Bosch, and in the scientific endeavours of Elizabeth of England's court magician John Dee. The Renaissance encouraged inquiry and therefore doubt; the true scholar must maintain a mind open to all sources of knowledge, which in practice meant dabbling in the occult and the Hermetic tradition of allegedly pre-Biblical science. The Faust tradition reflected this background perfectly: the story was published in Germany in 1587, translated into English and Dutch in 1592, and into French in 1598. Though early science was inevitably concerned with magic (such as the attempt to transmute metals), it was a magic that had nothing in common with naïve popular beliefs. Intellectuals were pursuing a truth that did not contradict or conflict with Christianity, but which on the other hand seemed to make Christianity irrelevant.

Throughout the sixteenth and seventeenth centuries, therefore, there was a significant but carefully disguised current of alternative belief. In Prague the Emperor Rudolf II (d. 1612) gathered round him a circle of scientists ('magicians') and free-thinkers. In England Sir Walter Ralegh and his friends denied the reality of heaven and hell, claiming that 'we die like beasts and when we are gone there is no more remembrance of us'. In France after the excesses of the civil wars there was a reaction that made La Noue observe that 'it was our wars of religion that made us forget religion'. The epicurean court of Henry IV, like that of James I in England, encouraged licence of belief or 'libertinism'. Some made a profit out of their irreligion, like Jérémie Ferrier, a Huguenot pastor who abjured his faith in 1613, drew large pensions as a priest till his death in 1626, and claimed that for fourteen years he had preached Christ without believing in him. Most unbelievers kept their attitude concealed. This was advisable particularly after the enormous shock in 1623, when the poet Théophile de Viau was arrested for blasphemy and later condemned to death, a sentence subsequently commuted to banishment. The result was, as Pierre Bayle claimed, that many 'die like everyone else, after confession and communion'. 'Unbelief', the sieur de Rochemont wrote in 1665, 'has its laws of prudence'.

The most famous French sceptics frequented the literary academies, such as the Rambouillet; or the philosophic academies, such as that of the humanist brothers Dupuy. Among them were the doctors Gabriel Naudé (d. 1653) and Guy Patin (d. 1672), and the priest Pierre Gassendi (d. 1655). The most active influences still came from Italy, which Naudé claimed was 'full of libertines and atheists and people who don't believe anything'. Among the restless spirits in Italy was the adept of Hermetic lore, Giordano Bruno, who proclaimed that man had 'by the light of sense and of reason, with the key of most diligent enquiry, thrown wide those doors of truth which it is within our power to open'. The Church, however, still had a powerful hand. Bruno perished at the stake in Rome in 1600; Vanini, a Neapolitan priest and former papal physician, was burnt outside his country, at Toulouse in 1619. Thomas Campanella (d. 1639) only just escaped execution but was imprisoned for twenty-seven years and tortured seven times.

These searchers after truth attempted to find a reality beyond official dogmas; they were excited by the possibility of rediscovering ancient lost arts. Freemasonry, which became historically significant only in the early seventeenth century, attracted many because of its implied access to long-hidden knowledge. It was this that led the English antiquarian Dr William Stukeley to join the movement and 'to be initiated into the mysteries of Masonry, suspecting it to be the remains of the mysteries of the ancients'. Perhaps the most remarkable of the groups that practised the new mystification were the Rosicrucians. Their supposed existence was announced with the publication in 1614 of the *Fama Fraternitatis*, a work which provoked widespread excitement and came out in nine editions in three years. Descartes, who was living at Frankfurt in 1619, tried in vain to join the group and concluded that it did not exist; Leibniz at the end of the century proclaimed it to be a fiction. The myth was created by the Lutheran thinker Johann Valentin Andreae (d. 1654), probable co-author of the *Fama*; according to it, a fifteenth-century German nobleman, Christian Rosenkreuz ('Rosy Cross'), had been given access to the ancient lore of Persia and India.

Élite, no less than popular belief, thus had its marginal zones. A newer development was the wholly non-theistic philosophy of the Levellers and Diggers. Gerrard Winstanley, the Digger leader, went so far as to define religion only in terms of social justice: 'True religion and undefiled is thus: to make restitution of the Earth which hath been taken and held from the common people by the power of Conquests formerly and so set the oppressed free.' Two centuries before Marx, Winstanley described religion as the opium of the people: 'This divining spiritual Doctrine is a cheat; for while men are gazing up to Heaven imagining after a happiness, or fearing a Hell after they are dead, their eyes are put out; that they see not what is their birthrights, and what is to be done by them here on Earth, while they are living.'

Literacy and the people

Although a knowledge of reading and writing was considered desirable in medieval Europe, it was still looked upon largely as a practical skill, a qualification rather than a cultural necessity. Many medieval monarchs and even prelates of the Church were illiterate: they were not however uncultured, for they had readers who read to them and scribes who wrote for them. The importance of literacy as a practical qualification is reflected in the statutes drawn up by an archbishop of York for a college he founded in 1483, in which one of the purposes of the foundation was said to be that 'youths may be rendered more capable for the mechanic arts and other worldly affairs'. This technical importance of literacy would always be important. The supreme technical use was, of course, in the service of the Church, for only a literate clergy could be the arbiters of religious (no less than social) life. In a very special sense, too, literacy was the preserve of the Church, which had a monopoly control over education.

The invention of printing, involving quicker and cheaper methods of book production, revolutionized the problem of illiteracy. Living in the century immediately after the development of the printing press by Gutenberg, Francis Bacon described it as one of three great inventions (the others were gunpowder and the compass) which had 'changed the appearance and state of the whole world'. Did printing bring about any change in the cultural level of the common people? In at least three distinct respects – in the promotion of education, in (mainly religious) propaganda, and in the development of popular taste – literacy and the printed book had an important part to play.

The advent of the printed book could not by itself promote literacy. Books were not widely distributed, as they are today, and in the villages people had to rely on obtaining them from strolling pedlars; these in any case carried booklets ('chap-books') and fly-sheets rather than weighty tomes. Printed matter, moreover, was expensive; so that the public resorted less to quality books than to the cheaply-produced tales of love and adventure (known in seventeenth- and eighteenth-century France as the Bibliothèque Bleu – Blue Library – from the colour of the binding) that pedlars hawked around. The greater accessibility of reading material helped to inspire an upsurge of interest in education. The theory of teaching developed significantly from the Renaissance onwards: possibly the most outstanding contribution came in the seventeenth century from Comenius. A literate education came to be considered desirable, not solely because literacy was useful but because it was right and proper to acquire knowledge. There is evidence that, in England at least, the essentials of reading and writing were being communicated to a high proportion of the common people. In the city of Norwich, for example, there was free elementary education for the children of the poor.

A writer in central Sweden in 1631 reported that the people were 'so fond of letters that although public schools are very few nevertheless the literate instruct the others with such enthusiasm that the greatest part of the common people and even the peasants are literate'. What, however, did it mean to be literate? Historians have usually judged literacy for this period by the ability of people to sign their own names; but, of course, many who knew how to sign were otherwise unable to write or even to read. In default of any other, the method may still give plausible results. Of the 1265 people in rural Surrey in 1642 who protested their loyalty to the government on paper, one-third signed their names and the rest made a mark. The variation in literacy according to social class was quite notable. In the English village of Limpsfield only 20 per cent of the servants but 62 per cent of the householders signed their names. In the Narbonne area in late sixteenth-century France, literacy among the bourgeoisie went up to about 90 per cent, among the urban artisans it was about 65 per cent, and among the rural population it varied from 10 to 30 per cent.

There may have been some rise in literacy rates during the early modern period. In Durham in about 1570, a fifth of the lay witnesses in a church court were literate; by the 1630s the proportion was 47 per cent. In Sweden the Lutheran church insisted on literacy as a condition of active membership, resulting in unusual levels of literacy: in one seventeenth-century parish (Möklinta) 21 per cent of adults were able to read in 1614, and 89 per cent by the 1690s. A constant rise in literacy cannot always be assumed: it improved in some social sectors but not in others, in cities but not in the countryside. London in the 1640s had a literacy rate of 78 per cent, but in the counties it was never higher than 38 per cent. Some groups in England were actually more illiterate in the seventeenth than in the sixteenth century, because educational opportunities had not been expanded for them. The most striking figures came from Protestant countries, but in Catholic countries there was no lack of emphasis on education. By 1700 most parishes in France were equipped with a school (59 per cent in the diocese of Toul, 87 per cent in that of Paris), though literacy still varied a great deal: in the Beauvaisis 60 per cent of men could sign their marriage acts, but less than 10 per cent could in the Limousin and Brittany; in general, literacy was much higher in the north than in the Mediterranean south. Religious reformers on both sides were concerned to educate their people to read the Bible and manuals of instruction. By contrast, a conscious effort was made by lay authorities not to allow so much education to the lower orders that they might get ideas above their station.

Elementary education was not necessarily a step towards greater literacy. In most countries the 'grammar' taught at school as an adjunct to reading and writing, was Latin grammar. The use of Latin was deliberately fostered by writers who believed that knowledge was the preserve of the few, and even innovators like Copernicus preferred to use Latin in the belief that the mysteries of science should not be communicated to the common public. Latin became a symbol of obscurantism to the Protestant reformers, and they fought against it bitterly on the grounds that it prevented the mass of the people gaining access to the truth. There can be no doubt that Latin had long ceased to be an adequate method of communicating with the people. Vernacular sermons and books assumed a greater importance than ever before, for they could change the minds and hearts of the population. When Sir Thomas More in 1533 claimed that nearly three-fifths of the English people could read English, and hence could read a vernacular translation of the Bible, his purpose was to express alarm at the evil that could be done by unlicenced literature. More's figures were certainly wrong, but the fear of literacy in the native tongue persisted. Though Catholics in this period were by no means hostile to education, political motives lay behind the introduction of controls. Philip II in 1559 imposed restrictions on Spaniards studying outside the peninsula, and in America the authorities were frankly restrictive. A sixteenth-century viceroy of New Spain, Gil de Lemos, said curtly to a deputation of settlers: 'Learn to read, write and say your prayers, for this is as much as any American ought to know.'

Promotion of literacy among the common people was undertaken seriously in Protestant countries. The Bible was the basis for faith, and the Bible must be read. 'The Scripture', Luther argued passionately, 'cannot be understood without the languages, and the languages can be learned only in school.' Much of the success of the Reformed movement in France was based on efforts at promoting literacy. Elementary textbooks and alphabet manuals were distributed among the population. In 1562 the Parlement of Paris was asked to prosecute a butcher who had given an heretical alphabet book to about 200 children. By the end of the seventeenth century the Protestant countries were the most literate in Europe. In England by the mid seventeenth century there was a school for every 4400 of the population. Among the Puritans, where piety presupposed literacy because of the heavy reliance on inspirational reading, there was a remarkably high level of culture. In Cromwell's army, the vast majority could sign their names.

The development of propaganda

In medieval times the pulpit had been the chief moderator of public opinion, and from the sixteenth century both Protestants and

Catholics rediscovered the potential of the sermon. The Jesuit Peter Canisius is said to have preserved Vienna for the faith by his preaching. It must not be supposed that successes were easily achieved. Most clergy, Protestant and Catholic, did not know how to preach: in pre-Reformation Europe sermons may have been frequent in the large towns but they were rare in rural areas. Congregations were quickly bored: in one parish in Cambridge in 1547, 'when the vicar goeth into the pulpit, then the multitude of the parish goeth straight out of the church, home to drink'. All over Spain in the 1560s pulpits had to be erected in parish churches where preaching had been unknown. Congregations had to be enjoined to listen reverently: silence in church was one of the great innovative achievements of both Reform and Counter-Reform.

Ecclesiastical permission was required in order to preach. The continental Reformation liberated the pulpit from Catholic episcopal control, but in episcopal England the bishops still kept a tight rein on the public expression of dissentient views. It was this that encouraged Puritan communities in the Anglican Church to appoint to their parishes unofficial 'lecturers' who, because they were not formally parish clergy, did not require a licence to preach. The lecturers might often put forward theological views that differed from those of the official Church. They were appointed by Puritan parishes, peers and city corporations. As a result Puritan attitudes were disseminated with impunity from hundreds of pulpits throughout the country and threatened to subvert the established order. Lecturers, stormed Archbishop Laud in 1629, 'are the people's creatures and blow the bellows of their sedition'. The struggle for the pulpit was a struggle for men's minds.

The spoken word was powerful, but transient: it was the permanency of the printed word that alarmed the authorities, encouraging them to repress and control information. Printers were in the front of the firing line. In the post-Reformation era many emigrated from Catholic to Protestant countries; from south to north Germany, from France to Geneva, from Belgium to Holland (among the exiles from Antwerp was the firm of Elsevier).

The battle of the books continued to be a religious one. Though there were opportunities for works on literature, travel, law and history, the religious book (devotional or controversial) was seldom displaced from its leading position. Of 169 books published in Paris in 1598, 32 per cent were in belles-lettres, 29 per cent on religion, 16 per cent on history, and 13 per cent on arts and sciences. In 1645 of

456 works published 38 per cent were on religion, 24 per cent in belles-lettres, 18 per cent on history, and 7 per cent on science. One-third of the books published between these two dates were on religion. This may have been influenced by the high-tide of the Counter Reformation in France, but even outside France religious controversy (Arminianism, Jansenism) continued to dominate.

Books were not the ideal vehicle for controversy or propaganda: they were still comparatively expensive and tended to be published in small editions (about 1250 to 1500 copies). The Bible was always a best-seller (possibly a million copies of Luther's Bible alone were printed in the sixteenth century). So were some devotional works: the *Imitation of Christ* (c. 1418), the great product of *devotio moderna* spirituality, went through innumerable editions in the course of the sixteenth century, and in France alone from 1550 to 1610 was issued in thirty editions; St Francis de Sales's *Introduction to the Devout Life* (1609) totalled over forty French editions by 1620, and by 1656 had been published in seventeen different languages. But books in the vernacular were often in a minority, judging from the catalogues of the international book fair at Frankfurt. From 1564 to 1600 this fair, the largest in Europe, displayed nearly 15,000 books of German origin. On average, no more than a third of these were in the German language. In 1601–5, of 1334 books at the fair, 813 were in Latin and 422 in German. Only after about 1680 did books in German come to be in the majority. In England the vernacular had a stronger hold on publishing, but despite this there was no notable attempt to use books in the moulding of opinion.

The literate public were less likely to read weighty books than chap-books, pamphlets and fly-sheets. Short, well-phrased tracts with a clear argument and simple language became the staple fare of the ideological conflict. From the pamphlet war of the Reformation to the often cruel propaganda of the Fronde and the Thirty Years War, it was this category that came closest to providing some sort of propaganda for the masses. The fly-sheets usually contained satirical illustrations brilliantly calculated to attract a reader's sympathy, or at least his attention. In most cases the text was a piece of doggerel verse, often several stanzas long. Though the entire early modern period was one of strife and controversy, pamphlet propaganda was not a continuous part of it. The overwhelming majority of surviving pamphlets date from one central epoch only, the middle decades of the seventeenth century, and are concerned with three key events: the Thirty Years War, the Fronde and the English Revolution.

The vast majority of German leaflets dealing with the Thirty Years War attempted to present the justice of one cause and the excesses of the opposing side. The volume of literary output this involved, signalled the emergence of a particular kind of writer: the professional publicist. The Germans were to produce many such in the course of the conflict, notably Kaspar Schoppe, who wrote for the Catholics, and Hoë von Hoënegg, court preacher to the elector of Saxony, for the Lutherans. All the techniques of crude propaganda – distortion, exaggeration, plain falsehood – were employed generously by these writers. Small wonder that to the historian the most interesting of the fly-sheets are not the blatantly partisan ones so much as those which react against all the protagonists and plead wearily for peace and humanity. Typical of these is one of 1642, protesting bitterly against the sufferings endured by the peasants at the hands of the nobles and soldiery:

> The splendour of the land can no longer be seen,
> War, robbery, murder and arson are laying it waste,
> The free Roman Empire is falling to barbarians.

The propaganda of the Thirty Years War seems often to have reflected popular attitudes, but for the most part it was produced by a handful of skilled publicists. The literature associated with the English Revolution and the Fronde was of a wholly different order.

To contemporaries one of the most alarming aspects of the troubles in England and France was that the rebel leaders had invited the common people to partake of mysteries forbidden to them: the literature of the 1640s was one of the first great exercises in revolutionary propaganda. 'The people entered into the holy of holies', Cardinal de Retz was to say with satisfaction of the Fronde. In England Clement Walker in his *History of Independency* (1661) criticized the proceedings of the Independents: 'They have cast all the mysteries and secrets of government before the vulgar, and taught the soldiery and the people to look into them and ravel back all governments to the first principles of nature.' Another English contemporary denounced 'the tumultuous risings of rude multitudes threatening blood and destruction, the preaching of cobblers, feltmakers, taylors, groomes and women', a list drawn up no doubt in ascending order of outrageousness.

The situation had to be faced: revolutionary propaganda was more than an exercise in persuasion; it frequently reflected genuine popular attitudes, it was committed not to the support of established

parties but to the questioning of all authority. As soon as the
floodgates of censorship had been opened, the sentiments of all
sections of the people burst through. In Paris the pamphlet war
centred on the period from January 1649 to October 1652. Moreau's
catalogue of these Mazarinades (so called after the best known
pamphlet, *La Mazarinade*, dated 11 March 1651 and directed
against Cardinal Mazarin) lists over 4000 items. It seems likely that
the actual total was about twice that figure. The circulation of the
pamphlets appears to have been fairly wide, and not restricted only
to Paris or even to France; the Dresden library, for example,
possesses over 3000 items presumably collected within Saxony and
Germany.

In the English Civil War the output was higher than any known
in Europe. The British Library collection lists nearly 2000 for the
year 1642 alone, an average of nearly six pamphlets a day. For the
years 1640 to 1661 the total of surviving pamphlets approaches
15,000. In general, the pamphlets in both England and France were
not sophisticated propaganda nor the handiwork of experienced
publicists. A very high proportion were totally irrelevant to the
crisis that produced them: these were simply the produce of
scribblers of doggerel. Among the rest, despite their ephemeral
character, were a great many that reflected the outlook of the
common people, pamphlets full of proverbs, slang, vulgarities and
outright obscenities. For sheer volume of publicity, the seventeenth
century was one of innovation.

This activity meant a very busy time for the presses. A Paris
printer commented in 1649: 'One half of Paris prints or sells
pamphlets, the other half writes for them.' As the leaflets rolled off
the presses, vendors would be on hand from early morning to take
them out to the streets. After the capital, came distribution to the
provinces, carried out with striking efficiency. Mazarin complained
in 1649 of one pamphlet that 'they have sent more than six thousand
copies of the leaflet against me and d'Hémery [the finance minister]
into all the provinces'. Since censorship regulations were
theoretically still in force, pamphleteers always needed to be wary.
The Levellers were among the most devious and successful
publicists of this time. John Lilburne made himself a thorn in the
side of authority by his ability to produce unlicensed pamphlets: 'I
am now determined to appeal to the whole kingdom and Army
against them [the Presbyterians]', he proclaimed in 1647. From
1648 to 1649 he was assisted by the existence of a newspaper, the

Moderate, which presented most of the principal Leveller news to the public. This was one of the first instances of a close-knit revolutionary group making extensive use of the press in order to change the climate of opinion. Incomparably the most important propaganda centre in Europe was the Dutch Republic. In Amsterdam and in Leiden the presses served the demands of nearly every leading European language. Amsterdam had a virtual monopoly in the production of anti-French propaganda, and subversive literature was also smuggled regularly into England, Scotland and other countries. With the freest press in Europe, the Dutch threatened the security of every state practising censorship.

The history of pamphlets overlaps that of the periodical press. The function of both was to appeal to the public forum, and a pamphlet that appeared periodically (the earliest example in England was the series of Marprelate tracts in 1588 and 1589) was already setting a precedent. The real distinction between the two, however, was that the periodical aspired to give news and was, in effect, a news-sheet. We are so accustomed to the daily communication of news that it now appears to us to be a harmless and necessary part of human intercourse. In the sixteenth century, on the other hand, as in some modern authoritarian states, news could be dangerous. A printer could be accused of betraying information to the enemy, or of deliberate distortion and slander, or of inflaming the people by seditious publication. The penalties for sedition could be severe: in England in 1637 William Prynne had his ears cut off, was heavily fined, and then imprisoned. In Rome in 1572 the pope waxed so indignant at the hostile tone of the *avvisi* that he forbade their publication, and his successor passed an edict against the spreaders of false and malicious news. One of the journalists who fell foul of these regulations in 1587 had his hand cut off and his tongue cut out, and was then hanged.

The *avvisi* were principally merchants' newsletters, and were the earliest form of Italian journalism. Those sent from Venice to the Fuggers in Augsburg in 1554–65 were among the earliest, but the first regular series were those sent from his agent in Rome to the duke of Urbino over the years 1554–1605. The information was collected by journalists called *menanti*. The best known of the newsletters patronized by a business firm were the Fugger newsletters, to which correspondents from every part of Europe contributed. They were not limited merely to business news, but gave information about everything that the writer considered worth reporting. It is not easy to define the difference between published newsletters such as the *avvisi*, and the early newspapers. Periodicity is perhaps the most important criterion. The official *Mercure français*, published at the beginning of the seventeenth century, was issued only annually. By general agreement the first 'newspaper' is dated to the early seventeenth century. This was the monthly *Relation*, first produced by the Strassburg printer Johann Carolus in 1609 and distributed also in Augsburg. It contained news reports from seventeen different European towns. Another contender for the title of being the first newspaper is the *Avisa, Relation oder Zeitung* which appeared at Helmstedt in the same year, 1609. A weekly seems not to have existed until the appearance in 1615 of the *Frankfurter Zeitung*, published by Egenolf Emmel. Germany may rightly claim to have been responsible for both the invention of printing and the beginnings of journalism. The first French newspaper was published in 1620, not in France however but in Amsterdam. It was in Amsterdam, too, that the first English newspaper came out, in the same year 1620. This was the *Corrant out of Italy, Germany etc.*, which gave regular news reports on the Thirty Years War.

Two considerations gave a great impetus to the growth of proper newspapers. In the first place, the state was concerned to publicize its views. Copies of state edicts were printed and distributed (for the years 1598–1643 alone the National Library at Paris possesses a total of over half a million different printed papers issued by the state). The desire to have a regular platform for official views led Théophraste Renaudot to found in 1631, with the support of Cardinal Richelieu, the *Gazette de France*, as a journal for 'kings and the powers that be'. But the *Gazette* was also to be a straightforward supplier of information, of use to the average citizen, so that 'the merchant will no longer trade in a besieged and ruined town, nor the soldier seek employment in a country where there is no war: not to speak of the comfort for those writing to their friends, who were formerly forced to give news that was either invented or based on hearsay'. It came out weekly and consisted of four (later eight) quarto pages. Other states followed suit. Florence got a weekly gazette in 1636, Rome in 1640, Genoa in 1642, the States General of the Dutch Republic in 1649, and in Spain the *Gaceta de Madrid* was first published by royal order in 1661.

The second reason for the growth of news organs was the desire of political factions to air their views regularly. News became particularly desirable during a political crisis, and any sort of information was seized on with avidity. 'From the great to the small', says a report on Paris during the Fronde, 'everyone discusses what is going on only through the *Gazette*. Those who can afford it, buy copies and collect them. Others are satisfied to pay in order to borrow and read it, or else they group together so as to buy a copy.'

In England the breakdown of censorship during the Civil War gave scope to an unprecedented flood of news-sheets: in the Thomason collection at the British Library there are only four newspapers for 1641, but 167 for 1642 and 722 for 1645. The two most important were the royalist *Mercurius Aulicus* (edited from Oxford) and the parliamentarian *Mercurius Britanicus*. The circulation of the former in London alone was about 500 copies, but each copy was read by several people; if other papers sold as many copies, the total public they reached must have been large. Censorship was reimposed with the Licensing Act of 1662, but in the later century when political parties appeared the demand for tracts was even greater. The common people of London (where the number of printing presses trebled from 1662 to 1695) became sensitive to the great issues of the day, particularly after the Licensing Act of 1695 abolished pre-publication censorship. Though 'the greatest part of the people cannot read at all', commented the editor of a newspaper founded in 1704, 'they will gather about one that can read, and listen'.

Censorship had been strict in the early sixteenth century, as it had been in medieval times even before the invention of printing. Printing became a major threat to established authority: it 'opened German eyes', wrote the German historian Sleidan in 1542. John Foxe commented that 'either the pope must abolish knowledge and printing or printing must at length root him out'. This optimistic view is reflected also in Hartlib's claim (1641) that 'the art of printing will so spread knowledge that the common people, knowing their own rights and liberties, will not be governed by way of oppression'. Every country had firm controls: in England the first list of prohibited books was issued in 1529, and in 1530 a licensing system was introduced. The notorious Star Chamber decree was passed in 1586. One of the first opponents of licensing was the Leveller leader Walwyn, who demanded in 1644 'that the Press may be free for any man that writes nothing highly scandalous or dangerous to the state'. John Milton made the same demand in his *Areopagitica* (1644). On the continent the Roman and Spanish authorities published guide-lists of forbidden books in their famous *Indexes*. The *Indexes* ironically became useful to bibliophiles seeking details of anti-Catholic publications: in 1627 the Bodley's librarian at Oxford suggested that they be consulted as a guide to books worth buying.

A major consequence of the spread of literacy, the diffusion of the printed word, and the imposition of new ideas through propaganda, was that the differences between élite and popular cultures were made sharper. It has been well argued that there was a 'withdrawal of the upper classes' in the early modern period, and that a fairly universal culture was succeeded by a split into two cultures: one, the dominant, for the élite; the other for the common people. It is possible, however, that this 'withdrawal' or split may be an optical illusion, and that the spread of printing merely brought into relief what had always been there: two traditions, previously less clearly defined but now increasingly defined as the upper classes maintained their monopoly of education and extended their domain over the means for diffusing knowledge. Printing appears not to have disturbed the levels of popular preference. Readers chose escapist literature, 'lewd Ballads', 'merry bookes', 'corrupted tales in Inke and Paper', to cite English critics of the genre. The 'Blue Library' in France consisted of romantic fiction of this sort. Attempts were of course made to change popular taste. Jerónimo de Zurita, chronicler of the history of Aragon and a sixteenth-century secretary of the Spanish Inquisition, felt that the suppression of superficial literature was one of the chief purposes of censorship. Of books of romance and chivalry, he felt that 'since they are without imagination or learning and it is a waste of time to read them, it is better to prohibit them'. Fortunately for the public, who would otherwise have had to feast on very dull fare, censors in practice paid less attention to superficial than to ideologically dangerous literature.

The European universities

So many new universities were founded in the age of the Counter Reformation that it was as though a new age of learning were coming into existence. In Germany there were Dillingen (1554), Jena (1558), Helmstedt (1569), Würzburg (1582), Herborn (1584), Graz (1586) and several others; in the United Provinces there were Leiden (1575), Franeker (1585), Groningen (1614), Harderwijk (1600) and Utrecht (1636); in Britain there were Trinity College,

Dublin (1591), Edinburgh (1583) and the new Protestant College at Aberdeen (1593). The expansion of universities took place throughout Europe. In the old universities new colleges were founded and the total student membership rose: Cambridge had 1267 students on its books in 1564 and 3050 in 1622.

The notable expansion of universities presents all the appearances of a boom in higher education. The truth is that, to some extent, the statistics of expansion are misleading. A great number of the new universities were foundations artificially created to serve an immediate religious or political bent, and without any real hope of attracting students. Of the twenty-two new German universities created between 1540 and 1700, only seven survived into the nineteenth century. Some of them never attracted more than 100 students, and served a purely local demand. The principal reason why so many new foundations came into existence was not primarily an increased demand for education: it was because Catholics and Protestants refused to attend each other's universities, and instead set up rival colleges of their own. The new establishment at Leiden, for example, was created because Louvain and Douai (the latter founded in 1562) were both in the Catholic southern Netherlands. The Lutherans had obviously taken care to fortify themselves in the institutions that passed to them at the Reformation, and the same was true for the Anglicans. Where the need for denominational education was still felt, the gap was filled by establishments such as Strassburg (1538, created a university in 1621). The Catholics in their turn had to create colleges for their refugees. The first great university created by the Counter Reformation was Würzburg (1582), which was under close Jesuit control and was staffed principally by former professors of Louvain. In Germany the two most famous Jesuit-orientated universities were Ingolstadt (a pre-Reformation university) and Dillingen (newly founded).

The coincidence of the rise in the volume of higher education, with the revolutionary changes of the post-Reformation period, might suggest that the educational impulse was breaking new ground. Once again, on the whole, this was not so. The education offered by the many new places of learning was very much a repetition of old methods and syllabuses. That there was an increase in the number of schools and universities, and in the number of scholars attending them, is indisputable. But there was no corresponding change in the methods of teaching, or in the subjects taught. Hartlib and Comenius were still struggling in the mid seventeenth century to bring in that 'revolution' in education which had till then occurred in numbers alone.

Part of the reason for the decay of academic learning in the universities, was, as we shall see, the rising tide of demand for civil office. Study of the liberal arts was neglected in favour of the two disciplines – civil and canon law – that offered a promising career. In the German universities the cultivation of the philosophical and natural sciences, of mathematics no less than of biology, was neglected. A fleeting stay at college became one's passport to a career. Besides, wealth could purchase degrees. The Wittenberg professor and poet Frederick Taubmann wrote in 1604 that 'nothing is easier today than to gain a doctorate, if you have money. Anyone can become a *doctor*, without being *doctus*'. There were numerous complaints of the type of education that Oxford and Cambridge offered. Giordano Bruno in 1583 described Oxford as 'the widow of good learning in philosophy and pure mathematics'. Chemistry and experimental science were apparently neglected and, reported William Harrison in 1587, 'arithmetic, geometry and astronomy . . . are now smally regarded'. 'The secrets of the creation', Gerrard Winstanley complained, 'have been locked up under the traditional, parrot-like speaking from the universities.' Aspects of the decay in Spain may be seen from the case of Salamanca university, which ceased teaching Hebrew in 1555, a year when only one student was registered for this subject. In 1578 the chair of mathematics had been vacant over three years. By 1648 the arts faculty there was described as 'totally lost'. If scientific method advanced in this period it was not, for the most part, at the universities. The great pioneers – Copernicus, Brahe, Kepler, Peiresc – were often educated at universities but did not hold chairs, and pursued their researches in a more independent environment. Perhaps the only significant exception was Italy, where the pursuit of knowledge in universities lingered on. Torricelli was professor of mathematics at Florence in the mid seventeenth century. Padua, thanks mainly to Vesalius, remained the principal medical school in Europe, and it was to Padua that Harvey went as a young man.

Learned disputation and scientific inquiry flourished less in the universities than in the independent colleges and private academies. Literary salons and philosophical circles were commonplace in late sixteenth-century France and Italy. By the early seventeenth century the scientific academies were much in evidence. The two outstanding Italian ones were the *Lincei* in Rome (founded in 1603), which counted Galileo among its members, and the *Cimento* in Florence (founded in 1657), which included Borelli and other scientists. In England, 1660 witnessed the formal establishment of the Royal Society, which could trace its origins back over a decade earlier. Many of the first members of the Society had been professors of Gresham College, an independent institution set up in 1596 to provide an alternative to the education offered by the major English universities.

Renaissance ideals of culture and education were certainly influential in the vogue for improvement, especially among the gentry and rising men who wished to give their children the best. In 1614 Sir Thomas Fairfax asked a Cambridge college to allocate a good tutor to his son, for 'my greatest care hitherto hath bene, and still is, to breed my sonne a scholar'. But higher education was never regarded as an unmixed blessing. At the French Estates General of 1614 some deputies of the clergy complained that higher education 'burdens the state with too many educated people, weakens the armed forces, destroys trade and the arts, depopulates agriculture, fills the courts with ignorant people, diminishes the *taille*, inflicts simony on the Church, supernumerary officials on the state, wages and pensions on the Exchequer, and in brief overturns all good order'. Cardinal Richelieu was strongly opposed to more education: 'the commerce of letters would totally drive out that of merchandise', he claimed in his *Political Testament*. A French writer of 1627 thought that the schools 'have produced a great number of literates but few educated people. If someone learns three words of Latin, of a sudden he ceases to pay the *taille*'. Education, it was felt, made one a privileged person. Not surprisingly, many political commentators blamed political turmoil on the pretensions of the great number of shiftless educated. The Swedish statesman, Magnus de la Gardie, claimed in 1655 that 'there are more *literati* and learned fellows, especially *in politicis*, than means or jobs available to provide for them, and they grow desperate and impatient'. 'It is a hard matter for men', Hobbes was to point out, 'who do all think highly of their own wits, when they have also acquired the learning of the university, to be persuaded that they want any ability requisite for the government of a commonwealth.' His conclusion in respect of 1640 was simple: 'The core of rebellion, as you have seen by this, and read of other rebellions, are the Universities. . . . The Universities have been to this nation, as the wooden horse was to the Trojans.'

This exaggerated viewpoint had little in common with reality. Students went into higher education to serve, not to overturn, the state. If they were to be criticized it was for a lack of interest in academic studies: 'the love of letters', observed a high court judge in Valladolid in 1638, 'brings only a very few to the colleges'. In most universities in central and western Europe two subjects predominated: canon law (in Catholic countries) and civil law. Then, as now, the legal profession was the gateway to employment by the state. Marburg had been the first post-Reformation university founded (in 1527) with the express aim of turning out graduates to serve the government; other German universities followed the trend of specializing in law. In Salamanca in the sixteenth century, enrolments for canon law exceeded those for all other faculties together; in the early seventeenth century civil law became popular, taking about half as many students as canon law. In England, those who did not go to Oxford or Cambridge went to the Inns of Court in London; many (50 per cent of entrants to the Inns) went to both university and Inns. The governing class in England became more educated: of 420 members of Parliament in 1563, 110 (or 26 per cent) had matriculated at university; by 1642 out of 552 members the figure was 276 (or 50 per cent). Most of the local Justices of the Peace in the country had by the 1640s been either to university or to the Inns.

The increase in university enrolments shows a consistent pattern in England, Germany and Spain; one may presume that it was the same elsewhere. Figures rose during the sixteenth century, with a pronounced increase from the 1550s until the second decade of the seventeenth century. Very roughly, matriculation totals doubled in Spain between about 1560 and 1590, in Oxford between about 1550 and 1580, in Leipzig between about 1560 and 1620. The common people did not, of course, participate in this increase. In England peasants were 70 per cent of the population, but at Cambridge they were only 15 per cent of the student body.

Though law was the main subject taught in most places of learning, it would be wrong to conclude that the universities thereby became the training-ground for the bourgeois bureaucracy. The bourgeois in Germany and Spain were conspicuous by their virtual absence from places of higher learning, and in England they were only a small proportion. Everywhere the nobles and gentry were in ascendance. The Venetian ambassador in 1612 reported that the

Inns of Court contained 'five hundred of the wealthiest gentlemen of this kingdom'; records of the Inns confirm that between 1570 and 1639 gentry were over 80 per cent of entrants. At Oxford, 39 per cent of those matriculating in 1575–9 were gentlemen, by 1600–9 the proportion was 52 per cent; correspondingly, the number of students of plebeian origin fell from 55 per cent in 1577–9 to 37 per cent in 1637–9 and 17 per cent in 1760. At the same time scholarships that had been reserved for the education of the poor were seized by the privileged. The picture was repeated in Germany: at Leipzig 289 poor students had matriculated in 1421–5, but only seventeen in 1556–60; at Cologne there had been 743 poor students in 1486–90, but only ten in 1556–60. It was the same in Spain, where in the course of the late sixteenth century the sons of the poor were crowded out of the places originally reserved for them. The university of Geneva (that is, Calvin's Academy, founded in 1559) had by the early seventeenth century become firmly aristocratic, the resort of the Calvinist nobility of Germany and France and of the premier families of Britain (Beauchamps, Cavendishes, Cecils, Douglases and Drummonds). Leipzig became dominated by the patriciates of central Europe and Poland: in the period 1559–1634 its students included six dukes of Saxony, four princes Radziwill, one crown prince (of Denmark) and numerous other higher nobles.

For the gentry, university was a convenient finishing school. William Harrison said in 1577 that 'they oft bring the university into much slander' with their extravagant way of life. Few bothered to stay the course and take a degree: this applied to half of all those enrolling at Cambridge in 1590–1640. Of the thirty-five government officials in the 1584 English Parliament, only thirteen had been to university and only four had a degree. In Heidelberg between 1550 and 1620 the proportion of matriculands taking their final degree never exceeded 5 per cent.

Nobles usually had private tutors for the formative years of their education. Universities – particularly foreign universities – were fitted in at the end in order to 'finish off'. Hence the Grand Tour, a product of the Renaissance which flourished no less in this period of confessional strife. When Sir Philip Sidney undertook it in 1572, the main aim was travel. 'Your purpose is, being a gentleman born', he was later to advise a younger brother, 'to furnish yourself with the knowledge of such things as may be serviceable to your country.' Leaving England at the age of 19 in the company of a tutor and three servants, Sidney travelled to Paris, Frankfurt,

Heidelberg, Strassburg, Vienna, Hungary, Padua, Germany, Poland, Prague and Antwerp, an absence of three years, only some of it spent in study. The whole of noble Europe practised the Tour, the '*nobilis et erudita peregrinatio*', as Justus Lipsius described it. Manuals were written, such as Jerome Turler's *De peregrinatione* (The Tour) (1574), and another by Thomas Palmer in 1606 which was prepared expressly 'for the youngest sort of such noble gentlemen as intend so recommendable a course'. Public service no less than personal edification was the purpose, if we judge by Sidney's remark above as well as by Sir Thomas Bodley's comment in 1647: 'I waxed desirous to travel beyond the seas for attaining to the knowledge of some special modern tongues and for the increase of my experience in the managing of affairs, being then wholly addicted to employ myself and all my cares into the public of the state.'

In the late sixteenth century Italy was far and away the most popular country visited by the nobility of western Europe. John Evelyn wrote in 1645: 'From the reports of divers curious and expert persons I've been assured there was little more to be seen in the rest of the civil world after Italy, France and the Low Countries but plain and prodigious barbarism.' The Dutch, according to Sir William Temple, travelled 'chiefly into England and France, not much into Italy, seldomer into Spain, nor often into the more northern countrys. The chief end of their breeding is to make them fit for the service of their country'. A tour might often be rapid (one German noble journeying abroad in 1578–80 spent, during his visit to Italy, a few days at Bologna, a few weeks in Perugia, three months in Siena and then one year in Padua, having probably inscribed himself at all these universities without necessarily studying anything). The Austrian nobility were one group to broaden their cultural horizons: the Protestants journeyed abroad to Wittenberg, Jena and Marburg universities, the Catholics to Vienna, Ingolstadt and Louvain; those of either faith who wished to study law went to Padua, Bologna and Siena. Through these travels they extended their knowledge of the romance languages (Spanish was in any case a requisite at the court of Vienna), and contacts with Italy brought them into the sphere of Renaissance literature. In private libraries of the Austrian nobility three books – all Latin in culture – took pride of place: Cicero's *De officiis*, Petrarch's *Canzionere*, and Ariosto's *Orlando furioso*.

The practice of the tour emphasizes what is easily forgotten, that even in the age of ideological conflict the universities had not lost their international character. The rise of state barriers, of *cuius regio eius religio*, did not peremptorily destroy the international republic of letters. Protestants still went to Italy, Calvinism helped to universalize academic study by opening the doors of its universities to all nations. Of the 161 names enrolled in the *Livre du Recteur* of Calvin's Academy at Geneva in 1559, nearly all were foreign to Switzerland. Of the 110 who matriculated at the Academy from late 1584 to early 1585, nine were Genevan, ten Polish, twenty Netherlandish, three Czech, three British, and nearly all the rest from France or Germany. As late as 1653 a Genevan pastor complained that 'there come to this city a great number of foreign nobility, who live in great licence'. Attendance in the late sixteenth century at Heidelberg, perhaps the most important of the Calvinist universities, included about 39 per cent foreigners.

Leiden university can serve to illustrate the continuing internationalism of higher education. Founded in 1575, it remained open to both Catholics and Protestants, but flourished chiefly as a centre of Calvinism. In its first twenty-six years, 41 per cent of its registered students came from outside the United Provinces; in the subsequent quarter century over 52 per cent were from outside the country, more than half of them from Germany. In 1639 there were more Germans matriculating at Leiden than at nearly every German university.

During the seventeenth century universities went into decline, for two quite distinct reasons. Demographic stagnation led to falling enrolments: in Spain matriculations nose-dived after the 1620s; and in Germany the disruption of the Thirty Years War created a huge drop in admissions between 1620 and 1645. The second reason was that by becoming little more than channels for the bureaucratic élite and leisure resorts for the aristocracy, universities suffered a lowering of standards and ceased to be desirable centres of learning. In Salamanca, for example, faculty chairs were prized because they were stepping-stones to high office: one chair of canon law was filled sixty-one times in the course of the century. Those, even from the aristocracy, who wished to offer their sons an academic training would send them to private academies or hire private tutors.

The discovery and loss of Utopia

At a time of rapid social change and shifting beliefs, one aspiration remained constant: the yearning for a better world in which man would cease to make mistakes and justice for all would be achieved. The search for a just society drew on ideas of the late medieval millennarians (particularly Joachim of Fiore), on classical mythology, and above all on the tradition of the simplicity of the early Christians. Successive thinkers and social rebels looked back to a mythical 'age of gold' which was, assuming that history moved in cycles, to come again. They contrasted it with their own 'age of iron' or 'iron century', in which strife and injustice were rampant. When they proposed improvements, however, their ideals tended inevitably to arrive at a confusing compromise between the unattainability of perfection and the reality of man's limitations.

In 1516 Thomas More published in Latin a little study called *Utopia*, which was not translated into English until 1551. The book described an imaginary society on the island of Utopia ('Nowhere'); to this More later added an introductory dialogue between himself, some friends and a traveller called Ralph Hythloday, on the main topics of the time. Inspired by medieval monastic ideals and by the communism of Plato, More presented his Utopia as a place where men lived in conditions of equality, elected their rulers freely, were all obliged to work, were guaranteed security, education and leisure, coexisted peacefully with other states and worshipped without dogmas. The subsequent reputation both of the book and of its author is somewhat misleading: *Utopia* was an exercise in imagination, not a blueprint for a communist paradise; it made no attempt to be explicitly Christian because the author was writing in the non-ideological humanist environment that preceded the Reformation.

The study had been provoked by tales of the lands discovered across the Atlantic. When Columbus and the early Spaniards reached the New World they were astounded by its felicity, the warmth of its climate, the luxuriance of its vegetation, the innocence of the natives who lived unspoiled by the possession of gold and silver. The perfections of America appealed immediately to all those who wished to compensate for the evils of the Old World. Montaigne evolved his myth of the 'noble savage', others resurrected legends of the 'earthly paradise'. The reality after the conquest was different: the Indians were ravaged by diseases against which they had no immunity, their lands were taken away, their villages broken up and the men taken off to perform labour services. All this horrified those Spanish missionaries who still treasured the early vision. Schooled in the humanists and in Erasmus, hopeful clergy tried to recreate for the Indians the environment they had lost. Vasco de Quiroga, first bishop of Michoacán, had spent some time reading and annotating More's *Utopia*. As a result he set up at Santa Fé an entire community based on the practicable principles of *Utopia*: all property and land was held in common, labour was communal, government was through elected representatives. For the first time in history, Utopia was actually put into practice. Similar programmes were attempted by Las Casas in his settlement of Vera Paz (True Peace) in Guatemala in the late 1530s. But one by one these schemes collapsed. By the 1550s Utopia was seen to be unrealizable.

After the 1550s the Utopian vision faded, to be overtaken by an epoch of inflation, epidemic and continuous religious conflict: for contemporaries this was the core of the 'iron century'. The only significant idealist scheme of the period was offered by an Italian bishop, Francesco Patrizi, in his *La città felice* (1553). Scholars were more concerned to salvage some order out of the ruins of their war-torn countries. When Jean Bodin published his *Six Books of the Republic* (1576) he disavowed any intention of writing about an impractical ideal state, ' a republic in the imagination and without effect, such as those which Plato and Thomas More have imagined'.

The years of strife were not without practical experiments. After the disastrous episode of Münster (1535), Anabaptists set about constructing peaceful communities in central Europe, notably in the mountains of Moravia. Meanwhile, Giordano Bruno in his *Expulsion of the Triumphant Beast* (1584) presented a proposal for sweeping changes in society. His radicalism of outlook, however, tended to be anarchical. The practical Utopias of minority groups were, by contrast, strictly regulated. In the 1560s when the Polish Arians visited the Moravian Brethren with a view to further unity, they were repelled by the authoritarian structure of their community. All Utopias, whether theoretical or practical, depended for their existence on rigid seclusion from the rest of the world; on total uniformity of thought and action, with a minimum of free choice; collectivization of functions, and in extreme cases even of the family; abolition of all distinctions of rank and wealth; and an extensive system of education for all. These principles might work among small groups in Moravia; they were more difficult to put into practice in south America, where the grandest of Utopias was created by the Jesuits.

In seventeenth-century Paraguay (a large area covering a third of Spanish territory in south America) the Jesuits attempted to liberate the Guaraní tribes from the colonial labour system. In 1611 the local authorities prohibited Indian slavery and permitted the Jesuits to set up Indian settlements (*reducciones*). By 1676 the Society had twenty-two *reducciones* with a total of over 58,000 Indians who held land in common, were given arms to defend themselves against marauding settlers (all whites other than Jesuits were excluded), and had negro slaves to do the heavy labour. The experiment continued until the Jesuits were expelled from America in the late eighteenth century. In one sense it was not a Utopia, for the Jesuits were doing little more than fulfilling local legislation in respect of the Indian. While it survived it seemed to work, stimulating the interest of social thinkers in Europe.

In the early seventeenth century the accumulation of crises seemed to provoke a resurgence of Utopian literature. All the significant writers were convinced Christians, yet curiously none of their projects was explicitly so. Common to the schemes of Campanella, Andreae, Bacon, Hartlib and Vairasse was an emphasis on rational order and a scientific structuring of society. Knowledge (and therefore education) became the key to a well-ordered state. Comenius described this outlook as 'pansophism', a term he borrowed from the *Pansophia sive Paedia Philosophica* published at Rostock in 1633 by Peter Laurenberg, which drew heavily on the ideas of the medieval Catalan philosopher Ramón Llull.

Tommaso Campanella (d. 1639), a native of Calabria, was a man of contradictions. A priest of the Roman Church, his fundamental commitment was to astrology and magic; a protagonist of Spain's universal dominion, he spent over twenty years in a Spanish prison in Naples; defender of Rome's supremacy, he was imprisoned by the pope and fled to France after three years in a Roman gaol. These contradictions emerge in his *City of the Sun*, which he wrote during his imprisonment from 1602 to 1626. Presented as a dialogue between a Grand Master of the Knights Hospitaller and a Genoese sea-captain, the work describes an ideal communistic society free from the corruptions of contemporary societies. Campanella's city has no private property: this is abolished because property encourages acquisitiveness and self-love. 'But when we have taken away self-love, there remains only love for the state.' All things are held in common, all activity done in common. Living, sleeping, eating are mass communal activities. The family is likewise abolished, and procreation is controlled by the state. Work is held to be noble: because everyone works tasks are completed rapidly and the average time worked is four hours a day. There is universal education from very early youth, and the sciences are encouraged. There is no explicit reference to Christianity, and the city is governed by magistrates who possess the names of the principal virtues. The physical layout of the city is magical and astrological. The chief priest who governs the city represents the sun. Procreation is undertaken at the right astral conjunction, and the careers of inhabitants are decided 'according to their inclination and the star under which they are born'.

When Johann Valentin Andreae (d. 1654) published his *Christianopolis* in 1619 his aim was not to describe an ideal state so much as a tiny community of like-minded people. He conceived of a settlement no larger than a small village: 'about four hundred citizens', he wrote of Christianopolis, 'live here in religious faith and peace of the highest order'. There was no private property, and 'no one has any money, nor is there any use for any private money'. Manual labour was honourable: everyone took part, and the working hours were short. After what we have already seen of Andreae's Rosicrucianism, it seems that Christianopolis was really an exclusivist society, and the citizens an élite of savants. Education was universal, and even 'their artisans are almost entirely educated men'. Despite the name of the city, Andreae's concern was with learning rather than religion.

It was the service of learning that also influenced Francis Bacon to describe the mysterious island of *New Atlantis* (written in about 1624, published 1627). The work was left unfinished, and is not strictly Utopian. New Atlantis was a monarchy which still possessed the standard features of property, wealth and rank, and Bacon showed little interest in discussing social improvements. The main interest of *New Atlantis* lies in the secret scientific society (the members of Salomon's House) that enjoyed a privileged position in the state. Its members could withhold scientific secrets from the state, and periodically sent agents out into other countries to learn their secrets. Most commentators have seen this as a pre-figuration of the Royal Society of London, founded in 1660.

Samuel Hartlib (d. 1662), of Baltic origin but resident in England after about 1628, was interested more in education than scientific learning. His brief work, *A description of the famous kingdome of*

Macaria, published in London in 1641, took the form of a dialogue between a scholar and a traveller, and returned to the more normal outline of an ideal society. Macaria was a monarchy, with a Great Council that sat annually for a short period. Below this Council were five lesser councils, dealing respectively with husbandry, fishing, trade by land, trade by sea, and overseas plantations. One-twentieth of the income from husbandry was taken by the state to finance improvements. Nobody in Macaria held more land than he could exploit. The kingdom was armed, in order to secure peace through strength. The health of its inhabitants was looked after by a college of medicine, and medicaments were distributed free. In many respects all this seems more modern than Utopian. We are also told, however, that there were neither Papists nor Protestants in Macaria, all were non-sectarian Christians. 'There are no diversitie of opinions among them', and a divine who comes up with novel opinions 'shall be accounted a disturber of the publick peace, and shall suffer death for it'. New opinions could not be published, but had first to be debated before the Great Council, which decided whether to sanction them.

The four authors we have noted were men of great learning, experience and liberal views, but their Utopias were less a reflection of society's shortcomings than of their own private vision. Andreae and Bacon were frankly élitist, Campanella openly exotic. Hartlib's *Macaria* was by far the most sober blueprint for society, but it was clear that his own concern for reunion among the churches was perhaps the chief rationale for the work. The only writer to base his scheme for the future squarely on the errors of the present, and to locate his ideal state not in some distant island but in his own native country, was Gerrard Winstanley, whose last and most important work, *The Law of Freedom*, was published in 1652.

Winstanley's career with the Diggers had been spent in trying to persuade the authorities to bring freedom and equality to England. Now in 1652, after the collapse of the Digger cause, he presented to Cromwell in book form a summary of his ideas for the new society. 'I have set the candle at your door', he addressed Cromwell, 'you have power in your hand to act for Common Freedom, if you will.' *The Law of Freedom* lacked some of the fire of his earlier published tracts, but in outline it presented most of Winstanley's essential ideas. All land and resources would be held in common by all the people. The economy would be mainly agricultural, practising barter and exchange, but there would be no commerce and no money. The family unit would remain sacred, and so would family property. Government would be under a parliament, elected annually. Knowledge would be made available to all, and education would be free and compulsory. Information would be circulated throughout the country, and general (rather than just religious) instruction would be given through the pulpit. Law would be codified and not depend on man's interpretation. These radical proposals contrast sharply with the more conventional ideas of James Harrington, whose *Oceana* (1656) was essentially a set of moderate constitutional reforms, based on the same scientific principles that inspired his colleagues in the educated élite.

The conservatism of late seventeenth-century society was not fertile ground for political innovation. The crisis of absolutism in Louis XIV's France was responsible however for a revival of speculative Utopias. Over a dozen projects appeared in French, the majority written by Protestants who used the genre as an oblique way of criticizing the régime. The Huguenot exile, Denis Vairasse, presented his *History of the Sevarambians* (1675 in English, 1677 in French) as a travel tale of Europeans shipwrecked in Australia who stumble across the people of Sevarambia. There are echoes of Campanella in the fact that worship of the sun is central to Sevarambia; government follows regular Utopian lines in being communistic, and all education is controlled by the state. The device of a travelogue was also used by Archbishop Fénelon of Cambrai in his *Télémaque* (1699), which followed the hero as he wandered through various countries and polities in search of his father Ulysses; but Fénelon's scheme was less Utopian than conservative, a summons to the classical virtues of the traditional pastoral way of life.

Utopian ideas were a reasoned response to the social and political problems of the time. Underlying the dreams was a desire to advance beyond contemporary illusions to the achievement of a perfect science and a just society. Winstanley, who had seen deliverance from the Iron Age and from 'the great red Dragon' within the people's grasp, had most cause to hope still for the achievement of his vision: 'that we may work in Righteousness and lay the foundation of making the Earth a Common Treasury for all, both rich and poor'.

9   Economic and political crisis

These days are days of shaking, and this shaking is universal.
    Sermon by Jeremiah Whittaker (1643)

The major political events of the mid seventeenth century took place against a background of economic and social crisis. All periods are, of course, subject to repeated crisis, and it may be an excessive simplification to group disparate developments together under one heading; but the notion of a crisis will serve here to describe the process of change from the energetic and expansionist sixteenth century to the more stable late seventeenth century. In between these two formative periods we find a half-century of anguish that begins in the 1580s and reaches its climax in the 1640s, during which so many significant crises can be identified that it has become habitual to talk of a 'general' crisis. Seven aspects that make the period significant will be touched on here.

First, the great inflation of the sixteenth century came to an end in the early seventeenth: prices levelled out and began to fall. Where the sixteenth century had been one of a disastrous fall in living standards for labourers and the poor, the seventeenth offered hope. That at any rate is the message conveyed by price trends. The reality turns out to be different: falling prices were themselves in part the consequence of agrarian problems, and the downward trend obscures very severe and frequent harvest fluctuations which brought rural misery without in any way offering the compensation of an expanding market. In Germany, for example, prices were falling from the 1620s, evidence of a recession that preceded the oncoming disasters of the Thirty Years War.

Second, from the 1580s there was a reversal of the demographic expansion of the sixteenth century. Epidemics seem to have struck with more force, and more frequency, after the late century. The Atlantic plague of 1596–1603 cost about a million lives, and there were other disasters throughout Europe: 1630 in the western Mediterranean, 1636 in northern and central Europe, 1648 in Spain, 1656 in Italy. The Mediterranean suffered worst: taking account also of the Morisco expulsions, Spain in this period lost at least 1.5 million out of a 1590 population of 8 million; Italy did not recover its 1600 population levels for one and a half centuries (in 1630–1 alone it lost 1.5 million). The rest of western Europe was more fortunate. Though Lower Normandy lost a quarter of its population in the plague of 1636–9, France continued to grow, but at a slower pace. In England growth between 1500 and 1600 has been put at 40 per cent, between 1600 and 1700 at 25 per cent. The United Provinces, too, continued to grow, aided, however, by considerable immigration from the southern Netherlands. The slowing down and decay of population growth affected agrarian production, depressed demand, and caused fiscal problems for states that required more taxation but had fewer heads to tax.

Third, agricultural production suffered. In part this may have been a Malthusian response, as some regions reached the limit of their output in the 1580s, and cut back thereafter in step with falling population. The Mediterranean, in particular, was a casualty. From about 1560 Spain became dependent on Sicilian then on Baltic wheat. From the 1580s Italy was no longer self-sufficient. By 1600 Sicily and the papal states, once exporters, became importers.

The fall in output was aggravated also by the incidence of war, which was responsible for agrarian crises in France, the Netherlands, Poland and other areas. In France in the 1590s the civil wars cut output in the Cambrésis by a half, in the Paris region by a quarter, in Auvergne and Burgundy by 40 per cent. The worst war effects were in Germany, where the production levels of 1625 were not again attained until 1704. Even without war, however, after the 1580s output fell sharply in Geneva, Zürich and Valladolid. Evidence for a climatic change at this time (the onset of a 'little ice age') is sometimes cited, but is not convincing. It is true, however, that harvests were generally poor, a consequence both of output and weather: the entire period 1596 to 1630 in England was one of agrarian disaster, including famine.

Fourth, there was a considerable disruption of European trade. The rapid decline of Antwerp's trade in the 1580s was soon balanced by the rise of Amsterdam, but this did not help all the trade routes that had formerly focused on Antwerp: the Spanish export trade, the transalpine routes from Italy and southern Germany. The international slump of 1620 was the most significant reflection of economic difficulties. It was provoked in part by currency problems. Scarcity of silver (American bullion imports, and American trade, began to decline after 1610) and plentiful Swedish copper encouraged several governments to solve their cash problems by issuing debased copper coinage: this happened in Spain after 1599, in central Europe after 1620. The result was a phase of monetary and price inflation (called in Germany the *Kipperzeit*, a time of coin-clipping) that seriously disrupted trade. Local currency devaluations (of the order of 25 per cent in Alsace and Württemberg, for example) raised the price of imported goods to local consumers, making it difficult for English and Dutch exporters to trade normally and maintain profit levels. England, in addition, was suffering the consequences of the disastrous 'Cokayne project' (1614–17) in the textile industry, which caused a trade clash with the Dutch, depressed exports by a third, and created unemployment. The slump in England went on until 1624, but had longer-lasting effects: London's export trade in textiles between 1606 and 1640 fell from 120,000 pieces a year to 45,000. Meanwhile, the Dutch were also suffering from the expiry in 1621 of the Twelve Years Truce with Spain: Spain cut all trade links (two-fifths of the Republic's ships had till then been committed to trade with the Spanish monarchy) and brought about an immediate slump in Holland. The trade dislocation had repercussions all through the Mediterranean, and obviously affected industrial production. Italy and Spain were badly hit: in Milan in 1600 there were seventy firms making woollens, by 1640 there were only fifteen; Florence in the 1580s produced 30,000 woollen cloths a year, in 1650 the figure was 5000; Segovia was producing 13,000 pieces a year in the 1580s, in the seventeenth century the level was 3000 pieces.

Fifth, western Europe from the 1580s moved into an epoch of war. Spain had been at peace for over half a century, but the Dutch and Turkish problems in the 1570s, and the universal war after 1580 against Portugal, England and Henry IV, established a new situation in which all state resources were geared to conflict: armies and navies increased in size, and military expenditure became the major component in the budgets of Holland, Spain, Sweden and France. The only way to pay for all this was through higher taxation: in Spain taxes increased fivefold under Philip II, in France the tax burden quintupled between 1609 and 1648. Fiscality, since it tested the capacity of both rich and poor to contribute to the unprecedented demands of the state, became the crucial ingredient of crisis.

Sixth, the cumulative difficulties of the period aggravated a social crisis. Many commentators looked on their age as a harsh, merciless time: 'this is the Iron Age', wrote Robert Greene in 1592; 'it is not the best of times, being an Iron Century', wrote Robert Menteith in 1649. The incidence of fiscality forced political activists to question the authority of governments; the popular classes in their turn reacted to hard times by rebelling. Reassessment of thought went beyond politics and entered the realm of moral authority: 'new philosophy calls all in doubt', claimed John Donne. Intellectual life was at a crossroads, because this was the very epoch that universities began to show a marked decline in the number of students. Some intellectuals followed their own reasoning and logic into a new era of rationality: such were Hugo Grotius and Galileo; others however, like Francisco de Quevedo in Spain, sought refuge from a shaken world in the traditional certainties of religion and medieval science.

Seventh, and finally, all these aspects interacted with each other and contributed to the political crisis of the decade 1640–50, when the tensions immanent in the attitudes and institutions of early modern Europe were made manifest. Many French thinkers of the early century, like Le Bret, argued that authority was best preserved through 'absolute' government. In England, by contrast, a large number of thinkers were committed to the belief that authority should be based on 'consent'. The divergent trends, and the conflicting interests of social classes, focused their attention on the problem of fiscality.

The broad lines of the crisis, then, came together and were expressed most forcibly in the political events of 1640–50. It was a turning-point with unmistakable consequences, not all of them negative: in philosophy the era of doubt, represented by Descartes, was succeeded by the assurance of the age of Locke; the irresolution of state authority was succeeded by an emphasis on power, most notably through the role of armies; the social crisis in the east and central Europe was resolved in favour of stability and serfdom; the primacy of the northern European nations was established, in contrast to the decay of the Mediterranean, which slipped into the role of being a colony of the north; the period of a sharp population and price rise was followed, after the epoch of crisis, by one of relative stability and moderate expansion in the later seventeenth century.

The English Revolution of 1640

In England a conflict between crown and Parliament had been a half-century in the making. Elizabeth in her declining years had already found it difficult to control the House of Commons. Under the first two Stuarts, James and Charles, tensions were magnified and confirmed. There were major conflicts about religion, finance and foreign policy; on the first and the last, in particular, the differences could be traced back well into Elizabeth's reign. Religion alone was so important an issue that it is possible to discuss the whole conflict of the early seventeenth century in terms of Puritanism, and it was once standard practice to refer to the events of mid century as a Puritan Revolution. But whatever the precise issue may have been, what really lay at stake was the exercise of power and the ability to control government policy. Sooner or later all disputed points came for discussion to Parliament, and all grievances, whether of religion or finance, were debated there as constitutional issues. It was the constitutional struggle, the struggle for sovereignty, that dominated events up to 1640.

The range of questions that obsessed Parliament, from finance in the Petition of Right (1628) to religion in the Grand Remonstrance (1641), and the successful attempts of the House of Commons to sit in judgement on monopolists as infringers of the constitution and destroyers of freedom of trade, demonstrate how wide-ranging was the front on which the struggle was fought. But there was no coherent revolutionary party or programme. The most prominent members of the opposition in the early 1620s, like Sir John Eliot and Sir Thomas Wentworth (later earl of Strafford), believed almost as explicitly in the sovereign rights of monarchy as the king himself. It was the Eleven Years Tyranny (1629–40), a period when no Parliament was summoned, that forced the opposition to consider its attitudes, and that turned the doubters into revolutionaries. When the Long Parliament met in 1640, a majority of the 500 or so members of the Commons had become convinced that what was required was a total dismantling of the apparatus of courtly absolutism. The legislation of 1641 – the Triennial Act, the act against dissolution of Parliament without its own consent, the abolition of the prerogative courts – was truly revolutionary in scope.

Once the process of dismantling had taken place, and the hated symbol of royal policy, Strafford, been executed (in 1641; it was not until much later, in 1645, that Laud went to the scaffold), the unity of the opposition broke apart. The Grand Remonstrance in November 1641 was passed by a bare majority of eleven votes. It was a deliberately aggressive document and it drove even long-standing rebels further towards support for the king. But, for the embattled core, it was the one necessary step of defiance. Had it not been passed, said one of the members present, Oliver Cromwell, 'I would have sold all I possess next morning and never seen England more'. The Remonstrance had been framed as an appeal to the country against the king. But was the country really a protagonist in the revolutionary struggle?

Even when the two parties, Royalists and Parliamentarians, went to war in 1642 there was no serious intention of recruiting the country, that is the mass of the people, to either side. As John Hotham, who served with Parliament in 1642 but joined the king in 1643, said: 'No man that hath any reasonable share in the commonwealth can desire that either side should be conqueror.' His fear was lest 'the necessitous people of the whole kingdom will presently rise in mighty numbers and . . . set up for themselves to the utter ruin of all the nobility and gentry'. The quarrel was essentially one that took place within the ruling class, and it is this that has caused considerable problems of interpretation, for there was no tidy division of interests. There was no exclusively bourgeois revolution against feudalists, nor was there a struggle of the rising gentry for their place in the sun, nor was there a neat religious struggle of Puritans against neo-Papists. All these conflicts did of course occur, but only within a framework that comprised them all. To explain the revolution by analysing the taking of sides has not been a very successful task, if only because men did not always take the side they favoured. We know, for example, that some London merchants supported the king only because they hoped thereby to recover his debts to them; it is also true that property counted for much, and about 100 members of the Commons who had opposed the king up to 1641 fought for him in the war because their estates were in royalist territory.

One division of interests that was clearly marked was that of 'court' against 'country'. Here 'court' refers to the royal system, the private individuals who were part of it, the control of taxation and lucrative sources of income, the monopoly of government offices, titles of rank and commercial privileges. By 'country' we understand those sections of the ruling class, based both in

Parliament and in the provinces and the city of London, who were for various reasons excluded from the workings of the system, and who aimed to seize control of it in order to reform it. Seen in these terms it was a conflict of property and power. Stability depended on the co-operation of the propertied classes in the city and in local government (on the co-operation, that is, of the 'country') with the court. But when property was threatened by arbitrary taxation, by wasteful court expenditure, by unpopular foreign policies, by the granting of monopolies in restraint of free trade: then a split severe enough to lead to civil war could occur in the ruling class.

This does not mean that the tension between 'court' and 'country' was a materialistic one, innocent of ideology. The conflict extended to the Church, to the law, and to other disputed areas. It was the 'court' conspiracy, after all, against which the Puritan gentry, peers and preachers fought in their struggle for a purified Church of England. The Puritans were by and large not separatists: they were dissident brethren, in fact the 'country' party within the established religion. As in the secular sphere, they wished to reform the top-heavy structure of ecclesiastical administration, to devolve authority from bishops to local synods, to reform the tithe system. The question of legal reform was much the same: what was required was decentralization, simplification, economy. In commerce the merchant classes of London were similarly concerned with an end to state interference and state monopolies, and a return to free competition.

Although we have just stressed that the constitutional conflict was primarily conducted by the upper classes, it remains true that the nation as a whole was drawn into the struggle. More than any other country in Europe, England in this decade could be said to have had a revolution that affected not merely the seat of government but nearly every corner of political life in the land. In this sense, as in many others, it was the most important revolution of the seventeenth century. Beginning in the upper strata of society, its effects filtered through to the common people. A pamphleteer of 1642 gave a warning of the populace that 'now they know their strength', and imagined them hatching revolutionary plots against their masters. Few, if any, plots existed; but the fears were reasonable enough. For, once they had set their hands to the wheel, the rebels of 1641 and 1642 were not sure where the tides would take them, and they were reluctant to follow the logic of revolution right through. 'If we beat the King ninety-nine times', said the earl of

Manchester, commander of the parliamentary armies, in 1644, 'yet he is King still.' 'My lord', Cromwell replied, 'if this be so why did we take up arms at first? This is against fighting ever hereafter.' Cromwell was no revolutionary, but he saw the situation through to its necesary conclusion, the execution of Charles I in 1649 and the establishment of a republic in England.

Analysis of the members of the House of Commons, of the royal household, and of other institutions in which sides were taken, shows little or no difference in the social composition of the parties. There were gentry, nobles, merchants and commoners on both sides equally. It would appear that there was little to distinguish the two. As the Latitudinarian bishop Chillingworth was to comment cynically at a later date, 'all the scribes and pharisees were on one side and all the publicans and sinners on the other'. But as soon as we move from Westminster and the court to the countryside, a more significant social pattern emerges. The economically more advanced south-east of England supported Parliament, royal support came from the less developed north and west. The commercial and industrial interests were almost solidly for Parliament: all the ports chose this side, and so did (as we are told by Clarendon in his *History of the Great Rebellion*) 'Leeds, Halifax and Bradford, three very populous and rich towns, depending wholly upon clothiers'. Most important of all, London after 1643 came out for Parliament. The king's support came naturally from traditional interests, from the greater proportion of the nobility and gentry; 'and also', reported Richard Baxter, 'most of the poorest of the people, whom the other call the rabble, did follow the gentry and were for the King'.

What was revolutionary about the English Revolution? It would be wrong to think of its work principally in terms of the first acts of the Long Parliament, and the revolutionary period should really be thought of as extending from November 1640, when the Long Parliament assembled, to December 1653, when the Barebones Parliament was dissolved. Those thirteen years were probably the most astonishing in all English history. In them every conceivable proposal for the reformation of the country was put forward; a few passed into law, most passed into limbo. The most permanent and important part of the revolution consisted in the acts of the Long Parliament in 1641 abolishing conciliar and prerogative government. Ironically, few members thought these measures revolutionary; they were looked upon as a necessary remedy for abuses. The Council of the North, for example, was abolished principally through a clause introduced by the lawyer Sir Edward Hyde (a royalist during the Civil War, created earl of Clarendon at the Restoration).

It had been a simple matter to overthrow the structure of royal government. When it came to reform in matters of religion and property, the revolution dragged its feet. Some of the changes achieved in these fields, such as the abolition of bishops (they were excluded from Parliament in 1642, but not abolished until 1646), were superficial and perfunctory, and easily reversed at the Restoration. None of the religious experiments of these years, forced through by a small number of zealots, made any appreciable impact on the population: England became no more Puritan as a result of Puritan rule. There were important changes in property ownership as a result of penal legislation: crown lands were sold to the value of nearly three and a half million pounds, Church lands were sold to a value of nearly two and a half, and royalists had estates confiscated and sold to a value far exceeding one million pounds. But most royalists appear to have re-purchased their own land through intermediaries, and crown and Church property was returned at the Restoration. There was no social revolution, no passing of wealth from the old nobility to the new gentry. The Civil War delayed reforms. By 1647 the only real power in the country – the army – had impatiently begun to draw up its own plans for reform. In that year, as they lay encamped outside London, the officers drafted a reform document known as the Heads of the Proposals, while the Levellers produced their considerably more advanced programme, the Agreement of the People. These documents and others produced at this time are intrinsically interesting for the advanced and sophisticated political thinking that lay behind them. But the most relevant and significant thing was that it was being felt necessary to demand reforms. When Parliament (in effect, the Commons) prevaricated, the army marched on London and in December 1648 purged the members, leaving only a section of the House, to be known as the Rump.

The rule of the Rump Parliament coincided with that of the republican Commonwealth (1649–53). It also coincided with favourable economic circumstances, so that its members could claim with justice that England had not been so prosperous nor so strong abroad within living memory. But the Rump was little more than an oligarchy, unconcerned with reform and dedicated only to is own self-interest. In August 1652 the council of officers presented it with an ultimatum, asking for a number of listed reforms. The Rump instead drew up plans to make itself a self-perpetuating assembly. When he heard of this, Cromwell in April 1653 marched into the Commons with troops and expelled the members by force. In its place the Barebones Parliament was nominated: over 130 men of proven religion and virtue, not elected but hand-picked by the officers. Long held in derision by writers, this unique assembly, which sat from July to December 1653, was in fact one of the most promising ever to sit in Westminster. It took up again the tasks that its predecessors had neglected. Far-seeing measures were proposed in the committee for law reform; changes were discussed in education, the poor law, taxation and other matters. When it began discussing tithes, however, the men of property both inside and outside Westminster became alarmed. On 12 December troops marched in and cleared the House.

With the dispersal of the Leveller movement in 1649 and the end of republican rule in 1653 (in 1654 the Protectorate came into existence), the active phase of the revolutionary years came to a close. The trend after 1653 was a backwards one: back to stability and order if possible, back certainly to the Restoration of the monarchy.

The Fronde

The crisis conditions of 1647–8 in England also served in France to introduce the Fronde (1648–53), the last great political crisis of the pre-absolutist régime. Although not a nation-wide phenomenon, since most of its activity was in Paris and northern France, the Fronde provoked disorder simply by paralysing the central government and precipitating regional conflicts elsewhere in the country, notably in cities such as Bordeaux and Angers. The civil wars devastated huge areas and caused considerable loss of life. Louis XIV, and with him most Frenchmen, reacted strongly against these years of chaos; in 1668 the king ordered references to the rebellion to be excised from public documents. They were also the years of Vincent de Paul's great charitable missions to the victims of hunger and war.

The Fronde was not an unexpected crisis. Cardinal Richelieu's régime had left political tensions unresolved: as late as 1642 there were court plots against him, and the regular introduction of intendants and the restrictions imposed on the Parlement of Paris

(1641), gave cause for complaint. Cardinal Mazarin was threatened with a noble plot (the *cabale des Importants*, 1643) within a year of taking power. The fact that the realm was under a regency, with Queen Anne of Austria, proved once again the truth of the dictum that a royal minority is a time of political disorder. The régime, moreover, was faced with a war that had already provoked a steep rise in taxation. In January 1648 the tax proposals of Mazarin's finance minister d'Hémery, which included a further creation of senior judicial offices for sale, precipitated protests in Paris. All the higher judicial bodies met in the Chambre Saint-Louis of the Palais de Justice in July 1648 and drew up twenty-seven articles demanding that the new offices be suppressed, that intendants be abolished, that the *taille* be reduced by a quarter. It was a move by the administrators of France (the other parlements gave their support) to protect the monopoly of the officer-class, and to dismantle the system of war finance that Richelieu and Mazarin had created.

In August the arrest of the Parlement leader Broussel brought about a revolutionary day of barricades in Paris. A royalist, Madame de Motteville, commented that 'the Parlement began to claim for itself so exorbitant a power as gave cause to fear that the bad example the jurists saw in the Parliament of England had made some impression on them'. A writer of a 1649 pamphlet claimed that France was not alone in the fight for liberty, and that England, Catalonia and Naples had already shown the way. But at heart the bourgeois Fronde was non-revolutionary, anti-republican and pro-royalist. The execution of Charles I in England in 1649 caused horror everywhere in France and doomed any nascent republican sentiment (though even as late as December 1651 there was a small republican party in Paris). The demands of the rebels were often radical and far-reaching; their attacks on Mazarin were subversive of the existing régime; but their theory in the end tended only to confirm the divine right of absolute monarchy. 'You are, sire', said Omer Talon, advocate-general of the Parlement, in January 1648, 'our sovereign lord; Your Majesty's power comes from on high and is accountable, after God, to none save your conscience.' Unlike the parliamentarians of England, the Paris lawyers entertained no theory of popular sovereignty; they claimed to be supporting royal power against the minister and his régime.

The cause of the office-holders was supported in part by the nobles, who were divided into factions. The higher aristocracy were incomparably the most dangerous: the long and destructive princely Fronde (1650–3) was made possible quite simply by their military capacity. Condé's pretensions to power in the royal council, his hostility to Mazarin, his authority as army commander and later as patron of the Bordeaux rebellion, were crucial elements in the struggle. Eventually, however, the great nobles were undermined by two considerations: their persistent rivalries and inability to agree on the division of gains, and the fact that at no time were they able to offer alternative institutions which might act as an effective temporary government.

The lower nobility identified themselves in part with the aristocracy, but in part also with the office-holders (who were of identical status, as *noblesse de robe*). Though no Estates General met in France after 1614, assemblies of the nobility did occasionally convene (as in 1625 and 1626), and it was at these – sometimes no more than local meetings – that they discussed their complaints. When the government in 1649 decided to summon an Estates General, some of the provincial nobility drew up *cahiers* in which they filed their grievances. The Estates never met, but the impatient nobles held a brief assembly at Paris in 1650 and 1651. The *cahiers* drawn up for the projected Estates by the nobles of Angoumois and Troyes reveal a state of serious discontent. The Angoumois nobles, who tended to concentrate on local issues, complained about taxation, foreign traders, the encroachment of royal judges on their jurisdictions, 'the notable prejudice suffered by the nobles from venality of offices . . . to which access is almost impossible because of their excessive cost', the *Paulette*, and the pretensions of the *noblesse de robe*.

All parties in the Fronde wanted peace abroad (Condé, and Bordeaux, went so far as to ally with Spain) and a change of government at home; they all agreed, however, on total loyalty to the crown. This conservatism was fatal to rebellion. Because the crown alone could guarantee the social ascendancy of the *noblesse de robe* office-holders, these, after their initial protest, very quickly adhered to the royal cause, opposing Mazarin at one stage and then Condé. The language of much of the protest at this period thus needs to be approached with caution. 'We are kings (*nos sumus reges*)', the Parlement of Aix had said in 1645; but it then went on to explain that this was because 'we represent the king (*vicem regis gerimus*)'. The lawyer class in France remained wedded to the institutions that gave it wealth and status, of which the foremost was the monarchy itself.

The feudal nobility, on the other hand, was being slowly deprived of any institutional basis; though it retained wealth and status, which it drew less from institutions than from land and regional influence, it quickly lost political power to the rising absolutist state.

Although the Fronde was a major political crisis, its positive achievement was insignificant. It solved no problems, gave birth to no reforms, altered nothing in the structure of the old régime. The history of the intendants is significant in this respect. They were suppressed by the government in 1648 on the request of the Parlement, and an undertaking was given not to reintroduce them. Despite this, the frontier military intendants were allowed to continue, and Mazarin brought the other intendants back surreptitiously under the name of *commissaires*; after his victory in 1653 they were openly reintroduced under their old name.

The Spanish peninsula

Spain in 1640 gave the appearance of unity: since 1580 Portugal had been under the Spanish crown and all the realms of the peninsula were one. When Olivares became chief minister of Philip IV at the latter's accession in 1621, there was a little danger of any internal constitutional challenge to royal authority. There was no effective parliament, the office-holding class was quiescent. But two tragic paradoxes lay behind this picture. Peninsula Spain was in fact totally disunited, for the king was absolute ruler only over Castile; and the greatest weakness of the powerful monarchy lay in what appeared to be its strength – the overseas empire. On both counts the government at Madrid was seriously inconvenienced. Within the peninsula the king's writ ran only over the territories of the crown of Castile. If he wished to act in Catalonia, Aragon or Valencia he had first to consult the Estates of those realms. These realms were not only constitutionally autonomous, they also (as a memorandum presented to Philip III in 1618 pointed out) 'contribute nothing to Your Majesty's expenses beyond their own frontiers, and money even has to be sent to them from Castile to pay their garrisons'. Some sort of income was regularly available from the overseas territories, particularly America, to pay for the rising expenses of the crown. But bullion from America was invariably diverted directly to the Netherlands and Milan to pay for military costs, and income from other territories (such as Naples) was likely to cause growing resentment on the part of those who had to pay the taxes. The ultimate result was that Castile and America became almost the sole contributors to Spain's war bill. By the early seventeenth century an influential group of royal advisers, among them Olivares, had come to the conclusion that the other member states of the monarchy should pay their fair share of the costs. 'It is quite unreasonable', the *arbitrista* Fernández de Navarrete wrote in 1626, 'that the head should be weakened while the other members, which are very rich and populous, should simply stand by and look on while it has to bear all these heavy charges.'

In fiscal terms, Spain was weak internally because Castile alone contributed satisfactorily to finances; it was weak externally because it had actually to spend money on supporting its far-flung empire. The difficulties were multiplied when it came to problems of government and military recruitment, since in both these matters the non-Castilian provinces enjoyed great autonomy. The political crisis precipitated by Olivares originated in an attempt by Castile to assert its control in real terms. As Olivares put it in his famous secret memorandum of 1624:

The most important thing in Your Majesty's Monarchy is for you to become King of Spain. By this I mean, Sir, that Your Majesty should not be content with being king of Portugal, of Aragon, of Valencia and count of Barcelona, but should secretly plan and work to reduce these kingdoms of which Spain is composed to the style and laws of Castile, with no difference whatsoever. And if Your Majesty achieves this, you will be the most powerful prince in the world.

The events of 1640 in the peninsula – the Catalan rebellion in the spring and the Portuguese revolt in December – were reflections of an essentially Castilian crisis. Castile's inability to govern a peninsula province; its incapability of paying for the troops billeted there; the failure to raise troops in Catalonia; the refusal of the Castilian nobility to render military service; Olivares's own failure to rally support for his policies in the Castilian ruling class; the plot of the duke of Medina Sidonia in 1641 to set up an independent Andalucia: all these were symptoms of crumbling authority. Set in the context of a decaying Atlantic trade, mounting inflation at home and military expenditure unattended by success abroad, the events of 1640 mark a turning point in Castile's status as a world power. Olivares fell from power in January 1643, but the decline could not be arrested. The defeat of the Spanish infantry at Rocroi in May 1643 confirmed the diminishing returns from Spain's intervention in

Germany. In 1647 the government again declared itself bankrupt. In 1647 Naples revolted against the crown. In 1648 a plot to make Aragon independent under the duke of Hijar was discovered. In October that year the Treaty of Münster gave the United Provinces their independence from Spain.

These harrowing years exposed Spain's weaknesses as an imperial power. A poor country with a small population and few resources, Spain had managed to maintain the Habsburg inheritance by making enormous efforts, but the collapse of empire could not fail to raise doubts and questioning. The emergence of localism in the provinces – in 1630 in the Basque country, in 1640 in Catalonia and Portugal, in 1641 in Andalucia, and 1648 in Aragon – reflected the disillusion of local élites that saw little to gain from an association with Castile. Within those provinces, however, popular movements were also dissatisfied with the élites. After the murder of the viceroy in Barcelona on Corpus Christi day 1640, agitators turned their protest against the nobles and gentry; in Manresa in September they turned against certain rich and powerful citizens, calling them traitors, and said that they would burn down their houses. The popular protest in Andalucia was delayed until 1648 and later (see Chapter 10). Meanwhile, commentators began to criticize the régime in Madrid, and *arbitristas* continued to insist on sweeping changes in government and in the fiscal structure. The ravages of the plague epidemic of 1647–52, which cost half a million lives, completed the spectre of dissolution.

Conflict in northern Europe

In their separate ways the United Provinces and Sweden were thrown into a period of crisis by the coming of a general European peace in 1648. In the Dutch Republic the old split between the republican Hollanders and the House of Orange came to the fore again. Viewed as a struggle between the burgher oligarchy and the Orangeist court, or between a peace party and a war party, it had led in 1619 to the victory of the Orangeists and the execution of the revered republican leader Oldenbarnevelt. The alignment of parties remained the same on the conclusion of peace in 1648. Immediately after the Treaty of Münster the province of Holland, led by the Amsterdam patriciate, urged a policy of commercial expansion and of peace with England. The first step towards this would have been the disbandment of the large number of troops under their commander-in-chief, William II, and a reduction in military subsidies. Peace with England was not merely a question of trade: the exiled Charles Stuart, brother-in-law of William, was living at The Hague, and a royalist Orange–Stuart alliance was objectionable in every way to Holland's interests. As the chief financial contributor to the Union, Holland seemed about to get its way. The military and William II thereupon decided to force the issue.

William's position was extremely powerful. He was *stadhouder* of six of the seven provinces in the Union (the seventh, Friesland, was governed by his cousin William Frederick), and therefore commanded the support of a majority in the States-General; he had an army of veteran soldiers under him, and all the Dutch fortresses were in the hands of his relatives and followers; the people and preachers supported him wholeheartedly everywhere except in Amsterdam. Although the disbandment of troops was the ostensible issue in dispute, what was obviously involved was control of the Republic. Holland openly kept up diplomatic relations with the regicide Commonwealth in England, and unilaterally began to disband those troops paid by its exchequer: both actions were interpreted as provocations. After failing to make any headway during a visit to the chief towns of Holland, William at the end of July 1650 took direct steps to achieve his ends.

On 30 July, at eight o'clock in the morning, six leading deputies of the States of Holland were arrested in The Hague on William's orders. At the same time an army under William Frederick was sent to seize Amsterdam. The siege failed, but the terms on which the city eventually opened its gates were clearly favourable to the Prince of Orange. Though William had not succeeded fully (Holland still blocked in the States-General a plan by him to help France in the war against Spain), he had been granted extraordinary powers and was poised to assume a dominant role in the Republic. At this juncture, on 6 November 1650, he suddenly died.

His untimely death had momentous consequences: a son and heir, later William III, was born a month afterwards. But the rule of the House of Orange had been decisively cut short, and a whole epoch in Dutch history, that of the rise and consolidation of the Republic, came to an end. The balance of power swung back immediately to the regent class of Holland, whose leadership under the de Witts was to determine the course of Dutch history for the next two decades.

In order to bypass the Orangeist-inspired States-General, the Hollanders invited all members of the Union to send fresh delegates to a 'Great Assembly' that met in The Hague from January to August 1651. At this meeting the differences of the past were erased, the leading role of the Prince of Orange was eliminated (William III was not appointed as *stadhouder* of Holland, the supreme posts of captain-general and admiral-general were suspended), and Holland seized the initiative in foreign policy.

William II's death interrupted the seemingly irresistible drift of the United Provinces towards absolutist rule. By this historical accident a bourgeois republic was brought into existence and those bourgeois virtues that Sir William Temple was to praise so highly became the norm of life in the state. Even the noble class vied to have their children marry into the regent families.

The Swedish crisis was comparable in some ways. It, too, was a consequence of the war and the peace; as in the United Provinces, 1650 was a temporary stage and absolutism was not confirmed until well over twenty years thereafter.

By the 1630s Sweden had found its war policy increasingly expensive to finance. Under Gustav Adolf it had been possible to live off subsidies, port-tolls and the countryside. After 1635 some ports ceased to pay tolls, the French were having to finance their own intervention in the war, and campaigns in Germany met greater resistance. It was in this period of the Regency that sales of royal land were multiplied, as an emergency measure. 'We were impelled to use these very necessary means to save the fatherland from danger', a royal official stated in 1638. When Christina (1644–54) came to the throne, such sales were an established expedient for raising money. From about 1648 she indulged in extensive sales not only for fiscal purposes but also in order to gratify favoured individuals. The results were unprecedented. By the end of her reign nearly two-thirds of royal land had passed out of the hands of the crown. The area of noble land in Sweden more than doubled between 1611 (when sales had first commenced) and 1652. Since crown revenue relied a great deal on income from its estates, a financial crisis came into being. Royal revenue dropped from 6.36 million silver dollars in 1644 to 3.79 at the end of Christina's reign.

The balance between social classes was seriously disturbed. The free peasantry on the former crown lands found that they had been transferred to aristocratic control, with a consequent depression in their status. Their grievances remained muted until the harvest failure of 1649–50, the worst in the century; then economic despair made them combine with the clergy and burgher estates to protest to the queen in the Diet of 1650. From the grievances of the people, Christina was told,

you will see into what an unheard-of state of servitude they have declined since private persons took hold of the country; for some treat their peasants ill, either by raising their dues, or by imposing intolerable burdens of day-work upon them, or by imprisonment, or threats, or evictions; until the poor peasant is totally ruined.

The parliamentary opposition occurred against a background of risings elsewhere in Europe and of threats of disaffection within the country. The Swedish peasants had important political privileges – notably their own Estate in the Diet – that they felt to be threatened. But their discontent was directed not so much at the crown as against the power which the nobility were now accumulating. The immediate cure demanded at the Diet of 1650, one calculated to restore revenue to the crown and to diminish the growth of aristocratic power, was the resumption of all alienated lands. This call for a *Reduktion* was skilfully exploited by Christina to enable her to win her main objective, the confirmation of her cousin Charles as hereditary heir to the throne. Having gained that, she dropped her allies in the lower Estates of the Diet, refused a *Reduktion*, and remained even more firmly in power. The parliamentary opposition had served only to strengthen the crown.

The threat of revolt in 1650 was not directed against the crown, despite the open wastefulness of Christina's court. Nor did the division of parties represent a class struggle: when the resumption of crown lands was eventually begun by Charles X in 1655 part of his support came from the lower nobility. As in the Fronde, the programme of the non-noble opposition called for serious reforms in the structure of power, but no serious attempt was made to touch the royal prerogatives for, as the supplication of the three lower Estates in the Diet of 1650 put it, 'we esteem Your Majesty's royal power as the buttress of our liberties, the one being bound up in the other, and both standing or falling together'.

Revolution in eastern Europe

In the mid sixteenth century the Cossacks in the region of the lower Dniepr obtained from the Polish king permission to settle in the country 'beyond the rapids' (*za porogi*) of the river. From this period the Zaporozhian Cossacks established themselves as a powerful nomadic military community. In time they laid claim to being a nation. The struggle of the Ukrainian Cossacks for their independence from Polish tutelage was of primary importance in east European history. In military terms the Cossacks were a powerful auxiliary of the Polish crown (Cossack regiments were specially recruited by King Stephen Báthory), and were invaluable as a frontier force against the Tatars and Turks. In political terms they were a rising force that held the balance in the east between a decaying Poland and an emergent Muscovy; every revolt against Poland brought closer the day of Muscovite dominance. In religious terms they were the ultimate frontier of Catholicism, in an area where defence of the Orthodox faith (the Cossacks were overwhelmingly Orthodox) was a burning issue. In social terms, they were the protectors of the peasantry, who rallied to them in times of distress: every major peasant revolt in Polish lands took place only with the armed support of the Cossack leaders, as in 1590 with Kosínsky and 1596 with Nalivaiko.

Every move of the Ukrainian Cossacks was likely to have profound repercussions in eastern Europe. The Polish government, which relied constantly on them for help against the Turks, made several efforts to crush the monster it had conjured up, and in 1597, after Nalivaiko's rising, the Sejm actually branded the Cossacks as *hostes patriae* and called for their extermination. But the unusual Cossack way of life – they lived as nomads, and their military action took the form of banditry and piracy – made it almost impossible to subdue them. In 1645 the Poles once again called on the Cossacks to join them in a campaign against the Tatars. Among the Cossack commanders in 1646 was Bohdan Khmelnitsky. A lesser noble with extensive military experience in Russia and in Flanders, Khmelnitsky at the end of the Tatar campaign turned against his masters and gathered a small force of dissident Cossacks around him. In April 1648 he was acclaimed as Hetman of the Zaporozhians. After a great victory over royalist forces in May (Khmelnitsky was helped by the Crimean Tatars), revolt spread through the Ukraine. The spur to revolt was the Cossack cavalry, but the real source of disaffection was the protest of the peasantry against their Polish landlords. The entire feudal structure of the Polish frontier lands was being uprooted. The peasant fury (*khlopskaya zloba*) was direct at three main enemies: the landlords, the Catholic clergy and the Jews. These were annihilated with a ferocity exceeded only by that used by some royalist leaders, such as the Volhynia nobleman Jerome Wiśnowiecki, against the peasantry.

Khmelnitsky's successes in battle opened both White Russia and Lithuania to him: his marches took him through Lwow and towards the Vistula. By October 1648 he was accepted in Kiev as 'the father and liberator of the country'. All these gains were accepted by the helpless Polish authorities, but the negotiation of agreed terms was more difficult to achieve. As the Poles delayed and spent the spring of 1649 collecting troops, Khmelnitsky was forced to look for external support. In 1649 only the Tatars would help him. Khmelnitsky was therefore obliged to accept an agreement which gave him the provinces of Kiev, Chernigov and Bratslav, but returned three others to Polish hands. No rights were guaranteed to the peasantry. Subsequent military reverses threatened even these gains. By 1653 Khmelnitsky's position was desperate. At this stage, after numerous embassies from the Hetman, the Muscovite tsar Alexei Mikhailovich announced that he had agreed to help the Zaporozhians. In January 1654 the Agreement of Pereyaslavl united the Ukraine to Great Russia.

Russia's intervention in the Ukraine and in Polish affairs arose out of a position of strength. The moment of crisis had come, as in France and the Ukraine, in 1648. The urban revolutions of that year (discussed below in Chapter 10) led directly to a conservative reaction in the form of the Law Code of 1649. Representative government also suffered the reaction. The Zemsky Sobor of 1653, which approved of the incorporation of the Ukraine into Russia, was the last to meet. Autocratic Russia was poised for expansion.

Politics and the crisis

War and taxation were the two direct precipitants of political crisis. In England it was the need for taxes to finance the war against the Scots that forced Charles I to summon Parliament after a lapse of eleven years. In France it was Richelieu's heavy programme of war taxation that undermined the régime he had set out to strengthen, and Mazarin may have been saved from disaster partly because the Thirty Years War ended in precisely the year that the first Fronde commenced. In Spain the war with France enabled Portugal and Catalonia to break free, and Olivares was not the last minister to be disgraced because of his inability to solve the fiscal problems of the world's biggest imperial power. In Naples it was the excessive tax demands of Spain for the war effort that alienated the propertied classes and drove them to rebellion. In Holland the vital question of control over the military precipitated the coup of 1650. In Sweden all major internal disputes were a backwash of the problems raised by Sweden's intervention in the wars of Germany. In the Slav lands war was the very determinant of politics, and through it the duchy of the Ukraine was born.

War and taxation were, however, little more than the issues over which the broader conflict was waged. For each social class, the crisis posed problems of adaptation and survival: for the first time the common people found a voice (see the discussion of propaganda, above p. 212) and attempted to reason their way into government, their aspirations being nowhere so nobly expressed as in Rainborowe's claim in 1647 that 'the poorest he that is in England hath a right to live as the greatest he'. Inevitably, however, the struggle focused more on the problems of the noble élite. In the face of the anti-aristocratic mood of the English Revolution, Lord Willoughby observed bitterly in 1645, 'I thought it a crime to be a nobleman'. During the siege of royalist Oxford in the Civil War a hungry sentry on watch cried down to the parliamentarians: 'Roundhead, fling me up half a mutton and I will fling thee down a Lord'. In Catalonia in 1640 the native nobility were terrorized by the popular insurgents and accused of being traitors to their country; 'and', reported a correspondent from Barcelona, 'they can expect no help from their vassals, who are so tired of them that they will put up with them no longer'. In the Paris of 1649 leaflets began to ask whether the people should any longer tolerate the nobles.

The principal threat to the élite came not from popular agitation but from crown policy. Active reliance on a vigorous minister (Strafford, Mazarin, Olivares) took political initiative away from the governing class. Laud's policy in the Court of Wards caused, according to Clarendon, 'all the rich families of England, of noblemen and gentlemen, [to be] exceedingly incensed and even indevoted to the crown'. Queen Christina of Sweden threatened the security of her nobility by opening their ranks to newcomers and selling off royal land to them. By mid century it seemed that strong monarchy was working against aristocracy. The French princes of the blood consequently combined against absolutism, and even accepted a temporary alliance with popular forces (as in Bordeaux). In England the Lords allied with the Commons to remove Strafford.

The defection of the Lords from the crown led inevitably to war. As the political theorist James Harrington was to observe, 'a monarchy divested of its nobility has no refuge under heaven but an army. Wherefore the dissolution of this government caused the war, not the war the dissolution of this government'.

In every European state that suffered upheaval the confrontation between the monarchy and the ruling class was played out before the representative bodies: social conflict became expressed in constitutional terminology. In England, for example, the Commons' Protestation of 1621 stated that 'the liberties, franchises, privileges and jurisdictions of Parliament are the ancient and undoubted birthright and inheritance of the subjects of England; . . . the arduous and urgent affairs concerning the king, state and defence of the realm and of the Church of England, and the maintenance and making of laws, redress of mischiefs and grievances . . . are proper subjects and matter of comment and debate in Parliament'. Reforming ministers felt strongly that such pleas for constitutionalism were a cover for the vested interests of élites, and refused to be swayed by them. Writing to the viceroy of Catalonia in 1640 when a new meeting of the Cortes was being planned, Olivares directed that 'nothing is to be discussed in them except the reform of government: we will have none of that usual business of prayers and petitions'. Mazarin rejected the pretensions of the Parlement of Paris to verify legislation, and made use of the *lit de justice*, a procedure whereby the king's presence in Parlement secured the passage of measures. The cardinal's attempt to call an Estates General in 1649 floundered, for it was clear that Mazarin merely wished to play off the upper Estates against the Third Estate. In practice, rulers assented to a popular assembly only when it served their ends. The Zemsky Sobor of 1648–9 was compliant, the Neapolitan parliament of 1642 was not; the former was given a brief lease of life, the latter was dissolved and did not meet again. In Sweden the struggle was carried out principally at the Diet of 1650.

For a few countries, internal difficulties of government, war taxation and social conflict were aggravated by the arrival of peace in 1648. The great treaties of that year, known collectively as the Peace of Westphalia, involved the shifting of frontiers, withdrawal of armed forces, pensioning-off of mercenary troops, readjustment of financial commitments, and the barter of a variety of political and territorial privileges. For many parts of Germany, particularly the Rhineland, it meant an end to thirty years – a whole lifetime – of war. For the Dutch the war had lasted even longer: a full eighty years of struggle for independence. In these circumstances the outbreak of peace could only have been unsettling. In the Swedish Estates in 1635 the bishop of Västerås had expressed fears of what wartime measures might bring, 'of what befell the Roman Republic, how the constitution was overthrown by the keeping up of great armies, which led to internal dissension, and broke out in dangerous seditions'. But peace brought the greater threat of a monarchy strengthened by habitual obedience in time of war, and this alone made possible the extravagances of Christina's rule. It was the outbreak of peace, likewise, that precipitated the constitutional crisis in the Dutch Republic and William II's attempted coup d'état; peace that released the French generals to participate in the struggles of the Fronde; peace that brought depression and unrest to the Swiss cantons. Whatever the social and economic causes may have been, it is clear that for some governments the general crisis was provoked by the general peace.

The revolutions of the 1640s were even in their own day looked upon as related events. 'These days are days of shaking, and this shaking is universal', a preacher announced to the House of Commons in 1643. 'Where previously ills came separately, now they have come all together', observed the author of *Le Siècle de Fer* (1648). It was logical that politics should be internationally connected: the revolts of Catalonia and Portugal owed their success to the French army, the revolt of Naples threatened the authority of Madrid, the Fronde in Bordeaux tempted Cromwell to spread the ideas of the English Revolution. All the revolts, moreover, owed something to the general conjuncture of factors outlined at the start of this chapter. The 'general' aspects of the crisis seem to attain even more cohesion if the revolutions, and related developments, are viewed in extremely broad terms as disputes over the source of 'authority'. This apparent universality in the events of 1640–50 must, nevertheless, be set beside the difficulty in formulating a detailed analysis that suits all the revolutions. England and Spain in 1640, Moscow and Paris in 1648, Amsterdam and Stockholm in 1650, shared little in common except the date. The social and constitutional context in each nation was likewise distinct; and, even more obviously, each produced a different outcome.

When the crisis had come and passed, all the revolutions proved to be stillborn. They were great attempts at change but none of them, not even the English one, proved itself able to surmount the crisis. The way lay open instead to unchallenged conservatism. The Iron Age made way for an age of aristocracy.

10   Popular rebellions

Steere said that it would only be a month's work to overrun the realm [England]; and that the poor once rose in Spain and cut down the gentry, since when they had lived merrily.

Testimony against Batholomew Steere, carpenter (1597)

Revolt in early modern Europe was an expression of discontent involving all levels of society. Though 'peasant' revolts were the best-known form of protest, generically there were few purely 'peasant' or rural revolts, since town and country were interconnected. Townsmen took an active part in rural protest and agricultural labourers were a potent force for discontent in the towns. Those who helped to gather in the harvest in the fields in July were pacing the streets of the city in December: the proletariat of seasonal labourers belonged equally to both town and country and unified social movements in both. Popular rebellion was not, for all that, limited to the popular classes. At a local level, discontent was a symptom of stresses and strains in the fabric of traditional social relationships; at a national level, it reflected the conflicting aspirations of status groups. At both levels, the motive and ideology for revolt did not necessarily originate among the popular classes, who were often the led rather than the leaders.

Revolts of the early sixteenth century

The late fifteenth century set an ample precedent for the social discontent of the early sixteenth. In Spain the famous incident at Fuenteovejuna (Andalucia) in 1476, when an entire village claimed joint responsibility for the murder of its lord, emphasized the tradition of communal revolt that continued into the Catalan and Castilian civil wars and was ended only with the accession of Ferdinand and Isabella. In Germany there were millennial movements such as that of the piper of Niklashausen (1476) and the Bundschuh (or 'peasant boot') rebellions (from 1493, mainly in the Black Forest). In England there was an important rising in Cornwall in 1497.

The first big revolt of the century was that of the Hungarian peasants in 1514. Responding to a crusade against the Turk declared by the archbishop of Esztergom in April, peasants abandoned their lords' estates and flocked to join the royal flag; by May they formed an army of 40,000. Wearing the cross of the crusade on their chests, they soon became transformed into an army of revolt, led by a soldier who was termed 'supreme captain of the blessed army of crusaders subject not to the nobles but to the king alone'. Franciscan clergy were prominent sympathizers of the rebels, whose army however was shattered in July by the forces of the governor of Transylvania, John Zapoloya. In the same year the 'Poor Conrad' revolt, a protest of the rural population against taxes, broke out in Württemberg.

In spring 1520, as Charles V was leaving Spain for Germany, the revolt of the Comunidades ('communities') broke out in Spain. Led by the major cities of northern Castile (and without any echo in the cities of the crown of Aragon), the revolt was a complex blend of political, economic and nationalist grievances, involving all social classes and, therefore, also including a strong element of popular rebellion. Both townspeople and peasantry rallied to the movement. 'When my villages rose', commented the constable of Castile, whose lands were around Burgos, 'I could not find a single reliable man throughout my lands.' Though the Comuneros were led by gentry and men of property, a strong radical wing emerged. In 1521 Valladolid, the most radical of the cities, urged peasants to defend 'your liberty and be treated like men not like slaves'. There were uprisings against seigneurial dues. In a village near Palencia the priest promised that 'by the end of this month there will be no more nobles'. Incipient radicalism split the Comuneros and frightened the great nobles. These brought in their troops to help crush the main rebel force under Juan de Padilla at Villalar in April 1521. Charles V returned to Spain in 1522, when he signed a general pardon (twenty-two rebels had by then been executed). Meanwhile, parallel rebellions (of the *Germanías*, 'brotherhoods') had broken out in Valencia and Mallorca. These were firmly dealt with, and peace was restored in Valencia by about 1522, in Mallorca by 1523.

The classic popular revolt of the early century was that of the 'German peasants' (1525). Confined neither to Germany nor to the peasants, it was in reality a vast unintegrated wave of protest that swept over the whole of central Europe and in some areas was primarily urban. The events have been described in terms of a 'war' or even a 'revolution'. Their long-term cause must be sought in the slow encroachment of seigneurs on the peasant economy: anxious to maintain their income levels, lords enforced and extended their fiscal and jurisdictional privileges. In so doing, they came into conflict with the strong village communities, whose leaders helped to co-ordinate resistance. The first resort to arms was in June 1524 in Stühlingen (Swabia). By the autumn there were risings all round lake Constance and towards the Black Forest. The core of risings in south and central Germany (February to May 1525) extended into Upper Swabia then spread along the Danube down to Bavaria and the Alps. From April there were risings by peasants, miners and townspeople in Württemberg, northern Switzerland, Alsace, Thuringia and the Rhineland down to Mainz, the Palatinate and Franche Comté. By summer the revolts had spread to Saxony, Salzburg, Styria and Austria, then into French-speaking Lorraine and Burgundy. In the Rhineland the movement was largely urban, with a notable city revolt in Frankfurt.

Each wave of revolt was distinct in time, motivation, leadership and duration. The heart of the revolution was in Upper Swabia, where the original Twelve Articles of the peasants were drawn up at Memmingen in March 1525 by Sebastian Lotzer, and where the rebels had three armies. In Thuringia the centre was the city of Mühlhausen, where the radical Thomas Müntzer was active; this phase ended in defeat at the battle of Frankenhausen (May), when Müntzer was captured and executed. In the upper Rhineland and in Alsace revolt spread rapidly, but again was broken by a crushing military defeat at Saverne (May). In the Tyrol the rebels were led by Michael Gaismair, who early in 1526 drew up a radical 'Tyrolean Constitution' calling for a communistic type of régime.

This astonishing series of uprisings was led for the most part not by peasants but by artisans, preachers, lesser nobles and bourgeois. Village communities which would in normal times refuse to co-operate with other villages, now combined together in a common cause. All groups found a common ideology, a universal legitimation, less in their social grievances than in the appeal to 'God's law'. It was a concept that Luther had pioneered, and many rebels looked to him for support, but he fiercely denounced the uprising. The Twelve Articles combined social and religious demands. 'Henceforth', says the first, 'we ought to have the authority for the whole community to appoint its own pastor.' 'Christ redeemed and bought us all with his precious blood, the lowliest as well as the greatest', says the third, 'thus the Bible proves that we are free and want to be free.' Articles four and five reiterate the claims of the 'whole community' over rights in fishing and hunting. The most persistent demand of the Articles and of the twenty-five other different versions which appeared within two months in other regions, was that serfdom be abolished.

Given the complexity of the revolt, it was not everywhere a failure. In some areas, such as Upper Swabia, peasants obtained written agreements modifying labour services. In the Tyrol some tithes were removed and labour services reduced. In Hesse the landgrave Philip made important concessions.

Of the urban revolts of this time the Grande Rebeyne at Lyon (April 1529) originated as a food riot. A crowd of 2000 rallied outside a church under the leadership of a swordsman and a baker, and went on to attack the houses of the rich bourgeois. A product of urban tensions, the riot also had hints of heresy (some church images were broken); but its lasting consequence was a profound fear of the poorer classes, and the establishment of the famous Aumône Générale whose purpose was 'to nourish the poor forever' and thus avoid any repetition of social violence. The great urban revolt at Ghent (1540) was fiscal and in defence of traditional privileges: Charles V marched overland from Spain with an army and suppressed it ruthlessly.

In England the Pilgrimage of Grace (1536) began in October in Lincolnshire with a protest against taxation and the dissolution of the monasteries. The discontent spread to Yorkshire, where local economic grievances combined with hostility to Henry VIII's church policy, and drew in the gentry, including a peer, Lord Darcy, and a lawyer, Robert Aske. Though social protest remained strong within the movement the Pilgrimage quickly became a traditionalist pro-Catholic rising. The regionalist element, as in all other European rebellions of the time, was fundamental.

In 1548 the first of a series of major uprisings broke out in Aquitaine in protest against introduction of a salt tax (*gabelle*), which these salt-producing regions had till then escaped paying. Rural areas set themselves up into communes, as at Saintonge and

Angoumois, and the revolt (of the 'Pitauts') spread into the city of Bordeaux, which was taken over by the rebels. So extensive was the uprising that a royal army was sent to suppress it (October), but the demands of the province were met and Aquitaine in 1549 was freed 'forever' from the *gabelle* (which, in fact, was introduced without incident during the seventeenth century). Anxiety for regional privileges encouraged rebels to hark back to the myth of a medieval age of freedom 'in the time of the English'; 'Guyenne, Guyenne', cried the rioters in the streets of Bordeaux.

Regionalism appeared again in England, where there were two major revolts in the bad harvest year 1549. The rising that summer in the West Country was, judging by the 'Articles of the Rebels', primarily religious: 'we will have the mass in Latin. . . . The new service is but like a Christmas game. . . . We Cornishmen, whereof certain of us understand no English, utterly refuse the new English'. In Norfolk and Suffolk the only overtly social and Protestant revolt of the century took place. Conflict between tenants and landlords, and a poor harvest, combined to spark off a rebellion led by Robert Ket, a middling tradesman who organized the peasants into a fighting force. In the summer of 1549 the rebels based themselves in Norwich, but on 27 August they were cut to pieces by the superior forces of the earl of Warwick.

Rebellions of the late sixteenth century

The Reformation had promised liberty, and for many harassed villagers this should have included liberty from having to pay tithes to the Catholic Church. In France, however, when it became clear that encouragement not to pay meant encouragement to social revolution, the Huguenot nobility meeting at Nîmes in 1562 passed a resolution condemning any refusal to pay dues, and urging the punishment of all who refused as 'sowers of sedition, disturbers of public order'. But so long as Protestant ideas played a part among the European peasantry, refusal to pay tithes would continue. By 1560 in Languedoc, even Catholic peasants had been drawn into opposition. In the uprising at Agen in 1560–1 the peasants 'are beginning in some places not to pay their tithes, and proclaim that they will no longer pay the *tailles* or their seigneurial dues'.

Opposition to tithes occurred also in the churches of the Reformation, both Lutheran and Anglican. In Sweden the Lutheran clergy of Stavanger complained in 1573 of 'the great hostility and disloyalty shown by the peasants every year over the tithe'. They claimed that if they demanded tithes in their sermons 'they were threatened by many and did not feel safe'. From 1570 to 1580 there were risings in Trondheim province, and from 1573 an organized rebellion led by Rolv de Lynge was in progress. In 1574 the peasants held their own national assembly in Nidaros; though Lynge and other leaders were executed in 1575 the rebellion went on for several years after.

Hungary had several rebellions, in 1562, in 1569–70, and in 1571–3 (in Slovenia). One of the largest risings to occur on this eastern frontier of Christendom was that of the Croat peasantry in 1573. The grievances of the Croats centred on labour services and tithes. An imperial decree of 1538 had virtually deprived them of freedom of movement; at the same time their dues were made more heavy. But their principal complaint was against the taxation levied to support the war against the Turks, particularly the *dica*, a war-tax that was levied on the peasants twenty times between 1543 and 1598. In April 1572 a local revolt broke out and a deputation went to Vienna to present grievances; when nothing came of this a country-wide uprising broke out in 1573. At its height it involved up to 60,000 peasants. The basic demand formulated by the peasants was for the return of their 'ancient rights'. But over and above this simple phrase their demands were revolutionary: the abolition of the ecclesiastical tithe, and reduction of seigneurial taxation. The democratic temper of the rebels is shown by their habitual use of the term 'brotherhood' to describe themselves, and of the word 'brother' as a form of address within the organization. By mid February 1573 the brief uprising had been crushed. The Emperor Maximilian, who directed its suppression, estimated that about 4000 Croat and Slovene peasants had been annihilated by his troops. The leaders, Matthew Gubec and Andrew Pasanec, were tortured and then executed in Zagreb in February.

The mid 1580s were a time of bad harvests, particularly the three years 1585–7. They were years of political crisis throughout western Europe, accompanied by wars in France and the Netherlands. Some of the more savage undertones of popular rebellion came to the fore in these years of blood. In the town of Romans, in Dauphiné, in the winter of 1580 a rebellious alliance was formed between the peasants of the countryside (this was a Protestant area) and the artisans of the town, led by a certain Jean Serve or Paulmier. The economic difficulties of the time aggravated discontent. Encouraged by support from the townsmen, the peasants refused to pay their tithes and *tailles*. They armed themselves, broke into châteaux, and threw the *terriers* (court rolls) into the flames. In Romans the artisans and peasants danced in the streets, threatening the rich and crying that 'before three days Christian flesh will be sold at sixpence a pound'. This symbolic language was directed at the upper classes of the town, which was now taken over by a popular commune. During the winter carnival Paulmier sat in the mayor's chair, dressed in a bear's skin, eating delicacies that passed for Christian flesh. When they had their carnival procession, the common people under Paulmier dressed themselves up as prelates and dignitaries, crying 'Christian flesh for sixpence!'. Horrified by this cannibalistic disrespect, the richer classes organized their own resources. On the eve of *mardi gras* (Shrove Tuesday, 15 February 1580) they descended on their opponents and massacred them. The slaughter went on for three days. Peasants from the countryside thronged in to save the cause, but it was too late. The resort to the savage symbols of cannibalism signals an interesting development in the morphology of social revolt. The eating of human flesh, here as in other popular revolts, stood for the revolutionary overturning of social values.

In 1585 in Naples a similar but more explicit event occurred. As in Romans, there was a popular uprising, with its heart in the town rather than in the country. The immediate cause of the 1585 rising was a bad harvest and severe shortage of food. Despite famine conditions the authorities raised the price of bread and authorized the export of flour. An angry mob, in May, thereupon lynched one of the magistrates responsible, named Starace. His body was mutilated (pieces of his flesh were offered for sale) and dragged through the streets, while his house and all his belongings were burnt and destroyed. Nothing was stolen: the proceedings were carried out like a ritual sacrifice. A big urban revolt followed, to cries of '*mora il malgoverno, e viva la giustizia*'. In the inevitably brutal repression that took place, over 800 people were brought to trial between the middle and end of July. In the same epoch, the city of Paris experienced an uprising provoked by the politics of the religious wars. On 12 May 1588, the 'day of barricades', a general rising of the population in favour of the duke of Guise took place. When the duke and the cardinal of Guise were assassinated on the king's orders, authority in the anarchic city devolved on to a commune led by a so-called Council of Sixteen.

The conditions of the 1590s were catastrophic: from 1590 to 1597 harvests were bad, prices crippling. There was famine in 1595 in parts of England, Languedoc, and Naples. Prices in Rome in 1590–9 were double those for 1570–9. The crisis touched England, France, Austria, Finland, Hungary, Lithuania and the Ukraine: possibly never before had the timing of so many popular rebellions coincided with each other. In Finland a peasant revolt occurred in 1596–7. A few English labourers in the Midlands attempted a rising in 1596, but it came to nothing. Roger Ibill, a miller of Hampton-Gay, claimed in the autumn of 1596 to have 'heard divers poor people say that there must be a rising soon, because of the high price of corn'. He was joined by Bartholomew Steere, a carpenter, who told him that 'there would be such a rising as had not been seen a great while'. Their hopes were extremely sanguine, and Steere, in particular, did not find enough popular support to match his revolutionary ardour. He said that 'he would cut off all the gentlemen's heads', and that 'we shall have a merrier world shortly'; he also planned 'to go to London, and be joined by the apprentices'. But though he built up a considerable following the authorities responded swiftly, arrested the leaders, and snuffed out the rising.

The great rising of the *Croquants* in France was concentrated in the years 1593–5. It started in Bas-Limousin, spread throughout Limousin, and at its widest extent covered Périgord, Quercy, Limousin and Languedoc. Originally a peasant rebellion, it became more complex in its social composition and included a large proportion of urban labourers in its ranks. The causes of the rising are easily found: the ravages of war, the depradation of the soldiery, the food crisis of the 1590s, the tax régime. The main grievance of the *Croquants* was the fiscal system. They firmly opposed both tithe and *taille*, as well as seigneurial taxes. In a manifesto of March 1594 they also denounced the soldiery, both Catholic and Protestant, 'who had reduced them to starvation, violated their wives and daughters, stolen their cattle and wasted their land'; and reserved for the bourgeoisie the bitter complaint that 'they seek only the ruin of the poor people, for our ruin is their wealth'. The rebel movement was democratically organized. All religious discrimination was prohibited, and they swore 'by faith and oath to love each other and cherish each other, as God commands'. The programme of social justice and religious unity was one that appealed strongly to the king, Henry IV, and in the early stages of the rebellion he had not disguised his sympathy for the *Croquants*; but as the rising progressed he and the authorities adopted a harsher attitude. The religious unity of the rebels proved to be their weakest point, and government agents worked to undermine this. The main assembly consisted two-thirds of Catholics and one-third of Protestants. Thanks to the diligent agents, the rebels finally, in 1595, voted to split up into confessional armies. This led immediately to a disastrous defeat by government forces at Limoges. By 1594 and 1595 the movement became centred on Périgord, but military engagements were few and invariably disastrous. The famine of 1595 marked the end of the *Croquant* uprising.

Upper Austria, or Austria 'beyond the river Enns' (*ob der Enns*), with Linz as its capital, was the theatre of almost continuous peasant uprisings from 1525 to 1648. The risings had a strong religious inspiration, since the territory was Lutheran, but secular grievances were deeply intermixed. The revolt of 1594–7 was a major one that lasted from May 1594 to September 1597. The pastors urged their Lutheran people to defend themselves against the Counter Reformation, promoted by Cardinal Khlesl in Lower Austria and Bishop Passauski in Upper Austria from the 1580s. The French historian de Thou reported that in 1595 'the peasants said that they had taken up arms only to free themselves from the unjust taxes with which the nobles oppressed them'. Troops were sent against the peasants, but in their turn mutinied because they had not been paid: 'the mutineers marched on Vienna', reports de Thou, 'snatched the standards from the hands of their officers, planted them on the city gate and threatened to set the suburbs on fire'. The Vienna correspondent of the Fuggers reported in November 1595:

The peasants are waxing ever stronger. They are said to be encamped not far from here, 40,000 strong, near the Danube. They have most stately and experienced leaders who keep strict discipline, so that much might be learned by us from them. Since all the towns in the country must needs send troops, those of Wels were but a short time ago attacked by the peasants and soundly trounced but not killed. Only their armour and weapons were taken from them, and they were sent back.

Despite the Lutheran faith of both peasants and leaders, contemporaries saw the social threat as greater than the religious.

Commenting on an earlier Protestant-led rising in 1588, the Lutheran city of Speyer had said of the rebels, that 'many, if not most, of them use religion only as a cover. In reality they are rebelling against the authorities in order to have their burdens lightened'. For the same reason, even the Lutheran authorities in Upper Austria were hostile to the 1594–7 revolt. An examination of the rebels' grievances shows that for them taxation was the main issue. 'First', they said, 'there is the *Freigeld*'. This was a feudal tax levied when any property of a dependent peasant was transferred by sale or death or in any other way. It had not been collected, the peasants claimed, 'within human memory', but now it was being imposed and consumed up to half of a peasant's income. The first three complaints of the rebels were all against taxation. The fourth concerned labour dues: 'many have to work for twenty, thirty or more days, and particularly at times when they should be tilling their own soil'.

In eastern Europe there was a large rising in the Ukraine in 1591–3 under the leadership of Christopher Kosinsky. It spread through the governorships of Kiev and Bratslav, and had repercussions as far as Mstislav and Minsk. In 1596 there was another rising in the Ukraine, led by Severin Nalivaiko. The last great rebellion of these crisis years was in Hungary in 1597, when the peasants, according to de Thou,

suddenly revolted, adopting as their leader George Brunner, a man of humble origin. They were at first very restrained, and shed no blood whatsoever. People they met were forced to join them, and the booty they obtained in forts and other places was equally divided. Those who were found guilty of having stolen or taken something by force, were severely punished.

They complained of being crushed by taxes and reduced to slavery by the nobility, so that they were unable to meet the demands made of them, and that they could not till or sow their lands when they were claimed for other tasks. They were, above all, obliged to give their lords one-third of all their produce. They were also, they said, exposed to pillaging by the soldiery.

An army was sent against them by the emperor, and the main peasant body, drawn from the Danube lands, was defeated in a battle near Gravenek. The remnants were routed at Sampelka and their leaders executed.

Banditry and social revolt

Popular discontent might erupt into uprisings; but it also expressed itself on a smaller scale in a resort to crime. The frequency of banditry was another symptom of those very conditions that could cause mass rebellions: heavy taxation, agrarian distress, class resentment. In general all banditry, both aristocratic and popular, was criminal; but it was a form of crime that rose out of political and social crisis. Viewed as crime, aristocratic and popular banditry also shared the common factor of thriving in areas usually inaccessible to the government; in mountainous regions and in woods.

Beyond this common ground, the two sorts of banditry differed widely. Aristocrats who operated robber bands were reverting to a purely feudal defiance of the state. This was the case with the great bandit-lords of central Italy in the late sixteenth century, most notable of whom was the duke of Montemarciano, Alfonso Piccolomini, who for thirteen years from 1578 to 1591 was the supreme head of the brigands in the Romagna. Several other distinguished nobles followed Piccolomini's precedent, not always with success: in 1587 when the Grand-Duke Ramberto Malatesta began to operate as a bandit the pope had him seized and executed. Piccolomini himself was hanged at Florence in 1591. So severe were the pope's measures against the bandits that 'this year', reported a Roman newsletter of September 1585, 'we have seen more heads on the Sant Angelo bridge than melons in the market'.

Popular banditry, on the other hand, tended to originate as a protest against misery, and seems to have thrived most in periods of economic crisis. Unlike rebellions, which aimed to secure broad support, banditry was at its strongest when its support was purely local. The men who fled to the mountains to join the bands were usually those whose crimes, although culpable in the eyes of the state, had not received general disapprobation in the locality. It was this regional sympathy which defeated all the efforts of governments to annihilate banditry, for denunciations were almost unheard of.

In western Europe the mountainous regions of central France and the Pyrenees were prominent in the sixteenth century as centres of banditry. When Charles Estienne published his *Guide des Chemins de France* in the mid sixteenth century, he took care to list some of the roads that were infested by brigands, but no

information on their activity has come down to us. Catalan banditry
south of the Pyrenees is better known, and has a considerable
literature. The peak period for activity here was in the reign of
Philip III (1598–1621), under whom the most famous of all the
Catalan bandits, Perot Rocaguinarda, began his career in 1602.
Much of his fame derives from the appearance he makes in
Cervantes's *Don Quixote*. A diarist of his day reported that
'Rocaguinarda was the most courteous bandit to have been in that
region for many years: never did he dishonour or touch the
churches, and God aided him'. He ended his career in what became
a traditional way, accepting the pardon of the viceroy in 1611 and
going overseas to Italy to serve with the troops.

As in Catalonia, the Italian bandits emerged from an agrarian
background, and periods of agrarian crisis seemed to provoke
further bandit activity. The critical years of the 1580s, followed by
a harvest crisis in 1590–1, initiated widespread disturbances. A
Roman newsletter of 1590 reported incidents in the Romagna,
where 'numerous peasants have joined the bandits, and commit
murders publicly in the streets'. The resurgence of banditry was
part and parcel of an agrarian revolt: one of the most prominent
leaders to reflect this was Marco Sciarra.

Sciarra, a native of Castiglione, had been a bandit since 1584–5,
when he emerged as the leader of a group which had its
headquarters in the Abruzzi. For nearly seven years this group
operated in the Marches, Romagna and contiguous regions. His
activities were viewed as an anti-Spanish revolt, which helped to
bring him popularity. More significant was the fact that he practised
that redistribution of wealth that is the classic hallmark of the
'Robin Hood' type of bandit. He was loved by the poor of Naples
'who used to say', reports a contemporary, 'that he would soon
come to occupy Naples, and make himself king'. Around Rome the
countryside was virtually under his control, as the bandits held
courts, created magistrates and carried out marriages. Sciarra's
decline began in 1592 when he offered his services to the Republic
of Venice. Strong papal protests led Venice to betray him to the
troops. He escaped but was eventually murdered, by a former
friend and companion, in 1593. Sciarra's career exhibits most of the
essential characteristics of popular banditry: strong popular
support, the cult of the hero, some redistribution of stolen wealth
to the poor, the choice of mercenary service as an alternative to
punishment, and the final betrayal by former friends.

The combination of peasant agitation and banditry can be seen again in early seventeenth-century France, where the regularity of popular uprisings, particularly under Cardinal Richelieu, gave ample scope to rebels. In Périgord in this period the principal bandit was Pierre Grellety. After the collapse of the big uprising led by La Mothe La Forêt, some of the Périgord peasants in the area, known as the Paréage, continued their agitation and offered the leadership of their movement to Grellety. He accepted the role, and continued the struggle from a base in the woods of Périgord. Grellety was never caught and eventually in 1642, in the now accepted way, took up a military commission to serve in Italy, which Richelieu had offered him.

The Spanish bandits of this period operated not only in Catalonia but also in Valencia, Murcia and Castile. Their lives displayed a curious mixture of crime and charity, religion and impiety, the very combination of opposites that made social banditry a unique phenomenon. One bandit of the time of Philip II was called *el caballero de la Cruz*, because he always left a crucifix on the graves of his victims. Most bandits wore medals and scapulars around their neck, and practised the official religion; but they also drew on a wealth of superstition, and were known to recite prayers to make themselves invisible to their pursuers. Women were sometimes leaders of the bandit groups, as happened in Granada. One of the more curious groups active in the early century in Andalucia operated in the sierra de Cabrilla. They dressed as gentlemen, were always kind and courteous to their victims, and robbed them of only half their goods: this charitable form of property redistribution earned them the title of *los beatos de Cabrilla* – the holy ones of Cabrilla. Of a bandit active in Castile in 1644 it was reported that 'he never kills anyone but only takes part of their money, leaving them with enough to continue their journey; he borrows money from villages and individuals, giving his word as a pledge, and is punctual in payment'.

The Russian state and its frontiers were the principal victims of brigandage in the east, for two main reasons. First, many of the bands were tribal and racial groups which were actively at war against Muscovy. Both the Tatars and Cossacks were long-standing enemies. All the major peasant revolts in the Russian lands and in Lithuania and the Ukraine were made possible because of the active help of the Cossacks. Banditry became an essential arm of agrarian revolt, and the bandits in turn were accepted as defenders of the people, heroes of a popular tradition that persisted through Russian history. The second reason for the strength of banditry was the chaos caused in Muscovy by the growth of feudalism and the bitter internal struggles of the period. The breakdown of order during the Time of Troubles, for instance, was particularly fruitful in promoting brigandage; the schism in the Russian Church likewise drove many clergy and others to the same occupation. Peasants fleeing from feudal obligations were perhaps the largest single group of people to swell the growth of banditry. In popular estimation, the work of the bandits was a form of social justice, since their principal victims were merchants and other rich travellers, government officials and tax-collectors. In the Russian songs, the *bylini* (that were devoted to their deeds), they emerged as folk heroes whose work to redress the evils of the time earned them legendary status.

Revolts of the early seventeenth century

Rural agitation was continuous in areas of conflict between landlords and tenants, as in Upper Austria. In Russia there was an extensive famine from 1601 to 1603, followed by serious disturbances. The first great year of continent-wide rebellion was 1607. In England the conflict over enclosures precipitated the Midlands Revolt. Stow's *Annals* gives the following account:

About the middle of this month of May 1607 a great number of common persons suddenly assembled themselves in Northamptonshire, and then others of like nature assembled themselves in Warwickshire, and some in Leicestershire. They violently cut and brake down hedges, filled up ditches, and laid open all such enclosures of commons and other grounds as they found enclosed. . . . These tumultuous persons grew very strong, being in some places of men, women and children a thousand together, and at Hill Norton in Warwickshire there were 3,000, and at Cottebich there assembled of men, women and children to the number of full 5,000.

Rioters assured Justices of the Peace that their revolt was not against the king 'but only for reformation of those late inclosures, which made them of ye porest sorte reddy to pyne for want'. The leader, John Reynolds, was called Captain Pouch 'because of a great leather pouch which he wore by his side'. Now for the first time, the terms 'leveller' and 'digger' appeared in England: 'levellers' were simply those who levelled down enclosures, without any hint of radical social doctrine. The 'diggers' appeared in a well-known petition addressed in this year from *The Diggers of Warwickshire to all other Diggers*. Contemporary opinion was unsympathetic to these agitators. Preaching at Northampton in June 1607, after the suppression of the revolt, a parson claimed that 'they professe nothing but to throwe downe enclosures, but afterward they will reckon for other matters. They will acompt with Clergiemen, and counsell is given to kill up Gentlemen, and they will levell all states as they levelled bankes and ditches, and some of them boasted, that now they hoped to worke no more'.

In the late spring of 1607 a large revolt broke out in eastern Hungary. It was made up principally of Haiducks (peasant bandits) who by November numbered about 20,000 and were joined by large forces of serfs. The uprising was only one part of the wider struggle, led chiefly by Stephen Bocskay, by all sections of the Hungarian nation against the Habsburgs and against German influence. The most important rebellion of these years occurred in Russia. The Bolotnikov uprising of 1606–7 coincided with the dynastic struggles that followed the death of Tsar Boris Godunov in 1605. In 1606 the boyar prince Shuisky seized the throne, but his rule was opposed by other nobles, who raised armies and marched on Moscow. The core of their support was the peasant movement led by Bolotnikov, a former slave who had fled from his master, been captured by the Turks and after adventures in Italy and Germany had returned through Poland to Russia. Identifying himself with the opposition to Shuisky, Bolotnikov became allied to the noble party and raised the peasants for them. The main body of the rebel peasants came from the area to the south-west of Moscow and was also supported by the Cossacks. By October 1606 the rebels were under the walls of Moscow. It was then that the differences among them came out into the open. Terrified by the implications of the social struggle for which Bolotnikov was calling, the noble commander Pashkov went over to Shuisky, and Bolotnikov was forced to withdraw from Moscow after an initial defeat. In the spring of 1607 Bolotnikov and his forces found themselves trapped in the fortress town of Tula. After a long and cruel siege Tula capitulated in October. Bolotnikov was captured and executed.

In Upper Austria in 1626 the biggest popular uprising of the entire Thirty Years War period took place. Nearly all the nobility of Upper Austria were Lutheran, and their religion was guaranteed by the emperor. But precisely in the early seventeenth century the

Land ob der Enns was put under Bavarian administration, and a Catholic reaction took place. In 1624 the exercise of the Protestant religion in Upper Austria was prohibited by decree, a perfectly permissible procedure that followed the principle of *cuius regio eius religio*. The old faith was introduced with the use of force, provoking several of the bourgeoisie and nobility of the region, including the count of Ortenburg and the Freiherr von Zinzendorf, to plot rebellion. In 1626 the Catholic authorities in Linz began a house to house collection of Protestant books, and in four days managed to fill twenty wagons full. Protestant piety, which relied entirely on books such as the Bible, was outraged.

The revolt began in May 1626 when the peasants along the Danube were rallied together by their two principal leaders, Stefan Fadinger and Christoph Zeller. The peasants waged a full-scale war against the imperial armies, laying seige to several towns and at one stage besieging Linz itself. It was during this siege that Fadinger was killed. He was the true inspiration of the rising, a folk hero whose memory remained for centuries among the people of Upper Austria. His place as leader was taken by a nobleman, Achaz Willinger. By spring 1627 the rebellion was over: on 26 March Willinger and nine other leaders were executed. After Easter another twenty were also executed. Despite the participation of several nobles in the rising only one, Willinger, was hanged. No such mercy was shown to the common people. By the end of the war over 12,000 peasants had been killed, and numberless others crippled or driven into exile.

The 1626 peasant war was widely publicized throughout the German lands. News-sheets and pamphlets about it (and against it) were issued in Linz, Augsburg, Frankfurt, Vienna and other cities. The peasants themselves had their own publicity, in the form of songs which they sang when they marched or when they rested. The most famous of these was their theme, the *Baurenlied* or *Fadingerlied*, which celebrated the end of the old order, the destruction of lords and priests, and the emergence of the peasant as master:

> Das gantz Landt muss sich bekehren
> weil wir Bawrn jetzt werdn Herrn,
> können wol sitzen im Schatten.

(The whole country must be overturned, for we peasants are now to be the lords, it is we who will sit in the shade.) The day of clerical tyranny was over:

> Die Pfaffen sollen ihre Clöster lassen,
> die Bawrn seyndt jetzundt Herrn.

(The priests must quit their cloisters, for the peasants are now the masters.) The land had passed from the seigneurs to the peasants:

> Jetz wöllen wirs gantz Landt ausziehen,
> unsere aigne Herrn müssen fliehen.

(Now will we sweep throughout the land, and our own lords must flee.) The end of the rising led to Catholicization of the territory. In May 1627 an imperial patent gave the ruling classes a choice between conversion or exile. Though thousands of Austrians left their homeland, the majority conformed.

The years 1628–31 in the western counties of England witnessed what has been described as the 'largest single outbreak of popular discontent in the thirty-five years preceding the civil war'. Riots occurred in scattered areas in Gillingham forest (Dorset), Braydon forest (Wiltshire) and in the Forest of Dean. They were given unity by the leadership of the mysterious 'Lady Skimmington', a pseudonym used by several leaders but in particular by one John Williams. Complaints were directed against enclosures. The number of rebels was not negligible: eighteen townships of the area entered into a confederation and the strength of the rebels was put at over 1000 armed men. There were reports that the rioters had 'received private encouragement from some gentleman of quality', and that one clergyman, the curate of Newland, Peter Simon, had encouraged them with words 'constructed as if spoken in maintenance of the doctrine of the equality of all Mankind'.

Popular agitation continued in Upper Austria in the 1630s, and in the winter of 1633–4 the biggest uprising to take place on German territory during the Thirty Years War occurred in Upper Bavaria, in the Benediktbeuren area. About 10,000 peasants participated: the rising was put down by the troops of both sides, imperialist and Spanish as well as Swedish.

In France, thanks to Richelieu's need for money to finance diplomacy and war, the tax-burden in real terms doubled between 1630 and 1650. Up to the period of the Fronde there were four main waves of revolt: in the Quercy region in 1624; in several provinces of the south-west in 1636–7; in Normandy in 1639; and in areas of the south, west and north in 1643–5. By their nature urban revolts were more frequent (and briefer) than rural revolts; they can be found in many large towns and cities for every year from 1623 to 1647.

The nature of the French risings can be illustrated by looking at the two largest outbreaks, that of the *Croquants* in 1636, and the Norman revolt of 1639. The date 1636 helps to explain popular discontent, for this was the year after the entry of France into the Thirty Years War, and the correspondence of government officials in the provinces (above all in Burgundy and Picardy) reported widespread misery and anger caused by the plague, by poor harvests and by the passage of troops. Already in 1635 there had been a series of uprisings in the cities of the south, notably in Agen. The peasant revolt broke out in May 1636 and was crushed only in November 1637. It came to cover so wide an area – most of the territory between the Garonne and the Loire, an area approximating to one-fourth of France – that it may well be regarded as the biggest peasant rising in French history. It was not a unified, organized revolt, but consisted of the sporadic activity of numbers of wandering bands. The first explosion was in the city of Angoulême and its region, where a massacre of royal tax-agents occurred. In one town, twelve tax officials were murdered, and one (in Saintonge) was cut to pieces while alive. The uprising became so great and widespread that only a royal army could have crushed it, as one of the intendants reported to Richelieu. But the army was occupied elsewhere, in defending France's frontiers, so the government was obliged to arrive at a compromise. In August 1636 the governor and the intendant of Angoulême opened talks with the rebels. Several tax concessions were made, which pacified the rising for the winter. In spring it broke out again, largely provoked by the fact that the intendant had used troops to help him collect taxes. The new centre of the rising became Périgord. There nearly 60,000 peasants had in 1636 taken up arms, killed the tax-collectors and cried, '*Vive le Roi sans la gabelle! Vive le Roi sans la taille!*'. The leader of the movement and ultimately of the greater part of the *Croquants*, was a nobleman named La Mothe La Forêt. In the summer of 1637 the repression started. The duke of La Valette caught the peasants in the town of Eymet and left over 1000 dead on the ground. By November further action had crushed all but isolated groups of *Croquants*.

Normandy, where the *Nu-Pieds* rebellion broke out, was one of the most heavily taxed provinces in France. Sully once boasted to the English ambassador that the king drew as many taxes from Normandy as from all the other provinces together. Under Richelieu's fiscal régime, the complaints of the estates of Normandy against the burden of *tailles* and *gabelles* went unrelieved. In 1638 the estates were told that circumstances made relief impossible. A rumour in 1639 that the tax on salt, one of Normandy's chief products, was to be raised, proved to be the last straw. In July 1639 an officer named Poupinel, arriving in the town of Avranches on some other business, was mistaken for a *gabeleur*, and gravely wounded during a riot created by the salt-producers. A few days after Poupinel's death a sheet of verse was found fixed to his tomb. The last stanza ran:

> Si quelque partisan s'arreste
> Pour s'en informer plus avant
> Di luy que *Jean Nuds* piedz s'appreste
> Pour luy en faire tout autant.

(If any tax-collector – *partisan* – should stop in order to find out more, tell him that Jean Nu-Pieds is ready to do as much to him.) The reason for the choice of the pseudonym *Nu-Pieds* was apparently because taxes had reduced the people to barefoot beggary. Unlike the *Croquants*, the Normans were well organized. The peasants were formed into an army called the Army of Suffering (*armée de souffrance*) and their leader signed himself 'General Nu-Pieds'. Both Caen and Rouen had popular riots which put them for a while under rebel control. The uprising was ended in 1640 by bringing over troops from Picardy. The revolt in Caen was crushed, then the royal troops met the main rebel force near Avranches and annihilated it, killing most of the leaders.

1648: the year of revolutions

The year 1648 was one of agrarian crisis throughout Europe. In England there were bad harvests from 1646 to 1649; the winter 1647–8 was particularly wet, and in London prices rose in 1647–9 to their highest level prior to 1661. In Andalucia, thanks to the rains of 1647, there was a severe bread shortage in 1647 and 1648. In southern Italy and Sicily the heavy rains of February 1647 were followed by a drought and therefore by famine conditions in 1647 and 1648. In Russia, too, the years leading to 1648 were ones of bad harvest. For many of these countries the worst year in terms of weather, harvest and prices was 1647: the popular explosion was often delayed by a few months.

The English Revolution was the most important political event of the seventeenth century. The monarchy was overthrown, a republic proclaimed. The Leveller movement, under the leadership of John Lilburne and of his colleagues including Richard Overton and William Walwyn, made its first effective appearance in July 1646 when it published a *Remonstrance of many thousand citizens* which called for the establishment of a republican democracy and of religious toleration in England. From this time, the Levellers published several successive policy programmes, drawn up in the form of a national constitution: each of these statements, of which the first appeared in 1647, was called the Agreement of the People.

Because the Levellers failed to create an insurrection, it is often easily forgotten how close they came to creating a revolution. In the critical year 1647, when the army quarrelled with Parliament both over policy and because it had not been paid, the Levellers succeeded in infiltrating the army and in dominating all its proceedings. In October the General Council of the army was obliged to sit down at Putney, near London, and discuss plans to adopt the Agreement of the People as the basis of future policy. Only the ruthless hand of Cromwell succeeded in breaking the Leveller threat. Facing an attempted mutiny by some regiments in November, he arrested the ringleaders and had one shot. It was Cromwell again who in April 1649 arrested a group of Leveller mutineers and had one, Robert Lockyer, executed; a month later, at Burford, he captured another group by treachery and executed three soldiers. But for these actions the Levellers might easily have taken over the army, which alone held power in England, and through the army England might have been given a constitution whose essential demands had to wait two centuries to be resurrected, by the Chartists.

Cromwell wisely did not underrate the strength of the Levellers, whose popular support in London could be seen clearly by the great crowds that turned out for Lockyer's funeral on 29 April 1649, and by the thousands who greeted Lilburne's release from arrest by the magistrates. From 1647 to 1649 the Levellers' support could be seen in the volume of protest they managed to stir up not only in London but also in the provinces. They made ample use of the presses, dispatched thousands of leaflets throughout the country, and had their own newspaper, the *Moderate*. Lilburne and his friends resorted regularly to the habit of petitioning Parliament, which was the only sovereign the Levellers recognized. Their petitions give valuable evidence of their support. Four days after the arrest in March 1649 of Lilburne and other Levellers, a petition bearing the signatures of 10,000 Londoners was presented to Parliament; proof not only of support but of the remarkable speed of Leveller organization. In September 1649 the Levellers produced their most revolutionary pamphlet, *The Remonstrance of many thousands of the free people of England*, which was signed by nearly 100,000 people.

In these years the Spanish monarchy was shaken by disaster both within and without the peninsula. In its Italian possessions the crisis led to major revolts in the two largest cities of the south – Naples and Palermo. Reacting to the famine of 1647, in May a popular procession marched into the cathedral in Palermo and stuck a pole crowned with bread on the high altar. There were shouts of 'Long live the king and down with taxes and bad government'. Mobs set fire to the town hall, opened the prisons and demolished the tax offices. There were risings in other parts of Sicily as well, especially in the villages round Messina. In Palermo in August a popular leader emerged in the form of a goldsmith named d'Alesi. Some reforms were agreed to in principle, such as the reduction of food taxes and increased guild representation in the government of the city. However, when quarrels within the popular movement produced fighting at the end of August, the authorities seized their opportunity. D'Alesi was murdered, and in September Spanish troops entered the city. The Palermo revolt exhibits the three main features of the urban troubles of 1647–8: a food shortage triggered the uprising, the main grievance was against taxes, and the most active enemies of the people were the nobility.

The problems of Naples were very much those of Spain, its overlord. Administratively the crown had only limited control over the kingdom, since the major part was in the hands of feudal lords. It was the oppression of the nobles that sparked off popular revolt. Already in 1638 a Spanish official had noted that 'the tyranny and injustice in that kingdom deserve severe punishment'. Taxation for the Spanish war effort was also extremely heavy. The main fury of the people of Naples on 7 July 1647, the day that a riot in the market-place exploded into a major revolt, was directed against the *gabelle*, the salt tax. Though the illiterate fisherman Masaniello emerged as the popular leader, the real power behind the rising was his adviser, the elderly (86 years old) priest Giulio Genoino. Masaniello's murder in mid July did not check the revolt, which now spready rapidly to other parts of southern Italy. In October a Spanish fleet sailed into the bay of Naples but though some troops disembarked they failed to recover the city. The rebels, under a new popular leader Gennaro Annese, celebrated their victory by declaring a republic, under the protection of France. French support was only half-hearted, thanks in part to problems at home, and by April 1648 the Spaniards were back in control.

The Spanish peninsula was also torn apart by rebellion and separatism. There was a potentially dangerous uprising in Granada in 1648. On 18 May the poorer people of the city, chanting 'Long live the king and death to the bad government', began a peaceful agitation that swelled the crowds in the streets; they managed to get the civil governor (*corregidor*) replaced. These years of famine and plague helped to precipitate further risings in 1652 in Granada, Seville and Córdoba. The Córdoba rising began early one morning in May 1652 when a poor woman went weeping through the streets of the poor quarter, holding the body of her son who had died of hunger. As other women responded to this scene of misery, they persuaded their men to join them in protest. The riot began in earnest when an armed body of about 600 men entered and sacked the house of the *corregidor*, who took refuge in a convent. By late morning a crowd of 2000 had taken over the city. Despite the fury of the rioters and the sacking of several houses, not a single person appears to have been killed by them. The king eventually sent extra food supplies and issued a general pardon. The Seville rising followed a similar pattern. It began in late May and lasted about a week; here, too, not a single person appears to have been murdered by the mob. As in Córdoba the people of Seville set up a commune, chose their own *corregidor*, and set up a popular militia to keep order in the city.

The Frondes in France were the most important of all the urban revolutions of the year 1648, but the popular struggle never assumed significant proportions. Even the famous barricades, which went up on Wednesday, 26 August 1648 and stayed up until Friday, were not a purely proletarian phenomenon, and were firmly under the control of the bourgeoisie. The Fronde in Bordeaux was more popular in inspiration. The first serious disturbances, in August 1648, were precipitated by the export of wheat from the city at a time when, as in the rest of France, starvation was beating on the doors. The parlement of Bordeaux joined the rebellion and outlawed the governor, the duke of Epernon, as a public enemy. This first stage of the Bordeaux Fronde ended with a peace in January 1650. The city was next caught up in the Parisian struggle when the princess of Condé won the leaders of Bordeaux over to her party. From 1651 a new force entered the struggle. The Ormée, a mass movement named after its initial meeting place near some elm trees, was based on popular support but had very divergent aims. It absorbed the Condé party and by June 1652 had set up a commune in the city. The Ormée had a membership of thousands. At the top it was run by a council of 500. Merchants, bourgeois and lawyers were (not always voluntarily) members, but the petits bourgeois and the lower classes were more typical participants. The movement appears to have had genuinely radical views. 'It is equality that makes for perfection', claimed one of its pamphlets. 'The real cause of sedition and political strife is the excessive wealth of the few.' Views favouring democracy and a republic were expressed. Cromwell exploited this by sending the ex-Leveller Sexby to Bordeaux with a specially revised edition of the Agreement of the People. Huguenots and Catholics were jointly members of the Ormée. But the unity of the movement was threatened by economic chaos and the cessation of trade. Some richer Ormistes plotted against the more radical wing. The leaders of the radicals, Villars and Dureteste, joined Condé in supporting an alliance with Spain. The royalists besieged Bordeaux by land and sea, cutting off aid from Spain. By July 1653 it was reported that 'the people are howling for bread and peace'. After a coup in the city, royalist troops marched in on 2 August. About 300 people were expelled from Bordeaux. Dureteste and a few other leaders were executed.

The risings of 1648 in Muscovy were, in their political effect, among the most important to occur in Europe. Over the whole area of the Moscow governmental region we can count about thirty urban uprisings from 1630 to 1650. In the city of Moscow itself they occurred in 1633–4, 1637, 1641, 1645 and 1648; the latter year saw the greatest concentration of riots, mostly in June and July. From 1645, Russia had been ruled nominally by 16-year-old Tsar Alexis Romanov, but the real power was wielded by the boyar Morozov. Taxes rose steeply under his régime and the burgher class was the first to protest. Opposition focused on the new salt tax, first levied in 1648. Poor harvest conditions, military reverses in the fight against Turks and Tatars, helped to foster discontent. In June a riot broke out in Moscow. When the royal musketeers (*streltsy*) were ordered to break up the crowds a group of them announced that 'they did not wish to fight for the boyars against the common people'. An eyewitness reports that

the Streltsies or life guard, consisting of some thousand Men, whose pay being lessened and diminished in so much that they were not able to live by, took the Commons part, and thereupon in the afternoone they seized on the Court of Morozov. . . . The sayd Court they plundred totally, all the stately and pretious things they found they hewed in pieces . . . the plate of gold and silver they did beate flat, the pretious pearles and other jewells they have bruised into powder, they stamped and trampled them under feet, they flung them out of the windowes, and they suffered not the least thing to bee carryed away, crying alowd: *To Naasi Kroof*, that is to say, this is our blood.

Officials were murdered, and Morozov was exiled by the tsar. Moscow, meanwhile, caught fire in the riot and a large part of the city was destroyed. As a gesture to the popular basis of the risings in Moscow and other cities, the government agreed to a summoning of the Zemsky Sobor. This met in 1648–9. It was one of the last moments of Russian constitutionalism. Already the victory of the anti-Morozov landed magnates was signalled by the issue in 1649 of a new code of laws, the Ulozhenie, which followed the wishes of the feudal landowners. Unwittingly, the populace which had rebelled against a hated government in 1648 had succeeded in subjecting Russia yet more firmly to the yoke of feudalism.

The successes of Bohdan Khmelnitsky in the Ukraine (above, p. 252) encouraged peasant disaffection in Lithuania, where the rising of 1648–9 was entirely dependent on him. 'Not only do the Cossacks support the rebels', complained the chancellor of Lithuania, Prince Radziwill, 'but all our peasants in Rus flock to swell the Cossack forces.' An adjunct to the Cossack rebellion was the Polish revolt of 1651 in Podhale. The leader of the rebellion, known as Alexander Napierski or simply Kostka, spent the year 1650 in Khmelnitsky's army in order to learn the techniques of armed struggle, but was not directly helped by the Cossacks. The peasant grievances were standard; against labour services, exploitation, and 'the szlachta and Jews'. The Polish Jesuit Peter Skarga wrote at the time that 'there is no country in the world where the peasants, subjects of the lords, would be oppressed as they are in our country'. The rebellion ended in July 1651 with the execution of Napierski.

Revolts of the later seventeenth century

The Swiss cantons were not free from agitation during the Thirty Years War. In some respects, nevertheless, the peasantry benefited from the rise in prices caused by the influx of refugees from the German lands. The coming of peace reversed the trend: prices tumbled, leading to an agricultural slump and currency devaluation. In December 1652 Bern and Lucerne devalued, followed by the other cantons in January 1653. Unfamiliar with the economics of devaluation, the lower classes rose in revolt.

The protest movement was led by Johannes Emmenegger, a wealthy peasant who owned 100 head of cattle and drank out of a silver goblet. His friends called him the *Edelstein der Bauern*, the jewel of the peasants. Other leaders included Niklaus Leuenberger, a wealthy peasant who later became supreme head of the whole movement, and Christian Schibi, military commander of the Lucerne peasants, who was looked upon as a magician and sorcerer. When the Lucerne peasants failed to get the devaluation revoked, their leaders met in January 1653 in the town of Entlebuch and took an oath to struggle together for freedom. At the meeting they also drew up a protest song, the *Tellenlied* (song of William Tell), which was to become the anthem of the peasants as they marched to war. In March 3000 peasants under Schibi marched on Lucerne and forced concessions; similar concessions were made in April by Basel and Solothurn. On 23 April a mass rally of several thousand Swiss rebels was held in Sumiswald. Secure in the justice of their cause and their strength in numbers, they took the offensive in a war campaign that covered several weeks in May and June. Their forces were immense. The main body of the rebel army, led by Leuenberger, exceeded 24,000 men. By the end of June, however, they were defeated and in disarray. Schibi was executed in July, Leuenberger in September.

The indomitable spirit of the Cossacks troubled Russia in the 1660s with the rise of Stepan (Stenka) Razin, leader of a section of the Cossacks of the river Don. Revered as a daring commander and as a sorcerer, Razin began raiding in 1667, when he announced that 'I have come to fight only the boyars and the wealthy lords'. In 1668–9 he made an astonishing expedition to the Caspian coast, where he scored a brilliant victory over Persian forces and won the legendary reputation that helped him, on the return to Astrakhan and the Don, to build up an army. Fired by the old dream of uniting all Cossacks he was, by March 1670, at the head of 7000 Don Cossacks and in open revolt against Moscow, his professed aim being 'to remove the traitor boyars and give freedom to the common people'. The forces took Tsaritsyn and then Astrakhan; his following soon became immense, swollen by the nomadic populations of the Don and Volga. Many monks and clergy rallied to his cause; as literate men, they helped to draw up the propaganda that was circulated through the countryside. Razin's failure to take Simbirsk in September 1670 allowed the royal army to arrive and scatter his forces, with a bloody repression of his humble followers. In April 1671 he was betrayed by dissident Cossacks and handed over to the government. Taken to Moscow in a cage, he was tortured and then quartered alive (June 1671). The most popular folk hero in all Russian history, his stature may be measured by the legends and *bylini* devoted to him. Revered as the 'shining sun' (*krasnoe solnyshko*), he was believed by his followers not to have died but to be in hiding, waiting for the call of his people.

Just as serfs succumbed to the feudal structure of eastern Europe, so in the France of Louis XIV the peasant tradition of revolt seemed to collapse. A revolt in the region of Boulogne in 1662 was brutally crushed. Apart from risings in 1664 (Gascony) and 1670 (Languedoc), the main disturbances were in 1675, directed specifically against taxation. In Bordeaux tax riots in March led to street riots, and for over four months the city remained under popular rule, with the number of urban and peasant rebels estimated at several thousand. The government took a harsh view of what it regarded as complicity by the city in tax-protests, and exiled the parlement. In Brittany, where tax revolts broke out at Rennes in April 1675, the movement became an extensive rebellion against taxes and seigneurial oppression and in favour of regional liberties. In Lower Brittany, where châteaux were pillaged, a 'Code Paysan' was drawn up by delegates of village communities of the 'pays armorique': they wanted social peace on the basis of inter-class marriages, a revision of peasant labour services, abolition of the corvée as being against 'Armorican liberty', and all legal proceedings to be free, with judges being elected by peasants. The peasants wore red bonnets as symbols of the liberty of the province. Only towards the end of the reign, with the spread of urban disorder in the great subsistence crises of 1693–4 and 1709–10, did rebellion again attain the ascendancy it had held during the early century.

Peninsula Spain experienced some of its most threatening insurrections at the very end of the century. In 1688 the first stage of a prolonged revolt broke out in Catalonia. Since 1640, when social order in the principality had almost totally collapsed, the Catalan communities had lived in peace. The approach of war with France renewed the problem of contributions for the troops, and minor clashes with cavalry provoked a chain of uprisings. In April 1688 all the villages of lower Catalonia rose, and a peasant host of 18,000 besieged Barcelona. The crisis continued into late 1689, when once again the peasants laid siege to the capital. This time, however, energetic action by a new viceroy pacified the rebels and scattered their leaders. A few years later, in 1693, the peasant communities of central Valencia rose in protest at their seigneurial burdens and formed themselves into an 'Army of the Germanías' (after the movement of 1520), but were easily suppressed.

The structure of popular revolt

Although much of the preceding narrative has concentrated on isolated peaks of revolt and on those that were politically significant, in fact popular unrest was more frequent than the peaks suggest and did not necessarily take the form of political rebellion. The great uprisings were the tip of an iceberg: below them lay a society, both urban and rural, that was not dormant but in a continuous state of evolution and tension. The apparent tranquillity of the European countryside was permeated with low-level violence. A study of the rural communities of Provence has unearthed a total of 374 insurrections, both large and small, over the period 1596–1715. A study of Aquitaine over the same period has discovered some 500 revolts. The overwhelming majority of these incidents were not directed outward at the state but were restricted to the confines of the local community, thus confirming the apparent peacefulness of traditional society.

By the sixteenth century the local communities – the fundamental unit of early modern Europe (see above p. 16) – were changing their external status and their internal structure. Socio-economic tensions emerged both within and between communities, and were often sublimated through mechanisms such as feasts and carnivals. Hard times did not necessarily provoke the village, and indeed created greater solidarity and a determination among all social levels to step up mutual help and to endure difficulties.

Heavier taxes and seigneurial oppression thus did not necessarily lead to revolt, which was not an automatic response to outside pressure. The idea of 'spontaneous' rebellion is difficult to sustain, because villagers did not react instinctively to external stimuli. Why then did peasants revolt? The model of Fuenteovejuna (above, p. 258) offers part of an answer. Here was a small community acting in unison to eradicate a common problem, but otherwise uninterested in revolt and refusing to combine with other communities in a general protest. Problems that did not threaten the basic structure of the community were solved through internal conflict (murder of the lord, riots of tax-payers against tax-exempt, persecution of 'witches') and seldom led to an outward explosion. Rural incidents were thus frequent, but 'revolt' was exceptional.

For revolt to occur, two things were essential: an outrage or threat to the moral conscience of the community; and the projection of protest from a local to a universal plane. On the first point, a threat might come in the form of a violation of subsistence norms (crippling taxes and maldistribution of food would both threaten a basic right, the right to exist), and would instantly lower the threshold of violence, precipitating collective action that might not occur at other times. Any violence would naturally be conservative, not revolutionary; it would aim to conserve and restore disregarded norms. On the second point, the universalization of protest was a difficult step for the self-centred, conservative local community to take; and tended to happen under the influence of outside ideologies and leaders. Revolt in these circumstances was not a blind, unthinking act of violence, but a carefully co-ordinated movement, usually agreed by the leadership of several villages at some regional function such as a fair (in Swabia in 1524), a religious festival (Corpus Christi in Barcelona in 1640), or a carnival (Romans in 1580), and carried out with maximum coercion against those individuals or villages that refused to take part.

In early modern Europe the precipitants of revolt can be reduced very generally to three: bad harvests, extraordinary taxation, and the soldiery. The *causes* of revolt did not necessarily coincide with these precipitants. Food shortages did not by themselves cause discontent; bad harvests were a normal occurrence, and so long as the common people could see that everyone else was starving they were long-suffering. Only when it was clear that others were profiting from distress did they rise: food-exporters and food-hoarders were the target in Naples in 1585, Bordeaux in 1648, Cordoba in 1653. In 1566 in Antwerp, 1648 in Granada, riots occurred after the food-crisis had passed; in the latter, reported a witness, 'the supply and price of grain improved, [but] disorder in the quality and supply of bread increased', causing indignation where there had been none during the actual shortage.

Extraordinary taxation features in nearly every revolt as a direct or proximate cause; in France, thanks to Richelieu's war policy, the fiscal burden quadrupled between 1620 and 1641. Though taxes may have been the provocation, they were, however, invariably no more than a trigger to release other longstanding grievances, so that few revolts can be considered merely fiscal in scope, and in some cases the question of taxes may be seen as the excuse for rather than the cause of insurrection. The soldiery – to take the third point noted above – were a notorious bringer of ruin to the countryside. Troop billeting provoked the rural uprisings in Catalonia in 1640 and 1688. In some cases the soldiers were an indirect cause of risings. A report on the French north-east border in 1645 noted that 'the administration of justice has been interrupted, through the passage and lodging of armies which have caused such disorder in the country that the peasants refuse to allow any judicial action to be taken, and instead rebel even against the judges'.

The tradition of revolt featured as a strong aspect of many insurrections. Geography was important: banditry tended to recur in mountainous areas (the Catalan Pyrenees, the Polish Tatr mountains), and frontier areas (such as the Habsburg frontier with the Turk) had a continuous history of agitation. Certain localities seem to have been in the forefront of rebellions: the little town of Gourdon in Quercy (France) was at the centre of peasant agitation three times in three centuries; the 1648 uprising in Seville started in the same quarter that had supported the *Comuneros* in 1520. On a larger scale, endemic regionalism was a self-evident reason for the persistence of a tradition of rebellion. In Spain, Catalonia was always looked upon as a source of disorder; in France, Marseille from 1591 to 1596 maintained itself as an independent state of the Catholic League and again in 1650 declared itself independent. At times the tradition took the form of a myth: names like *Croquants*, Levellers, *Germanías*, were adopted repeatedly by subsequent rebels, as if to draw legitimacy from their predecessors. The urge to legitimate a rebellion by establishing continuity from a respected past, was constant. The Swiss rebels of 1653 appealed directly to the national hero, William Tell, as the words of the Entlebuch *Tellenlied* make plain:

> Ach Tell! ich wollt dich fragen
> Wach auf von deinem Schlaf!

(Tell, I beseech you, wake up from your sleep!)

The leaders and inspirers of uprisings were drawn from the rural élite, urban artisans and, at the topmost level, nobility. This was not surprising since many major revolts, once they had transcended the local level of grievances, mushroomed out to become large movements embracing all classes and interests. The lords were in addition keen to protect their communities. In Normandy in 1643 it was reported that 'the gentry and seigneurs of the villages support and protect the revolt of their vassals'. Nobles also wished to rescue their people from the taxation and political authority of the state. Frequently rebels chose leaders from the upper classes: only nobles had the requisite military expertise, and only they had the status necessary to give respectability to the rebel cause.

Clergy were prominent participants and leaders. In the rebellion in Angoumois in 1548 the vicar of Cressac marched at the head of his parishioners 'in a green bonnet and blue sandals, with a large beard and a two-handed sword'. A *Croquant* priest in the same region justified his role 'because priests are not forbidden to go to war . . . and he was defending the public good'. In Spain clergy had a long tradition of rebellion: the preaching of friars in Salamanca in 1520 put the city firmly on the side of the Comunidades. The populist role of clergy is, however, deceptive. In general priests and friars participated less for ideological reasons than because their primary loyalty was to their flocks: their function in revolts was sociological rather than religious.

Town and country had varying roles in uprisings. In eastern Europe the rural economy dominated the life of the people and the towns, whereas in the west the towns and the bourgeoisie or nobility controlling them had begun to dominate the rural areas. In the east, therefore, the conditions of social conflict were radically different: the revolutionary impetus had to come not from the towns but from the countryside. When the common people rose in the east it was under Bolotnikov, Napierski, Khmelnitsky, men who had lived all their lives outside the towns. In the west, the radical movements tended to originate in and emerge from the towns, and as a rule they had a considerable bourgeois component. A brief look at the French revolts of the early seventeenth century is enough to establish that every significant outbreak began in a town, expanded its support from the town, and maintained its strength so long as it had urban help. By the 1640s all the major risings in the west were urban – in Naples, Paris, Granada, Bordeaux. The townspeople were beginning to take the initiative. In eastern Europe no such trend was forthcoming.

Popular agitation has often been viewed as fragmentary and short-lived, and consequently of no political importance. The duration of revolts depended in part on the solidarity of the local community. Where community structures were weak or even nomadic (as on the Russian frontier), peasant risings degenerated into skirmishes, all too easily suppressed. Where they were firmer, protracted struggle was possible: near Linz the peasants of Wildeneck maintained a ceaseless fight from 1601 to 1662 against the monastery of Mondsee. When communities and towns resolved themselves into 'communes' and held together, a revolt might survive for some time: the Catalan revolt of 1688 lasted for nearly two years, as did the *Croquant* rebellion of 1594; and the Austrian peasant rising of 1594 went on for three. In numbers, too, the uprisings could not be ignored, rebel armies amounting to 24,000 in Switzerland in 1653 and 40,000 in Austria in 1595.

A common misapprehension about popular uprisings is that they were sanguinary. Luther denounced the peasants as 'murderous', but the reality was different. Most rebels respected both life and property. The Austrian rebels of 1595, far from resorting to an orgy of looting, maintained 'perfect discipline'; and in one remarkable incident that year they did not kill the soldiers who were sent to attack them but merely disarmed and beat them, a practice repeated by the Catalan peasants in 1689. During the Spanish urban risings in 1648 and 1652 not a single death was caused directly by the populace.

The violence of revolts was none the less distinctive. The primary purpose of rebellion was always to achieve justice: justice was therefore visited, in a primaeval and almost symbolic way, on doers of evil and enemies of the community. Tax-collectors, particularly those who originated from outside the community, were regular victims. Bodily mutilation, as practised at Agen in 1635 (the private parts of a tax-collector were cut off), was common. The ritual of cannibalism as practised at Romans in 1580, and ritualistic mutilation of the sort committed on Starace in Naples in 1585 and at Saintonge in 1636, were further examples of a savagery that was little more than a resort to a form of justice older than civilization.

Property likewise was an object of popular justice, the emphasis here being on purification rites. The scene at the destruction of Morozov's palace in Moscow in 1648, with rioters throwing valuables out of the windows to cries of 'This is our blood!', can be found also in the Starace incident at Naples and in the Seville rising of 1652. The refusal of outraged rioters to touch tainted property was one of the most striking aspects of the purification ritual of popular rebellions. It can be seen in the Naples riots of 1647:

It was admirable what a regular method they observed in their fiery executions: for they used first to take all the goods out into the Market place to be burnt, crying out *it was the blood of the people* of Naples, and 'twas death to embeazle the least thing; insomuch that one who had stolen but a peep of Sausage was like to be hang'd by Masaniello; nor did they spare either gold, silver or jewels, but all was thrown into the flames, as also coaches and horses were burnt alive, most rich Tapistries and Pictures; but they saved books and pieces of Piety, which they sent to several Churches.

All rebels took great pains to establish their legitimacy. Lacking any basis for their authority, they appealed to history, to myth and to God. Side by side with this pseudo-ideology went a formal belief and trust in the king. Most movements appealed over the heads of local superiors to a distant ruler. It was rare for them to question the existence of monarchy, hence the shock felt throughout Europe when the English in 1649 got rid of theirs. It is exceptional to meet cases, such as that recorded by Marshal Monluc in his *Commentaires*, of peasant rebels in the late sixteenth century who reacted to a mention of the king by saying, 'What king? It is we who are the kings; the one you speak of is just a little turd.' Role reversal of this type – peasants as kings – was commonplace in most uprisings: rebels might dress themselves up as lords and clergy, men might dress up as women (in the Forest of Dean in 1627 and 1631 the male leader of the revolts assumed the name 'Lady Skimmington', a skimmington being one version of the charivari). The symbolism was subversive, but modelled on the otherwise non-subversive role reversal practised in carnivals. Failing secular legitimacy, rebels appealed to God. The religious radicals of the

German Peasant War wanted to bring the kingdom of heaven down to earth. The bandit Marco Sciarra titled himself *'flagellum Dei, et commissarius missus a Deo contra usurarios et detinentes pecunias otiosas'*, the scourge of God, sent against usurers and hoarders. Captain Pouch in the 1607 Midlands revolt claimed 'that he was sent of God to satisfie all degrees whatsoever, and that in this present worke hee was directed by the lord of Heaven'.

Authority, however, must be proved by deeds and miracles. The rebel leaders consequently became invested with supernatural powers in the eyes of their followers, and on occasion deliberately fostered this sense of magic. In the Normandy rebellion there was more than one mysterious Jean Nu-Pieds: a leader who was known yet unknown, who was one yet many, who was here yet also everywhere; this was the consciously cultivated image that made the leader appear ubiquitous, elusive, immune to all danger, immortal. In the folk songs, Stenka Razin hurls back the bullets fired by his enemies. Wherever the 1607 rising broke out, in the south, in the Forest of Dean, it was reported that Captain Pouch was there. In addition to this ubiquity Pouch was able to grant immunity, 'because of a great leather pouch which he wore by his side in which purse hee affirmed to his company, yt there was sufficient matter to defend them against all commers, but afterward when hee was apprehended his Powch was seearched and therein was onely a peece of greene cheese'.

The Lucerne peasant leader Schibi was famed as a magician and warlock. His superior, Leuenberger, maintained his authority by an outward symbol. He had been given a red cloak by the peasants of Entlebuch, which he wore wherever he rode. 'He had only to beckon with his hand', reported a Solothurn chronicler, 'or scribble a word and men, women and children would go by day or night, through rain, wind and snow, to deliver his message'. Catherine de Medici observed in 1579 of Paulmier, leader of the commune at Romans, that 'he has such great influence and authority that at his slightest word all the people of the town and round about will bestir themselves'. The Fugger correspondent at Linz in 1596 wrote of the Austrian rebels that 'they seem bewitched, for as soon as the word is given, even in this cold, they leave their wives and children, hasten from their houses and farms, yet attacking neither towns, castles nor even villages. They tell the populace, whom they drag along with them, that for all they care horses, oxen and cows, even the women, may perish and they pawn their cattle and drink away their gold'.

How revolutionary were rebels? Most, necessarily, looked to restore what had been lost, not to gain what they had never had. The Croat rising of 1573 demanded little more than the restoration of 'ancient rights'. One of the lords reported how his peasants came to him and asked him 'not to ally with anyone against them, since they had not risen against their lords, but only that their ancient rights be restored to them'. However limited their aims, they none the less, and despite themselves, threatened the social order. The Croat rebels demanded a reduction of taxes and the abolition of tithes; had either been granted the structure of authority would have been shaken. Moreover, the cry of 'ancient rights' was revolutionary because it appealed to a near-mythical age of freedom.

The yearning for equality was of course perpetual. In 1679 we encounter in Germany the couplet which John Ball had preached through England in the fourteenth century:

> Da Adam ackert und Eva spann,
> Wer war damals ein Edelmann?

(When Adam delved and Eve span, who was then a nobleman?) Egalitarianism was not new, but in many risings it became commonplace. 'We bear the nobility on our shoulders', observed a pamphleteer in Paris in 1649, 'but we have only to shrug our shoulders to throw them on to the ground.' An Essex labourer asked in 1594, 'What can rich men do against poor men if poor men rise and hold together?' The oppressors were not shaken off and the optimism of the rebels never bore fruit. Bartholomew Steere in 1596 informed a friend that 'he need not work for his living this dear year, for there would be a merry world shortly'. Despite all millennaristic hopes, this merry world receded farther and farther into the future, until overtaken by the gaunt realities of the Industrial Revolution.

11 Absolutism and the state

The great and chief end of men uniting into commonwealths, and putting themselves under government, is the preservation of their property.

John Locke, *Of Civil Government* (1690)

Emerging out of the decades of crisis, Europe in the late seventeenth century relaxed into a more quiescent, more stable, epoch. Over most of the continent levels of fertility appear to have stagnated or fallen (an exception was Spain, where the birth-rate rose as though in compensation for repeated epidemics). Scattered evidence exists of a new tendency to restrict family size by marrying later (between the sixteenth and the late seventeenth centuries the mean age of brides rose in Normandy from 21 to 24 years, in Amsterdam from about 24 to over 26 years, in Colyton from 27 to 29 years). The move to later marriage helped to stabilize population levels at a time when the dreaded bringer of mass mortality, plague, had been banished from northern Europe and would soon disappear from the Mediterranean. Subsistence crises were also much fewer in the late century: there were natural disasters – 1693 and 1709 in France, 1696 in Finland – but on a more regional scale.

Falling demographic levels were accompanied by falling prices. In southern Europe agricultural output decayed (again, with the exception of Spain): in Languedoc yield ratios of nearly 7:1 in the early century fell in the 1680s to under 5:1, in the Roman Campagna they stagnated at about 6.5:1. In northern Europe the response to what looked like recession was different. Yield ratios in England were maintained at about 8:1. Since prices were falling and demand decreasing, rather than cut back on production tenants and landlords preferred to improve and innovate. Ironically, therefore, the difficult economic climate in England encouraged greater investment in the soil. Agriculture benefited from manuals such as

Weston's *Discourse* (1645) and Houghton's *Letters for the Improvement of Husbandry* (1681); new field (clover, lucerne) and fodder (turnips) crops; and mechanical innovations (Jethro Tull's seed-drill, patented 1701). The diet of the poor improved, English corn output rose.

Though the late century displays some of the characteristics of a depression, therefore, it would be wrong to suggest that the economy was contracting. Falling prices did not dampen business; indeed, in northern Europe business activity increased. Bullion from America, far from decreasing in quantity as historians once suggested, actually increased. The metals did not, however, push up prices as in the inflation of the sixteenth century, but were re-exported out of Europe by the English and Dutch to pay for their purchases in Asia. The English East India Company in 1700–1 alone exported over £700,000, and Dutch bullion exports to Asia rose from half a million ducats in 1618 to 1.25 million in 1700. It was a period when the foundations of Europe's domination of the world economy were laid: the English, in particular, made spectacular gains in the Atlantic slave trade, the Asian trades, and the re-export trade from the colonies. Within Europe, cash shortages were remedied by the extension of credit facilities: bills of exchange were made more generally negotiable, and bank-cheques began to be issued (by the Bank of Amsterdam in 1682). In 1694 the Bank of England was founded; it issued 'bank-notes' and offered attractive interest rates to investors.

The economic difficulties of the early century seemed, then, to be largely surmounted in the period after 1660, which was an epoch of consolidation. Lower grain prices benefited the working poor and in effect raised real wages. Entrepreneur farmers, faced with limited profits, turned their energies to innovation and improvement. Regular popular revolts were becoming a thing of the past: régimes now enjoyed greater security. In most western states, the government began to legislate for social stability on the land and in commerce.

State intervention: land and mercantilism

Political stability in both eastern and western Europe favoured the consolidation of the social régime. Gentry and bourgeoisie committed their fortunes to the land, as the necessary prerequisite for social position and political office. In an economic climate where direct exploitation of the soil was costly, emphasis shifted to indirect exploitation through rentals; in the east, meanwhile, serfdom was intensified. The state stepped in to protect the landed régime of its élites.

In eastern Europe the ascendancy of the nobles was not new, for they had long been the natural rulers of the soil. The novelty was that this ascendancy was confirmed by the state in conditions where an extension of state power might have been expected. The noble estates were the backbone of the economy, and rulers such as the Great Elector of Brandenburg-Prussia chose to ally with them against the towns. In Brandenburg after 1660 excise taxes were levied on the produce of the towns but the nobility were exempted, giving them an obvious advantage. In Prussia the Estates granted the Elector an excise in 1662, but this likewise was used in favour of the nobles and against the towns. The story was repeated in Russia and other eastern lands.

In England feudal tenures and the Court of Wards were abolished by Parliament in 1646. This meant that the crown ceased to be the ultimate landlord in the realm. Landowners now gained full ownership of their estates. In 1647 a law of entail was first brought in: owners could settle their land on their eldest son and prevent alienation of the family estate. This prepared the way for the great consolidations of property in the eighteenth century. When an act was passed in 1660 to confirm the measure of 1646, no additional privileges were extended to lesser landowners. The smaller men failed to win that security of tenure which the big landowners had obtained. General insecurity was aggravated by the land sales of the interregnum. Royalist sympathizers alone (this does not include crown or Church lands) suffered confiscation of estates to the extent of about £1.25 million and a further £1.5 million was lost in fines. A number of people lost their lands permanently in this way, but no revolution ownership occurred. Many bought back their own property, and what was unredeemed often went to members of the same social class. Perhaps the most important result of the sales was the acceptance of greater mobility in agrarian relationships.

The sum total of this was a situation favourable to the interests of the big landowner. A property franchise made sure that only those with a material interest could vote for the government of England. To protest those whose incomes came from the soil, Corn Laws were brought in. In 1670 grain exports were allowed, and in

1673 bounties were granted on export shipments; finally in 1689 duties on corn exports were removed and were instead imposed on imports.

In Piedmont it was also a period of aristocratic consolidation on the land. The noble class – recruited both from the old families as well as from successful bourgeois – continued to accumulate estates and at the same time provided most of the capital for the bonds issued by the state from 1653 onwards. Clergy and aristocracy together provided two-thirds of these loans to the state. It was to preserve the economic power of this class that the rulers of Piedmont introduced legislation to protect noble holdings. The most important step was the edict of 1648 encouraging primogeniture. At the same time the burden of taxation on noble lands was lightened, until by the eighteenth century they were paying virtually no taxes. The power of the aristocracy was strengthened in all walks of life. Only under Victor Amadeus II in the early eighteenth century were any steps taken to reduce their hold on political life, but their economic and landed predominance remained undisturbed.

Whether freed from feudalism (as in England) or subjected to it (as in the east), the land became the mainstay of an aristocratic régime. State protection became normal policy, because the state protected the interests of the landed élite. Colbert's famous 1669 Ordinance on Waters and Forests restricted the rights of the non-propertied to cut wood, just as the English Game Law of 1671 restricted the rights of the rural classes to hunt. The unprecedented legislative activity of the state also had an effect on the formulation of 'mercantilist' policy.

'Mercantilism' did not exist as a formal theory: there were no specifically mercantilist writers and no governments consistently practised mercantilist policies. In retrospect, however, some historians have suggested that the word may be usefully applied to a number of principles that the emergent nation states of western Europe were putting into practice. The state seemed to be intervening for the first time in the formulation of economic policy, and the interests of the state therefore seemed to be coinciding with the wishes of the merchant oligarchies and the élite producers. In England and Holland there is clear evidence that commercial companies exercised influence on the formulation of foreign policy.

The state intervened in economic policy for three virtually self-explanatory reasons: to protect the sources of tax income, to control the movement of bullion, and to protect the trade of its merchants; in three words, fiscality, bullionism, and protectionism. All three aims are most commonly identified with the economic policy of France under Colbert, but can be found also in aspects of the policy of most other states, such as Piedmont under its minister Truchi. In practice the operation of these policies varied considerably. England and Holland gave less importance to 'bullionism', because their enormous entrepôt trade made it necessary for them to let a multilateral system of financial exchange come into existence. France, however, with a simpler trade system, wished logically to maintain a reasonable trade balance, and consequently limited the exit of precious metals.

Social structure and absolutism

Political institutions reflected the disposition of social forces. In England and a few other nations in the north of Europe and to the east of the Elbe, the medieval élite maintained their unity in the face of the king, who was consequently obliged to consult a bi-cameral body consisting of the landed classes (the lords) and the great cities (the commons). In France and most of the German lands the élite became split into interest groups, in accordance with feudalism in its most developed form: parliaments therefore became tri-cameral, with nobles, prelates and commons. Together king and consultative bodies represented an alliance of interests, a 'commonweal' (to use an English term). The tasks of government were minimal: to maintain the proper relationship between classes (that is, to secure order and protect property), and to defend the commonweal.

From the late fifteenth century the collapse of feudalism resulted in greater emphasis on the role of the 'prince'. Renaissance writers such as Machiavelli, Castiglione, Seyssel and Erasmus looked to the prince to bring some order out of the conflict created in post-feudal Europe. The excellent advice they tendered was, however, often wishful thinking; the princes of this time were like an only infant in a domestic nursery: despotic and destructive in the little zone to which he is confined, but powerless to range over the family house where he is by common consent the most important resident. France and Spain were still only embryonic nation-states and their rulers had very limited powers in finance and administration, but in theory their authority was considerable. Late medieval ideas, adapting the language of Roman law, had accepted that the crown should be absolute. Isabella of Castile referred repeatedly to her 'absolute royal power', a phrase which recurs several times in her testament. In France it had been held since the late thirteenth century that the king 'holds his power of none save God and himself'; and later theorists emphasized that he was the source of laws and not subject to them. There was a vast gap between such claims and political reality, but the long-standing theory helped to justify subsequent efforts by princes to free themselves from the control not only of their élites but also, most importantly, of the Church and papacy, which had also made far-reaching claims to political authority.

In the course of the sixteenth century princely pretensions were put to the test. The first great casualty was the papacy, which everywhere found its claims successfully contested not only by nations (it was against the papacy that Thomas Cromwell claimed that 'England is an empire' or sovereign state), but also by its own bishops in each nation. Prelates trained in law maintained in France, Germany, Spain and England that within the realm the crown had broad temporal authority over the Church. The Spanish monarchs by about 1510, the French crown by the Concordat of Bologna in 1516, won extensive control over their respective Churches; and the Reformation, when it came, took several other Churches completely out of papal control. The crown did not benefit from these changes as much as it might have expected. Indeed, the social changes of the sixteenth century seemed to pose new threats to orderly government: economic and social mobility gave a stronger voice to interests, notably the rural and municipal gentry, that sought political power; the price-rise created difficulties for state finance; in some countries (France, Germany) religious differences threatened to bring anarchy.

Ferdinand and Isabella, who were feudal rulers and in no way 'new monarchs', adopted a wholly feudal solution to their problems by allying with their noble and municipal élites. For later European rulers the situation was more complicated. Among the developments which helped them was the emergence of sedentary 'courts', with their ritual and their chivalric glamour, which created a visible centre of authority; the reorganization of laws and the legal system, which confirmed that legislation emanated from the prince; the growth of a bureaucracy, trained in the law faculties of the expanding university system; and the evolution of a modern army under the central command of the state, in place of the old feudal musters. Even while these steps were taking place and writers such as Bodin (*Republic*, 1576) were maintaining that sovereign power was absolute and entitled the king to raise taxes, make war and peace, and so on; in practice rulers were careful not to move a finger without receiving support from sections of the political nation. Autonomous sovereignty was still only an aspiration; 'absolutism' was an ideal construction, in which thinkers attempted to create order out of the disorder they saw around them.

The persistence of absolutist theory, however, is proof that Europeans felt a deep longing for order and peace: in this sense, the theories are a significant attempt to deal with a real problem. Governments were obliged to handle their aristocrats carefully. The Reformation was a powerful spur to the process of power-sharing between the princes and their élites: land-hungry gentry became natural allies of a prince who guaranteed them the property they had seized from the Church. At the same time the images of royal authority (in France, for example, the magical 'king's touch' which was supposed to heal scrofula) became divorced from the Church and more laicized. In England Shakespeare argued for a 'deputy anointed by the Lord' whose authority came from God but was not mediated by the Church, and Elizabeth I declared (in 1585) that 'sovereigns are not bound to render the reasons of their actions to any other but to God'. Despite such claims the rulers of the time acted with remarkable circumspection. Machiavelli in *The Prince* (1514) had been impatient with the weakness of rulers, and kings thereafter increased their personal authority significantly, but all as a rule operated within the limits sanctioned by tradition, with few forays into *raison d'état*.

At the dawn of the seventeenth century nation states were emerging but the power of the ruler was still inadequate. Kings were forced to contend with dissension, revolt, separatism and war at a time when the means available to them, in terms of both cash and personnel, were exiguous. Kingship itself was shaky: England and France survived a disputed succession, but the northern Netherlands had rejected their prince (Philip II) and the elective monarchies of Bohemia and Poland continued to suffer political uncertainty. Muscovy achieved peace in 1613 only after selecting a new dynasty, the Romanovs. All over Europe the privileged classes, sitting in their regional and national assemblies, continued to dispute authority with their rulers. In Upper Austria in 1610 a

Protestant lord actually claimed in the Estates that 'the people chose their prince and can also reject him, the territory decides for itself whether the ruler shall be hereditary'. Princes naturally responded to such claims with doctrines of absolute power. James I, when king of Scotland produced his *Trew Law of Free Monarchies* (1598), and when king of England engaged in a spirited controversy with the papacy and its theorists (Bellarmine and Suarez) over the right of kings to demand an oath of loyalty. Although undoubtedly important at the time, the controversy was over an issue (the relative spheres of papal and kingly authority) that became quickly outdated; the loyalty of nationals to their ruler, regardless of his religion, was never again seriously undermined by papal claims.

The early seventeenth century was the high-tide of absolutist theory in most countries, with the notable exception of Spain, where Mariana and a small group of others reacted against Protestant regalism by proposing instead the democratic foundations of political authority. In France the reaction against the assassination of Henry IV encouraged more extreme absolutist theories than were current elsewhere: notable among the several works that came out was Le Bret's *De la souveraineté du Roi* (1632), which held that 'the sovereign command resides in a single person, and obedience in all others'. In these same years attempts were being made – by Strafford in England, Richelieu in France and Olivares in Spain – to harness and rationalize the resources of the state and strengthen the power of the king. Claude Joly remarked later during the Fronde that 'France has never been a despotic government unless it be in the last thirty years, when we have been subject to the mercy of ministers'. His sentiments are in some degree testimony to the success of the western European experiments in absolutism.

Conflict was inevitable because there were multiple and sometimes contradictory sources of legitimate authority. Many petty princes and small state assemblies also laid claim to sovereignty. In Germany while the theorist Reinking in 1619 defended the emperor as being an absolute monarch, Hippolitus a Lapide in 1640 claimed the same absolute power for each state and for the Imperial Diet as a whole. In Aragon the kings were unable to interfere with the absolute powers (including powers of life and death over their peasants) of the nobility; and even in Castile many lords were virtually sovereign in their own estates. In Poland the nobles exercised sovereign power in their estates and blocked the emergence of a strong central monarchy. 'Absolutism', in short, was not exclusive to the crown; it was not a form of government but merely one way in which power could be exercised. By the mid seventeenth century, indeed, in England and Holland some thinkers had moved towards absolutist republicanism. After 1640 the English Parliament exercised powers far more absolute than any that the Stuart kings had dared use, and Henry Parker in various writings claimed for Parliament the ability even to abolish Magna Carta. In 1649 the Rump Parliament resolved that 'the Commons of England . . . being chosen by and representing the People, have the supreme power in this Nation'. In Holland Spinoza (*Tractatus Politicus*, 1677) argued that 'absolute sovereignty is the sovereignty held by the whole people', and Ulric Huber (*De jure civitatis*) held that the absolute rule of the upper classes was superior to monarchical absolutism because more broadly based and therefore more stable.

Even while advocating royal claims, theorists were aware of traditional and practical restrictions on the exercise of authority. Many apparently extreme writings can, when read carefully, be seen within their context to be realistic. A good example is Charles Loyseau who in his *Traité des Seigneuries* (1610) announced that 'sovereignty consists in absolute power, that is to say in full and complete authority in every respect, and is consequently without superior'. 'However', he goes on, 'since only God is all-powerful the authority of men can never be entirely absolute. There are three kinds of law which limit the sovereign's power without affecting his sovereignty: these are the laws of God, the natural rules of justice, and the fundamental laws of the state.' Similarly Le Bret in 1632, while declaring royal sovereignty to be unlimited, went on to specify that the monarch must respect private property, could not alter the succession to the throne, and could not issue a command contrary to divine law. Bossuet, well known as an exponent of Louis XIV's absolutism, declared in the late century that the absolute sovereign must abide by the laws of the kingdom. An absolute ruler claimed to be free (*absolutus legibus*) from subjection to the law, but only because he was the fount of law, not because he intended to break the law. Absolute power implied autonomy or sovereignty, not despotism.

Were any acts of European rulers 'absolute'? The question is potentially a philosophical rather than a historical one. In practice it would seem that any royal decrees issued on the prince's sole authority might be *ipso facto* absolute, hence the strong suspicion with which lawyers in Tudor and Stuart England regarded the crown's right to issue proclamations (as confirmed in a statute of 1539). Outstanding among occasions when governments in western Europe acted alone and without consultation, were those when *raison d'état* permitted political assassination (the murder of Wallenstein is a good example). Louis XIV's revocation of the Edict of Nantes, often quoted as an absolute act, is a particularly weak example of absolutism: it came only at the end of a decade or more of persecution and merely set the seal on a process that had originated not with the crown but in the lower levels of the administration. In practice 'absolute' acts are as difficult to identify as 'infallible' papal decrees. Contemporary critics of Philip II, Charles I and Louis XIV felt on surer grounds when they condemned 'tyranny', a familiar Graeco-Roman concept, whereas 'absolutism' fell into no recognized category and so could not be easily identified.

By the same token, though 'absolute' princes preferred to rule without Estates, government without Estates did not in itself signify absolutism. Bourbon France after 1614 had no Estates General but was by no means short of representative assemblies. As a general rule, no western governments thought they were free from the need to consult at least some of their traditional institutions (even in France, though the Estates were not called Richelieu convoked the Assembly of Notables; and though Habsburg Spain had no Cortes after 1665 the cities represented in Cortes were directly consulted). In a society that was a complex amalgam of many different interests, representative bodies were not the only guarantors of the rule of law. Rulers had to be wary of the Church, of city corporations, of regional assemblies. States that were beginning to evolve some form of central apparatus were far from achieving any authentic centralization, thanks to the existence of other autonomies within the nation. By the early seventeenth century the western monarchies all had consultative and executive bodies in their capital cities, but in the absence of a national bureaucracy they were virtually body-less heads. Even more important was the fact that the social structure proved an obstacle to the centralization of power.

It is too often assumed that where absolutism flourished the ruling élite was crushed, its privileges removed, the Church subjected, the common people overwhelmed by taxes. This negative view identifies state power with coercion. Yet perhaps the two most successful rulers in the period covered by this book – Isabella of Castile in about 1500, Henry IV of France in about 1600 – became living legends and won the hearts of their subjects precisely because they used the minimum of coercion. There is therefore good reason to argue that consent rather than coercion was the basis on which the power of the emergent state came to rest.

Perhaps the most convincing way to view royal absolutism is as an overall supervising authority arbitrating between conflicting interests. Theorists such as Loyseau and Le Bret felt a need to elevate the executive authority of the crown, and in so doing they expanded on medieval principles of sovereignty. But at every stage they recognized that interests such as the Church, the nobility and the law must be respected. In practice, of course, kings in numberless individual instances broke all the rules: they usurped ecclesiastical rights, arrested and executed nobles, levied taxes, and broke laws ranging from regional laws to laws regulating the succession. They were able to do this not because they were strong but because they were able to play off interests against each other. A particularly telling example is the way in which the crown at the French Estates General of 1614 was able to divide the Estates and annihilate their role in politics; thereafter the First and Second Estates were summoned separately, the Third not at all. Similarly the monarchy survived the Fronde not because it was strong but because its opponents were divided. From the early sixteenth to the late seventeenth century, the undoubted increase in royal authority was achieved without any significant diminution in the power of élites. This was possible because power shifted *within* the ruling class from the traditional aristocracy to the recently ennobled. The state was able to exploit this shift of power and use it to its own advantage.

The power of élites altered but did not diminish. In part this was because the nobility everywhere retained its monopoly of the bulk of national wealth; in part also because newer status groups – the noblesse de robe, the gentry – broadened the hold of the upper classes on political and economic life. In these circumstances the crown could hold and increase its authority only as an arbiter between interest groups, gratifying sections of the élite with honours and offices while taking care to protect its own position as the source of patronage. Progress towards 'absolutism' thus involved compromises at every stage. In times of strained relations the élite took refuge in traditional laws, thus making the crown seem to be the aggressor. In Aragon the appeal (in 1591 and 1640) was to the fueros, in England a tradition of Common Law was felt to be the force by which (Parliament declared in 1642) 'the nobility and gentry enjoy their estates, are protected from any sort of violence and power, and differenced from the meaner sort of people'. These, the meaner sort, in their turn responded by rebellions that could be used by some of their leaders (as Mousnier rightly argues) against the fiscal pretensions of the 'absolute' state.

It has rightly been argued that the power and role of the state in the sixteenth and seventeenth centuries was enhanced by the regularity of war. The declaration of war was reserved to the monarch alone; he obtained sole right to command the nation's armed forces; military needs provided a pretext to raise extra taxes. Possibly three-quarters of a state budget might be allotted to war (including defence and diplomacy). In the process, important structural changes would occur: new administrative personnel would be required; the armed forces might (in what has been called a 'military revolution') be made more professional, cutting out reliance on mercenary troops; the regularity of conflict would stimulate back-up industries (uniforms, weapons, food supplies) and so give an added boost to nascent capitalism. Though war might promote state initiative and administrative change, however, it did not necessarily lead to princely absolutism. No modern state could wage war properly without training an officer class, and in every case the increase in military activity boosted rather than diminished the power of the traditional élite: in Spain Philip II decentralized defence and put it in the hands of the local grandees; in Brandenburg the Great Elector relied on the nobles for the efficiency of his army organization. Moreover, the soaring costs of war, far from stabilizing the state, caused profound social conflicts over fiscality and eventually provoked revolutions against the monarchy.

One contradiction in early absolutism, then, was that more authority was being gained by the crown (in France, for example, aristocratic criminal activity declined during the seventeenth century), but effective political power remained in the hands of both the old and the new élites. Attempts by the crown to achieve greater autonomy led everywhere to a crisis confrontation. The outcome has sometimes, and unsatisfactorily, been presented as a victory of constitutionalism over the prince in part of northern Europe (England, the United Provinces), and of the prince over the constitution in the rest of the continent. In practice there was no outright victory by either side. Though revolutionary acts did take place – in England the abolition of the system of conciliar government, in France the subordination of the Parlement of Paris and later of the provincial estates – the social structure remained untouched and immobile, thus guaranteeing both continuity and stability. In the more favourable economic conditions of the late century, 'absolutism' changed its character. In the early seventeenth century absolutism was an extension of earlier attempts to consolidate authority in the person of the monarch. In the later period it had become a device to consolidate authority jointly in the monarch and the political nation.

The drift towards the newer absolutism (William III's coup in 1650, undertaken against the wishes of the bourgeois élite, was atypical) was accompanied by the demise of representative government. The disappearance of traditional institutions was not, however, necessarily a sign of tyranny. The Diet in Brandenburg lost its effective power after 1653, the Estates of Prussia after 1663. The last Zemsky Sobor met in Russia in 1653, the last Danish parliament in 1660. The Parlement of Paris was silenced in the 1660s, the French provincial Estates in the 1670s. Habsburg Castile had no Cortes after 1665, Sweden and Piedmont became absolutist in the 1680s. It would appear that freedom was being silenced all over Europe. In reality most of these bodies concurred (with an occasional protest) in their own demise. Their disappearance did little to change the balance of power. In the provinces the local élites were still in firm control. And even when there were no active Estates, every rational government had to continue to consult regularly with municipal corporations, courts of justice, trade guilds and other national and regional bodies. 'Absolutism' therefore succeeded for a while because it appeared to reconcile the interests of the élite and of the state. Only when it failed to keep in touch with opinion (this was why criticism arose in the later years of Louis XIV) did it begin to seem tyrannical.

No political class in Europe would have been so foolish as to sign away all its political privileges, and no king was so foolish as to believe that absolute power gave him the right to act against the economic interests of the élite. The theoreticians, like Spinoza in his *Tractatus* (1677), or Schumacher in the Danish 'Lex Regia' of

1709, envisaged the monarch as an epitome of state power: the king was the state, in the sense claimed by Louis XIV. But as with the omnipotent modern state, the absolute monarch was meant to be a reconciler of interests. In practical terms this meant that he must respect the interests, above all the property interests, of the élite. This is what Bossuet, Louis XIV's greatest apologist, meant when he argued that 'what is termed legitimate government is by its very nature the opposite of arbitrary government'. Viewed in these terms, the most realistic political philosopher of the new type of government was not the idealistic Hobbes with his *Leviathan* (1650), but the non-authoritarian Locke, with his claim in the *Second Treatise of Civil Government* (1690) that 'the great and chief end of men . . . putting themselves under government, is the preservation of their property'. Despite the many conceptual differences between Locke and the continental Europeans, his was the most faithful expression of the views of the propertied élite. And despite institutional differences the social basis of authority in England was not greatly different from that in France or Denmark: certainly the propertied citizens of these countries were no more enslaved than Englishmen were, despite the decay of their representative bodies. The rhetoric of absolutist theory should not therefore be confused with the reality of social experience. Though absolutism might mean the rule of a single person, that person could not maintain his power without the aid of the social structure; it was the governing class that supplied officers for the army, administrators for the machinery of state. Agrarian developments of the seventeenth century gave landlords a greater part in profits and in the political process: the state seemed to work hand in hand with the producing élite, thereby assuring dominance to the gentry in England, the Junkers in Prussia, the rural nobility in France. The stability of the late seventeenth century arose from a broadening of the previously narrow social base on which state power had precariously rested. Rebellions by the élite were now virtually a thing of the past: social and political relationships settled into the mould from which they were to be rudely shaken only by the French Revolution.

Select bibliography

Where available in translation, the English editions of foreign works are cited. Only limited reference is made to works on economic and political history.

General and regional studies

B. Bennassar, *Valladolid au Siècle d'Or*, Paris 1967.

C.R. Boxer, *The Dutch Seaborne Empire 1600–1800*, London 1965.

F. Braudel, *Capitalism and material life, 1400–1800*, London 1973.

F. Braudel, *The Mediterranean and the Mediterranean world in the age of Philip II*, 2 vols., London 1972–3.

P. Chaunu, *La civilisation de l'Europe classique*, Paris 1966.

C.M. Cipolla (ed.), *The Fontana Economic History of Europe*, vol. 2, *The sixteenth and seventeenth centuries*, London 1974.

G.N. Clark, *The seventeenth century*, Oxford 1947².

P. Clark, *English provincial society from the Reformation to the Revolution. Religion, politics and society in Kent 1500–1640*, London 1977.

D.C. Coleman, *The economy of England, 1450–1750*, Oxford 1977.

A. Croix, *La Bretagne aux XVIe et XVIIe siècles*, 2 vols., Paris 1980.

J. Delumeau, *Vie économique et sociale de Rome dans la seconde moitié du XVIe siècle*, 2 vols., Paris 1957–9.

P. Deyon, *Amiens, capitale provinciale*, Paris 1967.

G. Duby and A. Wallon (eds.), *Histoire de la France rurale*, vol. 2, *L'âge classique des paysans, 1340–1789*, Paris 1975.

L. Febvre, *Philippe II et la Franche-Comté*, Paris 1911.

L. Frey, M. Frey and J. Schneider, *Women in Western European History: a select bibliography from Antiquity to the French Revolution*, Brighton 1982.

P. Goubert, *Beauvais et le Beauvaisis de 1600 à 1730*, 2 vols., Paris 1960.

P. Goubert, *The Ancien Regime*, London 1973.

H. Kamen, *Spain in the Later Seventeenth Century, 1665–1700*, London 1981.

E. Le Roy Ladurie, *The Peasants of Languedoc*, Chicago 1974.

P. Léon (ed.), *Histoire économique et sociale du monde*, vol. 1, P. Chaunu and B. Bennassar (eds.), *L'ouverture du monde XIV–XVIe siècles*, Paris

1977; vol. 2, P. Deyon and J. Jacquart (eds.), *Les hésitations de la croissance, 1580–1740*, Paris 1978.

R. Mandrou, *Introduction to modern France, 1500–1640*, London 1976.

R. Mousnier, *Les XVIe et XVIIe et XVIIe siècles*, vol. 4 of *Histoire Générale des Civilisations*, Paris 1967[5].

N.J.G. Pounds, *An historical geography of Europe, 1500–1840*, Cambridge 1979.

E.E. Rich and C.H. Wilson (eds.), *The Cambridge Economic History of Europe*; vol. 4, *The economy of expanding Europe*, Cambridge 1967; vol. 5, *The economic organisation of early modern Europe*, Cambridge 1977.

J. Thirsk (ed.), *The agrarian history of England and Wales, vol. 4 1500–1640*, Cambridge 1967.

H.R. Trevor-Roper, *Religion, the Reformation and social change*, London 1967.

J. de Vries, *The economy of Europe in an age of crisis 1600–1750*, Cambridge 1976.

J. de Vries, *European urbanization 1500–1800*, London 1984.

I. Wallerstein, *The Modern World System*, 2 vols., New York 1974, 1980.

K. Wrightson, *English Society 1580–1680*, London 1982.

Chapter 1   Population structures

Population and community

A. Bellettini, 'Ricerche sulle crisi demografiche del seicento', *Società e Storia*, **1**, no. i, 1978.

J. Blum, 'The internal structure and policy of the European village community from the fifteenth to the nineteenth century', *Journal of Modern History*, **43**, 1971.

G. Cabourdin, *Terre et hommes en Lorraine 1550–1635*, 2 vols., Paris 1977.

C. Cipolla, *Clocks and culture 1300–1700*, London 1967.

M. Devèze, *La vie de la forêt française au XVIe siècle*, 2 vols., Paris 1961.

'Famiglia e Comunità', *Quaderni Storici*, **33**, September–December 1976.

M.W. Flinn, *The European Demographic System 1500–1820*, London 1981.

R. Gascon, 'Immigration et croissance au XVIe siècle: l'exemple de Lyon (1529–1563)', *Annales*, **XXV**, 1970.

D.V. Glass and D.E.C. Eversley (eds.), *Population in History*, London 1965.

D. Grigg, *Population growth and agrarian change*, Cambridge 1980.

J.P. Gutton, *La sociabilité villageoise dans l'Ancienne France: solidarités et voisinages du XVIe au XVIIe siècle*, Paris 1979.

L. Henry, *Anciennes familles genevoises. Etude démographique XVIe–XXe siècle*, Paris 1956.

T.H. Hollingsworth, *The demography of the British peerage*, Supplement to *Population Studies*, **18** no. 2, 1965.

R. Mols, *Introduction à la Démographie Historique des Villes d'Europe du XIVe au XVIIIe siècle*, 3 vols., Louvain 1955.

O. Placht, *Lidnatost a spolecenská skladba Ceského státu v. 16–18 stoleti* (The population and social structure of Bohemia in the 16th and 17th centuries), Prague 1957. With German summary.

J. Pitt-Rivers, *The People of the Sierra*, Chicago 1971[2].

E.A. Wrigley, *Population and history*, London 1969.

E.A. Wrigley and R.S. Schofield, *The Population History of England 1541–1871. A reconstruction*, London 1981.

The family

L.K. Berkner, 'The use and misuse of census data for the historical analysis of family structure', *Journal of Interdisciplinary History*, **5** no. 4, 1975.

'Le XVIIe siècle et la famille', *XVIIe Siècle*, nos. 102–3, 1974.

J.L. Flandrin, *Families in Former Times. Kinship, Household and Sexuality*, Cambridge 1979.

J.L. Flandrin, 'Repression and change in the sexual life of young people', *Journal of Family History*, **2**, 1977.

P. Goubert, 'Family and Province: a contribution to our knowledge of family structure in early modern France', *Journal of Family History*, **2**, 1977.

O. Hufton, 'Women in history', *Past and Present*, no. 101, 1983.

P. Laslett (ed.), *Household and Family in Past Time*, Cambridge 1972.

R. Burr Litchfield, 'Demographic characteristics of Florentine patrician families', *Journal of Economic History*, **29** no. 2, 1969.

A. Macfarlane, *The origins of English individualism: the family, property and social transition*, Oxford 1978.

L. de Mause (ed.), *The History of Childhood*, New York 1974.

M. Mitterauer and R. Sieder, *The European Family*, London 1982.

H. Medick, 'The proto-industrial family economy: the structural function of household and family during the transition from peasant society to industrial capitalism', *Social History*, **3**, 1976.

L. Stone, *The family, sex and marriage in England 1500–1800*, London 1977.

R. Thompson, *Women in Stuart England and America: a comparative study*, London 1974.

R. Wheaton, 'Family and kinship in western Europe: the problem of the Joint Family Household', *Journal of Interdisciplinary History*, **5** no. 4, 1975.

T.M. Safley, 'Marital litigation in the diocese of Constance, 1551–1620', *Sixteenth-Century Journal*, **12** no. 2, 1981.

T.M. Safley, 'The Basler Ehegericht, 1550–1592', *Journal of Family*

History, **7** no. 2, 1982.

Population checks

W. Abel, *Massenarmut und Hungerkrisen im vorindustriellen Europa*, Hamburg 1974.

A.B. Appleby, *Famine in Tudor and Stuart England*, Stanford 1978.

P. Ariès, *The Hour of our Death*, London 1981.

B. Bennassar, *Recherches sur les grands épidémies dans le nord de l'Espagne à la fin du XVIe siècle*, Paris 1969.

H. Bergues *et al.*, *La prévention des naissances dans la famille*, Paris 1960.

J.N. Biraben, *Les hommes et la peste en France et dans les pays européens et méditerranéens*, 2 vols., Paris 1975–6.

P. Chaunu, *La mort à Paris, XVIe, XVIIe et XVIIIe siècles*, Paris 1978.

L. Clarkson, *Death, Disease and Famine in pre-industrial England*, London 1975.

A. Feillet, *La misère au temps de la Fronde*, Paris 1862.

R. Finlay, *Population and Metropolis. The Demography of London, 1580–1640*, Cambridge 1981.

G. Franz, *Der Dreissigjährige Krieg und das deutsche Volk*, Stuttgart 1961.

C. Friedrichs, *Urban society in an age of war: Nordlingen 1580–1720*, Princeton 1979.

I. Gieysztorowa, 'Guerre et régression en Masovie aux XVIe et XVIIe siècles', *Annales*, **13**, 1958.

J. Jacquart, *La crise rurale en Ile de France 1550–1670*, Paris 1974.

H. Kamen, 'The social and economic consequences of the Thirty Years War', *Past and Present*, no. 39, 1968.

E. Keyser, 'Neue deutsche Forschungen über die Geschichte der Pest', *Vierteljahrschrift für Sozial– und Wirtschaftsgeschichte*, **44**, 1957.

E. Le Roy Ladurie, *Times of Feast, Times of Famine. A history of climate since the year 1000*, London 1972.

F. Lebrun, *Les hommes et la mort en Anjou aux XVIIe et XVIIIe siècles*, Paris 1971.

F. Lebrun, 'Les crises démographiques en France aux XVIIe et XVIIIe siècles', *Annales*, **35**, 1980.

G. Parker, 'War and economic change: the economic costs of the Dutch revolt', in *Spain and the Netherlands 1559–1659*, London 1979.

V. Pérez Moreda, *Las crisis de mortalidad en la Espana interior. Siglos XVI–XIX*, Madrid 1980.

A.-M. Piuz, 'Alimentation populaire et sous-alimentation au XVIIe siècle. Le cas de Genève', *Schweizerische Zeitschrift für Geschichte*, **18**, 1968.

E. Scholliers, *Loonarbeid en honger. De levenstandaard in de XVe en XVIe eeuw te Antwerpen*, Antwerp 1960. With French summary.

A. Sharlin, 'Natural decrease in early modern cities: a reconsideration', *Past and Present*, no. 79, 1978.

P. Slack, 'The disappearance of plague: an alternative view', *Economic History Review*, **34**, 1981.

E. Thoen, 'Warfare and the countryside: social and economic aspects of the military destruction in Flanders', *Acta Historica Neerlandica*, **13**, 1980.

J. Walter and K. Wrightson, 'Dearth and the social order in early modern England', *Past and Present*, no. 71, 1976.

C. Webster (ed.), *Health, medicine and mortality in the sixteenth century*, Cambridge 1979.

E.A. Wrigley, 'Family limitation in pre-industrial England', *Economic History Review*, **19** no. 1, 1966.

Chapter 2   Prices and change

W. Abel, *Agricultural fluctuations in Europe from the thirteenth to the twentieth centuries*, London 1980.

G. Bois, *Crise du féodalisme. Economie rurale et démographie en Normandie orientale du début du 14e siècle au milieu du 16e siècle*, Paris 1976.

Y.S. Brenner, 'The inflation of prices in early sixteenth-century England', *Economic History Review*, **14** no. 2, 1961.

A. Chabert, 'Encore la révolution des prix au XVIe siècle', *Annales*, **12**, 1957.

C. Cipolla, 'La prétendue révolution des prix. Réflexions sur l'expérience italienne', *Annales*, **10**, 1955.

P. Clark, 'The migrant in Kentish towns 1580–1640', in P. Clark and P. Slack, *Crisis and Order in English towns 1500–1700*, London 1972.

J.D. Gould, 'The price revolution reconsidered', *Economic History Review*, **17** no. 2, 1964.

E.J. Hamilton, *American Treasure and the price revolution in Spain 1501–1650*, Cambridge, Mass. 1934.

I. Hammarstrom, 'The Price Revolution of the sixteenth century: some Swedish evidence', *Scandinavian Economic History Review*, 1957.

S. Hoszowski, 'The revolution of prices in Poland in the 16th and 17th centuries', *Acta Poloniae Historica*, **2**, 1959.

P. Jeannin, *L'Europe du nord-ouest et du nord aux XVIIᵉ et XVIIIᵉ siècles*, Paris 1969.

P. Kriedte, *Feudalismo tardío y capital mercantil*, Barcelona 1982.

P. Laslett and J. Harrison, 'Clayworth and Cogenhoe', in H.E. Bell and R.L. Ollard (eds.), *Historical Essays 1660–1750 presented to David Ogg*, London 1963.

E. Le Roy Ladurie and P. Couperie, 'Le mouvement des loyers parisiens de la fin du Moyen Age au XVIIIᵉ siècle', *Annales*, **25**, 1970.

C. Lis and H. Soly, *Poverty and Capitalism in pre-industrial Europe*, London 1979.

A. de Maddalena, 'A Milano nei secoli XVI e XVII: Da ricchezza reale a ricchezza nominale?', *Rivista Storica Italiana*, **89**, 1977.

F. Mauro, *Le XVIᵉ siècle européen: aspects économiques*, Paris 1966.

E.H. Phelps Brown and S.V. Hopkins, 'Wage-rates and prices: evidence for population pressure in the sixteenth century', *Economica*, **24**, 1957.

E.H. Phelps Brown and S.V. Hopkins, 'Builders' wage-rates, prices and population: some further evidence', *Economica*, **26**, 1959.

R. Romano, 'Tra XVI e XVII secolo. Una crisi economica: 1619–1622', *Rivista Storica Italiana*, **74**, 1962.

I. Schoffer, 'Did Holland's golden age coincide with a period of crisis?', *Acta Historiae Neerlandica*, **1**, 1966.

L. Stone and A. Everitt, 'Social mobility in England 1500–1700', *Past and Present*, no. 33, 1966.

K. Thomas, 'Work and leisure in pre-industrial society', *Past and Present*, no. 29, 1964.

C. Verlinden *et al.*, 'Mouvements des prix et des salaires en Belgique au XVIᵉ siècle', *Annales*, **10**, 1955.

P. Vilar, *Or et monnaie dans l'histoire, 1450–1920*, Paris 1974.

D. Woodward, 'Wage rates and living standards in pre-industrial England', *Past and Present*, no. 91, 1981.

Chapter 3   Economic structures

V. Barbour, *Capitalism in Amsterdam*, Michigan 1963.

J.F. Bergier, *Naissance et croissance de la Suisse industrielle*, Bern 1974.

H.I. Bloom, *The economic activities of the Jews of Amsterdam in the seventeenth and eighteenth centuries*, Williamsport, Pa. 1936.

I. Bog (ed.), *Der Aussenhandel Ostmitteleuropas, 1450–1650*, Cologne 1971.

W. Bodmer, *Der Einfluss der Refugianten-einwanderung von 1550–1700 auf die schweizerische Wirtschaft*, Zurich 1946.

P. Boissonnade, *Le socialisme d'état. L'industrie et les classes industrielles pendant les deux premiers siècles de l'ère moderne (1453–1661)*, Paris 1927.

W. Brulez, 'De diaspora der Antwerpse kooplui op het einde van de 16e eeuw', *Bijdragen voor de Geschiedenis der Nederlanden*, **15** no. 4, 1960.

D.C. Coleman, 'Proto-industrialization. A concept too many', *Economic History Review*, **36** no. 3, 1983.

R. DuPlessis and M. Holwell, 'Reconsidering the early modern urban economy: the cases of Leiden and Lille', *Past and Present*, no. 94, 1982.

P. Earle (ed.), *Essays in European economic history, 1500–1800*, Oxford 1974.

A. Ernstberger, *Hans de Witte, finanzmann Wallensteins*, Wiesbaden 1954.

G. Fischer, *Aus zwei Jahrhunderten Leipziger Handelsgeschichte 1470–1650 (Die kaufmännische Einwanderung und ihre Auswirkungen)*,

Leipzig 1929.

J.T. Fuhrmann, *The origins of capitalism in Russia. Industry and progress in the sixteenth and seventeenth centuries*, Chicago 1972.

R. Gascon, *Grand commerce et vie urbaine au XVIe siècle: Lyon et ses marchands*, Paris 1971.

H. Hauser, *Les débuts du capitalisme*, Paris 1927.

R. Hilton (ed.), *The transition from feudalism to capitalism*, London 1976.

H. Kamen, 'The decline of Spain: a historical myth?', *Past and Present*, no. 8, 1978.

H. Kellenbenz, *The Rise of the European Economy. An economic history of continental Europe 1500–1750*, London 1976.

F. Krantz and P.M. Hohenberg (eds.), *Failed transition to modern industrial society: Renaissance Italy and seventeenth-century Holland*, Montreal 1975.

H. Lapeyre, 'La banque, les changes et le crédit au XVIe siècle', *Revue d'histoire moderne et contemporaine*, 3, 1956.

A. Maczak, 'Money and society in Poland and Lithuania in the sixteenth and seventeenth centuries', *Journal of European Economic History*, 5 no. 1, 1976.

F.A. Norwood, *The Reformation refugees as an economic force*, Chicago 1942.

A. Paul, 'Les réfugiés huguenots et wallons dans le Palatinat du Rhin du XVIe siècle à la Révolution', *Revue Historique*, 157, 1928.

R.T. Rapp, *Industry and economic decline in seventeenth-century Venice*, Harvard 1976.

H. Schilling, 'Innovation through migration: The settlements of Calvinistic Netherlanders in sixteenth- and seventeenth-century central and western Europe', *Histoire Sociale*, 16 no. 31, 1983.

E. Silberner, *La guerre dans la pensée économique du XVIe au XVIIIe siècle*, Paris 1939.

W. Sombart, *Der moderne Kapitalismus*, 3 vols. in 5 tomes, Munich-Leipzig 1916–27.

H. van der Wee, *The Growth of the Antwerp Market and the European Economy*, 3 vols., Antwerp 1963.

R.H. Tawney (ed.), *Thomas Wilson's Discourse upon Usury*, London 1925.

R. van Roosbroeck, *Emigranten. Nederlandse vluchtlingen in Duitsland (1500–1600)*, Louvain 1968.

Chapter 4   Nobles and gentlemen

G. d'Avenel, *La noblesse française sous Richelieu*, Paris 1901.

K. Agren, 'Rise and decline of an aristocracy', *Scandinavian Journal of History*, 1 nos. 1–2, 1976.

G. Baker, 'Nobilità in declino: il caso di Siena sotto i Medici e gli Asburgo-

Lorena', *Rivista Storica Italiana*, **84** no. 2, 1972.

Y.-M. Bercé, 'De la criminalité aux troubles sociaux: La noblesse rurale du Sud-Ouest de la France sous Louis XIII', *Annales du Midi*, **76**, 1964.

M. Berengo, *Nobili e mercanti nella Lucca del Cinquecento*, Turin 1965.

F. Bluche, 'The social origins of the secretaries of State under Louis XIV, 1661–1715', in R. Hatton (ed.), *Louis XIV and Absolutism*, London 1976.

O. Brunner, *Adeliges Landleben und Europäischer Geist*, Salzburg 1949.

O. Brunner, *Neue Wege der Sozialgeschichte*, Gottingen 1956.

J.C. Davis, *The decline of the Venetian nobility as a ruling class*, Baltimore 1962.

P. Deyon, 'A propos des rapports entre la noblesse française et la monarchie absolue pendant la première moitíe du XVIIe siècle', *Revue Historique*, **231**, 1964.

A. Domínguez Oritz, *La sociedad española en el siglo XVII*, Madrid 1963.

W. Dworzaczek, 'La mobilité sociale de la noblesse polonaise aux XVIe et XVIIe siècles', *Acta Poloniae Historica*, **36**, 1977.

M.-C. Gerbet, *La noblesse dans le royaume de Castille. Etude sur ses structures sociales en Estrémadure de 1454 à 1516*, Paris 1979.

E.F. Guarini (ed.), *Potere e società negli stati regionali italiani del '500 e '600*, Bologna 1978.

H. Kellenbenz, 'German aristocratic entrepreneurship. Economic activities of the Holstein nobility in the 16th and 17th centuries', *Explorations in Entrepreneurial History*, **6**, 1953–4.

J. Kowecki, 'Les transformations de la structure sociale en Pologne au XVIIe siècle: la noblesse et la bourgeoisie', *Acta Poloniae Historica*, **26**, 1972.

J.P. Labatut, *Les noblesses européennes de la fin du XVe à la fin du XVIIIe siècle*, Paris 1978.

R. Mazzei, *La società lucchese del Seicento*, Lucca 1977.

R. Mousnier, *The Institutions of France under the Absolute Monarchy 1598–1789*, Chicago 1979.

H. Nader, 'Noble income in sixteenth-century Castile: the case of the Marquises of Mondéjar, 1480–1580', *Economic History Review*, **30**, 1977.

E.L. Petersen, 'The crisis of the Danish nobility, 1580–1660', in M. Ferro (ed.), *Social historians in contemporary France. Essays from Annales*, New York 1972.

H. Rosenberg, 'The rise of the Junkers in Brandenburg-Prussia 1410–1653', *American Historical Review*, **49** nos. 1–2, 1943–4.

L. Stone, *The crisis of the aristocracy, 1558–1641*, Oxford 1965.

P. de Vaissière, *Gentilshommes campagnards de l'Ancienne France*, Paris 1903.

S.J. Woolf, 'Economic problems of the nobility in the early modern period: the example of Piedmont', *Economic History Review*, **17** no. 2, 1964.

L.P. Wright, 'The military orders in 16th and 17th century Spanish society', *Past and Present*, no. 43, 1969.

A. Wyczanski, *Studia nad folwarkiem szlacheckim w Polsce w latach 1500–1580* (Studies on the noble estates in Poland, 1500–1580), Warsaw 1960.

G. Zeller, 'La vie aventureuse des classes supérieures en France sous l'Ancien Régime: brigandage et piraterie', *Cahiers internationaux de Sociologie*, **28**, 1960.

G. Zeller, 'Une notion de caractère historico-social: la dérogeance', *Cahiers internationaux de Sociologie*, **22**, 1957.

G. Zenobi, *Ceti e potere nella Marca Pontificia. Formazione e organizzazione della piccola nobiltà fra '500 e '700*, Bologna 1976.

Chapter 5   The bourgeoisie

F. Angiolini and P. Malanima, 'Problemi della mobilità sociale a Firenze tra la metà del cinquecento e i primi decenni del seicento', *Società e Storia*, no. 4, 1979.

G. Barni, 'Mutamenti di ideali sociali del secolo XVI al secolo XVIII: giuristi, nobiltà, mercatura', *Rivista internazionale di filosofia del diritto*, 1957.

R. Baron, 'La bourgeoisie de Varzy au XVIIe siècle', *Annales de Bourgogne*, **36**, 1964.

S. Berner, 'The Florentine patriciate in the transition from republic to principato, 1530–1609', *Studies in Medieval and Renaissance History*, 1972.

L. Bulferetti, 'L'oro, la terra e la società', *Archivio Storico Lombardo*, series 8, vol. 4, 1953.

P. Burke, *Venice and Amsterdam: a study of seventeenth-century elites*, London 1974.

P. Bushkovich, *The Merchants of Moscow, 1580–1650*, Cambridge 1980.

B. Caizzi, *Il Comasco sotto il dominio spagnolo*, Como 1955.

J.T. Cliffe, *The Yorkshire gentry from the Reformation to the Civil War*, London 1969.

J. Dewald, *The formation of a provincial nobility. The magistrates of the Parlement of Rouen, 1490–1610*, London 1980.

H. van Dijk and D.J. Roorda, 'Social mobility under the regents of the Republic', *Acta Historica Neerlandica*, **9**, 1976.

J. Estèbe, 'La bourgeoisie marchande et la terre à Toulouse au XVIe siècle', *Annales du Midi*, **76**, 1964.

C.H. George, 'The making of the English bourgeoisie, 1500–1750', *Science and Society*, **35** no. 4, 1971.

R.B. Grassby, 'Social status and commercial enterprise under Louis XIV', *Economic History Review*, **13** no. 1, 1960.

R. Hellie, 'The stratification of Muscovite society: the townsmen', *Russian History*, **5** no. 2, 1978.

J. Kaufmann-Rochard, *Origines d'une bourgeoisie russe*, Paris 1969.

H.P. Liebel, 'The bourgeoisie in southwestern Germany, 1500–1789: a rising class?', *International Review of Social History*, **10**, 1965.

P. Malanima, *I Riccardi di Firenze. Una famiglia e un patrimonio nella Toscana dei Medici*, Florence 1977.

F. Mauro, 'La bourgeoisie portugaise au XVIIᵉ siècle', *XVII Siècle*, 1958.

R. Mousnier, *La vénalité des offices sous Henri IV et Louis XIII*, Rouen 1946.

R. Mousnier, 'L'opposition politique bourgeoise à la fin du XVIᵉ siècle et au début du XVIIᵉ siècle', *Revue Historique*, **212**, 1955.

R. Pernoud, *Histoire de la bourgeoisie en France*, 2 vols., Paris 1962.

T.K. Rabb, *Enterprise and Empire. Merchant and gentry investment in the expansion of England 1575–1630*, Harvard 1967.

D.J. Roorda, 'The ruling classes in Holland in the 17th century', in J.S. Bromley and E. Kossmann (eds.), *Britain and the Netherlands*, vol. 2, Groningen 1962.

G. Roupnel, *La ville et la campagne au XVIIᵉ siècle*, Paris 1922.

H. Soly, 'The Betrayal of the sixteenth-century Bourgeoisie: a Myth?', *Acta Historiae Neerlandicae*, **8**, 1975.

L. Stone, 'Social mobility in England, 1500–1700', *Past and Present*, no. 33, 1966.

K.W. Swart, *Sale of offices in the seventeenth century*, The Hague 1949.

H.R. Trevor-Roper, 'The Gentry', *Economic History Review*, supplement, 1953.

M. Venard, *Bourgeois et paysans au XVIIᵉ siècle*, Paris 1958.

Chapter 6   The peasantry

K. Blaschke, 'Das Bauernlegen in Sachsen', *Vierteljahrschrift für Sozial- und Wirtschaftsgeschichte*, **42**, 1955.

J. Blum, *Lord and peasant in Russia*, Princeton 1961.

R. Brenner, 'Agrarian class structure and economic development in pre-industrial Europe', *Past and Present*, **70**, 1976.

G. Delille, *Croissance d'une société rurale. Montesarchio et la Vallée Caudine aux XVIIᵉ et XVIIIᵉ siècles*, Naples 1973.

C. d'Eszlary, 'La situation des serfs en Hongrie de 1514 à 1848', *Revue d'Histoire économique et sociale*, **4**, 1960.

G. Franz (ed.), *Bauernschaft und Bauerstand 1500–1970*, Limburg 1975.

C.J. Fuchs, *Der Untergang des Bauernstandes und das Aufkommen der Gutsherrschaften in Neuvorpommern und Rügen*, Strassburg 1888.

G. Giorgetti, *Capitalismo e agricoltura*, Turin 1977.

P. Goubert, *La vie quotidienne des paysans français au XVIIᵉ siècle*, Paris 1982.

W.G. Hoskins, *The Midland peasant*, London 1957.

E. Kerridge, *The Agricultural Revolution*, London 1967.

E. Kerridge, *Agrarian problems in the sixteenth century and after*, London 1969.

W. Kula, *An economic theory of the feudal system. Towards a model of the Polish economy 1500–1800*, London 1976.

A. Lepre, *Feudi e Masserie. Problemi della società meridionale nel '600 e nel '700*, Naples 1973.

L. Makkai, 'Neo-serfdom: its origin and nature in east central Europe', *Slavic Review*, **34**, June 1975.

F. Lütge, *Geschichte der deutschen Agrarverfassung vom frühen Mittelalter bis zum 19. Jahrhundert*, Stuttgart 1963.

F. McArdle, *Altopascio. A study in Tuscan rural society, 1587–1784*, Cambridge 1978.

A. Mika, 'Feudalni velkostatek v jiznich cechach (XIV–XVII stol.)' (The great feudal estates in southern Bohemia), *Historicky Sbornik*, **1**, 1973.

T. Munck, 'The economic and social position of peasant freeholders in late seventeenth-century Denmark', *Scandinavian Economic History Review*, **25** no. 2, 1977.

Zs. Pach, *Die ungarische Agrarentwicklung im 16–17 Jahrhundert*, Budapest 1964.

P. Raveau, *L'agriculture et les classes paysannes dans le Haut Poitou au XVIe siècle*, Paris 1926.

D. Saalfeld, *Bauernwirtschaft und Gutsbetrieb in der vorindustriellen Zeit*, Stuttgart 1960.

N. Salomon, *La campagne de Nouvelle Castille à la fin du XVIe siècle*, Paris 1964.

T. Shanin, 'The nature and logic of the peasant economy', *Journal of Peasant Studies*, **1**, 1973.

S.O. Shmidt, 'Kizucheniyu agrarnoy istorii Rossii XVI veka' (Research into the agrarian history of 16th century Russia), *Voprosi Istorii*, **5**, 1968.

S.D. Skazkin, 'Osnovnie problemi tak nazivaemogo vtorogo isdaniya krepostnichestva v sredney i vostochnoy Evrope' (Basic problems of the 'second serfdom' in central and eastern Europe), *Voprosi Istorii*, **2**, 1958.

B.H. Slicher van Bath, *The agrarian history of western Europe A.D. 500–1850*, London 1963.

R.E.F. Smith, *The enserfment of the Russian peasantry*, Cambridge 1968.

M. Spufford, *Contrasting communities: English villagers in the sixteenth and seventeenth centuries*, Cambridge 1974.

R.H. Tawney, *The agrarian problem in the sixteenth century*, London 1912.

J. Topolski, 'The manorial serf economy in central and eastern Europe in the 16th and 17th centuries', *Agricultural History*, **48** no. 3, 1974.

D.E. Vassberg, *Land and Society in Golden Age Castile*, Cambridge 1984.

J. de Vries, *The Dutch rural economy in the Golden Age, 1500–1700*, New Haven 1974.

H.H. Wächter, *Ostpreussische Domänenvorwerke im 16. und 17. Jahrhundert*, Würzburg 1958.

H. van der Wee and E. van Cauwenberghe (eds.), *Productivity of land and agricultural innovation in the Low Countries (1250–1800)*, Louvain 1978.

K. Wrightson and D. Levine, *Poverty and Piety in an English village: Terling 1525–1700*, London 1979.

K. Wrightson, 'Aspects of social differentiation in rural England, c.1580–1660', *Journal of Peasant Studies*, **5**, 1977.

Chapter 7 The marginal population

J.L. Alonso Hernández, *El lenguaje de los maleantes españoles de los siglos XVI y XVII: la germanía*, Salamanca 1979.

A.L. Beier, 'Vagrants and the social order in Elizabethan England', *Past and Present*, no. 64, 1974.

A.L. Beier, 'Social problems in Elizabethan London', *Journal of Interdisciplinary History*, **9** no. 2, 1978.

B. Bennassar, 'Economie et société à Ségovie au milieu du XVIe siècle', *Anuario de Historia Económica y Social*, **2** no. 1, 1968.

Y.-M. Bercé, 'Aspects de la criminalité au XVIIe siècle', *Revue Historique*, 1968.

P. Bonenfant, *Le problème du paupérisme en Belgique à la fin de l'ancien régime*, Brussels 1934.

P. Camporesi (ed.), *Il Libro dei Vagabondi*, Turin 1973.

E. Chill, 'Religion and mendicity in seventeenth-century France', *International Review of Social History*, **7**, 1962.

P. Clark and P. Slack, *Crisis and Order in English Towns 1500–1700*, London 1972.

J.S. Cockburn (ed.), *Crime in England 1550–1800*, London 1977.

D.B. Davis, *The problem of slavery in western culture*, Cornell 1966.

J. Deleito y Pinuela, *La mala vida en la España de Felipe IV*, Madrid 1951.

P. Deyon, 'A propos du paupérisme au milieu du XVIIe siècle', *Annales*, 1967.

A. Domínguez Ortiz, 'La esclavitud en Castilla durante la edad moderna', *Estudios de Historia Social de Espana*, **2**, 1952.

C.C. Fairchilds, *Poverty and Charity in Aix-en-Provence, 1640–1789*, Baltimore 1976.

V.A.C. Gartrell, B. Lenman and G. Parker, *Crime and the Law. The social history of crime in western Europe since 1500*, London 1980.

B. Geremek, 'La popolazione marginale tra il medioevo e l'era moderna', *Studi storici*, **9** nos. 3–4, 1968.

B. Geremek, 'Criminalité, vagabondage, paupérisme: la marginalité à l'aube des temps modernes', *Revue d'Histoire Moderne et Contemporaine*, **21**, 1974.

J.P. Gutton, *La société et les pauvres: l'exemple de la généralité de Lyon, 1564–1789*, Paris 1971.

J.P. Gutton, *La société et les pauvres en Europe (XVIe–XVIIIe siècles)*, Paris 1974.

E.M. Hampson, *The treatment of poverty in Cambridgeshire 1597–1834*, Cambridge 1934.

R. Hellie, *Slavery in Russia, 1450–1725*, Chicago 1982.

M. Jiménez Salas, *Historia de la asistencia social en España en la edad moderna*, Madrid 1958.

H. Kamen, 'Public authority and popular crime: banditry in Valencia 1660–1714', *Journal of European Economic History*, 3, 1974.

W.K. Jordan, *Philanthropy in England 1480–1660*, London 1959.

E. von Kraemer, *Le type du faux mendiant dans les littératures romanes depuis le moyen age jusqu'au XVIIe siècle*, Helsinki 1944.

W. Kuhn, *Geschichte der deutsche Ostsiedlung in der Neuzeit*, vol. 1, Cologne 1955.

B. Leblon, *Les gitans d'Espagne. Recherches sur les divers aspects du problème gitan du XVe au XVIIIe siècle*, 3 vols., Montpellier 1979.

E.M. Leonard, *The early history of English poor relief*, Cambridge 1900.

R. Livi, *La schiavitù domestica nei tempi di mezzo e nei moderni*, Padua 1928.

G. Marrone, *La schiavitù nella società siciliana dell'età moderna*, Rome 1972.

C. Paultre, *La repression de la mendicité et du vagabondage en France sous l'Ancien Régime*, Paris 1906.

I. Pinchbeck and M. Hewitt, *Children in English society*, vol. 1, *From Tudor times to the eighteenth century*, London 1969.

B. Pullan, *Rich and poor in Renaissance Venice. The social institutions of a Catholic state to 1620*, Oxford 1971.

B. Pullan, 'Catholics and the poor in early modern Europe', *Transactions of the Royal Historical Society*, 26, 1976.

J. Samaha, *Law and order in historical perspective: the case of Elizabethan Essex*, London 1974.

A.C. and C.M. Saunders, *A social history of black slaves and freedmen in Portugal 1441–1555*, Cambridge 1982.

J.A. Sharpe, 'The history of crime in late medieval and early modern England: a review of the field', *Social History*, 7 no. 2, 1982.

P. Slack, 'Vagrants and vagrancy in England, 1598–1664', *Economic History Review*, 27, 1974.

P. Sorcinelli, *Miseria e malattie nel XVI secolo*, Milan 1979.

E.P. Thompson, 'Time, work-discipline and industrial capitalism', *Past and Present*, no. 38, 1967.

C. Verlinden, *L'esclavage dans l'Europe mediévale*, vol. 1, *Péninsule ibérique – France*, Bruges 1955.

A. Vexliard, *Introduction à la sociologie du vagabondage*, Paris 1956.

Chapter 8   Culture and communication

Cultural and religious change

J. Bossy, 'The Counter Reformation and the people of Catholic Europe', *Past and Present,* no. 47, 1970.

Y.-M. Bercé, *Fête et Révolte. Des mentalités populaires du XVIe au XVIIIe siècle,* Paris 1976.

P. Burke, *Popular culture in early modern Europe,* London 1978.

S. Clark, 'French historians and early modern popular culture', *Past and Present,* no. 100, 1983.

N.Z. Davis, *Society and culture in early modern France,* London 1975.

J. Delumeau, 'Les réformateurs et la superstition', *Bulletin de la Société d'Histoire du Protestantisme français,* 1974.

J. Delumeau, *Catholicism between Luther and Voltaire,* London 1977.

J. Delumeau, *Le Péché et la Peur. La culpabilisation en Occident. XIIIe– XVIIIe siècles,* Paris 1983.

C. Ginzburg, *The Cheese and the Worms. The cosmos of a sixteenth-century miller,* London 1980.

H. Kamen, *Inquisition and Society in Spain,* London 1985.

R. Muchembled, *Culture populaire et culture des élites dans la France moderne (XV–XVIIIe siècles),* Paris 1978.

M. Rosa, *Religione e società nel Mezzogiorno tra Cinque e Seicento,* Bari 1976.

R. Sauzet, *Contre-Réforme et Réforme Catholique en Bas Languedoc. Le diocèse de Nîmes au XVIIe siècle,* Brussels 1979.

G. Strauss, 'Success and failure in the German Reformation', *Past and Present,* no. 67, 1975.

Witchcraft

S. Anglo (ed.), *The Damned Art: essays in the literature of witchcraft,* London 1977.

K. Baschwitz, *Hexen und Hexenprozesse,* Munich 1963.

G. Bonomo, *Caccia alle streghe,* Palermo 1959.

P. Boyer and S. Nissenbaum, *Salem Possessed: the social origins of witchcraft,* Cambridge, Mass. 1974.

E. Delcambre, *Le concept de la sorcellerie dans le duché de Lorraine au XVIe et XVIIe siècles,* 3 vols., Nancy 1949–51.

M.-S. Dupont-Bouchat, W. Frijhoff and R. Muchembled, *Prophètes et sorciers dans les Pays Bas, XVIe–XVIIIe siècle,* Paris 1978.

C. Ginzburg, *The Night Battles: witchcraft and agrarian cult in the 16th and 17th centuries,* London 1983.

R.A. Horsley, 'Who were the witches? The social roles of the accused in the European witch trials', *Journal of Interdisciplinary History,* **9** no. 4, 1979.

H.C. Lea, *Materials towards a History of Witchcraft*, 3 vols., repr. New York 1957.

G.L. Kittredge, *Witchcraft in Old and New England*, New York 1956.

A.D.J. Macfarlane, *Witchcraft in Tudor and Stuart England*, London 1970.

R. Mandrou, *Magistrats et sorciers en France au XVIIe siècle*, Paris 1968.

H.C. Erik Midelfort, *Witchhunting in south-western Germany (1562–1684). The social and intellectual foundations*, Stanford 1972.

E.W. Monter, *Witchcraft in France and Switzerland: the borderlands during the Reformation*, Ithaca 1976.

A. Soman, 'Les procès de sorcellerie au parlement de Paris (1565–1640)', *Annales*, **32**, 1977.

K. Thomas, *Religion and the decline of magic*, London 1971.

R. Zguta, 'Witchcraft trials in seventeenth-century Russia', *American Historical Review*, **82**, 1977.

Scepticism

J.-R. Charbonnel, *Le pensée italienne au XVIe siècle et le courant libertin*, Paris 1919.

R. Pintard, *Le libertinage érudit dans la première moitié du XVIIe siècle*, 2 vols., Paris 1943.

R.H. Popkin, *The history of scepticism from Erasmus to Descartes*, Assen 1964.

G. Spini, *Ricerca dei Libertini*, Rome 1950.

F. Yates, *Giordano Bruno and the Hermetic tradition*, London 1964.

F. Yates, *The Rosicrucian Enlightenment*, London 1972.

Education and literacy

R. Chartier, D. Julia and M.M. Compère, *L'éducation en France du XVIe au XVIIIe siècle*, Paris 1976.

D. Cressy, *Literacy and the social order: reading and writing in Tudor and Stuart England*, Cambridge 1980.

E.L. Eisenstein, *The printing press as an agent of change*, 2 vols., Cambridge 1979.

R.L. Kagan, *Students and society in early modern Spain*, Baltimore 1974.

R. O'Day, *Education and Society 1500–1800. The social foundations of education in early modern Britain*, London 1982.

G. Gascio Pratilli, *L'Università e il principe. Gli Studi di Siena e di Pisa tra Rinascimento e Controriforma*, Florence 1975.

H.F. Kearney, *Scholars and Gentlemen: Universities and Society in pre-industrial Britain, 1500–1700*, London 1970.

H. Schneppen, *Niederländische Universitäten und deutsches Geistesleben*, Münster 1960.

S. Stelling-Michaud (ed.), *Le Livre du Recteur de l'Académie de Genève*

(1559–1878), Geneva 1959.

L. Stone, 'The educational revolution in England 1560–1640', *Past and Present*, no. 28, 1964.

L. Stone (ed.), *The University in Society*, vol. 1, *Oxford and Cambridge from the fourteenth to the early nineteenth century*, Oxford 1975.

Propaganda and press

E.A. Beller, *Propaganda in Germany during the Thirty Years War*, Princeton 1940.

M. Chrisman, 'From polemic to propaganda: the development of mass persuasion in the late sixteenth century', *Archiv für Reformationsgeschichte*, **73**, 1982.

J.A. Downie, *Robert Harley and the Press. Propaganda and public opinion in the age of Swift and Defoe*, Cambridge 1979.

J. Frank, *The beginnings of the English newspaper 1620–60*, Harvard 1961.

M.N. Grand-Mesnil, *Mazarin, la Fronde et la Presse 1647–1649*, Paris 1967.

J. Klaits, *Printed propaganda under Louis XIV. Absolute monarchy and public opinion*, Princeton 1976.

H.-J. Martin, *Livre, pouvoirs et société à Paris au XVIIᵉ siècle (1598–1701)*, 2 vols., Geneva 1969.

K. Schottenloher, *Bücher bewegten die Welt*, 2 vols., Stuttgart 1951–2.

A. Soman, 'Press, pulpit and censorship in France before Richelieu', *Proceedings of the American Philosophical Society*, **120**, 1976.

Utopia

M.L. Berneri, *Journey through Utopia*, London 1950.

L. Firpo, *Lo stato ideale della Controriforma*, Bari 1957.

F.E. and F.P. Manuel, *Utopian Thought in the Western World*, Oxford 1979.

M. Mörner, *The political and economic activities of the Jesuits in the La Plata region*, Stockholm 1953.

R. Ruyer, *L'Utopie et les Utopies*, Paris 1950.

M. Yardeni, *Utopie et révolte sous Louis XIV*, Paris 1980.

Chapter 9   Economic and political crisis

R. Bonney, 'The French Civil War 1649–53', *European Studies Review*, **8**, 1978.

J.H. Elliott, *The Revolt of the Catalans*, Cambridge 1963.

M. Fulbrook, 'The English Revolution and the revisionist revolt', *Social History*, **7** no. 3, 1982.

E.H. Kossmann, *La Fronde*, Leiden 1954.

J. Morrill, *The Revolt of the Provinces: conservatives and radicals in the English civil war 1630–1650*, London 1976.

M. Roberts, 'Queen Christina and the general crisis of the seventeenth century', *Past and Present*, no. 22, 1962.

H.H. Rowen, 'The revolution that wasn't: the coup d'état of 1650 in Holland', *European Studies Review*, **4**, 1974.

Chapter 10   Popular rebellions

A. d'Ambrosio, *Masaniello: rivoluzione e controrivoluzione nel Reame di Napoli (1647–1648)*, Milan 1962.

S.I. Arkhangelsky, *Krestyanskie dvizheniya v Anglii v 40–50kh godakh XVII veka* (Peasant movements in England in the 1640–50s), Moscow 1960.

P. Avrich, *Russian rebels, 1600–1800*, New York 1972.

P. Barbier and F. Vernillat, *Histoire de France par les chansons*, 8 vols., Paris 1956.

Y.-M. Bercé, *Histoire des Croquants. Etude des soulèvements populaires au 17e siècle dans le sud-ouest de la France*, 2 vols., Geneva 1974.

Y.-M. Bercé, *Croquants et Nu-Pieds. Les soulèvements paysans en France du XVIe au XIXe siècle*, Paris 1974.

Y.-M. Bercé, *Révoltes et révolutions dans l'Europe moderne, XVIe–XVIIIe siècles*, Paris 1980.

P. Blickle, *The Revolution of 1525*, Baltimore 1981.

H.N. Brailsford, *The Levellers and the English Revolution*, London 1961.

K.V. Chistov, *Russkie narodnie sotsialno-utopicheskie legendy XVII–XIXvv* (Popular socio-utopian legends of 17th–19th century Russia), Moscow 1967.

P. Clark, 'Popular protest and disturbance in Kent 1558–1640', *Economic History Review*, **29**, 1976.

C.S.L. Davies, 'Peasant revolt in France and England: a comparison', *Agricultural History Review*, **21** no. 2, 1973.

A. Dominguez Ortiz, *Alteraciones andaluzas*, Madrid 1973.

Y. Garlan and C. Nières, *Les révoltes bretonnes de 1675*, Paris 1975.

G. Grüll, *Bauer, Herr und Landesfürst*, Linz 1963.

C. Hill, *The world turned upside down: radical ideas during the English Revolution*, London 1972.

J.L.H. Keep, 'Bandits and the law in Muscovy', *Slavonic and East European Review*, **35**, 1956–7.

H.G. Koenigsberger, 'The revolt of Palermo in 1647', *Cambridge Historical Journal*, **8** no. 3, 1946.

E. Le Roy Ladurie, *Carnival. A people's uprising at Romans 1579–1580*, London 1980.

J.A. Maravall, *Las Comunidades de Castilla*, Madrid 1979.

R. Mousnier, *Peasant uprisings in 17th century France*, London 1971.

J. Pérez, *La Révolution des Comunidades de Castille (1520–1521)*, Bordeaux 1970.

R. Pillorget, *Les mouvements insurrectionels de Provence entre 1596 et 1715*, Paris 1975.

B. Porshnev, *Les soulèvements populaires en France 1613–1648*, Paris 1963.

J. Reglà and J. Fuster, *El bandolerisme català*, 2 vols., Barcelona 1962–3.

W. Schulze, *Bäuerliche Widerstand und feudale Herrschaft in der frühen Neuzeit*, Stuttgart 1980.

W. Schulze (ed.), *Europäische Bauernrevolten der frühen Neuzeit*, Frankfurt 1982.

W. Schulze (ed.), *Aufstände, Revolten, Prozesse*, Stuttgart 1983.

B. Sharp, *In contempt of all authority. Rural artisans and riot in the west of England, 1586–1660*, Berkeley 1980.

I.I. Smirnov, *Vosstanie Bolotnikova 1606–1607* (The Bolotnikov uprising 1606–1607), Leningrad 1951.

P. Smirnov, *Pravitelstvo B.I. Morozova i vosstanie v Moskve 1648g* (The government of B. Morozov and the 1648 Moscow rising), Tashkent 1929.

R. Villari, *La rivolta antispagnola a Napoli. Le origini (1585–1647)*, Bari 1967.

R. Villari, 'Rivolte e coscienza rivoluzionaria nel secolo XVII', *Studi Storici*, **12** no. 2, 1971.

H. Wahlen and E. Jaggi, *Der schweizerische Bauernkrieg 1653*, Bern 1952.

H.U. Wehler, *Der deutsche Bauernkrieg 1524–26*, Gottingen 1975.

S.A. Westrich, *The Ormée of Bordeaux*, Baltimore 1972.

Chapter 11   Absolutism and the state

T.M. Barker, 'Military entrepreneurship and absolutism: Habsburg models', *Journal of European Studies*, **4** no. 1, 1974.

D.C. Coleman (ed.), *Revisions in Mercantilism*, London 1969.

J.P. Cooper, 'Differences between English and continental governments in the early seventeenth century', in J.S. Bromley and E.H. Kossmann (eds.), *Britain and the Netherlands*, London 1960.

J. Daly, 'The idea of absolute monarchy in seventeenth-century England', *Historical Journal*, **21** no. 2, 1978.

R. Hatton, *Louis XIV and Absolutism*, London 1976.

D. Parker, *The social foundations of French absolutism*, London 1983.

T.K. Rabb, *The struggle for stability in early modern Europe*, New York 1975.

C. Tilly (ed.), *The formation of national states in western Europe*, Princeton 1975.

Index